THE GULF BETWEEN US

THE GULF BETWEEN US

A Story of Love and Survival in Desert Storm

Cynthia B. Acree

with

Colonel Cliff Acree, USMC

Brassey's

WASHINGTON, D.C.

Editorial Offices:
22883 Quicksilver Drive
Dulles, VA 20166

Order Department:
P.O. Box 960
Herndon, VA 20172

Brassey's books are available at special discounts for bulk purchases
for sales promotions, premiums, fund-raising, or educational use.

Library of Congress Cataloging-in-Publication Data

Acree, Cynthia B.
The Gulf between us : a story of love and survival in Desert Storm /
by Cynthia B. Acree with Cliff Acree. — 1st ed.
p.   cm.
ISBN 1-57488-370-4
1. Acree, Cliff. 2. Prisoners of war—United States—Biography.
3. Prisoner's spouses—United States. 4. Persian Gulf War, 1991—
Personal narratives, American. 5. Persian Gulf War, 1991—Aerial
operations, American. I. Acree, Cliff. II. Title.
DS79.74.A27 1998
956.7044'248—dc21   98-18347
CIP

Designed by Pen & Palette Unlimited

First Edition

10 9 8 7 6 5 4 3 2 1

Printed in Canada

To the unsung heroes of Desert Storm.

The measure of a man's character is what he would do if he would never be found out.
—Thomas Babington Macaulay

Contents

Acknowledgments

Cliff and I extend our heartfelt thanks to the American people for their unity and unwavering support of our armed forces during Operations Desert Shield and Desert Storm. We are especially grateful to those who sent words of encouragement, wore POW bracelets, and kept us in their prayers. Your energy, sincerity, and kindness gave us great strength.

Special gratitude is owed to my mother, Emily, and my late stepdad, Vince, for always being there when I needed them. Mom, there's a special place in heaven reserved for mothers like you and Dee Acree. Thanks also to Bill Acree, for the values you instilled in your son.

I'm grateful to my sister, Bonnie Romain, whose wit, wisdom, and friendship I will always treasure, and to Karen Critz, Mary Pat Hall, and Ethel Vogel for their unending encouragement and love.

Many cherished friends unselfishly gave their time and support during Cliff's captivity; Rosana Martinez and Debbie Mills stand at the forefront of these. It is impossible to name all the others, but they include: Kay and Don Beaver, Joel Lees, Ed Brandstoettner, Connie and John Borley, Lois and Marty Caverly, Dan and Nickie Kuhn, Jane and Rick Patton, Pam Pindrys, Chere and Tanny vanLigten, and Carol and Jim Treadwell. "Thank you" does not begin to express our appreciation.

For their unselfish and tireless assistance, our deepest appreciation to the founding members of the POW/MIA Liberty Alliance, especially Pat Antosh, Dee and Ken Barackman, Rosana Martinez, Marty and Lois Caverly, Carol Craven, Jane and Peyton DeHart, Catherine Gamboa, Bill Handel, and P. J. Jennings, and all the others who kept the vigil going.

We are also grateful to the Seattle POW/MIA Liberty Alliance members who worked equally hard on the letter-writing campaign, including Shirley

Grimnes, Joyce Hammond, Bert and Barbara Naiman, Jim and Mary Osborne, and Ann Siepak.

Special thanks to Chief Warrant Officer Michael Clark, a passionate advocate of POW/MIA families. He advised me along with the real experts—former Vietnam POWs Gary Thornton and Bill Stark—who took me under their wing and guided me so well.

To the tens of thousands of people around the world who took the trouble to write to the Iraqi ambassador to the United Nations, we extend our deepest gratitude. To Ben Schemmer and the others who made donations to the POW/MIA Liberty Alliance, we couldn't have accomplished our goals without you.

At Batsford Brassey, Inc., I was lucky to have as my editor Don McKeon, whose clarifying suggestions helped me write a better book. I also want to extend my appreciation to the friends who read my manuscript and provided helpful feedback, especially Kay Beaver, Jeff Douglass, Mary Pat Hall, Debbie Mills, Eric Bower, and Warren (Lefty) Wright.

For her guidance and enthusiasm for this book, I am forever indebted to the gifted journalist, Melinda Bargreen. Her unfailing encouragement inspired me to persevere during the six years it took me to obtain a publisher and complete the manuscript. Every first-time author should be so lucky to have such a talented, supportive friend as Melinda.

My thanks to all the many people who graciously gave me their time and recollections during our interviews, especially our dear friend Muhammed Mubarak, whose vivid recollections of captivity greatly enhanced the manuscript.

To my greatest treasures, Stephen and Mark, thank you for sharing Mommy so often with the computer. Someday you will understand why this project was so important to me and be even more proud of your great dad.

Finally, and most importantly, I'd like to thank my husband, Cliff, who worked as hard on this book as I did. He patiently answered my endless questions when he would have rather been doing anything else. His willingness to talk about his painful experiences in exacting detail, and in doing so, relive them, enabled me to share with others the story he is too modest to tell. Cliff, your unending devotion, love, and encouragement are my greatest sources of inspiration. You are my hero.

Preface

Desert Storm had many stories. This one is ours, an intimate look into the lives of two ordinary people caught in extraordinary circumstances.

This portrayal of the human side of war is based on Cliff's story as he told it to me as well as my remembrances. Every detail, circumstance, and event is depicted as we knew it to have happened.

Please join us for a tale of captivity and freedom, of hope and despair, and of love—the beacon in any storm.

Prologue I

Cliff

January 17, 1991

This was it.

The Super Bowl, D day, the ultimate testing ground.

When I climbed into the cockpit of my OV-10 Bronco observation plane, dawn hadn't yet broken in Saudi Arabia. It was cold outside, but I didn't feel it. All I felt was the incredible exhilaration of entering my first day of combat, knowing I was ready.

I would learn plenty about raw terror in the weeks to come, but this mission inspired me with confidence and excitement. No worries about "maybe I should have trained harder." No wondering "Am I ready for combat?" The homework was done and the preparations made. After years of rigorous flight training, I was as ready as I could ever be.

For my family and friends, it was a fear-inspiring day. They knew my job as commander of the Marine observation squadron, VMO-2, was to fly into the forward edge of the battle zone and locate targets for the Coalition aircraft. It's a high-risk mission; there's no getting around it. But like anybody who straps on an aircraft in the Marine Corps knows, you have an assumed risk and you accept that. It's part of the excitement, and the challenge I had trained for throughout my eighteen-year Marine career.

I had no feelings of doubt or trepidation that morning as I briefed with Chief Warrant Officer Guy Hunter prior to takeoff. We couldn't wait to get over enemy territory. I was confident in my abilities to handle our mission and especially assured with Warrant Officer Hunter in my back seat.

When I planned our course, I had no inkling that a day later I'd be seeing that patch of Kuwaiti sand close up. The chance to pit myself against the enemy was fast approaching, but I would battle the enemy closer than I had ever planned.

Prologue II

Cindy

January 18, 1991

They came without warning. Yet when the Marine officers appeared at my door, I knew why they had come. The moment all military wives dread had arrived.

That day was the culmination of five months of preparation. As my husband, Cliff, molded his squadron into a cohesive combat-ready unit, I, too, had faced the challenge of creating unity and preparedness, among the wives and families back home. And like our men, we had bonded into an equally capable "battle unit," a sisterhood of strength.

The months had passed in a blur of worrying, coping, and pressing on. As in other military communities across America, the squadron's wives and families struggled to stay calm despite failing peace talks, escalating tensions, and gloomy predictions of casualties. When the January 15 deadline passed, we, too, prepared ourselves for the worst.

Then the war began, with my husband flying in combat, low and slow, searching for enemy targets near the front lines. Would he return home to me? We'd had so little time together. For twenty years, circumstances had pulled us apart. When we finally married, we vowed never to be separated again.

Now, with a chime of the doorbell, that dream—and life as I knew it— would be shattered. Within hours, I would become a prisoner in my own home; within days, an activist founding an international organization dedicated to Desert Storm POWs and MIAs. Celebrities, political figures, and everyday people all over the world would join our crusade.

But as I walked toward the door that day, I only knew my life would never be the same.

1

A Bronco in Baghdad

King Abdul Aziz Airfield, Saudi Arabia
January 18, 1991

My aerial observer (AO) and I strode toward the flight line and the looming shadow of our OV-10 Bronco, eager to repeat our successes of the previous day. At 0400 the air was chilly, but the flight line was alive with activity so early on this second day of Operation Desert Storm, as the flight crews wrapped up preparing the aircraft for the day's missions.

Vehicles rumbled and maintenance crews scurried around aircraft. Jets thundered by overhead, already airborne to their objective areas in Iraq and Kuwait. We'd soon be up there with them, joining the fight against a brutal dictator armed with chemical and biological weapons.

Lights from the highway beyond cast an eerie glow, backlighting our two-seat turboprop Bronco. Used to locate the enemy and direct air attacks, artillery, or naval gunfire to destroy them, the Bronco and its crew were an invaluable resource for frontline ground units. The observation and light attack plane was armed with five-inch Zuni rockets to carry out some of the most dangerous missions of the war—missions that required its Marine crews to fly low and slow, often behind enemy lines. Some did not return.

I threw my helmet and navigation bag into the front cockpit of the Bronco. Though eager to get into the air, readying my aircraft was one thing I wouldn't hurry—especially in preparation for combat. Every detail counts.

But this morning, I felt dead tired. Not from rising at 0300 after five hours of sleep or from my early flight brief, but from fatigue that had been building for weeks from the nonstop demands of being the 350-member squadron's commanding officer. Even in normal times, with Cindy feeding

1

me a never-ending supply of her cookies and fresh bread, I had trouble keeping weight on. Now, after five months of living in "tent city," five months of grueling day-and-night training, insufficient sleep, and way too much to do, my flight suit fit looser every day.

Ducking under the high, arching tail section, I began working down an extensive checklist to prepare the Bronco for flight. In the dim light of predawn, I inspected engine compartments, landing gear, and external ordnance loads, periodically rubbing my hands to warm them. Someday I'd tell the folks back home about this adventure in person.

My adventure began in June 1990, when I took command of VMO-2, a Marine OV-10 squadron. Ten weeks later, I received orders to deploy my unit to the Middle East. Since OV-10s are not equipped for air-to-air refueling, and no aircraft carriers had available deck space, we flew our six planes to Saudi Arabia by hopscotching from airfield to airfield across the globe in fifty-five hours of flight time over twenty-six days. This had never been done before.

Immediately upon arrival, VMO-2 Marines set to work preparing for war. Over the next five months, we transformed ourselves into a more focused and capable fighting unit, disciplined, well trained, and conditioned like athletes. We had practiced our mission countless times, and we were ready.

By 0500 my preflight of the aircraft was complete. Now, everything should have been "all systems go" for our mission that morning, but as I reached for my olive-drab G suit, something tugged at me, a feeling in my gut—an apprehension, a warning. Yet, with time to launch upon us, I dismissed it. "Must be this strange weather," I thought.

I looked up at the unusual low, gray cloud formations that obscured some of the sky. They seemed secretive, as if shrouding an unforeseen opponent. Yanking up my G suit's inseam zipper from ankle to crotch, I forced my suspicions away.

Sergeant Major Warner, the senior enlisted Marine in the squadron, came to the flight line to see us off. His deep brown eyes radiated concern. "Go do it, sir," the tall, athletically built Marine told me in his husky voice. "Be careful out there."

I pulled my arms through the integrated torso harness, which held my pistol, survival equipment, and radio. Suited up, I turned to Chief Warrant Officer Guy Hunter, my aerial observer (AO) for the flight. "Ready, GW?"

"Yes, sir!" Guy answered with his typically confident smile. We climbed into the sand-colored plane, Guy sitting behind me in the rear cockpit. Kindhearted, easygoing, Guy had been raised in Georgia, and a Southern accent laced his soft voice. He was a likable man, and his humorous tales made everyone laugh. His crop of silvery-white hair had earned him the nickname of "Great White" Hunter, or "GW."

Hunter and I were seasoned Marines and our respect was mutual. If I, as CO, was the "dad" of the squadron, Marines regarded Guy, the almost legendary expert on the Bronco and its many missions, as the sage "grandfather."

We were a long way from Oceanside, California, and our families. Guy, married fourteen years, had two daughters and a son. I was married to Cindy, my high school sweetheart, and had an eleven-year-old daughter, Stephany, from an earlier marriage.

But at 0530, neither of us was thinking of his family. We climbed into the tandem cockpit, eager to launch. We'd have our hands full on this mission— flying the aircraft, calling for close air support, marking targets, and controlling aircraft attacking Iraqi forces. Patrolling the battle zone in our OV-10, Guy and I would be the "eyes in the sky" for ground and air forces. We'd call in targets for air strikes and alert the grunts (ground troops) of what enemy forces lay ahead of them.

Once we spotted a target, we would request an air strike, get approval to attack, then fire a white phosphorus rocket. The rocket's huge smoke plume would serve to mark the target for the bomb-laden jets (usually AV-8B Harriers, F/A-18 Hornets, or A-10 Warthogs) carrying out the strike. We would then provide a "talk on" to the target, supplying pinpoint directions as the jets moved in for the kill.

Ours was a job that has been done for centuries, that of the forward scout. But we were to accomplish our mission in a turboprop plane. Our slow-moving OV-10s would be easy prey for Iraqi MiGs or Mirage F-1 fighters.

I strapped into the aircraft by attaching my torso harness to the ejection seat, then situated my knee board and maps. I pulled the silver flight helmet over my head and swiveled the tinted visor down over my eyes. I glanced back at Guy. Any Marine would feel confident with Guy Hunter in his back seat. Husky and strong, Guy was in exceptionally good shape for his forty-six years. He had flown in the Bronco longer than most Marines had been in the Corps. Starting with back seat reconnaissance as a sergeant in 1966, Guy went on to fly many combat missions during four tours in Vietnam.

On today's mission, Guy would scan for targets, locate them on the map, and coordinate air or artillery strikes. He was the best AO the Marine Corps had in the OV-10, and we worked together well.

With our forward-looking infrared radar (FLIR), OV-10 crews could see people walking in the sand up to six miles away and spot a moving vehicle nearly ten miles away. By *not* swooshing in overhead at Mach airspeeds, our Broncos were a big comfort to the grunts. When they heard the drone of our engines overhead, they knew they had eyes aloft to help guide and protect them from being mistaken as enemy targets.

I adjusted the microphone over my mouth to relay messages over any of the four radios in the aircraft. I pulled on my gloves, then waggled one finger at the plane captain, signaling that I was ready to start the number-one engine. The props began to rotate, and the plane vibrated as both engines leapt to life. It was 0545, and we were ready to launch.

I gave a thumbs-up sign to ordnance personnel who approached my aircraft to arm the rocket pods and the AIM-9 (air-to-air) Sidewinder missile. When the ordnance crew moved away, I gave another thumbs-up to the plane captain to taxi us for launch.

"Let's go flying, Colonel!" Guy said with a grin. The sun creeping over the horizon was nearly hidden by the early morning haze. I returned the crisp salute of the plane captain. He stepped aside and we taxied to the runway.

I advanced the throttles for maximum takeoff power, and we headed down the runway. As the plane climbed quickly in the cool morning air, I felt an invigorating mix of power and excitement. It was 0600, and our plane was in the air, according to plan.

With our Bronco's landing gear raised, Guy Hunter and I headed north, straight for Kuwait, in search of Iraqi artillery positions. I checked my instruments and monitored our airspeed and rate of climb. Prowling the skies only 5,000 to 10,000 feet above enemy terrain, we would be vulnerable, but we needed that perspective to locate and identify targets for the attack jets. Flying above us at 450 knots, the jets caught only a quick glimpse of the target, and could easily confuse friendly and enemy forces during the excitement and confusion of combat.

Though two squadrons of OV-10s kept Broncos airborne twenty-four hours a day during Desert Storm, most Americans were unaware a mission as dangerous as ours existed. Watching televised briefings, most people imagined bombers moving in on Iraqi targets with sophisticated devices in tune with the latest satellite intelligence. But technology can never replace the human eye in the continually changing battlefield. Information that is days or even hours old can be useless. Despite their low billing, Bronco crews directly observed and reported what was going on during combat, one of the most difficult and dangerous jobs in the air war.

The plane rose through the morning haze and intermittent clouds. I patted the good luck charm in my pocket: Cindy's homemade oatmeal cookies. Guy and I had flown two successful missions as a crew the day before. When our last mission was complete and we were safely south into friendly airspace, Guy and I had celebrated our first day in combat and our safe return with a victory roll and by splitting a bag of cookies Cindy had mailed to me from California. Before my 0430 brief that morning, I'd tucked another bag into a pocket of my G suit.

I scanned the flat desert, looking for movement, my adrenaline pumping. After receiving clearance to proceed north over the border into Kuwait, I knew it wouldn't be long before we would find enemy targets.

My OV-10 Bronco squadron was located fifty miles south of the Iraq-Kuwait border, less than one mile inland from the shore of the Persian Gulf.

For five months, my Marines and I had trained day and night. There was little time off. There was no leave. There was no liberty. We just trained. But when January 15—the Desert Shield deadline set by President Bush and adopted by the UN—rolled around, we were ready. And when the war started I told my Marines, "It's time to go hand the enemy his ass on a platter!"

"Crossing the fence now," I said as Guy and I headed into enemy territory. I continually scanned the airspace around our plane for any airborne threat. With reports of antiaircraft artillery (AAA or triple-A) and possible SAMs, even the smallest mistake could be deadly.

A radio call interrupted my searching of the desert below. Marine positions were taking fire from unobserved Iraqi artillery. I keyed the intercom: "Guy, our Marines are getting hammered by enemy arty! We need to find that arty *fast!*"

On the desert floor, I saw what looked like a cluster of vehicles and equipment. I couldn't positively identify the target, thanks to a gauzy layer of clouds at 6,000 feet.

"Colonel, we've got to get below these clouds to confirm what the hell that target is," Guy said.

"Going down," I replied.

As we dove beneath the cloud deck at 5,800 feet, I saw five long, green vehicles on trailers. "Are these guys nuts?" I wondered.

The day before we had found an artillery battery in this exact location. We called in Harrier attack aircraft, which annihilated one Iraqi artillery battery and partially destroyed a second. While the Harriers had been bombing the artillery pieces on that previous mission, I saw what looked like little stick figures running toward trenches nearby. Seconds later, all four Harriers emptied their 25-millimeter guns on those trenches. No doubt few, if any, of the 150 or so Iraqis there survived.

Today, the ground around the battery was still blackened and charred like a discarded campfire. Then I saw something that caused a small knot in my stomach. "What the hell is that?" I wondered, surveying the site below me. "Fuel trucks? A chemical weapons site?" That equipment hadn't been there the previous day.

I realized we were directly above a staging area for what appeared to be five FROG (Free Rocket Over Ground) missiles readied for launch into Saudi Arabia. This was a high-priority target! I keyed the UHF radio switch and requested attack aircraft be immediately diverted to our position. The radio crackled an acknowledgment.

I banked sharply and circled the plane once over the target area, looking right, left, and below; right, left, and below—scanning every inch of the desert below us a thousand times. Our radar missile indicator was blessedly quiet. Yet something felt wrong. Very wrong. An unusual movement caught my eye to the left and below the aircraft. I focused on it and looked back at a horrifying sight: glinting metal followed by an incredibly fast gray-white vapor trail snaking toward us. A heat-seeking surface-to-air missile had locked on to our aircraft and was tracking us. The missile, pointed right at my face, was coming fast to blow us out of the sky. With less than 6,000 feet of altitude, I had no more than a second of warning to dodge the missile streaking toward us.

They say your whole life flashes before you when you look death in the face. Maybe that's true for some. For me, as I watched that incredibly fast vapor trail and saw the glinting metal of the missile heading inexorably for us, there was barely time to register what was happening. It's the same feeling you get in a car crash when you've hit the brakes hard and so has the other guy. You know the impact is coming all the same.

I knew all the evasive procedures from countless flight exercises and from memorizing the flight manual. But given our altitude, there was no time to execute them. I had time for only one thought: Acree, this is it. You're a dead man.

Somewhere over Southern Kuwait
January 18, 1991

It all happened between heartbeats—seeing the telltale plume of smoke and feeling the smashing impact of the enemy SAM. Before I took my next breath, the SAM rammed the Bronco like a freight train, thrusting it to the right. My helmet smashed against the left side of the canopy. A blinding white flash illuminated the cockpit. A split second later the warhead exploded, violently jerking my head to the right. Shards of metal whistled into the canopy as 150-knot winds pounded our faces. There was no time for astonishment at being alive—the detonation of the missile had blown off most of the number-one engine and had torn away the left side of the canopy. Immediately, burning metal fragments sliced through the plane, hitting Guy and me.

Flames erupted instantly. Black smoke and fumes flooded the cockpit. The left engine was in flames. Then, one by one, the fuel cells on top of the wing ignited each other. *FFOOOMPH! FFOOOMPH! FFOOOMPH!* As the last fuel cell exploded on the right, the number-two engine caught fire. My cockpit warning lights lit up red. Warning horns sounded.

At incredibly high speed, my plane was being destroyed around me. The second engine fire spewed more smoke and fumes in the cockpit and crippled the electrical system. In a matter of seconds the whole plane could be a torch—an exploding torch.

Smoke and fumes half obscured my instrument panel. The Bronco became difficult to fly. I wanted to hang on as long as I could. Guy and I would be sitting ducks if we ejected into enemy territory. But if we didn't eject, we'd be dead. I didn't even know whether Guy had survived the impact of the missile.

Think! Think! Maybe it'd be possible to coax the Bronco back to friendly airspace if it stayed intact. Even without engines, it could fly like a glider. I had to get back over the fence.

I jammed the right rudder pedal full forward to counter the loss of thrust from the destroyed left engine. I started the step-by-step emergency procedures I had rehearsed so many times as I swung the plane into a left-hand turn, south toward the Saudi border. I rolled the wings level and adjusted the nose attitude to achieve 130 knots of airspeed. This airspeed would give me the best glide range if my second engine failed. I might even be able to glide back to Saudi Arabia. Then the stick froze. The flight controls were jammed and the plane was no longer flyable. Any hope of gliding back to friendly territory was forever lost. We weren't gliding; we were falling like a ten-ton brick.

My eyes burned from the acrid smoke. I had only seconds to sort out my options and react. We rolled to a left thirty-degree angle of bank and began to plunge, nose-low, on a crash course toward the desert. The ground was coming up fast. I didn't want to leave the airplane. Even if it was on fire, I'd rather ride than eject into enemy hands.

Our plane wasn't exactly unobserved—we had the missile to prove it. Iraqis would be eagerly awaiting our arrival via parachute. But we all knew stories of pilots who died because they delayed ejection until it was too late, hoping to save the airplane. Lectures on ejection stressed, "Know when it's time to go."

It was time to go, all right. The flight controls were jammed; we were rapidly descending and becoming a fireball. We had already lost 2,000 feet of altitude. Hoping my radio was operative, I broadcast: "Mayday! Mayday! Mayday!" I said the international distress call three times as required. "Hostage Seven-six has been hit by a surface-to-air missile, six miles north of Kuwait border. We're going down! Mayday! Mayday! Mayday! Hostage Seven-six is going down."

No acknowledgment, only static.

I keyed the intercom. "Guy, we have to eject!" No answer. "Guy, can you hear me? Stand by to eject!" Silence. "Guy!" I yelled at the top of my lungs without the ICS. "Stand by! Stand by! Here it comes!"

I remembered looking back at Guy in the rear cockpit seconds before the missile hit. He was looking down and must have never seen it coming. The missile had hit even closer to Guy's section of the plane. Had he been knocked unconscious—or worse? If Guy had been knocked out he would be unable to pull his ejection handle. By pulling the pilot's command ejection handle, I could eject us both.

Once I knew the plane was no longer flyable, time slowed to a crawl. I had no choice but to pull the pilot's ejection handle at the front of my seat. We'd be taking our chances on the ground, but it was better than remaining in an uncontrollable plane going down in flames.

I yanked the handle. The Bronco's ejection system is designed so that four-tenths of a second after the pilot pulls the handle, the person in the back seat ejects. After Guy ejected, it would be my turn. I waited. One second . . . I waited . . . Guy still wasn't gone. I began counting: "One, one thousand, two, one thousand . . ." He still wasn't gone! Just as I got to "Three, one thousand" *BANG!* The rocket detonated beneath Guy's seat. *Whoosh!* Guy blasted off as the rocket motor ignited. *Crack!* The breaker bar on top of Guy's ejection seat shattered the canopy as he exploded into the sky like a human cannonball. Shards of broken glass exploded; the smoke and fumes were gone. Air surged into the cockpit, tearing at the pages of the aerial chart on my knee.

The rocket motor burned out and it was quiet again. Eight-tenths of a second after I pulled the pilot's ejection seat handle, my seat should fire. I waited. And waited. Nothing happened. I wasn't going anywhere. The ground was coming up fast. "I'm going to ride this plane down to the sand. That'll be the end of it," I told myself.

In desperation, I looked between my knees to tug on the yellow ejection handle one more time. The instant I lowered my head the seat fired, violently wrenching my neck, forcing my head toward my waist. The loud bang of the explosive charge under my ejection seat roused me a second later. I felt a hard jolt as the rocket motor initiated. Brutally forced through the glass canopy, every part of my body reacted to the shock as I rode a rocket seat out of my plane.

The cockpit bow moved down below me as I surged into the sky. Icy wind tore at my face, and a blast of air ripped the visor off my helmet. The smoldering instrument panel dropped beneath me as the ejection seat catapulted me out of my burning cockpit with a force twelve times that of gravity.

I was out of the plane! Things came into focus and blurred out again . . . there was no time to think about what had just happened and why. I squinted as the cold breeze rushed over me. Slowly my senses cleared. My eyes opened as I heard the flutter of my parachute before its white silk canopy popped open. A hard jerk on the harness straps on my waist and shoulders, a loud pop, and my body shuddered from a tremendous jolt as my parachute jerked me up after fully opening. The noise and confusion vanished. In deathly quiet, I floated in the vast sky.

I descended toward the desert over what appeared to be Iraqi infantry fortifications—very near the area I had targeted. But what about Guy? Had he survived the missile impact? Had his chute opened? If we'd both made it this far, we should have the worst behind us. I couldn't have been more wrong.

I scanned the surrounding terrain to determine in which direction my parachute was headed. If I could drift south toward the border of Saudi Arabia, I might evade capture. Normally, the prevailing winds in Kuwait blow southward to the Saudi Arabian border. But on this day, the winds blew me in the opposite direction, farther into enemy territory, an area thick with Iraqi soldiers and artillery.

I glanced over my left shoulder toward our aircraft. It took a tremendous effort to move my neck. Though I couldn't see the abandoned plane, I heard it descending noisily down to the desert. Less than twenty seconds after we ejected—half the time it takes to cross a room—I heard a thunderous explosion in the distance.

I couldn't see the fiery crash as the plane slammed into the ground on its belly five miles from the Saudi border. Much later, crash photos would show the twin booms extending behind the twisted, charred plane ripped away and the left engine torn completely off the wing. That engine is why I survived. The warhead of the missile had hit the engine casing at its hardest part. The engine cushioned the impact, saving my life. Had the missile hit just twelve inches away, we would both have been killed instantly.

As I tilted my head back to inspect my parachute canopy, a scorching pain shot down my neck, long and sharp as a knife, stabbing into my flesh. I remembered my neck snapping back upon ejection. That stiletto jab of pain was from the injury I'd received. With effort, I scrutinized my chute, and what I saw drove my pulse rate higher. My parachute was on fire!

Taking few precious seconds, I assessed the damage. The missile's explosion had burned out two panels. A third, charred black and smoldering, flapped in the breeze. Would the damaged chute hold my weight? My heart pounded hard and fast. "There's nothing you can do about it," I told myself. "Stop looking."

Descending more rapidly because of the damaged panels in my parachute, I knew I'd land hard. I turned my attention to where I was headed. The flat terrain was bleak and empty of life, but foxholes and bunkers had been built into the sand. Were they abandoned or filled with troops lying in wait for my arrival? I couldn't see a soul. But I figured the Iraqis would soon be here to greet us.

In preparation for war, I had attended graphic briefings on the atrocities of the Iran-Iraq war. Intelligence told us that the Iraqis brutally mutilated Kuwaiti and Iranian prisoners. Horror stories—of fingers cut off and arms pulled out of sockets with vehicles—were legion. Prisoners endured long, lingering, torturous deaths. Saddam Hussein had taunted Coalition forces, trumpeting in the world press, "We will drink your blood!" Most pilots assumed they'd be better off dead than captured.

I'd accepted that risk when I climbed into the cockpit, but the thought of being in Iraqi hands terrified me just the same. "If they're watching... *don't think about it*," I commanded. "Think logically." I forced myself to control my emotions and concentrate on what I must do next: land safely. I couldn't afford an injured leg or spine. I hoped my burning chute was strong enough to break my fall. It was disintegrating above me. What *else* could go wrong?

I breathed deeply, trying to slow my heart rate, then looked down to check my flight path. I couldn't believe my rotten luck: I was careening into the only high-voltage electrical lines in southern Kuwait. With electricity coursing through them, they had enough power to shock a damn elephant.

Had I survived being blown from the sky only to be electrocuted on the way down? The freak weather that had brought in the strange clouds and winds, and that had thrust me farther into enemy territory, was now sweeping me into the only high-tension power lines in southern Kuwait. Like an insect snared in a giant wire web, I was being pushed into the huge, lethal lines.

Even with a steerable parachute I could not avoid the thick power wires. The shroud lines resisted my hard tugs. A puppet on a string, I spiraled, the lines dead ahead. As I swooped toward them, I picked up my feet. I descended so rapidly that only the top of my smoldering parachute tipped the lines. My body slipped by with inches to spare. Thankfully, my nylon chute wasn't a good conductor of electricity. By the grace of God, I got past those wires. I felt like a cat with nine lives. But my luck was fragile.

With my parachute partially burned out, I was falling at twice the normal speed of eight feet per second. The horizon was coming up fast. Guy was descending in his parachute about 200 yards to my right. His head was slumped forward and his body was limp. I didn't know if he was dead or alive.

It was time to concentrate on landing. I had parachuted before and remembered the procedure. "I've got this thing wired," I assured myself, before I realized how rapidly I was hurling to the ground.

I prepared for the jolt of landing, ready to make my best five-point roll. "Okay, parachute landing fall... toes, heels, knees..." The ground swept up beneath me. Touching down hard, I landed on my toes... then on my face!

"Oooomf!" I grunted loudly, expelling the air from my chest. My face and helmet sunk into the surprisingly soft earth—a farmer's field, recently plowed and damp from rainfall. The two-feet-high furrows cushioned my abrupt landing. Too stunned to move, I lay facedown in the dirt for a moment. I spit out a mouthful of wet sand, then picked myself up. With the back of my hand, I wiped a thick layer of mud and sand off my face. My black visor dangled off the back of my helmet. Still shaken, I released the torso harness from my parachute. Something hard bounced against my calves. It was my seat pan, still attached to my torso harness.

That seat was important. It contained a survival kit and a beacon that automatically transmitted an emergency location signal. The beacon was firing, and I hoped the signal was being picked up by the Airborne Warning and Control System (AWACS) or another Coalition radio site.

I pulled off my helmet, disconnected my seat pan and harness, and threw them to the ground. I ripped off my knee board, containing my flight plans and aerial chart, and buried them under a bush. Was anyone watching? I didn't want any Iraqis to get those.

I made a beeline for Guy. He was alive! He picked himself up from the ground, his parachute billowing behind him. As soon as I broke into a jog, my neck hurt like a son of a bitch.

As I ran closer to Guy, he raised his head. His gold wire-rim glasses were missing. Extremely nearsighted, Guy needed glasses to find his way around the house. He took one look at me and ran the other way! Seeing double, Guy saw a couple of stick figures headed toward him. He thought they were Iraqi soldiers.

I yelled as loud as I could. "Hey, Gunner, it's me!" Guy stopped and turned to face me.

"Colonel? Is that you?"

The whole left side of his face was bloody from a gash over his eye. "Can you see?" I asked when I reached him.

"Not very well." Guy wiped his eyes, and his hand came away slick with blood. "I think I'm all right."

"Hold still. Let me look at your eye. Are you hurting anywhere?" A piece of hot metal had punctured his left eyelid, ripping it into two bloody flaps. Even with his eyes closed, Guy could see through the slit in his eyelid. With his eye injured and no glasses, Guy's vision was severely handicapped. Both of us were in shock.

"How are *you* doing?" Guy asked. "You've got quite a bit of blood dripping from the back of your head." I had hardly noticed the shrapnel wound I'd received from the exploding missile. The pain from my neck injury masked every other sensation.

"The blast from the missile knocked me out," Guy said. "When I came to, we were going downhill. I grabbed the stick, but it wouldn't budge. I was reaching for the D-ring to eject when I lost consciousness again." Thank God I'd been able to eject us both; Guy woke up in his parachute.

We'd been trained to "escape and evade" if downed in enemy territory. But our chances of evasion were slim to none. We couldn't have picked a worse spot to land in if we'd tried—we were in the heart of an Iraqi division that had taken a serious pounding by Allied forces the previous day, and were within a mile of the artillery batteries we'd been trying to trash ten minutes before. The area we'd landed in was so heavily fortified that you could run half a mile in any direction and bump into somebody or something.

Could Guy and I make it to the coast? Bleeding and still in shock, neither of us was in any shape to run our fastest mile. With bad guys positioned in cottages all along the coast, our getaway through the desert moonscape would prove the old boxing maxim: "You can run, but you can't hide." Almost devoid of hills, furrows, or vegetation, the desert sand would retain footprints deep enough for even an amateur tracker to find. Our only hope was to get picked up by a search-and-rescue (SAR) helicopter.

We pulled our small survival radios from our torso harnesses. "Mayday! Mayday! Mayday!" We tried to get *anybody* to respond. No response, only static. The Iraqis would soon arrive—time was running out. I scanned the sky. A Huey helicopter with two Cobra escorts would be a gift from heaven right now.

Before I could devise an evasion plan, I heard a rumble in the distance. To the southeast a tan vehicle, possibly a hum-vee, jounced over the sand. "Marines got across the border already?" I was amazed: I hadn't known hum-vees could do over fifty miles an hour. "Thank you, God," I prayed.

But my heart sank as the vehicle swooped down on us.

We were cornered.

Oceanside, California
January 17, 1991

"Honey, I wish I knew what you were going through right now," I said, speaking into the handheld recorder. Since Cliff's departure five months earlier, I had recorded brief messages throughout the day—while driving, cooking in the kitchen, lying in bed at night. He cherished the tiny tapes of my voice. They often lulled him to sleep late at night as he lay on his cot holding the cassette player on his chest. "Whatever you're doing, I know you're doing it well . . ." I paused.

Since the war had started, I had felt a deep sense of foreboding, a feeling of impending disaster. "Every wife must feel this way when her husband is in a war," I reminded myself. I released the red record button.

For those with loved ones in the Gulf, the wait had been agonizing as the days marched toward January 15. After midnight on that date, Coalition forces were to commence military operations if Iraq had not withdrawn its forces from Kuwait.

On January 9, Secretary of State James Baker met with Iraqi Foreign Minister Tariq Aziz. My hopes were high that this last-ditch effort might work. Surely Saddam must be starting to sweat. Six hours later the meeting concluded. Secretary Baker's first word—"Regrettably"—immediately fore-told the unfortunate result.

The fears of the American people multiplied. Demonstrators gathered in the streets and in front of government buildings. Citizens held candlelight vigils and special church services. Along with family and friends, nonmilitary families now shared our burden. The U.S. public rallied behind our troops with care packages, letters addressed to "any soldier," yellow ribbons, flags, bumper stickers, and other symbols of patriotism and support.

The American people waited, feeling helpless. The world was on the brink of war. As the clock ticked toward the January 15 deadline, I became increasingly jittery, preoccupied with Cliff's safety in combat.

Late on the afternoon of January 16, the television announcement stunned me: "The liberation of Kuwait has begun." The war had given birth to new graphics, new music, and a new name: Operation Desert Storm. I stared at the TV. All I wanted was a little more time—for Cliff to fly more combat exercises in Saudi Arabia, for me to fortify his food cache, to prepare myself. Now no packages could be delivered to frontline units.

Now that the long-discussed, long-debated war was on, I felt a strange sense of relief. "This is better," I thought. "We'll get it over with and know the outcome that much sooner." But tears slid down my cheeks. The media and many politicians had predicted thousands of casualties in the first weeks, tens of thousands after the ground war began.

That night, calls poured in from squadron wives, friends, and family—some lending support, others seeking it. The phone lines were jammed, crackling with fear. My sister called from Seattle. "You're so calm," Bonnie said, surprised at my composure.

"I can't fall apart now. Squadron families are depending on me.... Besides, worse things could happen."

That first night of the war, people all over the world were glued to their televisions. Crime rates were down as even lawbreakers watched the progress of the war. I attended an emergency meeting aboard Marine Corps Base Camp Pendleton to prepare for war casualties and official notifications. The topics discussed at the meeting frightened me: Hostile Fire pay, 800 numbers for casualty information, and the eerily named Death Gratuity.

We learned that sixty-three hospitals, two hospital ships, and eighteen thousand beds awaited casualties in the war zone. If those spaces filled, additional wounded would be flown to Camp Pendleton. The number of potential casualties, especially from Iraq's hidden chemical, biological, and nuclear arsenal, was terrifying.

Wives raised questions about their concerns. "What is the policy for notifying families of POWs and MIAs?" one wife had asked. I was impressed at her foresight. I, for one, had not even considered that possibility.

As I drove home from the emergency meeting that night, my head was swimming with details. If we had a squadron casualty, would I remember what to do? Would I say the right thing? Who might it be... Cliff?

When Cliff became a commanding officer, I had worried about being the perfect CO's wife. Most wives of senior officers have several years to gain

experience before their husbands take command; even Cliff trained for eighteen years for his job. But having been married less than two years, I knew
little about military life with its unique protocol and way of living. As a Marine
wife, I was a rookie. I had no idea I'd perform my role during wartime.

As the CO's wife I expected to chair the squadron's Officers' Wives Club
(OWC), an organization where new wives make friends, contribute to charitable projects, and receive emotional support during deployments. The ties
created between wives are invaluable during emergencies, times of high-
stress deployments, and when an aircraft mishap occurs. And tragedies
occur—even during peacetime and to the best of pilots.

Especially daunting to me was the prospect of accompanying Cliff on an
"official call," the heartbreaking task of notifying next of kin that their loved
one has died. The personal involvement of a commander and his wife can
ease a family's pain of loss.

Intent on becoming a proper CO's wife, I hosted a brunch for several
commanders' wives I admired, hoping to glean some insight into the things
that made them—and now me—different from civilian and even other military wives. I learned more from those commanders' wives than from any of
my books on military etiquette.

After Cliff's change of command, I threw myself wholeheartedly into my
role as CO's wife. At my first monthly OWC meeting, I shared ideas for
family and charitable activities and told the wives about the monthly
newsletter I planned to publish. We searched for a name that tied in with
"Bronco," the nickname of the OV-10, or "Hostage," the squadron's radio call
sign. We considered "Bronco Tales" and "The Horse's Mouth," but as an eerie
harbinger of things to come, VMO-2 wives selected "The Hostage Release."

Cliff's chosen profession was inherently dangerous, even in peacetime. In
the first year after we married, six of Cliff's fellow Marine pilots had died in
aircraft mishaps. The death of a Marine comrade was like losing a family
member.

When we married, I had been surprised at how our lives entwined with his
Marine Corps career. "You must realize your husband does not sell shoes," a
Marine friend once explained. "He is a Marine twenty-four hours a day."

During those early months of marriage, I quickly learned the truth to the
Marine's statement. Cliff never put his job as the executive officer, or XO, of
his helicopter squadron behind him when he left work at night. When problems or emergencies arose at the squadron, he received the initial call, frequently in the middle of the night. After deciding on a course of action, he
briefed the commanding officer before putting his plan into effect. With
three hundred squadron members and twenty-eight helicopters, often
deployed across the country, Cliff seemed to work seven days a week.

Most Marines work long hours, have unpredictable schedules, and deploy
all over the world, sometimes on short notice—making life interesting for

their spouses. Marine wives joke that the designation "Dependent Wife"— or its abbreviation, "D/W"—stands for "doing without"—without your family, your friends, a consistent address, and more often than not, your husband. Far from being dependent, military wives were some of the most capable women I had met.

Cliff and I had celebrated our first anniversary with a four-day camping trip to Big Bear Mountain in the California Sierras. Our tent site in a secluded forest provided a rare opportunity for solitude, and surprisingly, my first glimpse of an OV-10.

On the second morning of our getaway, we awoke to a continuous humming sound in the cloudless sky above our campsite. Cliff and I climbed out of our tent, curious to discover the source of the noise high above the towering pine trees.

Stephany stumbled out after us, yawning and stretching. Then ten years old, with her long, slender legs and pale green eyes, she looked more like her father every day. Stephany and I had hit it off immediately, and I grew to love her as my own. When the three of us debated an issue, Cliff said he was outnumbered two to one. Through her, I understood the joys of having children and came to wish for one of my own—when Cliff's schedule slowed down.

The humming noise overhead grew louder. Shielding his eyes, Cliff scanned the blue, high-mountain sky. "Looks like OV-10s." He pointed above the treeline to the plane with the distinctive twin tail. "A flight of two. Wonder what they're doing up here."

The two planes were 240 miles from their home base of Camp Pendleton and flew in tight formation, as if searching for something.

Two days later, we headed down the mountain to our home in Oceanside, forty-five minutes north of San Diego, near Camp Pendleton, the Marine base where Cliff was stationed. Our two-story stucco house with a red-tile roof sat high on a hill with a bird's-eye view of the Pacific Ocean, four miles away.

After we arrived home Cliff called his helicopter squadron and learned the reason for the planes' search. An OV-10 Bronco and its crew of two had disappeared. The next morning, he climbed into the cockpit of a Cobra attack helicopter to join the search that had already gone on for nearly a week.

The search was especially frustrating because the squadron's commanding officer had no idea where the plane might have gone down. The possible crash sites encompassed most of southern California and western Arizona. Though every flight crew is required to conduct an extended flight briefing to review its mission, route of flight, and emergency procedures, pilots in this squadron had bypassed their own procedures. The search continued every day.

Two weeks later, Cliff came home from work and told me the missing plane had been found. Both the pilot and the aerial observer had ejected moments before the plane crashed into a mountain in southern California. Unfortunately, neither man had survived.

The grisly images Cliff described of the charred OV-10 and its victims added fuel to my active imagination. Though I trusted Cliff's flying skills, I worried about his safety—especially when I was lying in bed late at night, waiting for his return after a night flight training with night vision goggles (NVGs). Aware of my late-night worries, he always called home after landing with the same short message of assurance: "Safe on deck."

With nearly ten years of experience and 2,000 hours of flight time, he was considered a "good stick" in the Cobra. And he reassured me that his days of hot dog stunts were behind him. "I've got too much to come home to now," he had said, giving me a hug.

"I don't know why," Cliff told me that night as we talked about the Bronco crash, "but the OV-10 community has always had a high rate of mishaps."

"I'm glad you fly Cobras," I told Cliff, squeezing his hand. "Even if they don't have ejection seats—they didn't help these poor men."

A few weeks later, Cliff arrived home long after dinner and surprised me with his news. That afternoon, he had been called to the office of his air group commander, Colonel Dan Kuhn, a soft-spoken man of quiet strength whose kindly blue eyes were framed with gold wire-rimmed glasses.

Eagerly, I listened to Cliff retell their conversation. Colonel Kuhn, a man of integrity who cared deeply about his Marines, was not only a respected Marine superior but a trusted friend. That afternoon, he and Cliff had discussed the efficiency and morale problems plaguing VMO-2, the OV-10 squadron that had lost the Bronco months earlier. After the fatal plane crash, VMO-2's morale had plummeted. Colonel Kuhn needed someone to step in to provide new leadership, order, and discipline, the glue that holds military units together.

"I want you to take command of VMO-2 by June of 1990," Colonel Kuhn said. "I've selected you because of your judgment, your high standards, your attention to detail, and most of all, your ability to lead Marines."

"What was your reaction?" I asked Cliff, trying to keep my voice light.

"I was stunned."

"Did you say yes?"

Cliff laughed. "He's my group commander. He didn't *give* me an option."

I felt proud. Cliff a commanding officer! It was every Marine officer's dream, and he was tailor-made for this challenge. But flying a completely different aircraft? His earlier observation about OV-10s and frequent mishaps haunted me.

Now, late on the second night of Operation Desert Storm, my worries over Cliff's safety multiplied as never before. But the war was going well for Coalition forces. Allied attacks had achieved what General Colin Powell described as "tactical surprise." Spirits were high, the stock market soared, and people celebrated our air superiority and our near invincibility: only three allied planes had been shot down. The spectacle of public joy magnified my private pain. I became angry. "Why is everyone so happy? How would they feel if someone *they* loved was in one of those planes?"

President Bush tried to rein in the increasing euphoria of the American public. "There will be losses," he reminded us. "War is never cheap or easy."

I pressed the red record button to continue my audiotape to Cliff.

"I hosted our monthly Officers' Wives Club meeting at the Olive Garden tonight," I began, forcing my voice to sound lighthearted. Yet in the hours before the meeting, several wives had called to ask if our meeting was still on. "This is why we have our wives support group," I told them. "To support each other during these difficult times." What better way to face our fears than with a group of supportive peers? But some worried that our group of military wives might be targeted for a terrorist attack.

Driving to the Olive Garden earlier that night, I had reminded myself to put on a brave face. Moods are contagious, and I had to set an example of calmness, of steadiness. The wives' strength and courage were infectious. Our conversations—though centered on our absent husbands—were a pleasant diversion. We laughed about Baghdad Betty, descendant of Tokyo Rose and Hanoi Hanna, who bombarded American troops with Iraqi propaganda over the radio. Her English wasn't good, nor were her facts. "While you are here," she taunted, "your wives and girlfriends are dating American movie stars . . . like Tom Selleck, Paul Newman, and Bart Simpson!"

It felt good to laugh for a change.

Even Rosana Martinez, bravely attending her first meeting after the unexpected death of her infant daughter, laughed with us. The wives shared ideas on ways to make the separation easier. A pregnant wife made a body cast of her burgeoning belly. A husband sent his wife a soiled T-shirt to put on the pillow next to hers. His familiar masculine scent comforted her as she lay alone in bed at night. Even their dog liked it.

Before bed that night, I finished my tape to Cliff and requested he send home a worn T-shirt. "Not *too* dirty, please!" I added.

I wondered how to conclude this tape. What could I say to give him strength in combat? Finally, I simply said, "Just remember, wherever you are, no matter how long it takes, I'll be here waiting for you. . . ." My voice started to quaver.

Consumed by my feeling of dread, I removed my tape and inserted the last one Cliff had sent me. The sound of his voice was soothing.

"I'm loving you so much right now. By the time you receive this tape, the war will have started. I've done everything I possibly can to be ready. Please don't worry about me; I *will* be home as soon as this war is over. My life will never be complete until I'm home where I belong with you. I love you, C."

I heaved a huge sigh and laid the recorder on the bed next to me. Was Cliff flying in combat yet? With the eleven-hour time difference between Saudi Arabia and California, it was already early morning in Saudi Arabia. The gulf between us was so vast that as night was falling for me, morning had already broken for him.

Two hours later I awoke from a troubled sleep. A dark fear haunted me. "Please, God, keep him safe," I prayed. Beside me, Cliff's pillow lay cold and empty. I hugged it to me, as if by doing so I could shield him from harm.

But it was too late. No one could do that now.

Southern Kuwait
January 18, 1991

"Mayday!" I radioed. With my heart pounding in my throat, I continued to broadcast my desperate call. "Mayday, Mayday! Hostage Seven-six is down. . . ." I said, stating my official call sign. My eyes were fixated on the four-door Toyota pickup truck bearing down on us. It came to an abrupt halt 200 yards away on an asphalt paved road. Could Guy and I take out these guys? We each had fourteen rounds in our nine-millimeter automatic pistols and were expert marksmen. In a battle of two-on-two I felt confident I could drill them before they took me out. If we drew our weapons before they fired their AK-47s, we might have a chance. . . .

"What am I thinking?" I chided myself. "We're both injured. Without his glasses Guy can't see the broad side of a camel. Within five minutes more Iraqi army regulars are going to arrive—*really* pissed off." I left the pistol in my pouch.

Four Iraqi soldiers in olive-green uniforms leapt out, wielding AK-47 assault rifles. They shouted angrily in Arabic as they sprinted across the sand toward us, rifles aimed. Their message was clear: "Drop your survival radio!"

"This is Hostage-Seven-six." I was talking at the speed of heat to get out my Mayday call. "Downed aircraft . . . Acree and Hunter are alive and on Kuwaiti soil. . . ." Each word I broadcast was priceless.

The Iraqi soldiers were 100 yards away, yelling louder. I considered our chances of escape. If Guy and I sprinted our best three-mile time, it would take at least thirty minutes to slog through the sand to the border. But it would be crazy! Guy was blind, and we were both bleeding with shrapnel wounds. To escape and evade would cost us our lives.

The Iraqi soldiers gestured frantically for us to raise our hands. We hesitated, wanting to keep broadcasting. Twenty-five yards away and closing, two soldiers pulled the bolts of their weapons, chambering rounds, preparing to fire. Both barrels pointed at my head. There's a time when you have to call it quits. Staring down the barrels of AK-47s, I knew this was it.

"Guy, they want us to drop our radios. They're going to shoot if we don't."
I lowered my radio and held it to my side in submission. "Guy, put your
radio down." We raised our hands in surrender and became prisoners of war.

It was seven A.M. and freezing cold. We had been on the ground less than
ten minutes. I didn't know it then, but the Coalition High Command in
Riyadh had received sketchy information about our Mayday transmissions.
They knew our OV-10 Bronco had been shot down and that the crew was
on the ground alive. But for days our families would be told there had been
no sign of us or our missing plane. Even though it would make all the difference to the grieving families, no one below the level of Headquarters
Marine Corps, not even the families, could be given this classified information.
One of the cruelties of war is that sometimes loved ones must be denied information that would relieve them but endanger others.

Four uniformed Iraqis circled us. With the high gloss on their black boots,
their well-maintained rifles, and their pressed uniforms, these weren't the raff-
ish soldiers in tattered clothing we had expected. They looked well fed and clean
shaven. The soldiers displayed discipline, and in all honesty I respected their
military demeanor and the way they captured us.

The soldiers tried in vain to remove our complicated flight gear. After
repeated attempts to remove our G suits and torso harnesses, it was obvious
they didn't know how to deal with our life-support equipment. Guy pulled
out his survival knife, which a soldier used to cut off the gear. The soldiers
tore the radios from our hands and slammed them down to the hard-packed
dirt. But the radios bounced back. They were still attached to our survival
vests by thin nylon lines.

The soldiers took our pistols and other gear, including our "blood chits,"
promissory notes printed in English and Arabic that offered a reward for
returning downed allied pilots to friendly forces. Saddam Hussein was also
offering rewards—up to $50,000 for each downed Coalition pilot.

I could only watch as the soldiers removed my equipment and emptied
my pockets. I didn't get mad until one of them lifted out the clear plastic bag
containing Cindy's cookies. He held the zippered bag as if he suspected it
might explode. A puzzled look on his face, he turned the bag over in his
hands, apparently wondering what specialized equipment or nutrition it
contained. He threw the bag in a pile with the rest of the equipment. "You
lucky bastards!" I thought. "Those are the best cookies you'll ever eat."

At least they wouldn't be able to steal Guy's wallet. Before flying in combat, aircrew members normally "sanitize" themselves. We remove all insignias,
patches, and personal effects from our uniforms—wallet, credit cards, or pictures of loved ones—anything that would link us to a particular squadron,
family, or address or that could be used against us by the enemy. For some
reason, that day Guy had forgotten to remove his wallet and his wedding
ring. When he landed he clawed the sand as quickly as he could and buried

the billfold. He was afraid the Iraqis would use the wallet's contents to track down his family.

Guy's eye was bleeding badly. The soldiers directed him to sit on the ground. One of them took a gauze bandage from his first aid pouch. I watched in amazement as he tended Guy's wounded eye. One of the other four soldiers saw my surprise.

"This is the Muslim way," he explained in accented English. Another soldier bandaged my bleeding head.

"Maybe these guys aren't as bad as we've made them out to be," I reflected, "Maybe there's some good in them after all."

And for the first twenty minutes of our captivity our treatment was fair, in accordance with the Geneva Convention. It might have been just as well that I couldn't foresee the brutality ahead, for this was the last humane treatment I would receive for many days.

The soldiers bound our hands behind our backs and walked us 300 yards to a small cinder block building, the electrical substation for the power lines I had nearly plowed into. They ordered Guy and me to sit against the north wall so we wouldn't be seen by any SAR force looking for us from the south. The four Iraqis split up their duties to ensure that there was no possibility we could escape. One Iraqi, near the truck, surveyed the surrounding terrain. Two others guarded us at gunpoint. A fourth searched for the source of an intermittent beeping sound.

I knew the sound was the signal beacon from the seat pan of my ejection seat, automatically beeping every other second. Lying 100 feet directly in front of the substation, it was so close I could hear its electronic beep. Unfortunately, it was close enough for the Iraqis to hear, too.

I shifted around and mumbled to Guy, trying to make enough noise to mask the seat's emergency beacon. If the homing signals could be heard by AWACS or any other Coalition aircraft, a search-and-rescue team could be launched before it was too late.

We talked quietly. "No speak!" one of the Iraqi guards said sternly. The soldier scrutinizing the desert continued to cock his head, straining to better hear as he searched for the location of the series of beeps. With our voices interfering, he couldn't determine its source. Once again the guard warned us, *"No speak!"* Then the soldier searching for the noise spotted the seat pan. He raised his rifle above his head then smashed the pan with the butt of his rifle. The seat was silent. Our last chance to contact the "outside world" was gone. It wouldn't have mattered anyway. Coalition forces never received the signal.

Our final hope of rescue dashed, we waited to see what our captors had in store for us. Ten minutes later a white two-door Toyota pickup with red Arabic lettering pulled up, a tangle of rope, wood, tools, and canvas in the back. Three haggard and scraggly men jumped out.

The scruffy men loaded our collapsed parachutes, our helmets, and our survival gear into the back of the truck. Guy and I were the next payload. The guards motioned for us to stand up. Feeling faint and nauseous, I steadied myself enough to sit on the tailgate of the truck. We were shoved onto the floor of the truck. Two Iraqi soldiers climbed alongside us with their AK-47s raised. One of them motioned for me to move all the way up to the cab where a driver and another soldier rode shotgun.

Slumped against the truck cab, my head felt like a dead weight. No matter what position I was in, the neck pain was excruciating. Each time the truck bounced on the road another blast of pain hit me. I scooted down into the truck bed and rolled onto my left side to support my neck against the angry, irregular rhythm of the ride. As the truck jounced along the highway, the cold wind numbed the side of my face exposed to the sky. The other side of my face was cushioned and warm. My head was resting on my parachute, which served to ease a second frightful journey.

For the first time I was able to reflect on what had happened. An hour before I had been in the cockpit of my OV-10 aircraft. That cockpit was now smashed somewhere in the desert. VMO-2 Marines were now without a CO.

It had been seven months since I assumed command of VMO-2 on a warm, breezy day in June 1990. The Camp Pendleton airfield blazed with color that day as nearly 100 flags of the United States, foreign countries, and other military services waved in the summer breeze. The Marine band played Sousa marches throughout the change-of-command ceremony. As I turned to face the 250 Marines standing at attention in squadron formation, I felt a mixture of pride, excitement, and determination.

"We must always be ready," I said to the assembled Marines and spectators. "We must always be prepared. Marines who have gone before us and given their lives in defense of our nation deserve nothing less." I silently vowed to elevate the reputation of the squadron and create a high degree of combat readiness.

I concluded my change-of-command speech by saying, "Twenty-five centuries ago the Chinese warrior-philosopher Sun Tzu advised, 'If you know the enemy and know yourself, you need not fear the result of a hundred battles.'" On that June day in 1990, I couldn't have predicted the battle I would fight against our next enemy, an Iraqi dictator.

As the crowd applauded, an official Marine Corps photographer kneeled in front of the lectern snapping photographs of me. Weeks later, Cindy would gasp as she reviewed the prints of me standing in my green camouflage utilities in front of the backdrop of colorful flags. A black-and-white flag nearly obscured the rest. Its stark profile of a man's bowed head loomed over me like a grim omen; it was the POW/MIA flag.

Now, seven months later, the omen's prediction had come true. I was a

POW, in the hands of Iraqi captors, being transported to an unknown destination. But the overpowering pain from my injured neck nearly surpassed my concern for my future.

After a ten-minute drive, the truck abruptly halted. I looked around. We had stopped next to a relatively new asphalt road near what appeared to be an underground bunker. The Iraqis yelled at Guy and me, then jumped from the truck. They dragged us out, pitching us onto the ground. We regained our balance and stood briefly, surrounded by about five Iraqi officers and twenty troops.

Once again, the appearance of the Iraqis didn't match my images. Although I wasn't allowed to look up, in a glimpse I saw they were fit and healthy, not gaunt and sick as newscasts had reported. They were well dressed, well armed, and confident. But my perusal was brief: In Arabic societies, eye contact is an assumption of equality.

Two soldiers approached us yelling in Arabic. They pushed us to our knees, then shoved us facedown onto the gritty road. My neck was forced back as my face scraped the wet asphalt. I heard the sound of someone cranking up a field telephone. An Iraqi squatted over the metal box, speaking quickly in Arabic. I guessed he was asking someone of authority, "Hey, we've got these two pilots here; what do you want us to do with them?" Silence, then a grunt of affirmation. A decision had been made.

A horde of Iraqis descended upon us. Forcing my head onto the ground, one of them grabbed my arms and wrenched them behind my back. He removed my wristwatch, then applied the first handcuff, digging two metal prongs on either side of the handcuff into my wrist for increased control. To get the device as tight as possible, the soldier placed my manacled wrist on the ground and stood on it. I grunted in pain as the metal prongs dug into my flesh. The guards looking on snickered. Spurred on by this, the soldier tightened my metal handcuff another notch. The second handcuff went on even tighter, and the Iraqi kicked it for good measure. The pressure and pain in my wrists were incredible. The metal claws of the cuffs had been forced into the protruding knuckles of my wrist bones, and the cuffs themselves were so tight they were cutting off the circulation. My hands immediately began to swell. A few feet away, Guy groaned as he received the same treatment.

I was blindfolded and hurled back into the truck. As I collapsed onto the floor, our captors manhandled Guy in beside me. The truck lurched forward. I began the journey I would remember as "the trip to hell."

2

The Gathering Storm

Oceanside, California
Early August 1990

"Why are *we* getting involved?" I asked Cliff as we discussed Iraq's unprovoked invasion of Kuwait. We talked as we often did at the kitchen table, the hub of our house. Here we ate our meals, planned our future, shared our successes and challenges.

Until now I had watched Iraq's invasion of Kuwait in a distant, "doesn't affect me" sort of way—like watching news of a faraway plane crash, thinking, "Too bad for those people over there." I didn't know anyone involved. It wasn't my news.

Wasn't there always one Middle Eastern country or another in a border dispute, a feud they could settle among themselves? Why was this one any different?

Cliff once told me that, historically, a major war occurs about every twenty years. We were coming up on twenty years since Vietnam, but I felt assured that this time world events would disprove his prediction. Relations with countries of the former Soviet Union had improved, the Berlin Wall had been torn down, and communism itself was crumbling. The U.S. government even planned to downsize our armed forces now that there was no worry of a war between the superpowers. But that day, as I listened to President Bush deliver his "line in the sand" speech, I realized the world was still an uncertain one.

"There's more at stake than one small country or the rights to its oil," Cliff explained. "Iraq brutally attacked and pillaged Kuwait, a small, peaceful country. Saddam Hussein has produced chemical and biological weapons, and he's working on a nuclear bomb. We have to stop him." Such was the goal of the first contingent of American troops heading to the Persian Gulf. "Marine squadrons from Camp Pendleton might be going, too," Cliff added.

I stared at Cliff. The invasion of Kuwait, seemingly so remote, had become my news. In the days following, several Marine friends readied to deploy. The line in the sand had moved closer to home.

I felt sorry for the wives whose husbands were going, so suddenly deployed into an unknown situation. And they couldn't share their burden. A military bulletin advised service members not to discuss which units were deploying, where they were going, when they would arrive, and how many people were involved. Officially they could only confirm to loved ones that they would be deploying "in the near future to the Middle East" as a part of Operation Desert Shield and that "the duration of the deployment is indefinite." The emphasis on secrecy added to family members' anxiety.

A second bulletin advised spouses to "keep letters from loved ones private and not speculate about ongoing or upcoming operations." Appearing on camera or being quoted in other media could make spouses a "news source" for local media.

On August 15, I hosted an Officers' Wives Club meeting. Women crowded into our living room, on the couch, chairs, floor, and sprawled up the stairs. Sitting together, we wives felt as if we were in a game of Russian roulette. Would my husband be next to leave, or would it be the husband of the woman next to me?

The apprehensive group of wives listened intently as Cliff described the squadron's involvement. He provided as much unclassified information as he could. When he didn't have an answer to a question or was not at liberty to share an answer, he told the wives so. He jokingly cautioned, "If you quote me on this, they'll string me up by my thumbs!"

I passed out an emergency information sheet I had designed with Cliff's help. On this form, wives were to list their nearest relative, their religious preference, and whom they wanted me to call in case of an "emergency" (read: your husband has been injured or killed).

VMO-2 wife Catherine Gamboa recalls, "Listening to your presentation felt like listening to a flight attendant review emergency procedures on an airplane. Throughout the safety lecture you're thinking, 'This plane will never have a sudden loss of cabin pressure or an emergency landing over water. It's good to practice, but it will never happen to me.' We're used to watching television and seeing all the disasters happen to other people. Then I realized this disaster could happen to me."

After the meeting, Cliff spoke privately with Rosana Martinez, a squadron wife gifted with keen insight into people. Her wavy brown hair framed a heart-shaped face that often held a teasing grin. Her laugh was contagious. Rosana and Marty's second child was due in less than three months; when their daughter was born, Marty had been deployed to Okinawa, missing the birth.

"How would you feel if Marty was deployed?" Cliff asked her as they sat alone in the living room. If Cliff's squadron was deployed to Saudi Arabia, he would need to decide who would go, and who would stay behind at Camp Pendleton.

"Wherever Marty's needed most, that's where I want him to go," she answered, without a hint of self-pity. "Besides," she said, smiling, "he wouldn't be much help in the delivery room anyway."

I couldn't imagine being so magnanimous if Cliff was suddenly deployed. We had known each other since high school, but for nearly twenty years it always seemed like something—other people, my career, his deployments— kept getting in the way. Now that we were finally married, I wanted to make up for lost time, not be pulled apart again.

I wrote in my journal:

> I feel selfish, but I'm glad Cliff is staying home and will be safe.... He will stay behind with the bulk of the squadron and call the shots for both detachments. What a relief! Everything is highly confidential and I can't discuss it with family or friends.

The Middle East crisis snowballed. Each night, Cliff had come home later and later, with a keen sense of urgency in everything he did. The demands on the United States military gathered momentum like a tidal wave, engulfing everything in its path. I feared that before long, Cliff would be swept up, too. The news was frightening, with more American troops being deployed daily.

One night Cliff arrived home with a mixture of excitement and concern on his face. "We need to talk," he said, leading me to the kitchen table. The scope of the mission had enlarged, he explained, involving more people and planes from his squadron. "And I'm going, too," he added quickly, as if slipping it in would soften the blow. As he watched my face for a reaction, a chill came over me despite the eighty-degree August heat. I had wanted to believe Cliff's training was only war games, guys out having fun, taking themselves too seriously. Now, as he revealed his plans, I swallowed hard. The line in the sand had reached the kitchen table, tearing us apart once more.

Oceanside, California
Mid-August 1990

"Damn!" I said, watching the Cable News Network (CNN) coverage of Operation Desert Shield. "That's where I should be." I saw my former helicopter squadron on the TV screen, unloading their gear from a huge cargo plane under the hot sun of Saudi Arabia. Watching with me, Cindy grimaced at my eagerness.

The action in the Middle East was heating up. Iraq continued to pillage Kuwait and terrorize its people. Two Air Force F-15 squadrons and several B-52 bombers had already gone over on the first wave. Camp Pendleton had moved into high gear, loading convoys of trucks and trailers with military equipment to sail to the Persian Gulf aboard ships. Railroad cars packed with equipment left for destinations unknown. Cars crowded the parking lots twenty-four hours a day. Everyone was putting in long hours, but no one seemed to mind, excited at the possibility of deploying on short notice.

Watching my helicopter buddies already setting up in Saudi Arabia, I felt the "A Team" had formed and we hadn't been selected to play. I was anxious to get to where the action was. This time flying an OV-10.

The transition from helicopters to fixed-wing aircraft in early 1990 had entailed a major shift in my flying career. I hadn't flown fixed-wing aircraft since flight school ten years before. Before taking command in June 1990, I spent three months at Davis Monthan Air Force Base in Arizona, learning to fly the OV-10 Bronco.

My OV-10 training at Davis Monthan began in the classroom. At thirty-eight years of age, I felt like an old man next to the lieutenants and captains in my flight program. But flying the OV-10, pressing the plane to its limits, was a pleasure. Broncos can fly as low as 100 feet and as high as 25,000 feet, and can travel nearly twice as fast as the Cobra helicopter. Though it lacks the explosive acceleration of a jet, the Bronco maneuvers easily through loops, spins, barrel rolls, and other aerobatics. I practiced until these skills became second nature. The proficiency and confidence I gained could save my life someday if I had to evade enemy fire or recover from an airborne emergency.

My days away were intense and challenging, but I wrote to Cindy nearly every night. I loved being a Marine. Every job, every duty station, taught me something. But I was ready to give up my nomadic lifestyle. Cindy was a loving, supportive wife, and our home was my haven. A letter to Cindy explained this change in priorities:

> I always considered being away from home an adventure. No longer. Since we've been married, the *last* place I want to be is away from you. We were meant to share our lives together, Cindy. I *know* there's no other place for me.

I had vivid memories of her—an athletic, ambitious sixteen-year-old—the summer we met in a Seattle karate dojo. I drew a mental picture of her dressed in her white karate gi, with long, shiny hair falling to the narrow waist cinched by an orange karate belt. With her sparkling green eyes and inviting smile, Cindy stood out among the other students—most of whom were male.

Twenty years later, I still admired her intelligence, her drive, and her zest for life. But after less than two years of marriage, we found ourselves parting again.

"Look at the bright side," I had told her before I headed to Arizona. "This should be the last time we're separated. After this I'll probably leave the fleet for a staff position. If I'm assigned overseas, you and I will go together."

After completing my OV-10 training, I flew my NATOPS check—the final test to fully qualify me to pilot the OV-10. This NATOPS check or "check ride" includes written and oral exams followed by a flight during which the pilot performs all maneuvers and emergency procedures.

I had studied hard for this check ride, reviewing emergency procedures every night with Cindy drilling me. "Single engine failure," she'd say, and I would methodically rattle off the step-by-step procedures. By the time I flew my qualification flight in April, I knew them cold.

The first "emergency" my instructor put the plane into during my check ride was a stall. I went through the procedures and we leveled off. Then he shut down one of the engines. I went through the procedures for a single engine failure. The engine engaged. Fifteen seconds later it shut down again. "This guy's giving me a hard time!" I thought. As I started through the procedures again he spoke to me over the headset. "This is the real thing!"

The instructor declared an airborne emergency, and I began the emergency procedures to land the plane with a single engine. We touched down safely on the runway amid five emergency vehicles with lights flashing and firefighters in thermal suits aiming hoses at the plane. After shutting down the remaining engine, I stepped onto the runway. I felt an enormous sense of pride at passing a true test of my OV-10 flying skills, not unlike the pride I felt for the Marines of my squadron.

After my change of command, I had my hands full with exercises, inspections, deployments, training, personnel problems, and turning around the troubled squadron. The daily "report card" of the squadron, the Aircraft Maintenance Report, is reviewed by each level of command, including the commanding general. It states by percentage the combat readiness of each squadron's aircraft. When I took command, the squadron scored in the low sixtieth percentile.

For eight months, squadron maintenance members had worked at least one day on every weekend. Though most Marines of VMO-2 routinely worked six days a week, the squadron still couldn't meet its maintenance or flight hour quotas. Most squadron members were counting the days until they left for a new assignment.

"You've been working a long seven days a week," I told them. "From now on, we'll work a smart five."

For ten days after my change of command, I ordered a safety and maintenance stand-down. All planes were grounded until I was satisfied they were safe and combat ready. "When you get eighty percent or better on aircraft readiness," I told the Marines of my unit, "we're on our way to being safer and more combat ready. You'll get this and every weekend off that you achieve eighty percent or higher."

I set about building a new team. Each workday I focused on a different department, talking to its staff, asking about their problems, and showing a genuine interest in their actions and responsibilities. I continually reinforced their contributions so each member of the squadron realized how his or her efforts counted toward the greater whole. I encouraged people to talk to me, to be themselves, and above all, to be honest. "If you've screwed up," I told them, "tell me and we'll fix it together, then we'll train not to repeat the mistake."

I strived to be an exacting and decisive CO. A squadron formation called at 7:45 was not to take place at 7:46. I required accurate, thorough documentation. Any paperwork sent to me for my signature that was incorrect or incomplete was returned to the originator. Meticulous records tracked equipment usage and expenditures. Previously, records documenting flight training had been submitted late or not at all. Now instructor pilots were required to submit training forms within twenty-four hours of completing a flight.

My temper stayed even until I had to fight for my Marines. I remained at the squadron each night until the aircraft maintenance night crew came on duty. Before leaving, I often checked the sack lunches the mess hall prepared for them. One night I found sandwiches on stale, smashed bread, no fruit or vegetables, and many drinks missing.

Fuming, I drove straight to the mess hall. "I wouldn't feed these lunches to my dog!" I thrust a lunch into the hands of the senior Marine in the mess hall. "If we ask our Marines to work at night, the least we can do is give them a decent meal!"

As the Marine pulled out a dry, flattened sandwich, I told him, "I never again want to witness an evening meal like this for the Marines of VMO-2. If I do, I promise that you and I will meet with your CO for a visit you won't soon forget." Thirty minutes later, I arrived back at the squadron with dinners I had purchased.

I demanded a lot of the Marines in VMO-2 and gave them as much in return. Before long, my efforts began to have their rewards. Thirty days after the change of command, weekend work was rare. A month after that, the squadron routinely scored above 87 percent on aircraft readiness, better than any squadron in the air group. Unauthorized absences, formerly one or two per week, went to zero per month. Reenlistment rates went up across the board. Marines who had purposely avoided assignment to the squadron requested to come aboard. Squadron members felt a sense of teamwork, efficiency, and pride in VMO-2. The squadron had become a cohesive team, and smiles returned to many faces.

A wife visiting the squadron confided in me, "I don't know what you're doing, but for the first time in months, my husband is excited about going to work in the morning."

I had pushed VMO-2 Marines to achieve the goals they were capable of, and had pushed myself even harder. Now I could pull back a little and concentrate on my flying abilities in the OV-10.

In July 1990, we celebrated the squadron's success by hosting our first squadron party. Sixty-five people attended our Bronco Bash, including the wives of husbands who were deployed to Okinawa. While I led the wives in a line dance to music of Diana Ross and the Supremes, several Marines sneaked into my well-organized garage and rearranged the systematic placements of my tools and turned our car sideways. They followed that prank by reversing the living room and dining room furniture.

I laughed when I saw their antics. The Marines knew I had a sense of humor and that they could trust me to not take offense. Late that night Cindy and I crawled into bed. Our laughter bubbled up again when we drew up the bedsheet and the bottom pulled past our ankles. As a final prank the Marines had short-sheeted our bed.

That night in bed, we talked about our Bronco Bash and the bonding it had fostered. I had nearly achieved my goal at VMO-2. My OV-10 training was behind me. Now we could make time for ourselves.

But three weeks later, Iraq invaded Kuwait. VMO-2 was given a Warning Order, which means "Stand by to deploy." Though I didn't know when or how, my squadron was to immediately ready a group of Marines. When called, this advance detachment of four to six officers plus 120 support personnel would head to the Middle East.

I was eager to get to the Middle East myself and test my flying skills again, maybe this time in combat. I had to downplay my excitement around Cindy. "It's not that I want to leave *you*," I kept reminding her. "This is what I've spent seventeen years of my life training for. It's what I've wanted to experience ever since I came into the Marine Corps."

"I guess I don't have enough testosterone to relate!" she replied. She'd rather stay home where it was safe, but for any Marine, staying behind would never do. I was proud to fly a tactical aircraft, and like the other pilots I knew, I yearned to test myself in the only arena that mattered: combat. Our Super Bowl was about to begin, and for the first time I'd be the quarterback, calling the shots for my own team.

My biggest challenge was getting our planes to the Middle East. The planes couldn't be flown there in even the largest military cargo plane—the wingspan of the OV-10 is too wide for it to fit inside even the C5A Galaxy aircraft. They couldn't travel by ship—every Navy ship large enough to carry us was either en route to Saudi Arabia or already being loaded with aircraft, tanks, ammunition, fuel, food, and medical supplies. VMO-2 pilots could fly the slow-moving planes to the Middle East, but not without considerable risk. Too many things could happen along the way—running out of parts or people, bad weather, lack of logistical support. It was too far, out of the scope of what had reasonably been accomplished in the past.

VMO-2 Marines weren't about to sit back and wait for someone to tell us how we'd get our planes there. We took the initiative and studied the problem from every angle, settling on a strategy to fly the OV-10s to the Middle East.

OV-10s are not equipped for air-to-air refueling, so the plan developed by VMO-2 Marines called for the Broncos to fly to southwestern Asia in 800-to-1,000-mile hops. With the length of the route and the unpredictably stormy weather near Greenland and Iceland, our planning had to be thorough. This nearly 10,000-mile journey had never been attempted before with this aircraft.

We put the final touches on our plan and I presented it to Colonel Kuhn, the commanding officer of the air group. "That's a long flight, full of risk," he said. He preferred transporting the aircraft aboard ship via the Panama Canal. Though much slower, it involved less peril. He requested we augment our plan with solutions to any conceivable "what if" situations such as engine failures en route, especially while flying over water.

We added detailed contingency plans for every imaginable emergency, including ditching in the icy waters off Greenland. Four days later, I briefed the wing commanding general. He sent our proposal up the chain of command, and I waited for the response.

"We need to be ready, whatever the decision," I told my Marines. From that moment on, there was a warlike urgency in everything we did. The Marines in my squadron raced against the clock to prepare for this first-ever OV-10 global crossing.

The squadron would fly to Saudi Arabia in two groups. The advance party of six planes with eight pilots and eight aerial observers would leave first, accompanied by two C-130 transport planes. The C-130s carried spare parts and a maintenance crew, and would provide backup navigation. A week later, the main body of 130 men would fly to the Middle East in a C-141. Their two-day flight would arrive three weeks ahead of the advance party.

The operations staff finalized plans for the OV-10s' route of flight, planning every leg of the journey down to the most minute detail. The squadron maintenance department readied aircraft parts, tested equipment, and packed everything needed to support life and aircraft in the desert for an undetermined length of time. The squadron logistics office packed tents, field desks, cots, sleeping bags, chemical protection garments, and other necessities, and loaded them onto pallets to be flown with the main body of 130 Marines from the squadron.

Our squadron flight surgeon, Navy commander Dr. Joel Lees, a slender man with brown hair and eyes and a quick sense of humor, was just as busy readying the Marines to deploy. He quickly immunized them, completed medical examinations, updated medical records, and ordered glasses, last-minute dental work, and prescriptions.

Choosing which Marines to take to Saudi Arabia and which to leave behind at Camp Pendleton was difficult. Both roles were important. I needed competent men to continue training new pilots who arrived at the squadron and, if needed, to serve as replacements for combat losses. No man left behind would be happy assigned—as he would see it—to the role of bench-warmer. Any Marine worth his salt was doing his best to make sure he was included in the game.

I felt the same way. This flight over was a golden opportunity to do well or to screw up—in a big way. If something went wrong, we'd get high-level attention. If we made it, we'd achieve something everyone in the squadron could be proud of, a boost needed by a squadron too long the underdog.

A couple of days later, we received word from the Commander of Marine Forces in Saudi Arabia that he was "frankly disappointed" the OV-10s were not there yet. He made it clear he wanted his OV-10s "in-country" as soon as possible. Suddenly senior Marine commanders were hustling to get us there the fastest way: fly.

Two days later, Colonel Kuhn called me into his office. "They've approved your route of flight to Saudi Arabia," he said. "How soon can you be ready to go?"

"Forty-eight hours." The planes and equipment were ready. Two days would give my Marines time to handle last-minute personal affairs and say good-bye to family. As Colonel Kuhn walked me out of his office, I thought about saying good-bye to Cindy again. During our twenty-three-month marriage, driving home from work had been a pleasure, knowing she'd be there waiting for me—along with the black Labrador-mix dog we'd adopted and named Cami after Camano Island, my boyhood retreat. Cami's constant companion was Murphy, a fifteen-pound bundle of orange-and-white fur. Pretending to resent the cat's privileged and spoiled life, I called him "His Murphness."

After living in more than twenty different locations during my Marine Corps career, living with Cindy and our animals left me feeling content in a way I never had before. My wandering soul had finally come home.

Colonel Kuhn walked down the hall with me. Stopping outside the operations office, he turned and put his arm on my shoulder. "Well, Cliff, how
would you like to go to war?"

Cindy once asked a similar question: "If you had a choice to be in a war,
would you go?" It was a hypothetical question, but I told her the truth.

"If my country was at war? Of course I'd want to go."

"Even if you knew you might be killed and leave me alone?" I'd seen the
hurt in her eyes.

"Protecting the national interest of our country is what my job is all
about. It's what I've trained my entire career to do."

Now my commander had asked me that no-longer-hypothetical question.
I answered quickly, "VMO-2 is ready and willing to go . . . *anytime*, sir."

Oceanside, California
Mid-August 1990

Cliff was aching to get to the Middle East. As soon as he secured transportation needed for planes, people, and supplies, he would be on his way.

I prayed the crisis would be resolved diplomatically before then, but news
from the Gulf remained grim. Responding to movement of U.S. troops,
Saddam Hussein proclaimed, "Thousands of Americans whom you have
pushed into this dark tunnel will go home shrouded in sad coffins."

Squadron wives called each night, most of them asking the same question:
"When do you think they're coming home?" "I wish I knew!" I wanted to
say. Instead I repeated what Cliff told me: "Plan on at least four to five
months. When it's over, they'll come home."

My mom, a kind, loving woman who never complained about her own
troubles, called one night from Seattle. "Cliff would never have to go, would
he?" she asked. Her voice expressed concern. "It's possible," I fibbed. Cliff
had warned me to assume that when I talked on the phone, someone was listening. Disclosing any information over the phone was strictly taboo.
Technically, *I* wasn't even supposed to know he was being deployed. Though
I didn't want to worry Mom, I hoped my tone of voice would relay Cliff's
imminent departure.

Journal—August 19, 1990

People everywhere are talking about this deployment. I hear conversations at
work, on the radio and in places I shop. When clerks at the grocery store, see
"LtCol" on our checks they ask, "Oh . . . Is *your* husband going?" I always have
to say "I'm sorry, I can't discuss it." I'm so glad I have Debbie to talk to.

Debbie Mills, a slender long-distance runner, was a Marine wife of four-teen years with pretty blue eyes and springy blond curls touching her shoulders. Her husband, Buzz, a longtime helicopter buddy of Cliff's, had already arrived in the Gulf. Besides our concern for our husbands, we shared a love of animals and athletics.

Despite her soft-spoken demeanor, Debbie was a no-nonsense person who held the position of comptroller for a defense contracting firm. I enjoyed her energy, sense of humor, and North Carolinian accent.

Like me, Debbie had taken on the awesome task of establishing a support group for the spouses in her husband's squadron, fitting the responsibility in around the duties of her full-time job. But even after her years of experience with the Marine Corps, she had found it a daunting task. "I'm running scared," she told me. Fears were running high amid this sudden and secretive deployment. I was scared, too. So new to the Marine Corps, I felt especially unprepared to organize a support group for our 200 VMO-2 families whose Marines were deployed in three geographic locations.

One group of VMO-2 Marines was in Okinawa, originally due home from its six-month deployment in January 1991; its return date was now "undetermined." A second group was prepared to deploy to the Middle East. A third group would remain stateside to continue training and operations at Camp Pendleton. This "rear det" would supply replacements to Okinawa and Saudi Arabia if needed. Though wives of men remaining behind might feel relieved, they had their own challenges. It wasn't easy living with a Marine who felt he'd been left behind to "mind the store."

Sergeant Major Warner, still with the rear detachment at Camp Pendleton in August, helped me. Cliff had told me his powerfully built senior enlisted Marine was "tough as nails," a man who did not settle for second best. I suspected the soft-spoken sergeant major was another Marine whose tall, rugged frame hid a sensitive side.

We formed all the squadron wives whose husbands were deployed any-where in the world into one large support group. Fifteen "key wives" volunteered their time and knowledge to act as a liaison between the command and the families left behind.

Organizing the Squadron Wives Support Group kept me busy. Each night I spent hours reading predeployment literature, attending meetings, making phone calls to seek volunteers, planning squadron support group meetings, and doing my best to answer questions.

One night after work, I volunteered with other squadron wives to baby-sit for mothers in Debbie Mills's husband's squadron while they attended a predeployment briefing. During the meeting, to be held on base, mothers would leave their small children with us in an adjoining room; it would be hard enough for them to concentrate on the detailed, complex, and often frightening predeployment instructions without having to deal with the needs of their children.

That night the Mainside chapel was as packed with emotional tension as it was with wives. Many were angry because they had been kept in the dark about their husbands' departures. Among the first to deploy, these men could say *nothing* about where they were going and when. Wives heard more about the squadron's imminent departure from neighbors and television than from the men they slept beside.

The sight of a mother's burgeoning belly reminded me of my visit that week to the base medical clinic. "Your test was negative," the nurse had said kindly. "This has been happening to a lot of wives lately."

That night we baby-sat children whose ages ranged from six months to nine years. Their dads had been gone one week, and their houses were in turmoil. Some kids misbehaved, while others cried continually. Others sat by themselves, clutching the coloring book "Daddy's Days Away."

Having little experience with babies, I took charge of the older children. Two little boys about five and seven sat quietly at a table, their coloring books and crayons untouched. "Not in the mood to color?" I asked as I took a chair beside them.

The older boy replied without looking up. "All I like is airplanes . . . and Ninja Turtles."

"Why do you like airplanes so much?"

He looked up. Showing the first spark of interest, he said proudly, "Because my dad fixes 'em!"

"Anything that flies, my dad can fix!" his brother chimed in. The boys listened intently as I explained how pilots relied on their dad to keep their planes safe.

The older boy looked at me with sad eyes. "My dad's at the war. Have you heard about it?"

"Your dad's not in a war," I said softly. "He's helping people far away protect their country."

At 9:45 P.M. exhausted mothers retrieved their children. For two hours they had listened to frightening presentations on Red Cross emergency notifications, death benefits, wills and powers of attorney requirements, and notification procedures should their husbands be declared either killed in action (KIA) or missing (MIA). The mothers had been warned about sexual assaults and terrorists. Their husbands' locations remained a mystery. They left with only an APO address in San Francisco.

"What an extra burden they must carry," I thought as I watched the mothers hugging their small children. At least I had only myself to worry about. Driving home, I cried for the kids, I cried for their mothers, and I cried for myself.

The following night I returned to my personal to-do list of things to accomplish. Cliff's deployment had instantly reordered our priorities. Now, each night I found myself concerned with updating our wills, compiling emergency information, finding important papers, completing legal forms, securing a power of attorney, and comparing life insurance policies. Cliff was not eligible for many policies since he had no time to supply the required medical tests and blood work. Other policies had a war clause that precluded payments for death during war.

I wanted to freeze time, doubting I'd ever be prepared. There was too much to absorb, and I was doing it with half a brain, the other half filled with fear and the inability to think logically. As Cliff's departure drew near, I became distracted, forgetful, unable to concentrate. I'd forget where my car was parked, or walk upstairs only to forget why I was there. Our once-stable routines were fragmented. Increasingly I awakened at night, often remembering questions I needed to ask Cliff before he left.

During the day, I struggled to focus on my job managing the Southern California branch of an executive search firm. After working as training director for a huge banking corporation in Seattle, I enjoyed working solo in this new line of work. My job was to locate senior management for biotech firms who retained our company. I was satisfyingly successful. But these days, reminders of the Gulf crisis came at me from all directions. Driving to work, I heard a radio advertisement touting "How *you* can profit from the current crisis in the Gulf!" As I walked past the open door of a capital investment firm, its members discussed excitedly the wealth they hoped to acquire. "Is my husband risking his life so other people can make money?" I thought. They had nothing to risk but profits.

As the clock counted down toward Cliff's departure, I had to remind myself to enjoy each day with him, even if our only time together was in bed—asleep. After an eighteen-hour day at the squadron, Cliff often received calls during the night with questions or status reports on preparation of planes and equipment. When a high-level classified message came in, he drove back to the base to read the message and respond on a secure-voice telephone.

Cliff had guided me in my new role as a CO's wife, tutoring me, encouraging me, bolstering my confidence. But now, when I needed him the most, my tutor was leaving. "You can do this!" I'd tell myself, but the next minute I would feel overwhelmed.

Cliff had grown involved and distracted by the urgency of his work. Like an athlete in training for the Olympics, he was preoccupied, agitated, of a singular purpose. At times I found myself wishing he were already gone. Before I knew it, he was.

The night before his early morning departure I drove in to the squadron to join several other wives for our ribbon-tying morale booster. The yellow ribbons we tied would be symbols of good luck and lasting reminders of our deployed men.

As I entered the huge squadron hangar I searched for Cliff's lanky frame. Knowing he'd be taking off from this airfield in the morning for the Persian Gulf brought powerful emotions to the surface. I had to keep them in check.

I spotted Cliff dressed in his flight gear, walking back into the hangar after preflighting his airplane. My heart ached at the sight of him carrying his oxygen mask and other flight equipment. He smiled and waved, then pushed himself on to his next task, gathering the maps and charts he needed to navigate to Saudi Arabia.

Our decorating brigade tied yards of yellow material onto railings, doorknobs, pipes, bulletin boards—anything we could find. The Marines appreciated our cheerleading squad. We chatted and laughed as we scurried about, while underneath our hearts ached.

After the last ribbon was hung, several pilots and their wives gathered on the flight line for picture taking. The advance party of six planes would leave in less than twenty-four hours, followed by the main body of men and equipment, to be flown out by cargo plane three days later.

The planes of the advance party had been newly painted, their standard green camouflage colors replaced by a blue-gray, sky-colored bottom and a desert-sand-colored top. Cliff proudly showed me the plane he would fly. The crew had surprised him by stenciling his name below the pilot's window.

After the picture-taking session, Cliff sent the advance party home. Everyone had last-minute projects, and he was no exception. He still needed to pack. On the way home, I did my final shopping for items on Cliff's list. I picked up a shortwave radio, mapmaking supplies, and Tabasco sauce to spice his "Meals Ready to Eat" (MREs), the modern-day C ration.

Driving through the Oceanside area, I felt a distinct change of atmosphere in the military-based town. Thousands of troops were being deployed from Camp Pendleton. An eerie silence blanketed the streets—even the traffic seemed muted. Except for the final scurrying for supplies, everyone wanted to retreat with their loved ones, savoring those last precious days.

When Cliff arrived home at 6:30, we ate quickly, aware of the clock ticking. We wanted to finish packing by nine o'clock so we could spend a precious hour together then be in bed by ten. Out in the garage, I crossed the items off the list as he packed them into his huge green duffel bag: field gear, earplugs, sunglasses, stamps, survival knife. . . .

Cliff was as meticulous about packing as he was with other aspects of his life—a trait that had taken me some time to get used to. It was one thing to be together for a long weekend and quite another to live daily with each other's idiosyncrasies.

As in his childhood, Cliff's lifestyle emphasized order and routine. Even his closet was organized, with the clothing—even jeans and T-shirts—hung by category on hangers spaced evenly apart. His polished shoes formed a neat line on shelves he had built himself, and his green Marine Corps T-shirts were folded in symmetrical rectangles, the edges aligned like thick pages of a book. In his neatly painted garage, tools above the neat workbench hung on a pegboard in graduated order of size. Banks of plastic drawers and neatly stacked cans held carefully separated nails, screws, and hardware. Every tool had its own spot; in his life neatness reigned.

When I was single, my garage was organized if I could squeeze in the car. Opening its cupboards, I had to duck to avoid the avalanche of junk stuffed into them. Happiest doing five things at once, my style was "quick and dirty." I accomplished projects in half the time it took Cliff but left a wake of clutter in my path. And while he was mortified to arrive after the stated time for a dinner party, I considered it a favor to the hostess.

Our different styles caused a few battles early on. But we learned to compromise. I kept my projects neater and more contained and promised to be ready on time. He learned to be more flexible and to live with a certain amount of chaos. By now we balanced each other. But on this night before his journey to the Middle East, Cliff's normally tidy ways went by the wayside. Now piles of equipment cluttered his normally tidy workbench.

I went into the kitchen to retrieve the "care package" food—mostly cookies—I had baked for Cliff's journey. Walking back to the garage with my load, I stood in the doorway for a moment and watched Cliff. Never had I seen him look so tired—or so thin. As usual, he was pushing himself too hard. In the strain of the past three weeks, he had lost a lot of sleep and eight pounds. I stuffed as many packages of cookies into his bag as I could. Cliff later removed some to fit in other gear. When he wasn't looking, I jammed them back in. After we married I had been determined to add at least five pounds to his slender frame. But he always shared his huge lunches. Soon the "Acree Bakery" had the reputation of supplying most of his staff with cookies.

To complete his packing, Cliff placed a black-and-tan stuffed animal—a striking replica of our dog, Cami—on top of his green duffel bag. It would accompany him in the cockpit as he flew across the globe. The pairing of the soft, huggable dog atop the rough canvas military bag symbolized the duality that had always attracted me to Cliff: the disciplined, rock-hard Marine equally capable of being the pillow-soft, tenderhearted husband and father.

Cliff's final task was to call Stephany and then our families in Seattle to say good-bye. "I may be leaving the area soon," he told them, unable to reveal when he was going or where.

By the time we headed to bed at eleven, Cliff looked drained, the creases in his forehead deeper than I'd ever seen. Taking over a troubled squadron as CO, learning to fly the OV-10, then quickly preparing his squadron for potential combat had been a heavy load to bear.

After kneeling to say his prayers, Cliff climbed into bed. When he reached for his thick OV-10 manual, I couldn't disguise my disappointment. "I just need twenty minutes to study emergency procedures," he said. "The plane is going to be heavy and I've never taken off with such a full load."

I waited, watching the clock, anxious about our dwindling time together. Finally he laid the manual down. He laid his head on the pillow and closed his eyes. "Just give me five minutes to rest." He sounded so tired he seemed almost drugged. Less than a minute later, his breathing became deep and even.

I didn't have the heart to waken him. The alarm was set for four A.M.— four hours from now. The precious hour we had hoped to share on our last night was not to be. I curled up behind him, circling my arm around his waist. Tucking my chin securely beneath his shoulder blades, I bit back sobs that would awaken him.

On Tuesday morning, August 28, the alarm awoke us to the day of his departure. Without speaking we jumped out of bed, at once relieved and sorry that our long-anticipated farewell was near. Cliff had to dress, eat, and be out the door by 4:30. Downstairs, I prepared his breakfast and gave myself a pep talk. "No more lunches to make and dinners to plan," I said silently. "Fewer groceries to shop for, no more ugly green T-shirts to wash. I can come and go as I please."

After eating, it was time for Cliff to go. He knelt on the floor to say good-bye to Cami. But his tremulous voice and pained expression confused her. She backed away. He pulled the frightened dog into a tight bear hug. "I'll miss you, Cami." His eyes filled with tears.

At the front door, we held each other without speaking. What was there to say? Things had happened so quickly. It seemed one day we looked forward to our busy lives settling down—the next, he was journeying across the world.

Cliff patted my back. "Gotta go, Babe," he gently said. We broke apart, still holding hands. I tried to force a smile. The penetrating look in Cliff's eyes told me he, too, wondered when he would return. We froze for a moment, reluctant to face our final good-bye.

"Time to go," Cliff reminded me. We walked out into the early morning chill. He swung his heavy duffel bag into the bed of the pickup, then turned and put his hands around my shoulders.

"Nobody's shooting over there. This is only a show of force." He squeezed my shoulders. "In the time it takes us to fly over there, this whole situation may blow over. Then I'll turn around and fly home." He looked at me with a forced smile. "It'll be the world's greatest cross-country flight ever!"

I nodded, unable to speak for fear my pent-up tears would flood out. "I'll call you before I take off," he promised, brushing my cheek. "I love you, Babe."

"Love you, too," I managed.

He hugged me tightly. Then, without speaking, he climbed into the cab of the truck. He lifted a hand in farewell, then backed out of the driveway. I waved as the truck rumbled down the street in the dark. My best friend was gone. As the red taillights bled off into the distance, I felt tears gathering in my throat. "What if I never see him again?"

With an emptiness in my heart, I turned and walked back into the house. I knelt beside Cami and petted her soft black head. The house felt eerily empty and quiet. The stillness was broken only by an unbridled sob that had been building yet contained for so many days.

Camp Pendleton, California
August 28, 1990

"The eyes of the Marine Corps are upon you," I told the Marines assembled on the flight line that morning before takeoff. "You're taking part in something that has never been done in the history of our Corps. Our goal is six OV-10s, and all our personnel arriving safely in Saudi Arabia. It's time to prove we can handle any mission assigned to us."

After the flight crew posed for pictures with Colonel Kuhn, we nearly raced to our planes, primed to begin our long journey. The energy level was high as we taxied out with six planes and twelve aircrew. Reaching 110 knots of airspeed, I pulled back on the stick and we lifted off the runway. "If we make it in one piece, we'll make Marine Corps aviation history," I thought. "If we screw up, we'll never recover."

Our first-of-its-kind expedition started in California, flying east to North Carolina. As the plane sped down the runway, I could hardly contain my eagerness. How many people have the chance to fly a plane halfway around the world and get paid to do it?

Leading this flight of OV-10s to the Middle East was a risky move. But if our squadron waited to send them by ship, the planes would arrive at their destination six to eight weeks later, covered with rust and corrosion. By flying them over, aircrews would land with six planes fully operational and ready to fight. We had many hurdles—and oceans—to cross before then. I prayed our group of planes would make it safely.

After two days of flying across the United States to Cherry Point, North Carolina, we'd link up with two C-130 planes and their crews. The planes would accompany us the rest of the way to Saudi Arabia and provide transportation for our maintenance crew, spare parts, and test equipment.

From Cherry Point, we'd continue north to Goose Bay, Canada, then head north on the polar route, reaching Greenland via a long overwater leg—our most dangerous segment of flight. After a stop in England, we would head south to Spain, Italy, Crete, and Egypt, eventually joining the rest of our detachment in Saudi Arabia. We would log nearly 10,000 miles on the journey, which we dubbed "The Excellent Adventure."

Until we made it to England, unpredictable weather would be our biggest concern. The heavy cloud layer, cold temperatures, and quickly moving fronts in the far north would test our flying skills—especially mine, having recently received my initial qualification for solo flight barely two months prior.

I could fly anywhere in a Cobra helicopter, but in the Bronco, I was only building the confidence that comes with 200 to 300 flight hours under your belt. Now I was taking a flight of planes nearly 10,000 miles over foreign countries, often in marginal weather conditions.

The powerful thrust of the engines drove me into my seat, and as the plane arched into the sky, I grinned like a kid on the first day of summer vacation. Minutes later, Camp Pendleton was a dot on the horizon.

Frequently during the next three weeks, we landed each night in a new air base, tired and hungry. Before unpacking my plane and finding something to eat, I checked on the Marines and airplanes of my squadron. By the time I got to my quarters each night, it was nearly midnight. That's when my additional duties began: handling administrative details, calling the squadron in California to handle problems and keep updated on the status of the main body of 125 Marines that had already arrived in Saudi Arabia. Early each morning, I briefed for the next leg of our journey and, when I could, squeezed in a letter or phone call to Cindy.

The most challenging leg of the flight came in treacherous weather high above the Atlantic Ocean. We were halfway to Greenland, past the point of no return. If our plane ditched, even with the protection of full-length exposure suits, the frigid water would incapacitate any crewman in the water within fourteen minutes. Your muscles freeze and your hands become paws, unable to use your survival equipment. Thirty to forty minutes after hitting that icy water you're dead. "Wouldn't that be the pits?" I thought. "To freeze to death getting to the deserts of Saudi Arabia."

We were "in the soup"—thick, heavy clouds that obscured our view of anything beyond fifty feet. I couldn't see an ocean liner in the water below, much less five OV-10s and two C-130s flying with me "in the goo." We were too far from any airfield to use radar to identify our cluster of planes or other aircraft nearby. We had a ceiling of less than 1,000 feet and were headed toward a short island runway surrounded by mountainous terrain and a layer of disorienting clouds.

One minute before landing I worked my way through the landing checklist as the OV-10s joined in sections of two in close formation with the C-130s. With everyone in tight formation, we descended through clouds so dense they blocked the view of the lead aircraft four feet off my wing. The planes held position until we broke through the clouds. I approached the short runway, made even shorter now with five airplanes collected on it. I felt their turbulence as I touched down, breathing a sigh of relief. Everyone had landed safely, the planes were operational, and the most dangerous leg of our journey was behind us.

After flights to Iceland, then Scotland, we landed at Lakenheath Air Force Base, near London. In England we discovered that one of the aircraft rudder cables had frayed to within the last seven strands of the original fifty. Without that cable, the plane would have no directional control, but since it wasn't a high-usage item, we hadn't brought a spare. A replacement had to be flown from North Carolina on an Air Force cargo plane. I decided all six OV-10s would remain in England until the plane was repaired and then leave as a team.

Four days later the Air Force cargo plane arrived in England. I threw up my hands in frustration when I learned the part was not aboard; someone had forgotten to load it. So we waited another three days.

While grounded in England, I handled my operational duties and also acted as prison guard, counselor, father, friend, and judge to the forty-five Marines in our group. By mid-September, the squeeze was on to keep everyone in-country, and the stated policy of the Commanding General of Marine Forces in Saudi Arabia was "*Nobody* goes home." The only exceptions: a critical family emergency or death. Once you were on your way to the Persian Gulf, you were committed—regardless of the tactics your family might use to get you home.

By now, I knew a conflict was inevitable. "You will take part in something that has never been done before," I told my men. "Rather than reading about history, we are going to *make* history." I summed up my prophesy by paraphrasing George C. Scott in the movie *Patton:* "When you're old and gray with your grandson on your knee, and he asks you what you did during the Persian Gulf War," I said, quoting Scott with considerable license, "you won't have to say you stayed home and shoveled shit in Louisiana!"

At Lakenheath Air Base, I shared a room with Dr. Joel Lees. In addition to being a top-notch doctor, he could expertly handle backseat navigation in an OV-10. Choosing him to fly as an alternate backseater on our "Excellent Adventure" made a strong statement about his importance to our team.

A quiet and caring man, well respected in the medical community, Doc Lees was a good companion to me. Since I'd have no XO in Saudi Arabia, the saying "It's lonely at the top" would aptly describe my situation. I valued Joel's advice in the many decisions I alone could make. We talked often in our room in the old B-52 ready alert quarters. A soft-spoken, devout Christian and a devoted father of four, he provided the sounding board I needed when faced with tough personnel decisions. Sharing thoughts on both a personal and a professional level, we soon became friends.

When the replacement part arrived in England, we installed it, flew a test hop, then launched with all six aircraft to Zaragoza, Spain. A blown propeller seal kept us there overnight. From Spain we flew to Sigonella, Italy. The next morning we flew to Cairo, Egypt, then on to an air base in central Saudi Arabia for our last refueling stop.

Finally, late on September 26, nearly a month after heading east from Camp Pendleton, I boarded my plane feeling exhilarated, knowing we were about to fly the last hop, to an unknown airfield in Saudi Arabia. Near dusk that evening, during a swirling sandstorm, our group of planes launched. The desert dust boiled up from the surface to 5,000 feet.

"We're going to make it," I thought as we launched. "We're going to take these six airplanes to the other side of the world and prove to ourselves and the rest of the Marine Corps that VMO-2 can do it." My excitement was tempered with apprehension. We weren't yet safely on the deck.

As we climbed through the hazy darkness, the ground and sky blended, eliminating key visual cues. The few glimmering lights below mirrored the stars above with mesmerizing similarity.

I looked forward to the moment we'd link up with the advance party who had been in Saudi Arabia for nearly three weeks. I had never directly spoken to the Marines in-country; all my communication had been through the squadron in California. Among the Marines with the advance party in Saudi Arabia was a new squadron member, Warrant Officer Guy Hunter. "What a great piece of luck," I had thought the day Guy checked in to the squadron. He had more experience as an aerial observer than anyone in the Marine Corps, and had trained every one of my squadron aerial observers during his tour as an instructor at the AO school. He would boost the strength of our team in Saudi Arabia.

Now I prepared to take off for the last of my journey into Saudi Arabia to join Guy and the other VMO-2 Marines in the advance party. Between aircraft mechanical problems, hazardous flying conditions, and family crises, it had been a long four weeks on top of weeks of intense preparation before that. I was tired, but the finish line was near. "I hope this is only a two-hour flight," I thought. That morning we had flown five hours from Egypt into Saudi Arabia, then waited five hours for fuel. I had already been up seventeen hours, and my hunger intensified my fatigue.

I forced myself to concentrate on flying. "You've got one more leg," I told myself. "Don't screw it up." The tiny red and green lights of my wingmen blended with countless stars. If I got 100 yards away from them, I might as well have been miles away. I had to stay close, but not close enough to collide with one of the OV-10s beside me or a C-130 in front and above me.

We still didn't know *where* in Saudi Arabia we were going to land. For days, we had requested our specific destination from the commanding general in Saudi Arabia. Now we were airborne on the last leg of our journey, heading for a remote airfield. We still didn't know which one.

I continuously scanned the black sky for signs of the other aircraft and periodically checked my instrument panel to verify everything was normal. I looked up and saw black sky with flickering stars. I looked down and saw black earth with flickering lights. Sky and earth seemed to merge. Which way was up? Which way was down? The world seemed reversed.

Were we flying straight or descending? Checking my instruments, I noticed something was wrong. Very wrong. My attitude indicator showed right wing down and almost fifteen degrees nose down. We were falling out—quickly losing altitude. How could that be when we were flying straight and level?

Quickly checking the remaining instruments, I saw we were increasing airspeed and descending at nearly 2,000 feet per minute. We were in a steep rate of descent, but my mind and body told me I was flying straight and level. "What's going on here?" I struggled to reconcile the difference between what my perception told me and what my instruments said. The realization hit me: I was experiencing "vertigo"—the disorientation pilots feel when visual cues aren't available to determine the position or attitude of the plane. The lack of a discernible horizon, the mild turbulence, the confusing patterns of lights flickering above and below us, and my fatigue had all contributed to my disorientation.

I had to trust my attitude instruments instead of my sensory judgment or I'd lose control of the aircraft. I pushed the stick to level the wings, and abruptly raised the nose to force the plane back up into the sky. I rechecked my instruments, then breathed a sigh of relief. We were back in position, on course.

A radio call caught my attention. One of the C-130 pilots requested our destination from the air command and control center in Saudi Arabia: "We are inbound. We need to know where these guys are going." Thirty minutes before we landed, they informed us of our destination. It had been a nineteen-hour day and an ugly last leg of flight. Thank God we were almost there.

Finally we got into the vicinity of our airfield. We could barely find the airfield because the runway was crude, run-down, and very poorly lit. Our group of planes started landing, one plane at a time, on an unfamiliar runway we could barely see. The lower my altitude got, the hotter the air temperature became. Descending through 1,500 feet, I felt as if someone had lowered me into a dry sauna. Sweat broke out on my forehead, then built up at my midsection where my flight suit, G suit, and torso harness intersected. My socks became soaked, and water pooled in my boots.

The OV-10s began stacking up at the end of the short, dark runway. I was the last to land. It took all my skill to stop the airplane before it came dangerously close to the plane of my section leader, parked at the end of the runway. I made it with minimal distance to spare.

It was 10:30 P.M. local time when I opened the cockpit and a blast of hot air rushed in. Drained of energy, I gathered my gear. Flying six airplanes halfway around the world was harder than I had anticipated, but we'd arrived safely. I felt proud of these Marines. They'd proved to themselves they could do it. They were stronger because of this journey.

I slung my gear over my shoulder and headed for the rows of canvas tents outlined against the sky. A dark, hulking shadow of a stadium loomed in the distance. Except for a few floodlights shining in the distance and the occasional headlight of a motor vehicle, only red and blue runway lights broke the unrelenting darkness.

Late that night, after being reunited with VMO-2 Marines, showering, and finding my tent, I fell asleep on my cot, dreaming of being with Cindy and Cami in the backyard, tossing a tennis ball.

Oceanside, California
Mid-September 1990

> Our first task is to keep up our own morale. Men separated from their families do much better when they feel their families are coping well and support their separation. They're counting on us to take care of the home front while they're gone, so let's take care of each other. . . .

I sat at the computer in the upstairs study, reviewing my suggestion in our first VMO-2 wives support group newsletter for wives whose husbands were deployed.

By early September, President Bush had authorized the call-up of 200,000 reservists and National Guardsmen to bolster combat forces in the Gulf. The fear of impending war settled over me like a cloud. Filled with dread and doubt, keeping up my morale became a challenge.

At least I had the assurance of knowing Cliff was doing a job he loved for a just cause. Colonel Kuhn had called soon after Cliff's departure. "I saw your husband take off and he was beaming," he reported. Colonel Kuhn also told me that Cliff had been selected for Top Level School, an honor bestowed on only the top 5 percent of lieutenant colonels. I noted in my journal, "With all the uncertainty now, it comforts me to focus on Cliff going to school (a safe job!) in a year."

Something heavy landed in my lap. The jolt was quickly followed by a warm, wet nose nuzzling my cheek. "Murphy! You're right, it's time for dinner."

I stroked his soft fur, hoping I had the courage to take my own advice. Having no date for Cliff's return from the Middle East was disheartening. There had been six-month rotations in Vietnam, but the Marine commanding general in Saudi Arabia had ordered commanding officers to stay "for the duration." Even if his men rotated home in six months, Cliff would remain.

My CO's wife's duties—answering phone calls, seeking volunteers, writing newsletters, holding food drives, attending meetings, and supplying occasional taxi service to wives who were ill or had no transportation—consumed thirty-five to forty hours per week in addition to my daytime job.

The enormity of my task was eased by Marines left behind at the squadron, especially Captain Warren Wright—or "Lefty," as he was affectionately called by his fellow Marines. He explained policies and procedures, provided second opinions, and handled many problems before I even knew about them. More than once his positive attitude and sense of humor cheered me up on a bad day. I didn't have to be "Mrs. CO" with him and could talk to him honestly about my questions—and my fears.

I teasingly called Lefty my "substitute husband." I spoke to him more often than I did to Cliff. Often the communication link between me and Cliff, he relayed personal messages between the two of us.

With the news that Cliff had arrived safely in Saudi Arabia, I shifted to worrying about his safety "in-country." I had visions of enemy mines, booby traps, and mad terrorists. For weeks, experts had voiced fears that Iraq might use chemical and biological weapons on our troops stationed in Saudi Arabia. Several Marine wives fearfully recalled the tragic Beruit bombing of a Marine barracks in 1983 when a terrorist attack killed 220 Marines.

I tried to not look too far ahead and to follow the advice of Hewlett-Packard CEO, John Young. He advised "just-in-time worrying." "If you worry too soon, things will change in the interim," he said. "So you end up having to deal with them twice." His advice would be uncannily accurate for my situation.

The media's predictions grew gloomier. A columnist with the *Los Angeles Times* declared, "War could be disastrous . . . we would be fighting a ruthless tyrant who could tolerate 100,000 fatalities better than we could tolerate 10,000."

Then one calamity followed another. A temporary roommate borrowed my car without asking, then plowed into another car, adding insurance forms to my list of duties. Three days after the accident, I rushed to a meeting on base, my third trip there inside twenty-four hours. As I drove past the guard station, a military policeman (MP) flagged me down. "Are these factory-tinted windows?" she asked.

"I assume so." I had bought the car in April while Cliff was training in Arizona, then had my car inspected and approved for a base sticker by the

MPs on base. Frowning, the MP scraped the window with her fingernail. "These are *not* factory-tinted windows. You are in violation of base rules!"

My heart sank as she scraped the base sticker—my passport onto the base—from the windshield. From now on I would need to go into the base office for approval each time I drove on base.

"You will need to have the tinting removed by a body shop," she ordered. "Just add that to the list of repairs," I thought.

A second MP approached my car. "I need to see your military identification, driver's license, and proof of insurance," he said sternly. I searched the glove compartment for the insurance papers and then my wallet for my identification card and license. "Where are they?" I wondered. I had left everything at home on the kitchen table.

I explained my predicament to the MP.

"You will be cited for two violations," the officer answered. "One for having tinted windows and one for driving without a valid license."

"Is your husband here or in the Gulf?" the first MP asked.

"In the Gulf," I answered glumly.

"Then the ticket will be sent to him there."

My troubles continued at work. For weeks the stock market had been in a slump and business at our search firm had fallen off. There were no longer enough clients to justify keeping our branch open. My boss informed me that he was closing the office and that I would soon be unemployed. I had lost my safe haven of distraction and the support I enjoyed from employees of other businesses on my floor. "Maybe it's a blessing in disguise," I told myself. I had felt overloaded with my two "jobs."

Around dusk, a few nights later, I heard Cami barking wildly. Frantically, she tried to jump over the five-foot fence of the vacant house next door. When I heard a cat's bloodcurdling screech, I dove through the bushes and pushed open the neighbor's gate. As Cami burst through the entrance before me, a coyote sailed over the back fence, dropping Murphy from its mouth.

The vet at the emergency clinic couldn't give me much hope. He'd never seen a cat survive a coyote attack. "All we can do is make him comfortable," he said. But tough little Murphy survived. When I visited the next morning, he lifted his shaved, bruised head and purred. One eye was swollen shut and the other was barely a slit; deep tooth marks punctured his head. Multiple bite wounds on his stomach showed how many times the coyote had tried to get a grip on his rotund shape. He had been trying to drag Murphy off by the head when Cami barreled in. When Murphy arrived home a week later, Cami would not leave his side, and Murphy purred so loudly I could hear him two rooms away.

Meanwhile, my challenges as the commander's wife mounted. Emotional difficulties were on the rise. We had trouble locating wives who had moved and not told anyone. Two teenage sons desperate for their fathers to come home had attempted suicide. Two wives had miscarried. I struggled to create solidarity between the wives of officers and those of enlisted Marines, thwart rumors of terrorists, and reassure wives afraid to answer the phone. "You would be notified personally," I reassured them. Protocol was strict on that point.

As the weeks passed, I learned to incorporate Cliff's absence into a new lifestyle, a burden that stayed with me. I had shifted my attention from being with him to doing for him, long distance. I deluged him with daily letters, "desert faxes," and hours of taped messages. My weekly care packages were filled with items to make his desert life easier: light socket outlet, extension cord, flashlight, dustpan and broom, camping mattress for his cot, bug spray.... By November, I had sent him nineteen boxes, each loaded with food—especially the cookies he loved. Deluged with so many cans of food and homemade treats, he had protested, "My tent is starting to look like a 7-Eleven Store!"

On November 8, President Bush ordered 230,000 additional troops to the Gulf, and he minced no words about their mission: "to ensure that the Coalition has an adequate *offensive* military option." They faced the fourth-largest military power in the world.

My letter that night to Cliff expressed my fears:

> Signals are pointing more and more to a war. Some now say January. I hate the thought of you being involved. I don't know how I could function day to day knowing you were in danger of being killed. I'd want to take sedatives and say, "Wake me up when it's over." I know you'll do your best however you're involved and I'll support you in whatever you do.

The following Saturday, I headed toward Camp Pendleton, excited about my opportunity to speak to Cliff. We had not spoken for longer than five minutes at a time since he left. He called the squadron from Saudi Arabia at a prearranged time each week to discuss squadron matters. Since I had official business—about wives support group issues—after finishing his squadron business, they would put him through to me. It would be a relief to ask Cliff questions and get immediate answers.

To my dismay, Lefty had transferred from the squadron and was not replaced. Before his departure, he tried to allay my fears. "Cindy, you've already done more in one month than most COs' wives do in an entire year," he said. "You'll do fine without me." I wasn't so sure.

Now I especially needed Cliff's advice and moral support. I reminded myself not to burden him with my fears; the weight I carried was nothing compared to what he bore.

The town of Oceanside had undergone a dramatic change since thousands of Marines had been deployed en masse. Rental occupancy and school attendance were down as many younger wives moved home to be with their families. Electronics stores, barbershops, furniture stores, and car dealerships were barely surviving due to lack of business. The whole mood of the town seemed to have darkened.

Traffic driving onto Camp Pendleton funneled into a single lane flanked with concrete barricades and barbed wire. Dressed in full battle gear, Marines carrying rifles checked every driver's identification. The airfield, once crowded with helicopters, people, and planes, looked eerily devoid of life. Cars in the once-full parking lots had vanished, and the helicopter hangars were dark and deserted. With the secrecy surrounding the abrupt departure of men and aircraft, it seemed they had been spirited away, leaving behind a ghost town.

Climbing the stairs to Cliff's office, I remembered the pride I'd felt the first time I visited him there. The Marines had treated me like visiting royalty, and one of them had confided in me, "We would rather take a beating than let down Lieutenant Colonel Acree." Another said, "If the CO said tomorrow, 'Dig a hole in the asphalt and look for the devil,' the next morning, everyone would be out there with a pick and a shovel. He'd just have to paint an *X* where he wanted us to start." I hoped sight of Cliff's tidy office would ease the ache I felt without him.

I stopped short in the doorway of Cliff's office. Gone were his familiar pictures, coffee mug, neat pile of papers, and lined-up pens. The office had been stripped of his personal possessions, his presence erased as if he had never been there. And was never coming back.

When his prearranged phone call came in, I discussed my issues with Cliff. Working down my list, I felt the weight of the world on my shoulders. "Anything else?" Cliff asked. "No, that's everything," I said, pushing back tears so hard my throat ached. Sitting in his barren office, I felt alone, afraid, and overwhelmed with responsibility. Families looked to me for guidance, just when my tutor—and source of emotional support—was halfway around the world. So long suppressed, my tears flowed forth as did my doubts and fears.

Hanging up the phone, I regretted my lapse in strength. I wiped my eyes and vowed that whatever worries I carried, I could not impose them again on Cliff. What if something happened to him and the last thing he remembered was me crying and complaining? I drove home, determined to face my fears, cope, and move on.

My family rallied around me to ease my loneliness on Thanksgiving: Eleven-year-old Stephany came for three days; and my mom and Vince, my stepdad, flew down from Seattle. Aunt Ethel, a sharp-witted retired nurse, flew in from Florida. Like everyone on Dad's side of the family, Ethel had blond hair, a pretty smile, and huge blue eyes. The only sister of my late father, she and I shared a deep and devoted bond.

Cliff's Navy friend Ed Brandstoettner, a quiet, six-foot-four-inch bachelor with a gangly build, joined us for a few days on his way to the Persian Gulf. Nicknamed "Scooter" by Cliff because of his ingenious dance steps, he had been Cliff's roommate during a tour in Korea years before and had been making appearances since. An avid music lover, he recorded several CDs on cassette tapes to send to Cliff in the Gulf and amused us all during his stay with his satirical sense of humor.

Scooter was a Navy intelligence officer assigned to the amphibious assault ship USS *Tripoli*. Patiently, he answered my incessant questions about Cliff's deployment and possible combat operations. After many of my inquiries, he answered, "I cannot confirm or deny," his hazel eyes behind gold-rimmed glasses disclosing nothing, though his lips turned up in a semismile.

By dinnertime on Thanksgiving, I was covered with flour after baking bread and three pies. Mom and Aunt Ethel helped me with final meal preparations while Stephany and Scooter danced around the living room to rock music. Vince watched their antics, enjoying Stephany's giggles and the wonderful smells from the kitchen.

After eating, we watched a videotape of greetings from VMO-2 Marines in Saudi Arabia. "Rosana, by the time you see this, we'll have a son," a beaming Marty Martinez told his wife, whose recent sonogram had revealed the sex of their unborn child.

At the airport two days later, my eyes stung as I hugged my company good-bye. I was alone again.

By December, Cliff's occasional phone calls from Saudi Arabia became even more sporadic. Thousands of service people crowded onto Cliff's air base in Saudi Arabia. Now the wait in line to make a personal phone call stretched to two or more hours—time Cliff could scarcely afford. When weeks passed without hearing his voice, the gulf between us felt greater than ever. I found myself migrating to Camp Pendleton, feeling somehow closer to Cliff. Seeing a tall slender Marine dressed in camouflage utilities, for a fleeting moment I wondered, "Could it be Cliff?" My mind conjured up that glimmer of hope against the ever more frightening news from the Middle East.

On November 29, the UN had voted to authorize the use of force if Iraq did not withdraw from Kuwait by January 15. We began a forty-one-day countdown to war. That the allies would suffer many casualties was a foregone conclusion.

The December 24, 1990, issue of *U.S. News & World Report* reported: "U.S. Commanders are preparing for a war that could take months, not weeks, and could produce a level of casualties America has not seen since Korea." Columnists predicted thousands of body bags coming to America.

Robert McNamara warned of "thousands and thousands and thousands of casualties." One of the most respected computer models estimated 10,000. The Pentagon ordered 16,000 medals, most of them Purple Hearts.

The most ominous prediction of all came from Saddam Hussein. The Iraqi dictator promised to fight the "Mother of All Battles" that would cause "rivers of blood" to flow.

King Abdul Aziz Air Base, Saudi Arabia
Mid-September 1990

"I waited seventeen years for all this luxury!" I thought when I first saw my desert home. As CO, my tent was unlike the others: seven feet by twelve feet, with a peaked ceiling, two overhead lightbulbs, and a plywood floor.

Dirt, sand, and fine dust permeated everything. Each time I swept my tent, I removed a quart of sand as fine as talcum powder. After my nightly shower I walked through dust to my tent—"step-*poof*-step-*poof*"—by the time I arrived back at my tent, a dust layer cloaked my legs. Swift desert lizards, big black beetles, sand vipers, and three kinds of scorpions, two of them poisonous, made nighttime visits to the bathroom interesting.

Our tent city had been erected near a soccer stadium that had hastily been converted to an airfield. The advance party had erected a tent camp for living areas, work spaces for aircraft maintenance, and tables for squadron gatherings.

After arriving in Saudi Arabia, I quickly became used to working, eating, and sleeping with my nine-millimeter pistol and my gas mask. Standing in line for showers, food, and phones became routine. I had no choice but to get used to eating MREs with selections like "Beef Slice—chunked and formed." Troops joked that MRE stood for Meals Rejected by Ethiopia. Our squadron would eat these dehydrated food packets three meals a day until a mess hall was set up.

Living in the inhospitable desert among a sea of tents was a spartan existence. The Marines scrounged building supplies, tent liners, and discarded packaging material and built a weight room. Arnold Schwarzenegger had donated thousands of dollars of weight equipment to deployed troops. When it went to troops living in comfortable apartments and condominium complexes miles to the rear, we pitched in and bought two sets of Olympic weights.

Everything our all-male unit accomplished in those first months was done in sweltering heat. Midday temperatures soared above 110 degrees in the shade—and there was very little shade. Even after midnight, temperatures in our tents hovered at 90 degrees. I wrote to my Navy friend Scooter:

Life at this desert resort area is truly in the bottom five worst places I've ever deployed to. Hot, dusty, sandy and no liberty. Who wants liberty in a country that has no beer anyway?

Tensions in the Middle East were even hotter than the weather. The atmosphere those first few weeks was of high pressure and uncertainty. Iraqi forces massed on the Kuwait border and clearly outnumbered Coalition forces. VMO-2 was the farthest forward fixed-wing squadron in the theater. With the threat of war looming over us, uncertainties flourished. We exercised, trained, and prepared for that possibility. While the Marine Corps has a proud tradition of always being ready to deploy at a moment's notice, each potential conflict has its own dangers. In the Gulf War, one of our greatest concerns was chemical attack.

Security around the base, especially preparing bunkers for chemical warfare, was high priority. I called random reaction drills. "This is a drill, this is a drill. Execute your reaction drill now." Marines scrambled out of their bunks and made tracks to their assigned bunkers, each grabbing his pack filled with a helmet, flak jacket, weapon, gas mask, canteens, ammunition, and chemical protective suit.

We upgraded the flight line and aircraft protection. We improved maintenance and ordnance. With the help of a Navy construction battalion, Marines dug foxholes, lined them with sandbags, and erected solid roofs. Medical supplies and hundreds of troops arrived to our encampment at a furious pace. Airstrips were built, and every square foot of ground seemed crammed with tents, jeeps, tanks, trucks, and aircraft. If it turned into a shooting match, I'd be glad to see every person and each piece of equipment.

Flying overhead, I had a bird's-eye view of the bustling airfield; our base, which we called the "Scudbowl"; and the sun-baked "Big Sandbox" beyond. Dust plumes rose from jeeps and trucks rumbling over unpaved roads. Wild camels roamed across sand dotted with scrub growth.

The other services and our Western allies got liberty. In the front lines, our Marines routinely worked twelve-to-sixteen-hour days, seven days a week. Running on adrenaline, all the Marines were tired, but if I asked them to take a day off, not one of them would have done it. Ours was a collective spirit of optimism. We never had a problem with morale or the "unbearable boredom" the press talked about.

Eventually we shared the airfield with three Marine Harrier squadrons. AV-8B Harriers are high-performance single-engine jets famous for their ability to hover. We were so close to Kuwait that the Harriers never required aerial refueling during the war.

The area where we lived was noisy twenty-four hours a day with aircraft turn-ups for maintenance checks and flight operations. But most nights, I could fall asleep in the heat, with Harriers and helicopters whining overhead. Sleep was a precious commodity.

No other squadron was spread so thinly across the globe. I envied squadron COs who had all their people, equipment, and support structure intact, in one location. As the only Marine commander with a squadron based in three different countries, I wore several hats, working with a partial staff. There were not enough hours in the day to accomplish all I had to do: training for an impending war, handling troop problems, flying, attending meetings, coordinating the staff, and dealing with higher headquarters. We worked extensively with Marine ground units to ensure everyone used the right communications plan and procedures to request and coordinate air support.

Most nights I slept only four hours, often being awakened at two or three in the morning with new intelligence information. Staff Sergeant Korsmo was my smart, diligent intelligence chief. He prided himself in keeping me more informed than most COs. Gregarious and good-looking, with friendly blue eyes and a trim, athletic build, he loved a joke, but he took his position seriously. Twenty-four hours a day, he knew to interrupt me if he obtained essential intelligence information.

As VMO-2 Marines prepared themselves for war, Red Cross "emergency" messages came in from family members who wanted their Marines home. The farther you are from home and the longer you're gone, the more distorted the truth gets. But except for the death or critical injury of a family member, no one was leaving Saudi Arabia once they arrived. I denied all requests to return stateside—except one: Marty Martinez needed to return to California, where his five-day-old daughter, Loren, was critically ill with a congenital heart defect. She would only survive with heart surgery or a transplant. We got him on a plane back home within twenty-four hours.

On November 29, the UN Security Council authorized the use of force if Iraq did not withdraw from Kuwait by January 15. I had six weeks to prepare my squadron and myself for war.

Besides my CO duties, I had to become combat qualified in the OV-10 as quickly as possible. Flying to Saudi Arabia, although a major feat in itself, was only a small part of a long list of tasks to accomplish. In the cockpit of a Cobra, my flying reactions were second nature. I had to develop the same confidence in an OV-10.

I had to become proficient in shooting ordnance, flying at night using the forward-looking infrared radar (FLIR) and the laser, and in evasive maneuvering against Triple-A and SAMs. I practiced night surveillance and reconnaissance, flying at low altitudes, and navigating over desert terrain with hampered visibility. The atmosphere was a brown-gray haze from winds sweeping across the desert and casting sand into the upper air. The reduced visibility—coupled with land barren of mountains, rivers, or any identifiable terrain—made navigating off a map demanding and difficult.

Though I couldn't share tactical information with Cindy, I described my training flights to her on my cassette tapes:

> Today I flew a one versus one flight, air-to-air, against another OV-10. Everyone goes ten miles away, then turns their aircraft into a general tactical area. Whoever sees the other one first calls the fight on and you go for it. For an hour we mix it up hard, a "furball," with lots of "G" stress and erratic maneuvering that puts your stomach in the back of the airplane. My opponent "killed" me twice, I "killed" him once, and his backseater threw up from vertigo.

Other flights I flew a two-versus-two hop, two OV-10s pitted against two Harriers. I told Cindy:

> I had an interesting 2 v 2 hop against 2 Harriers this morning. The dogfight gets real busy with four aircraft in one small piece of airspace—a good challenge to keep everyone in sight while maneuvering for a kill shot. *You* would really enjoy ACM (Aerial Combat Maneuvers) because you're inverted several times during the fight & the rest is like riding a roller coaster!

I flew four to five days a week, compressing years of training into whatever time I had before the war started. Countless practice flights honed my skills. In addition to flying and handling my command duties, I prepared myself for combat. I did most of my preparations in "the dungeon," my office in the basement of the old soccer stadium.

I analyzed friendly forces on the ground in my sector of operations and studied the allied forces' communication plan. I prepared my maps. After cutting and laminating them, I marked them with helo and fixed-wing ingress and egress routes, preplanned attack positions, and command and control checkpoints.

Between my CO's duties and individual preparations, I felt like I was in a blender. Push the button and twenty hours later stop. Work—eat—work—sleep—work. Spare moments I spent writing return letters to family, friends, schoolchildren, and other citizens who had written to me or VMO-2. Three to four nights a week I ran and lifted weights to prepare myself for the rigors of combat, then showered and hit the rack. Day after day of long hours makes you a tired person. At the end of each day, the fold-out cot against the canvas wall of my tent provided welcome solitude.

Sergeant Major Warner arrived in Saudi Arabia in mid-December. He saw my punishing schedule. "Colonel, you're looking beat; you need some sleep," he'd say. We shared a mutual respect and commitment to make the squadron something every Marine in it would respect. Our special closeness was never stated in words but understood with a nod or a grin. Without an effective CO *and* an effective sergeant major, the squadron would fail. I had a *great* sergeant major.

In those months before Desert Storm, Marines in my squadron asked what our future held regarding possible combat operations. I answered in three words: "Bush doesn't bluff."

Seattle, Washington
December 25, 1990

The snow crunched under my boots and Cami's chain jingled as she frolicked around me in the tranquil whiteness of newly fallen snow. Light flakes of snow fell as I walked the three miles to my sister Bonnie's house to spend Christmas morning with her family of four. Unusually deep for Seattle, the snow seemed to purify everything around me, creating peace amid my apprehensions.

In the previous weeks, my efforts to support squadron families had multiplied rapidly. There were real fears of terrorism, and by then, war looked inevitable. Financial and psychological problems had increased even among the most stable of families. Some wives were afraid to answer the phone. But by avoiding their fears, they encouraged them. Base wide, attempted suicides had increased dramatically. As chairperson, I was advised, "Tell your wives that attempting suicide won't bring their husbands home. If they try it, they must be hospitalized for two days. An agency will take their kids away, and they will be charged with child endangerment."

Many Marine families had financial difficulties without the additional income of their husbands' moonlighting jobs. Other lonely wives had accrued huge long-distance phone bills calling friends and relatives and accepting collect calls from Saudi Arabia. Our squadron wives group collected a truckload of food to deliver to the overburdened family relief organization.

Focusing so much of my energy supporting others, I had depended upon Cliff's almost daily letters as my emotional lifeline. But now their delivery had become erratic. When several days passed with no mail, my spirits began to sag. After a week or ten days, especially when we hadn't spoken for several weeks, I felt myself faltering. It was hard keeping my letters upbeat when my spirits were low. Just when I would give in to feeling sorry for myself, a pile of two-week-old letters from Cliff would arrive.

Christmas, with its spirit of peace, hope, and love, granted a brief respite from my worries. No one expected anything notable to happen in the Gulf during the holidays, but once they were over—watch out.

My ten-day trip to Seattle would give me time to relax, recuperate, and regroup for the challenges certain to be ahead. But trudging through the snow, I realized I was anxious to return home. Even being with family and longtime friends, the solace I had sought escaped me. With people laughing and going about their business, I felt isolated and alone. I realized I felt nearer to Cliff when I was around my Marine Corps friends. Here, talk of a potential Gulf War was mixed in with chatter about sports and weekend plans, the Gulf situation not necessarily taking precedence over the other two. At home, it was foremost on everyone's mind. I wrote in my journal:

> I now feel closer to my "new friends," my Marine Corps family. In some ways
> I feel like a stranger to my civilian friends. I'm on a journey they can't take
> with me and they can't understand. Life goes on for them. My life is on hold.

Still, my visits in Seattle with family and friends helped them understand the challenges I faced at home and why I devoted so much time to the Marine families of Cliff's squadron.

With the dawning of the new year, the incredible tensions returned. Wives and families could only hope for the best and brace themselves for the worst. I threw myself back into supporting the squadron families and Cliff. Military officials had warned that if war began, only lightweight letters could be delivered to frontline units. I doubled the rate and size of my care packages.

Cliff's last call from Saudi Arabia came on January 10. The line hummed as we held back our fears and emotions. But through the phone line, I sensed the strain he was under 10,000 miles away.

"How are you doing, honey?" I asked.

"Fine . . . busy. Are you doing okay?"

"Everything's fine on this end. You just concentrate on what you need to do."

I wanted to ask him about the future. Were we going to war? Would he be safe? But I knew he couldn't give me any clues about military moves planned after the January 15 deadline.

"Everyone's getting pretty tense here," I offered, referring to the Marine families.

He released a pent-up breath. "Same here."

Precious seconds ticked by of silence, filled with unasked questions. For the first time we ran out of things to say. Normal conversation seemed ridiculous. I didn't want to burden him with details of home repair dilemmas or tell him I was losing my job. Life's everyday problems seem trivial when the one you love is going into war.

After four minutes, the line clicked with a thousand things left unsaid. Many times I would replay that conversation in my mind and wish I had told him one more time, "I love you."

That following afternoon, I picked up Stephany for the weekend. Late that night I awoke to the sound of her whimpering. She tossed in her sleep, looking agitated. "Are you having a bad dream, honey?" I understood about having bad dreams. Cliff often appeared in mine, but as soon as we were together, he disappeared. In one dream, I found myself entering a large open area crowded with people talking excitedly.

I spotted another squadron wife in the crowd. "Are you here to meet Cliff off the ship?" she asked. "Oh . . . I guess I am!" I was amazed at the good news. I turned to see a long line of uniformed Marines slowly migrating toward us. Halfway down, dressed in his flight suit, stood Cliff. He winked, grinning widely as if to say, "Surprise!"

I waited impatiently, and finally he reached me. My body relaxed as we locked in a long hug. Clasping hands tightly, we moved away from the crowd. What a huge sense of relief I felt, having him safely at my side.

"Could you go somewhere for a couple of minutes?" Cliff asked. He hinted that he had brought a surprise for me and wanted to get it ready.

"Okay. I'll go to the rest room and be right back," I suggested. Five minutes later, I walked out to rejoin him. He had vanished.

I rubbed Stephany's back and she awoke, looking confused. "I dreamed that Dad and I were having our picture taken and we were hugging each other. Then I looked over and he was gone." He even disappeared in Stephany's dreams.

Sunday evening, two days before the UN January 15 deadline, Debbie Mills and I went to see the Kevin Costner film *Dances With Wolves*. Expecting a love story, we were dismayed when the film opened with a Civil War battle. "Great, a war movie," we both thought. But soon the battle was over and we found ourselves wrapped up in the story. A later scene reminded us of our fears when Indian wives bid farewell to their warrior husbands. In an especially poignant scene, Kevin Costner's wife worries about her missing husband, not knowing he has been captured and nearly killed by Army cavalry. Riding slumped over on her horse, disheartened and fearful, she tries not to look over her shoulder for his return.

That night, after the movie, Debbie and I talked, both fatalistic about the future. There was going to be a war, we both agreed, and our husbands were likely to be killed or injured. Their jobs as pilots were too dangerous to turn out otherwise. We promised to call each other immediately should we receive such "bad news."

My sister, Bonnie, sympathized in a letter: "Every time I hear something about Iraq on the radio or TV I get a horrible feeling in my stomach. I can only imagine how you must feel. Every day the news changes and you don't know whether to feel hopeful or to despair. It must be hard to live a 'normal' life when you don't feel at all normal. . . ."

King Abdul Aziz Air Base, Saudi Arabia
December 21, 1990

By December, the weather had turned cool, "imminent danger" pay had kicked in, and war seemed inevitable. I felt a great sense of urgency to make my Marines as protected and prepared as possible. The pressure I felt was growing, but my outlook and attitude improved dramatically each time I talked to Cindy. By then the single international telephone on base was being shared by nearly 4,000 sailors and Marines. As a CO, I had higher priority to use the phone, but I never abused the privilege and very rarely called home. Letters and tapes supplied the mainstay of communication between Cindy and me. Mine chronicled my preparations for war and my longings for home:

> *Audiotape—December 21, 1990*
>
> Honey, no matter what happens over here, once things start, you need to know I'm going to communicate with you just the same as I am right now, unless I am so overcome by flying constantly, or if the situation gets ugly early on. I have not been in combat before, but I do know the initial kickoff is very demanding. . . . If I get to a point, honey, where I am really OBE (overcome by events), you'll see it on TV and know what's going on. . . . We'll take this one day at a time and I don't want you to worry about me. . . . I'm coming home. Not as soon as you want me to, but I'm coming home. . . .

On Christmas Eve I attended a church service that ended with candle lighting and singing of "Silent Night." On Christmas Day, my heart yearned for the comforts of home and the joy of being with Cindy for the holidays. I spent Christmas morning briefing a visiting general.

After lunch I returned to my tent. Sitting on my cot, I opened my Christmas gifts under the glow of the overhead lightbulb. The living conditions underscored the underlying loneliness I had felt since arriving in this faraway land. Holding a brightly colored package, I missed anew the comfort and joys of being with my family, but my spirits lifted when I saw their efforts to make my desert tent more like a home.

Our friend Mary Pat had sent a miniature plastic Christmas tree. Cindy had sent—along with another load of cookies—a king-size pillow that threatened to consume my narrow cot; her mother, Emily, had sent a plush blue rug to protect my bare feet from the gritty floor.

The rest of the day I caught up on letter writing to family, friends, and schoolchildren, then headed to the dungeon (my office) to record a cassette tape to Cindy.

> *25 Dec*—Sure missed you today. . . . I spent from 0830 to 1130 with other squadron COs briefing a three-star general, after which he told us things we already knew. No one knew why he was wasting our time on Christmas day. Can you imagine having a *choice* and leaving your home and family to come *here?*

That night the squadron held a Christmas party with Guy Hunter appearing as Santa Claus. The men performed funny skits mimicking several people in the squadron, including me, and everyone enjoyed whacking the Saddam Hussein piñata.

A week later, on New Year's Eve, the Marines surprised me with a candlelit MRE cake for my thirty-ninth birthday. In my tent that night, I wrote to Cindy:

31 Dec—Love you a lot, always will. It's 2100 and I'm ready to call it a night. Your birthday gift and card was the highlight of my day. Everything else was a far distant 2nd place—to include meeting and briefing Vice President Quayle . . . I'm actually glad the holidays are over so I can focus on knowing I'll see you *this* year as soon as we're finished here. I sure miss even the simple pleasures of being with you, C. Walks, talks, cuddles in bed, calling you at work, going out to dinner, coffee on weekend mornings . . . you're my best friend, Babe, and my life is half of what it is when we're together . . . I'm trying my best to stay safe for my return to your arms. . . .

1 Jan—The mess hall is closed all day tomorrow so it's three MREs. The good news is that beginning 3 Jan we'll be served three hot meals a day, no more MREs! This I will believe when it happens.

By now, 80 percent of the Marine Corps was in Saudi Arabia. Everyone was anxious to fulfill our mission and return to our families. Sergeant Major Warner sent a letter of encouragement to Marine families back home:

We know you are fulfilling many roles—mother, housekeeper, employee, story reader, mechanic, bills payer . . . we appreciate all the hard work. I, the Sergeant Major, clearly can say from my heart that the men over here are doing excellent only because all of you back there are doing outstanding tasks by taking care of the family business . . . Special thanks to the "Key Wives" for all the hard work and planning . . . To all wives: Keep the meetings going and please don't quit on me now . . . We need you to be strong back home and pray for peace. Remember, you are in our hearts and we can't do well without your support. Kiss the kids and pet the dogs and cats. . . .

As the January 15 deadline approached, the climate around our air base became busy and tense. Morale remained high and Marines in my squadron were as ready as possible. I worried increasingly about Cindy's safety and reminded her, "Wear your seat belt always, OK? You survive the highways of California and I'll survive the skyways of Saudi Arabia."

11 Jan—We're not flying for 3 straight days beginning today so we can get our aircraft as ready as possible . . . until then, aircrews will finish any last minute preparations while maintenance crews prepare the aircraft. I need to disassemble and completely repack my g-suit and torso harness to make sure everything is working—plus we can add up to 5 pounds of additional gear (water, food, ammo, survival gear, etc) . . . We've done everything possible to be prepared so I think we're ready. My combat crew will be CWO-4 Guy Hunter or

Captain John Gamboa every time I launch. They're both real strong back-seaters so I feel good about that. They're both also nice gents all around. . . .

On January 12, both houses of Congress voted to give President Bush the authority to use "all necessary means" to kick Saddam Hussein out of Kuwait after the January 15 deadline.

13 Jan—It's raining hard right now and has been for three hours. Most of our tents are leaking. I'd like to be trapped in this tent with you for days while listening to the raindrops and keeping each other warm by snuggling . . . The day I'm told to leave here will be the *second* happiest day of 1991. I hope Cami still loves me when I come home. Tell her I'll still microwave her dinners. . . .

On Sunday, January 13, I attended a religious service. Marines filled all the benches and seats and sprawled onto the floor. Everyone had concluded war was inevitable. The service closed with "Where He Leads Me, I Will Follow." We prayed deeply for God's blessing and guidance for whatever the days to come would bring.

14 Jan—It's been raining for 24 hours now. What a mess this place is. Most of the tents are partially—if not mostly—soaked inside and out. It's also cold and *windy* . . . We've not received any mail for 4 days now. We've been told outgoing mail is getting out of country, but incoming mail is taking a lower priority behind last minute parts, ammunition, people and equipment to meet the 15 January deadline. This whole camp changes mood when the mail stops—and for good reason—it's our only connection to "the real world" as we call it.

15 Jan—Things are "moving right along" over here and the climate is becoming busy & tense. I think I've done everything possible to get the squadron ready and the Sergeant Major has been a great help to carry out my guidance. As an OV-10 pilot I'm as prepared as I can be and would prefer to get this show started *soon* so we can finish it and begin to focus on returning to our homes and family. It will never be soon enough for me to return to your arms and caring love.

The January 15 UN deadline passed with Saddam Hussein firmly entrenched in Kuwait.

16 Jan—By the time you receive this letter the war will have commenced at least a week earlier . . . My first brief for combat operations will begin at 0500. CWO-4 Guy Hunter and I will launch at 0715 and recover at 1045. I'll do my best to be safe. You be careful too, Babe, I worry about you even driving on California freeways . . . I *will* be home as soon as this war is over. . . .

Shortly after midnight on January 17, the aerial bombardment of Baghdad began, and Operation Desert Shield officially became Desert Storm. Marines were fortunate to be commanded by Lieutenant General Walter Boomer, Commanding General, Marine Forces Central Command.

President Bush announced the offensive action in a televised press conference: "Just two hours ago allied attacks began ... these attacks continue as I speak ..." Hundreds of warplanes relentlessly pounded military targets across Iraq and the Kuwaiti theater of operations (KTO).

On the first day of Desert Storm, Guy and I were the first daylight launch. As commanding officer, I had to lead from the front, and for an aviation squadron commander, that means leading from the air. Guy and I returned from our successful mission to cheering and slaps on the back.

I awakened early on the second morning of Operation Desert Storm. After briefing, I readied myself for the dawn launch of my second combat mission with Guy Hunter. In the left calf pocket of my G suit I placed my survival maps, and in the right, a plastic bag of Cindy's cookies. Little did I know I'd never eat them.

3

The Trip to Hell

Somewhere in Southern Kuwait
January 18, 1991

Guy and I were being driven by our captors along a rugged highway in Kuwait. I peered beneath my cloth blindfold. Thankfully, my captors were less proficient at putting on blindfolds than they were handcuffs. Seeing my feet gave me a measure of assurance. Twenty minutes later, the truck lurched to a stop. Guy and I were dragged out and walked a short distance to what appeared to be an underground bunker that served as a lower-level head-quarters.

Two Iraqis half carried, half walked me. Control of my damaged neck muscles was nearly gone, and my head flopped to one side at a crazy angle. Excruciating pain surged from my neck down the length of my back.

The bunker was dug deep into the desert. Raised beams covered with tin roofing were topped with sand as camouflage. Like others I would be taken to, this bunker was cold and damp and reeked of smoke, sweat, and stale piss. Each time I descended into a bunker, I felt I was walking into a grave. Maybe my own.

We were led straight down into the underground bunker. As I staggered down the stairs, I saw they were covered with cheap-looking green indoor/outdoor carpeting. I guessed the bunker belonged to a battalion-level commander.

Inside the main room of the bunker, I heard movement and muffled Arabic voices. I sensed that several Iraqi officers were sitting around huge conference tables. Guy and I were taken into separate rooms. My blindfold was removed and I saw a long, narrow room, crudely built and rustically furnished. An Iraqi captain sat in front of me at a wooden desk. A young enlisted

61

man who appeared to be a bodyguard for the captain was standing next to the table. Also present was another man, slender, well groomed, articulate, and dressed in a green Iraqi uniform. This man turned out to be an interpreter.

They sat me down in a small wooden chair, my head slumped to the side, pointed down. I was hurting. I felt a "snap, crackle, and pop" in my neck with any movement. It was getting progressively stiffer and throbbed like hell.

"Are you hurt?" the interpreter asked in heavily accented English.

"Yes." My voice was hoarse. My tongue was dry, my mouth parched as the desert—signs of dehydration.

"Would you like some water?"

"Does Warrant Officer Hunter have water?"

"Yes, he will have water," the man replied.

"Then yes."

"Tea?"

"No."

The interpreter held a bottle of water to my cracked lips. Grateful, I took a swig.

The interpreter began by asking two questions I learned to expect at every interrogation: "Are you an American?" he asked.

I nodded.

"Are you a pilot?"

"Yes," I answered. *Wham!* His fist slugged my nose. Though it was only the second day of the war, I sensed that Coalition bombing had already dealt a serious blow.

"What do Americans think of the Iraqi army?"

I tried not to antagonize them. "Americans respect the military capabilities of the Iraqi army."

"Why are you here?" he demanded. Before I could think of a diplomatic answer, he said, his voice bitter and hard, "You have been brought here to kill our children and ruin our nation. You do not deserve good treatment. You are a murderer."

Silent, I waited for the questions.

"Where are you from? What air base do you fly from?"

"I took off from Saudi Arabia," I answered. The interpreter waited a moment for me to continue. When he realized I had finished, a scowl settled on his face.

"No!" he shouted. "What *air base* did you take off from?"

The interrogator did not move gradually up the scale of intensity. "You must answer all our questions right now. We do not have the time or patience for an American pilot who does not answer our questions."

I said nothing, staring at the interpreter. The captain at the desk immediately grew red in the face, indignant that I, a prisoner, refused to answer this question. The young bodyguard, seeing the captain's anger, jumped up like a spark had ignited under his butt. He drew the pistol out of his holster and chambered a round. Then, squinting down the sight, he raised the pistol to my head. My whole body tensed. He looked at the captain for permission to shoot.

The captain conferred with the interpreter in Arabic. The interpreter turned back to me. "You must answer this question *immediately* or you will be shot," he translated the captain's warning.

The young soldier squared off in a stance. With a two-handed grip, he positioned the gun against my skull, his dark eyes glaring. I knew I could not give them the information they sought. They would have to kill me.

"I guess this is what God has decided for me," I thought. "It's my turn." Surprisingly, I wasn't crying and screaming inside. I just hated to go this way, without saying good-bye to Cindy.

I looked directly at the captain instead of the interpreter. "You tell *him*," I said, "that if *he* is going to shoot me," and I looked at the guard, "I want to pray first."

The interpreter spoke to the young guard in Arabic. Looking displeased, the soldier safed his pistol and took his position against the wall. I breathed deeply. I'd made it through that one. How many times would this happen? I heard Guy being interrogated in a nearby room and wondered what threats he was receiving.

Afterward, Guy and I were blindfolded, then brought back outside and thrown into a jeep. The air inside the jeep was warm, but thick with the smell of dirt and cigarette smoke. Someone told us we were going to Baghdad. We were somewhere in the southern area of Kuwait, so Baghdad was several hours' drive away. I expected a long ride and maybe a chance to rest. We rode only twenty minutes before the truck stopped. We were being sent up the chain of command before being delivered to the heavyweights in Baghdad.

We were led down a short flight of sandbag stairs into a second bunker. Through my blindfold I could tell that the light in the room was dim. This place, too, was foul smelling. The stench of kerosene, stale urine, and sweat permeated the room.

The Iraqis marched us around to various rooms as though they were showing us off to their staff members. We stopped in a smoke-filled office. Eight to ten Iraqis descended upon Guy and me and began pummeling us. They hit and kicked us in the head, the stomach, the groin, you name it. Handcuffed and blindfolded, we never knew where the blows were coming from and were helpless to dodge them.

The angry men screamed insults as they kicked and hit us, their frustrations pouring into their blows. "Why are you here? Why you want to kill us?"

Even if we had wanted to answer, we were too busy grunting from the avalanche of blows. They were like a bunch of hoodlums looking for someone to vent their anger upon, and Guy and I were convenient targets. Each blow to my head made my neck feel like it was being slashed with a knife. Unable to shield myself, I gritted my teeth as more thugs joined in the beating frenzy. The men shouted and laughed hysterically, relishing their chance at revenge.

After several minutes of gang battering, they took off our blindfolds. Blood trickled down to my chin.

"What type of aircraft do you fly?" one of them asked. Guy and I kept silent. "What air base did you launch from? How many aircraft are at your base? What is the location and size of ground units there?"

We refused to supply any information beyond our name, rank, and nationality. As if newly incited by our lack of cooperation, several men pounced on us again, striking us about the head and shoulders, yelling wildly. Guy was taken to another room. Every time they dragged him off, I feared the worst. It's tough not knowing what your fellow Marine is facing—or whether you're being used against each other in interrogations.

A group of people—a young captain accompanied by several much older Iraqi soldiers—entered the room. Skinny and arrogant, this captain walked with a swagger. Though he looked young—in his late twenties, perhaps—he was obviously the man in charge. Clearly many years his senior, the older soldiers treated him with nearly fearful respect. He strutted toward me with his hands thrust into his front pockets.

I'd like to meet up with this captain again someday. He was a real prick. He stood above me with an air of cocky self-assurance and assumed a military stance with his feet set wide. When I tried to stand, he shoved me to the floor. One of his subordinates pushed me backward onto the floor with my handcuffs beneath me. My body weight put more pressure on the steel piercing my wrists. I felt painful twinges in my shoulders; my hands tingled, almost numb.

The captain stood over me gloating, his stance that of a high school senior who knows he's tougher than the younger kids. Radiating arrogance, he taunted me. "Are you thirsty? Would you like a drink?"

He stood on top of me with one foot pressing into each hip. Leering down at me, the son-of-a-bitch unbuttoned the fly of his pants. All I could do was watch. He motioned as if readying himself to piss on my face. Then, laughing wildly, he zipped up his pants. He stomped his heel into my stomach and jumped off me like I was a trampoline.

His forty-year old lackeys sprang onto me and continued their brutality with fists and boots. They yelled at me in Arabic, and someone demanded in English, "Why did you come here to bomb us?" The beating lasted about twenty minutes. I was amazed at how vicious they were. Guy was brought back into the room. He looked like he had been beaten up, too.

We were finally jerked to our feet and shoved up the stairs. They stood us against a wall of the building. My legs were going weak beneath me. A short, fat Iraqi man with a large video camera approached. "Now what?" I wondered. The Iraqi was accompanied by two or three helpers who were carrying more camera equipment. Then a dozen Iraqi military men gathered around us.

By their rank insignia and demeanor, I could tell these junior officers were too far down in the chain of command to use us or our information anyway. They just wanted a piece of us before we were sent to Baghdad for whatever fate awaited us.

Before they took our pictures the soldiers took the opportunity to pummel us for a few more minutes. The day was turning into one beating after the other. The Iraqis seemed whipped into a frenzy. Then the camera crew took our pictures for a minute or two. Our blindfolds were put back on and the mob pounded us some more. All we could do was clench our teeth and wait for it to end. It's a horribly insecure feeling to be beaten and not see the blows coming. Blood was dripping onto my flight suit. I gasped for breath when they shoved us back into the truck. We were on our way again. Our captors seemed to be in a hurry to move us around. They got their thumps in and then we were taken to the next echelon in the chain of command.

After a thirty-minute drive we were brought to a building for a third round of interrogations. We were still in Kuwait. It was very cold. Our captors led us into the basement of a narrow concrete building. From under my blindfold I saw that the floor was wet and dirty. There were small offices off to the left and right. I was taken to a room at the far end of the hall, lit by a single low-wattage bulb. Someone pushed me down onto a wooden chair in the middle of the room. I felt cold and started to shiver as I slumped into the chair. I must have looked odd shaking, with my neck twisted and my head lying crookedly to one side.

I heard voices speaking in low tones and people shuffling around the room. When my blindfold was removed, I faced several Iraqi soldiers and a neatly dressed Iraqi colonel, an Arab rendition of the British actor David Niven, only taller and heavier. Though he looked to be in his late forties, his ashen pallor was that of someone twice his age—someone dying. His face looked like it hadn't glimpsed daylight in twenty years, and deep furrows around his eyes gave him a ghastly, deathlike appearance. I had a haunting feeling I'd seen this colonel somewhere in my military career.

He eyed me shrewdly. Speaking perfect English with a slight British accent, the colonel began to interrogate me. "You must tell us everything you know and you must not deceive us in any way."

"This man is *wicked*," I thought, listening to his European accent. He impressed me as the battle-hardened type who would be chosen to run a concentration camp, and not a native Iraqi. His hollow voice turned my blood to ice. "What is your name and rank?" he asked. I answered his question.

"What air base did you take off from?" he continued, his expression hard as carved rock.

When I did not answer, the colonel's pallid face darkened into a scowl. "Colonel Ah-*cree*," he said coldly, accenting the last syllable and rolling the *r*. "You must understand. You are now a prisoner and we will treat you in any manner we desire. You *will* tell us everything you know about the Marine Corps...without deception...accurately and completely. And if you are very lucky," he sneered, "you will not die. But you are going to tell us, one way or the other. I have seen these people cut off fingers. I have seen them cut their prisoners into many pieces before they finally died. They will do the same to you."

"Colonel Doom" asked me several more questions, one right after the other. His voice was full of hatred and contempt. "How many days of ordnance and fuel have you stockpiled at your base? Schwarzkopf and his allies—how do they plan to invade? When will they invade Iraq? How many Syrian soldiers are preparing to invade Iraq from Syria? Will Israel invade Iraq? How many tanks are there ready to invade Iraq?"

I refused to answer.

"You must change your attitude immediately!" He pushed his chair from the table. "You must answer all questions or you will be subject to extreme pain and torture." He stared into my face. "The last Iranian prisoner of war I interrogated was a pilot who would not cooperate with us," he said. I stiffened, holding my breath. "They removed one testicle from him—over a period of three days. Then they removed his other." He seemed to find the memory pleasing. "Then they cut off his toes and then they cut off his fingers. He begged them to kill him." Sweat ran down my back.

The door burst open. An immaculately dressed two-star general marched in, replete with beautifully polished brown boots and an olive-green cape swaying over the shoulders of his neatly pressed and finely tailored uniform. A red beret crowned his striking, dark features, which reminded me of Omar Sharif in the film *Dr. Zhivago*. With cool precision, he strode toward me, his head held high, his mustache neatly trimmed, his hair barbered, his nails manicured. He smelled of fine cologne.

"This guy looks like he's going to a fucking parade!" I thought. Yet I was impressed; I hadn't thought they had anybody like him in the field. We had assumed these guys were ragtag and disheveled, not like this high-ranking officer, a recruiting poster for the Iraqi army.

The interrogator immediately stood up. Bowing his head, he seized the general's hands and kissed them.

The wicked colonel turned his deeply seamed face toward me. "He is here to ask you questions," he snarled.

I stood and tried to come to some form of attention despite the fact that I could no longer move my neck and had to turn my whole body to see anyone. I brought my heels together, saying, "Sir. Lieutenant Colonel Acree, United States Marine Corps."

The general nodded, and with a slight smile gestured for me to take my seat.

"This guy is probably a pretty good general," I mused, studying his face. "A highly respected battlefield commander people would want to follow in combat, not a prick who would force them like Saddam Hussein." The general looked honorable, almost kindhearted, as he conversed with the interrogator in Arabic.

The interrogator turned back to me. "Are you injured? Do you have family?" Through the interpreter, the general asked several more questions, none of them hard. He was evaluating my demeanor, sizing up his opponent. He completed his questioning, then nodded, half smiling, as if to relay some form of soldierly respect. He walked out of the room and I was left with Colonel Doom.

"You would be wise to take our advice. Great harm will come to you if you fail to cooperate fully."

"I understand what you're saying," I said, knowing this mean, vindictive bastard would enjoy every minute. "I cannot answer your questions."

Finally, Colonel Doom looked disgusted, as if he had no further time to deal with me and wouldn't be allowed to kill me. "Do you need to go to the bathroom?" he asked. Later I realized he had used the western term "bathroom" rather than "WC" or "water closet," as did the Iraqis.

They led me to a filthy bathroom with a wet concrete floor and a long trough filled with stale excrement. In the sick-sour stench, a wave of nausea overcame me. Shivering, I barely kept my balance while I relieved myself. When I finished, they led me to a dark hallway and plopped me down on the floor against a wall. Guy was led off to one of the small offices flanking the corridor. I had been instructed to sit on the cold concrete, but a sickening wave of pain came over me. I keeled over onto the gritty floor.

I had been in captivity barely five hours. How long would this god-awful day last?

A few minutes later an Iraqi came behind me and wrenched my handcuffed arms farther behind my back. A sharp pain tore at my shoulder joints. He tied my wrists with rope, making sure I could not possibly escape on this next leg of our journey. He tied on a blindfold so tightly I couldn't blink, then bound a second one over that, even tighter. The pitch-black darkness was disorienting. Wherever our captors were taking Guy and me next, they absolutely did not want us to know. If we drove for an hour or so, we'd still be in Kuwait; any drive beyond an hour meant we were headed for Iraq—and probably to Baghdad.

Oceanside, California
January 18, 1991

Every military wife has a worst nightmare, a vision she hopes and prays will never come to pass. Mine came true on the third day of Operation Desert Storm.

Dressed in shorts and a T-shirt, I was absorbed in writing a letter to Cliff when the phone rang. I startled, though I knew the strict protocol for notifying next of kin. "Don't be afraid to answer the phone," I had told my squadron wives. "If there is 'bad news,' a Marine Casualty Officer will notify you in person." But dreading the bearer of bad news myself, I jumped each time the phone rang.

Once Desert Storm had begun, knowing the danger of Cliff's mission, I almost expected something to happen to him. More than once I visualized the dreaded "Official Call." I never dreamed it would come so soon.

It was a warm afternoon in Oceanside, a brilliant blue-sky Friday. Yet a storm cloud of apprehension hung over me. I was expecting a call from Rosana Martinez, a fellow squadron wife whose optimism and sense of humor I thoroughly enjoyed. Rosana had planned to drive to Los Angeles with me that afternoon for the filming of the television show "Major Dad."

But earlier this morning she had called to cancel the trip. Something mysterious was happening with her Marine husband, Marty, a gentle, soft-spoken man with a broad smile and the physique of a linebacker. Though vague about why, Marty had asked Rosana to remain home and wait for his call. I hoped Marty wasn't being sent back to Saudi Arabia.

Shortly before Thanksgiving, their then-five-day-old daughter, Loren, had become seriously ill with a heart defect. Within twenty-four hours, Cliff had put Marty on a plane headed home from Saudi Arabia. But before a heart transplant or surgery could be considered, their infant daughter suffered irreparable brain damage. Marty and Rosana brought her home from the Neonatal Intensive Care Unit, and in early December, Loren had died peacefully at home. Soft-spoken but strong-willed, Rosana had put on a brave, cheerful face at the Olive Garden wives club dinner the night before.

Now, when the phone rang again, I put down my pen and snatched it up. The caller was not Rosana but my aunt. "Is Cliff flying yet?" she asked.

I couldn't say for sure. We hadn't spoken for two weeks, and unlike the Stealth fighter-bomber, the F-16, the F-18, the A-10, or other aircraft they loved to glamorize, the little-known OV-10 Bronco had not received media attention. My aunt and I talked about our fears for the casualties to come. There had been only two so far, fewer than anyone expected. As we talked, the television screen flashed the latest casualty statistic. Two American pilots were now listed as missing in action.

"I feel *so* sorry for the wives of those missing men," I said. Just then the doorbell chimed. My chest tightened. "I have to go," I said. "Someone's at the door."

I pushed myself from the table and walked toward the front door. Through its small upper window, I saw the unmistakable outline of a Marine officer's "cover" (hat). I froze. Who was this Marine formally dressed in Marine Corps "Alphas"? In my heart I knew.

Trying to keep my hand steady, I turned the knob. As the door swung open, the funereal looks on the faces told me the moment I dreaded had arrived. Colonel Don Beaver, the short, stocky commander of the air group, strode into our living room with Kay, his trim, petite, blond-haired wife. The other Marine officer followed.

Kay took me firmly by the arm and steered me toward the couch. I had imagined the dreaded official call. Now, as in a dream, they were here. We sat on the couch, Colonel Beaver on my right and Kay to my left, her hand gripping mine. I scarcely noticed the other Marine officer—my assigned casualty assistance officer—as he quietly seated himself in a chair.

In those first few seconds of shock, I experienced an unexpected absence of emotion, as if watching myself on television. I had rehearsed the script many times over and now came the actual performance. But instead of being center stage, I was in the audience, watching myself. I braced myself to hear the news every pilot's wife dreads.

Colonel Beaver told me briskly but kindly that Cliff's plane was overdue. He was officially listed as missing in action.

"Missing?" I repeated. That was an option I had not imagined. My nightmares had conjured gruesome images of crashes and death and crippling injuries. I never imagined he would disappear.

"Where was Cliff flying?" I asked. "Were there any witnesses?"

Colonel Beaver told me all he knew, and it wasn't much. Cliff's plane was overdue by more than sixteen hours. Search-and-rescue teams had found nothing. Cliff's plane had vanished.

"Were there any signal beacons or emergency radio calls?"

"No one saw a chute," Colonel Beaver said. "They didn't see a plane crash; they didn't see *anything*." Wisely, he withheld the authorities' prediction: "It doesn't look good." No one expected survivors. "Now, listen," Colonel Beaver said. "If no one saw anything, they don't know if they bailed out or bellied into the desert." He paused. "No news is good news."

I turned to face him. "Who was in his backseat?"

"Warrant Officer Guy Hunter."

Cliff spoke highly of Guy. He added strength and experience to Cliff's team. I imagined them running together across the desert.

"Have Cliff's parents and Stephany been notified?" I asked. When Don gave the word, notification teams would be dispatched to them. Cliff's parents were vacationing in Arizona; finding them might be a challenge. My heart turned over as I pictured Stephany's angelic face clouding at the bewildering news. She barely understood the meaning of war.

"Is this why Rosana received the mysterious phone call?"

Colonel Beaver nodded. When the squadron received unofficial word early that morning, they stalled our trip to Los Angeles—without letting Rosana know the reason.

My questions answered, I suppressed my emotions. "If Cliff ejected, he'll be all right," I told myself. "He doesn't get rattled. He does everything right! If he punched out before it went down, he'll make it." I held on tight to that hope.

Colonel Beaver left to meet the notification team telling Guy Hunter's wife, Mary. Kay stayed to begin the task of breaking the news to our friends and family. "Who would you like to call first?" she asked. Without hesitation I dialed the number of my only sibling, Bonnie, a talented flutist and mother of two toddlers whose friendly smile matched my own.

"Are you teaching?" I asked her. "This is an emergency. I need to talk to you. *Now.*"

She threw down the phone. "Mom? *Mom!*" she screamed. "It's Cindy!"

Luckily our mother, an exceptionally kind and giving woman, now retired, was there helping Bonnie on a project. The minute Bonnie walked into the room, her face stark, Mom recalls, she knew it was about Cliff.

"Cliff went out on a mission and never came back," I told them. There was little else to tell. Knowing I needed her, Mom immediately made plans to fly down to San Diego.

Kay offered to make the rest of the notification calls, but I hated the thought of our friends' receiving such devastating news from a stranger. I mechanically worked down the list of family and friends, wanting to notify them Cliff was missing before they heard it on the news. Many of the calls went to our home state of Washington.

Although Cliff was born and raised in Seattle, I grew up in Anacortes, a small town seventy-five miles to the north. Our country home on nearly an acre of land near the San Juan Islands overlooked snowcapped Mount Baker. A grassy cliffside trail led to a saltwater bay filled with a bounty of oysters and clams.

A medical technologist, Mom performed clinical chemistry tests and X rays for a doctor's office. Known as a miracle worker at home and at work, she had the energy of five people and seemed never to rest or even sit still for long. A kindhearted, generous, and fun-loving man, Dad was a machinist for an oil refinery. He was an outdoorsman who enjoyed hunting, fishing, and boating, but his real love was breeding and training black Labrador retrievers.

With all my kicking before birth, Dad was convinced I would be a football player—named Jimmy. But I proved I was tougher and more athletic than any boy. Though it was sometimes lonely with no friends nearby, I enjoyed long walks on the beach, playing in the grassy fields that surrounded our tree-shaded backyard, and helping Dad with our black Labs. Then one day when I was ten, everything changed.

That afternoon, my sister and I were doing our homework in the kitchen, eager to be done. Bonnie—a pretty, blue-eyed, blond-haired eighth-grader— was eager to finish and call a girlfriend about an upcoming party. A fifth-grader, I couldn't wait to change into playclothes and escape to the outdoors.

Something distracted me from my homework—wheezing sounds—from the living room, where Dad was lying on the couch. Experiencing chest pains, Dad had been tested that morning at the doctor's office where Mom worked. His electrocardiogram was normal. Relieved, Mom dropped him off at home, then returned to her job in town.

I dismissed the noises as Dad teasing my dog, Queenie, who kept vigil beside him. I returned to my homework. Suddenly the noises intensified to a raw, powerful sucking in of air. As Bonnie and I lifted our heads in unison, the noises stopped.

We jumped up from the table and ran into the living room. Dad was sleeping peacefully on the couch. As I came closer, he looked different somehow. "Dad?" He lay so still. I grabbed a stocking-covered foot and shook it. "Dad? Dad!" Bonnie rushed to call Mom. Twenty minutes later, she arrived with the doctor.

I can still see the dark-suited man rising from the couch where Dad lay so still. The doctor put down his stethoscope and turned to Mom. His words knifed through me. "I'm sorry, Mrs. Blanchard . . . His heart has stopped beating."

I turned to Bonnie, watching with me from the doorway. "Is he going to be all right?" I whispered.

"No!" she shot back. "He's dead!"

He was forty-nine.

Later, two men covered Dad's face and rolled him away on a stretcher. I wanted to push them away. "He's *my* Dad!" I wanted to scream. Hugging Queenie, I thought, "Why didn't I do something to save him?" My life was never the same.

Now a widow with two children to raise, Mom was busier than ever working full-time and maintaining a spotless house. Never one to wallow in self-pity, she thought the best way for our family to recover was to maintain life as it had been before Dad's death—an event that was never discussed. Rather than mourning our loss, she put all her energy toward that end. With her strength and organization, Mom taught me that a woman had better be self-reliant and able to support herself and her children—whether she had a husband or not. I decided it was better not to depend on any man. Fate could throw you a curveball and leave you alone.

My beloved country home became a nightmare of maintenance problems and isolation for my capable mother. Two years after my father's death, she announced that we were moving to Seattle, closer to our extended family. I felt cooped up and miserable in our city apartment. Even Queenie had been sent to a new home with relatives in the country.

I enjoyed watching the detective television show "Mannix," and at fifteen years of age, decided to take karate lessons. Studying karate taught me focus and self-discipline. Each time I earned a new colored belt, I worked even harder to achieve the next ranking. I learned I could achieve any goal if I worked hard enough.

Karate had opened up a whole new world to me. It also started me down a path toward the man I would eventually marry, and share everything, including the nightmare of his captivity.

Now, on an afternoon in January 1991, I used a reserve of strength from the example my mother had set to call friends and family with the news that Cliff was missing. People were devastated. "No! Why Cliff? How could this happen?" Speechless with shock and disbelief, some simply sobbed. I was not yet willing to let myself feel my hurt and fear, but their reactions brought my emotions to the surface. Finally I handed the phone to Kay.

"Don't get your hopes up," I told myself as I listened to her break the news. "Better assume he's dead." Nothing would be worse than imagining Cliff being found alive, only to suffer a huge letdown when things turned out differently.

Bad news travels fast, and within minutes the phone was ringing as friends and relatives called with their condolences. Luckily, the news media had not been given Cliff's name since his parents had not yet been notified.

Our navy friend, Scooter, was sent—via the captain of the *Tripoli*—an unclassified personal message: "LT, regret to inform you that your close friend LtCol Cliff Acree and his AO, CWO4 Hunter failed to return from their mission on 18 Jan 91 . . . Cliff is listed MIA. Cindy wanted you advised..." But Scooter would learn of Cliff's status from a CNN report.

I hesitated to call my friend Debbie Mills to fulfill our pact to call each other first should we receive the dreaded knock on the door. Now that the worst had happened, I hated to burden Debbie with my bad news. Just yesterday she had told me how behind she was at work after taking time off to attend the emergency chairpersons' meeting. "Let's not call her yet," I told Kay.

Thanks to the lightning-fast wives' grapevine, Debbie appeared at my doorstep within two hours. "Cindy, this is *not* what we planned!" she scolded as she hugged me tightly.

The events of the next few hours were a blur. I remember the overpowering urge to clean. I was scouring the kitchen sink when our friends Lois and Marty Caverly, a couple in their early fifties, arrived from nearby Leucadia. They had heard the news from friends in Seattle and arrived with pizzas and a jug of wine. Lois was an attractive blond with a heartwarming smile, who managed their rental properties. Marty, a well-read man with a dry sense of humor and a prominent Bostonian accent, wrapped me in a gentle hug. I worried that I stained his sport coat with my tears.

A house full of company eating pizza was Cami's idea of a party. Everyone at the table gave in to her begging. Insisting that she work for her treats, I ran her through the dog tricks I had taught her. Cami ate up all the attention— and plenty of pizza. Afterward, hoping to be fed more, she repeated each of the seven tricks on her own, in rapid succession. We all laughed, and she was a pleasant diversion. Then my mind flashed to the reason everyone was there. Such a contradiction, to be laughing at Cami when Cliff might be dead.

That evening, I called Stephany and tried to lift her spirits. If Cliff was dead, would I lose her, too? We had become so happy in this marriage that took twenty years to happen. Our two-year marriage had been preceded by a seventeen-year on-again-off-again courtship fated to be interrupted by the wrong time, the wrong place, the wrong goals.

But we finally found the right time and place and were married. Now after celebrating only one anniversary, we were separated again. Would death cause our final parting? Or had some twist of fate brought us together again?

Believing in destiny, Cliff's only sister, Ann, was convinced he was alive: "It was meant for you to find each other again," she said. "You're the reason he'll survive."

Somewhere in Kuwait
January 18, 1990

I leaned forward to relieve some of the pressure from my cramping handcuffs. With no fat on my wrists to cushion them, the metal was digging deep into my flesh. Guy's handcuffs were tight, too. But tight handcuffs were a lesser concern than the three bastards riding in the cargo compartment behind us.

We had been dragged into a large jeep-type vehicle with two Iraqi soldiers in the front seat. We sat in the middle of the backseat with an Iraqi guard squeezed on either side of us. It was a tight fit.

Periodically, and without warning, they beat Guy and me with their fists, with the butts of their rifles, and with blackjacks, leather-covered bludgeons that act like spring-loaded whips. For seven or eight hours they beat us. The awkward position of my wrists cinched up behind my back was excruciating, but the cuffs tightened automatically if I tried to move. By now my hands were swollen to twice their size. They had no feeling and were turning blue. Metal prongs skewered my wrists; the handcuffs were severing nerves. Early in the ride, Guy made the mistake of asking if they'd loosen our handcuffs. In response, one of them reached behind Guy and cinched his even tighter. I tried to lean forward to keep the pressure off my handcuffs.

As the truck rumbled along, revolutionary, martial-style music blared from the vehicle's radio and seemed to excite our captors even more. The riotous drums, brass instruments, and roaring men's and women's voices added to the chaos of the random beatings. The Iraqis would sing along and seem to lose control. A certain song came on the radio several times. It ended with an Arabic-speaking voice shouting a question. A throng of people responded and then galloped off on horses, accompanied by the ringing of bells. Another song with a distinctive beat came on repeatedly. I grimaced the moment I heard the opening stanza. At several points in the song, the musical phrase ended with three marked beats. With each staccato beat, we were beaten on the head with rifle butts in time to the music.

Every so often our vehicle slowed down to enter a military checkpoint and I heard people yelling and shouting. When the vehicle stopped, the windows were rolled down. The excited voices of the guards told me they were saying, "Look what we've got! Here's our prize!" Then hands reached in through the windows to take potshots at us. Emotions were running high, and the crowds were jubilant. When the truck stopped at the side of the road, people yelled and screamed at each other in Arabic. Everyone along the way was given the opportunity to reach in the windows and join the beatings, too. Some of them shouted at us in broken English, saying things like "You kill our children!"

The painful ride continued, with the vehicle sometimes slowing down or driving off the smooth road. I envisioned them detouring around a barricade, mine craters, or bombing damage. I worried that allied planes would find us moving and blow us away. But I was being beaten too often to worry long. During this entire drive to Baghdad, the three bastards in the back beat the snot out of us. I felt my head becoming a massive bunch of knots. My neck was in agony. Guy recalls, "Those were heavy-duty thumpings. And it was getting worse. I wasn't thinking a whole lot, but I started praying for God to help us."

The car stopped. The windows were rolled down and an Iraqi soldier taunted us in broken English. "George Boosh. Washington, D.C. You no Washington, D.C. You Iraq. You no Kuwait, you Iraq!" Didn't we know it.

The hellish ride was finally over when we arrived in the outskirts of Baghdad. My injured neck felt like a weakened rubber band stretched to the breaking point. Guy and I were injured, weak from hunger and thirst, and exhausted. I lost consciousness more than once and slumped against Guy. Neither of us was in any condition to face the ordeal that lay ahead.

We were taken to a holding area, a cavelike cell dug into the side of a mountain and closed off by a rolling steel-walled door. In the dark, I could barely make out who was there. An Italian and three to four other captives were placed in the cave with us. The Italian was wounded and, in English, complained throughout the night of his injured arm. He begged the Iraqis to loosen his handcuffs.

The first night of my captivity was eerily quiet. The cave was damp and cold on that January night. I was still blindfolded and handcuffed, and my shoulders ached from the cramped position of my arms. My captors had bound my ankles with black communications wire. (As if I was going any-where.) That wire is so strong you can almost tow a car with it. They wound five or six pieces around my ankles. From behind my blindfold, I sensed that the only light was the glow of a kerosene lamp.

Late that evening in the Iraqi cave, I was startled by the sound of foot-steps. Moments later I felt something press against my lips. I recoiled. "Bread, bread," a man said as he prodded my chin with something soft. I opened my mouth, and he shoved in chunks of bread. Then the man pushed my head back and gave me a drink of water. Later I heard buckets moving down the line of prisoners. A man squatted in front of me. "Food, food." He pushed a spoonful of corn gruel into my mouth. I hadn't real-ized how hungry I was. It was about one in the morning, and this was the first food I'd eaten since four the previous morning. I would have savored that meal if I'd known it would have to last me several days.

I spent the night slumped on the damp stone floor. My neck was numb, except for intermittent electrical shock pains. I was determined to maintain my focus, but felt myself getting weaker. I tried to concentrate, to marshal my strength. But it was bugger cold. I laid my head on my knees and blew hot breath over the tops of my legs to warm my chest.

My tethered ankles ached from the wire cinching them. When no one was looking, I tried to exercise them. My purple hands felt like two heavy clubs on the ends of my wrists. Periodically throughout the night, an Iraqi guard slid open the door of the cell and held a lantern in the doorway to inspect our group. The opening in the door let in just enough light so that if I cocked my head a certain way, I could see under my blindfold. I guessed there were three, maybe four, other prisoners with me, but in the shadows I could make out only the Italian and Guy. Actually, I knew Guy was there without sneaking a look. I'd have recognized his snoring anywhere.

Though exhausted, I felt too overwhelmed by my predicament to sleep. Throughout my captivity, and especially during the first few days, I was in a state of hypervigilance—alert, orienting to my surroundings, attending to every detail. It was hard to believe that just the day before I had been leading a normal life—or as normal as life could be during a war. I'd awakened at three, briefed, had breakfast, and launched before six. An hour later I was a prisoner of war. It would have given me small comfort to know that of the sixty-four airmen shot down in the Gulf War, only nine were on the ground longer than thirty minutes before being captured.

But all I felt that night was shock over the drastic turn my life had taken: from commanding officer to helpless captive. The only thing I could control was my decision about how to get through each moment. I sat awake all night shivering, wondering what daylight would bring.

About four o'clock on the second morning of my captivity, several Iraqis entered my cell. One of them removed the wire restricting my ankles. "You want WC?" he asked. "WC? WC?" he repeated. As I stood up to walk outside into the cold and damp, I realized how much physical damage I'd sustained during my ejection and the marathon of beatings. My equilibrium was gone. Standing or walking was difficult, especially since I couldn't hold my head upright without using my hands. My hands had swollen to nearly twice their size. They felt like numb stumps. My wrists were raw and bleeding, and fluid oozed from them where the ratchets had bitten into my wrist bones.

Limping stiffly, bolstered by two Iraqis, I was allowed to urinate before they escorted me about a hundred yards to an underground bunker. This one seemed more permanent than those I'd visited the day before. I was taken inside to a cluttered, rustic office. An Iraqi major who seemed to be in his fifties sat at a desk flanked by a small kerosene heater on one side and an interpreter on the other side. A guard stood at attention in a corner by the door.

"What is your name?" the interrogator demanded. "Where are you from? . . . Why are you here?"

I told him my name and rank.

"What is the name of your aircraft?"

"I fly an OV-10 plane."

"How fast can your airplane fly?"

These questions were unsophisticated; they could find most of the answers at the library. Then the questions got tougher.

"What was your mission? . . . How many planes were at the air bases? . . . How many observation planes and how many fighter jets?" the interrogator asked. "What was your mission?" I didn't answer. Surprisingly, I wasn't beaten. After this brief questioning session, my captors put me in front of a waiting bus.

As I stood hunched over, blindfolded and handcuffed, I was approached by an Iraqi soldier. He wanted me to stand up straight so he could see my face. He placed one palm under my chin and forced my head back. I screamed.

"Are you hurt?" the Iraqi asked.

"Yes!" I screamed, gritting my teeth from horrendous pain. "My neck! My neck!"

I shouldn't have done that.

I was loaded with the other prisoners onto a bus. Someone threw blankets on top of us. I envisioned the civilian population, ready to attack the bus and seek revenge for the Coalition bombings that had taken place. I was glad to have my identity temporarily concealed.

After what seemed to be a one-hour ride, the bus stopped. Someone climbed aboard and walked down the aisle. He randomly slapped prisoners on the shoulder as if to establish his authority. When he asked them questions, his voice had no trace of an accent—like someone you'd find in line at a hardware store.

"What is your nationality?" the soldier asked. Anyone who answered "American" was slapped hard in the face.

"Italian," one prisoner responded.

"Oh," said the Iraqi. "Soon we've got to go to a café and have some pasta, wine, and cappuccino!" His speech transitioned to fluent Italian. Then I heard a loud smack as he slapped the Italian across the face.

Hauled out of the bus, we were taken into a building and walked downstairs into a small holding room. The prisoners sat against a wall, shoulder to shoulder, in silence. I guessed there were about eight of us. I didn't realize it, but Guy was sitting right beside me.

The situation felt menacing and creepy. I heard a lot of Arabic voices outside the room, commotion, and feet walking quickly. "This must be where all the heavies are," I thought. When certain voices barked orders, people jumped. I would spend the next four days in this two-story building, later known to me as the Iraqi Interrogation Center.

An Iraqi soldier stopped in front of our group of prisoners. "You George Boosh is donkey!" he said. Then he squatted in front of me and put his face close to mine.

"What is your nationality?" he asked.

"American."

"Ah, George Boosh. Boosh is donkey. *You* say that."

I didn't answer.

He struck me across the face, making it sting. "I want you to say 'George Boosh is donkey!'"

"No. I will not say that. He is my president."

He paused. "You *will* say it later."

Iraqi Interrogation Center, Baghdad
January 19, 1991

My hands are shackled and my head is bowed. "God hear my prayer, things are getting bad down here. I can't last much longer." Helpless and blindfolded, a prisoner of war in a hostile and barbaric country, I prepare myself to undergo yet another session of torture.

Behind the blackness of my blindfold I don't know if it's day or night or when the next vicious blow is coming. Breathing heavily, my imagination works overtime. I hear the raw screams of the other victims. Is one of them Guy? What is he telling the torturers—what am I going to tell them?

By the time I arrived at the Iraqi Interrogation Center on the second day of my captivity, my neck was too weak and painful to hold my head erect. My chin was locked to my chest. Breathing was painful. I tried to prop my elbows onto my knees and support my head in my hands. Seeing my hunched-over position, my captors knew my neck was damaged. I was about to learn the first of many painful lessons. Lessons that no book or even Survival Escape Rescue and Evasion (SERE) school could teach. Lessons I would have to learn the hard way.

Within thirty minutes of arriving at the interrogation center, I was taken away for my first interrogation. Before long I realized that the Iraqis were convinced I was in the CIA. I wore a sand-colored flight suit they'd never seen. Our OV-10, an aircraft they'd never heard of, was one of the first planes shot down. The strange plane I was flying was crewed by an older guy in an olive-drab flight suit with the rank "Warrant Officer" who wasn't really an officer. I fell into only one category: spy.

"I am a Marine," I insisted.

"No, Colonel Acree," he said, putting his face close up to mine. "You are a CIA agent. We will soon find that out. We know how to get information."

"Why are you flying this secret plane? We have never heard of an OV-10. What were you doing in that plane?"

"I was flying an observation and reconnaissance mission," I explained. "The OV-10 is a very old, slow airplane. That's probably why you haven't heard of it."

"Admit it. You are CIA. You are spy!" The interrogator slammed his fist into my neck. My neck muscles went into spasm.

"I'm not in the CIA. . . . I am in the Marine Corps."

"No, no!" he said angrily. "You are dressed like a spy." He landed another blow on my neck. I gritted my teeth against the searing pain.

"Every Marine pilot in Saudi Arabia wears this uniform," I said.

"You are lying! You are lying! We have never seen this uniform before. If you continue lying, you will soon die." After the next blow, it took every ounce of my control not to cry out. I felt a wall to my left and momentarily leaned against it. The pain was unbearable. I had learned an important lesson: Conceal your injuries.

"Who is this man flying with you? He is too old to be on this mission. And his rank, warrant officer, no one has heard of an officer with this title."

I explained why I was flying with a forty-six-year-old Marine who was not a regular commissioned officer. My interrogator didn't buy a word of it.

"Colonel Acree. If you do not cooperate, we are going to kill you. Do you want us to turn you over to the Iraqi people? They will gladly carve you up and feed you to their animals. Tell me what you were doing."

"I am *not* a CIA agent; I am a Marine Corps officer," I told them again and again. Finally they accepted my answer.

"What is your rank?" the interrogator asked.

"Lieutenant colonel."

He jerked his head and didn't speak for a moment, as if digesting the information. "Are you a squadron lee-der?" he asked, eyeing me.

"What do you mean?" I answered.

"If you are in squadron and you are lieutenant colonel, *you* are squadron lee-der." He gave me an acid glance.

Reluctantly, I nodded. If I lied about that simple fact, they'd believe I was lying about everything. But once they established I was a squadron leader, they assumed I had details about Coalition strategic or operational plans. My captors were hell-bent on getting information out of me. I had no hope of playing dumb. My interrogations took an ugly turn.

My captivity would teach me a lot about Einstein's theory of relativity. He used to illustrate that theory by saying, "When a man sits with a pretty girl for an hour, it seems like a minute. But let him sit on a hot stove for a minute and it's longer than any hour." Being savagely beaten for a minute would feel like Einstein's idea of eternity. The minutes go on and on, and you have no idea if they'll ever stop—or stop before you're dead.

Desperate for information, the Iraqis felt they had found the answer to that problem—me. As an early captive, a senior Marine, and an aviator, I was a lucrative source of information to the Iraqis. Most important, I was the commanding officer of a tactical squadron.

There's a greater assumed risk for a squadron CO. As a commanding officer, I held a top secret clearance and had access to information off-limits to most other people who might be captured. I had prided myself on keeping well informed. I read every classified document I could regarding Coalition capabilities and upcoming operations. I attended countless briefings on military activities, locations, equipment, operations, and targets. Extensively briefed, I knew too much.

My memory held details of the four phases of the air war, the artillery raids into Kuwait, and the massive amphibious landing. My brain contained more secret information than I ever wanted to know as a prisoner. Leaking the smallest bit could harm many people.

Though I only suspected it at the time, as the first Marine pilot shot down in the war, I was especially valuable. The Iraqis had information about the U.S. Army and Air Force. Our forces had helped train Iraqis in formal schools, field training, and colleges in the United States. The Iraqis knew little about Marine Corps capabilities and combat operations. Yet they knew enough about the Marine Corps's reputation to have a healthy concern for its abilities.

Marines have traditionally been "first to fight." Since World War II, the Marine Corps hallmark has been its ability to land assault troops on hostile shores from seaborne transports. The Iraqis were gravely concerned about how and when Marine forces might invade Kuwait from the sea. I was the only person captured who could supply that critical information. As a chief warrant officer, Guy Hunter was not privy to sensitive intelligence information. Classified briefings of in-depth plans for Desert Storm were normally given down to the commanding officer level only.

Because tactics change quickly in a war, my inquisitors had to extract as much information as possible, as soon as possible.

"Where did you take off from?"

"Saudi Arabia," I said.

"Aziz?" he asked.

"Saudi Arabia."

He tried again. "How many airplanes were at your base? What kind of airplanes?"

I remained silent.

"Tell us about F-18s."

"I don't fly F-18s," I said.

My silence and refusals antagonized them.

"How many days of ordnance and fuel have you stockpiled at your base?"

I remained silent. *Wham!* The Iraqi soldier's bludgeon detonated an explosion of pain inside my skull, swelling the mass of welts. Just then I would have sold my soul for ten minutes without pain. Just ten minutes. "God, help me." *Smash!* The next blow knocked me gasping off the chair, dumping me facedown onto the floor.

Someone hauled me back into the chair. "Colonel Acree. We have ways to make you talk." The voice again. "How are you resupplied? What is the Saudi government giving you?"

Like a gunshot, the next kick went off into my stomach. I doubled over, collapsing onto the floor. I coughed, spewing blood. Another blow to my neck. Then I was manhandled back into the chair. My neck was on fire. "Hold on, hold on," I told myself.

Hands grabbed me by the head and dragged me back onto the chair. My mouth gulped for air, bypassing my broken nose. As the interrogation continued, I felt warm drops of blood dripping on my cold legs. "You cannot endure this for long. Why aren't you cooperating with us? Why won't you answer our questions?"

I had to withhold information to protect my fellow Marines, to preserve my honor. My body said *"Talk."* Deep in my soul, deep in my gut, my hatred and resolve prevailed. I didn't have much left, but I did have my honor. Honor and hate—they kept me alive.

The next blow bashed my weakened neck. My muscles felt like they'd been slashed with a razor blade. More kicks, more slaps, more punches to the neck. I felt more blood trickling down my face.

"You are going to die soon. You will never go home alive."

I kept silent.

My captors pounded me with unrestrained savagery. At the mercy of blackjacks, clubs, fists, and boots, I kept my head down and clenched my teeth. My breathing became raspy and ragged. "Don't cry out," I told myself, clenching my teeth until my jaw ached. But pain demands an outlet. My screams escaped. "No. No! No-o-o-o!"

After hours of beatings I had learned my most important lesson since capture: The hard-ass act of not cooperating doesn't work. Hardballing them, I could last only so long. I was getting exhausted. It was hard to shut out the pain long enough to think. I had read numerous accounts of Vietnam-era POWs and realized I had only three options: say nothing, tell them classified information, or lie. So I gave them a little generic information they could get out of an aviation magazine or even *Time* or *Newsweek*—nothing of use against Coalition forces.

I tried to downplay my job. "I'm driving an old, inefficient, twin-engine, turboprop airplane. My mission is insignificant. I'm just up there looking around with a pair of binoculars." I didn't want them to find out I used forward-looking infrared radar (FLIR) and an onboard laser designator to locate and mark targets.

"You must understand. I have a job to do," the interrogator said sternly. His questions, pointed, urgent, seemed to go on forever: "Who is your chain of command? . . . Where is the command center for your squadron and higher headquarters?...Tell us the type and location of all Marine aircraft....How do you gather information on Iraqi forces?...What airplanes have sensors and equipment for gathering intelligence?...Which airplanes have day capabilities and night capabilities?...Which airplanes have infrared sensors?...Tell us about Marine ground forces. What sensors do they have?...Where are they?...Are they mobile?...How are they resupplied?...If they are fixed, how long does it take to break them down and move them?...Are they manned?...Who are they manned with?...How are they protected?...By what weapons?...Can they operate twenty-four hours a day?"

I didn't answer.

"We are not making much progress," the interrogator said after several hours. I had been asked every question imaginable about the U.S. Marine Corps and all Coalition forces while I heard someone scribbling notes.

"This is no good. We shall have to get this out of you another way."

I didn't expect to be treated like a guest, but the viciousness and cruelty of the interrogators stunned me. Not that they didn't have plenty of reasons to act that way. The Iraqis had been at war with Iran for more than eight years; they didn't eat well and they didn't live well. Their own families were blackmailed into spying against them. They were used to pain and suffering and deprivation. They didn't like Americans, and they had Saddam Hussein for a president. It was far easier to beat up an uncooperative American prisoner of war than to stand up as an individual under a corrupt regime and suffer the consequences.

Each interrogation session lasted from twenty minutes to several hours. They were held in several interrogation rooms. Sometimes I was shuttled from one room to another. Other times I remained in the room and they brought in a new interrogator for another round. Most were experienced. There seemed to be an endless supply of Iraqi interrogators who spoke perfect English. They were focused, impatient, and asked detailed, penetrating questions. Others were knucklehead novices. These "B Team" interrogators didn't care as much about gathering information as they did about getting their hits in. Their moods ranged from calm and methodical to agitated and violent. Once I mentioned the Geneva Conventions. That made them even angrier.

I had stumbled into a time warp. We were fighting a sophisticated twentieth-century war with "smart bombs" against an opponent who used the brute force interrogation techniques of an eighteenth-century war.

During my interrogations the muffled sounds of other prisoners being interrogated came from adjoining rooms. I couldn't hear the questions asked, but I could hear people being hit over and over again and their screams of pain. Each prisoner had a signature sound, a distinctive response to pain. Their grunts, moans, horrible shrieks, and shudders pierced my heart. Hearing them was almost as bad as being beaten myself—especially when I heard Guy Hunter. Guy's Southern voice was easy for me to recognize, but after the first day of interrogations I never heard him again.

Questions continued: "How many men does it take to repair an F-18 engine?... Tell me about Harriers.... Who is your chain of command?... Where is the command center for your squadron and higher headquarters?... Tell us every type of aircraft in all the services.... What type of equipment has the Army brought to this theater?... Where are their logistics bases?... What types of aircraft has your Air Force brought?... Where are their bases?... Where will the amphibious landing take place?"

While dredging my brain for lies, I had to memorize what I'd already said and think of what to say next, while hearing other prisoners' beatings. Overwhelmed with fear, my brain was on overload.

I was not going to give them classified information. I had to uphold the principles I was raised with and had continued to assimilate as a Marine officer. I would make it through my captivity with honor—I would not compromise for my own life. Survival was secondary.

From an early age, I had learned to take life seriously, work hard, and never settle for less than my best. "If you do something, do it right the first time," my father, Bill, always said as he pointed out my mistakes. The values I absorbed through his example—loyalty, determination, responsibility, and discipline—had sustained me throughout my Marine Corps career.

Dad cared deeply about our family. To him, being a good father meant being a good provider, and he took pains to ensure that our upbringing was better than his. Frugal and hardworking, he was the epitome of a man who "pulled himself up by his bootstraps."

"If you want to make something of yourself or succeed in anything, hard work is the only way to get it done," he often reminded me. He worked as a skilled supervisor for a large vending machine company and could build or repair anything. He built our family's two-story house with his own hands.

When I joined the Marine Corps, my sister Ann, a bright, articulate educator, was married with three young children, living in Seattle. From our mother, Ann learned unconditional love. I worshipped my mother, Dee. "Mom has never said a bad word about anyone," I always said, and I wasn't exaggerating.

With her gentle nature, soft-spoken voice, and slight frame, my mother appears demure and fragile. Yet underneath her quiet demeanor exists unwavering strength and a fierce love for her children. Kind to a fault, she was a devoted wife and mother and the emotional hub of our family, caring for our needs while putting aside her own.

I shared a special relationship with Mom. Even as a young boy, I tried to protect and take care of her. At night I rubbed her arthritic neck when it ached from hours of typing at her job as a school secretary. We seemed to understand each other without speaking. Mom had a sixth sense that warned her if I faced danger or difficulty. (It proved uncannily accurate during Desert Storm.)

My happiest childhood memories were of my family's summer beach cabin on Camano Island, one hour north of Seattle. I loved to plunge into the fifty-five-degree ocean to swim, skim board, scuba dive, or water-ski. Dad often kept me busy hauling wood and helping him with the repair and upkeep of the cabin and our small powerboat. Whether throwing a baseball, baiting a hook, or painting a room, everything I did had to be perfect. I worked hard to make him proud, but as a kid, never felt I succeeded. My demanding father instilled in me a drive for perfection.

In time I took over his role, pushing myself hard, becoming my own worst taskmaster. Setting high standards had been driven deep inside me, and for nearly twenty years I had focused on being the best Marine I could be. Now that I was fighting for my life, those high standards helped me endure.

My captors planned to execute me anyway. They told me that many times. The thought of those bastards torturing me for information and then killing me made me livid. It was going to be bad no matter what I did. If they planned to take my life, I'd be damned if I'd give them anything on the way out. Later that first day I learned another lesson: Tell lies, but don't forget them.

At least I was blindfolded during interrogations. By restricting eye contact, captors dehumanize their victims and create the delusion that they are dealing with a subhuman species. The blindfolds also protected my interrogators from my identifying them someday. But they didn't know they were doing me a favor. Because I didn't have to look at anyone, it was easier to lie with a blindfold on. I've never been a good liar, and they say the eyes don't lie. With my eyes covered, I lied my ass off.

I lied about what I did the first day of the war, about fuel requirements, and about other noncritical information. I told them things that made sense but were a sham. The best lies were based on the truth. In captivity, I earned a Ph.D. in lying.

The problem with lying is that I had to make up the lie, tell it, and remember it for future interrogations. And once I went down that path, there was no turning back. I couldn't forget the lie once I told it. The pressure was tremendous to memorize my answer while I listened to the next question. My brain was woozy from beatings, lack of sleep, hunger, and thirst. I was scared to death I'd slip up and give my captors contradictory information.

Another device to mislead them worked great once I caught on. During my early interrogations I wasn't smart about how to respond to questions. When they asked for unclassified information, I was relieved and answered quickly. The problem came with the hard questions, like "How many airplanes do you have? . . . How many days of ammunition do you have at your air base? . . . Where did you take off from?"

I stalled on the questions with classified answers, trying to buy time until I'd formulated a plausible lie. It was obvious to them I was withholding information. Because of my pause prior to answering, I took my hits.

Eventually I learned to slow down my response to *all* questions. I became amnesic, a slow dimwit, hesitating with every answer.

"What is your name?"

I paused, counting to myself before answering. "Lieutenant . . . Colonel . . . Cliff . . . Acree," I said as slowly as I dared. The questions kept coming: "Who is your chain of command? . . . Where is the command center for your squadron and higher headquarters? . . . Which airplanes have day capabilities and night capabilities? . . . Tell us about the ground forces. . . . "

After every question, I paused, answering as slowly as I could. Sometime during almost every interrogation, the Iraqis would blame me for their problems and threaten to retaliate. "Your country is killing thousands of our people. Our children are dying of starvation. Many people have died because of your bombs. Now it is time for you to die."

Late in my first day at the interrogation center I was dragged into an outdoor corridor. Though blindfolded and handcuffed, I pictured this concourse to be a balcony running around the outside of the building. The concourse was heavily used; people continually passed us. Other prisoners were out there with me. I heard their grunts when passersby kicked, punched, or otherwise harassed them. These tormentors pulled out prisoners' hair, poked them with burning cigarettes, and cursed them with angry Arabic epithets. Over the next three days, I would be brought to this corridor between interrogations.

The staccato beat of feet tromped down the corridor. Then they stopped. Near me. I froze, almost afraid to breathe. Was he coming for me or the next guy? I heard scuffling and knew that, for the moment, I was spared. I released my held breath. My turn at interrogation would come. The dread, the apprehension, the fear—waiting to be hauled to my feet was pure terror. I worried about my own ordeal and what was happening to Guy, too—wherever he was. Overwhelmed, never knowing what would happen next, I took it a circumstance at a time.

Even when lying in the corridor, I never relaxed for a moment—not with the ever-present fear, the grinding pain, the pangs of hunger, and the unbearable cold. Fifteen minutes to an hour or two later, guards would haul me to my feet and drag me down the stairs on the soon-familiar route back to the interrogation room.

The interrogations were gruesomely the same: me in a chair, blindfolded and handcuffed; an interrogator; and three to five heavy-handed types with a gung-ho enthusiasm for brutality. That first day at the interrogation center, the beatings continued around the clock. Every beating started out with fists and then graduated to a variety of instruments. Those bastards hit me with fists, feet, clubs, and then moved on to leaded gloves and a blackjack. Another of their instruments of torture was a mitten—like the kind your mom made you wear when it was cold outside, but this mitten had a pocket filled with lead weights or steel balls. My captors knocked the shit out of me for a long time. These guys were mean, vicious bastards who were desperate for information and in a hurry to extract it. Their blatant disregard of any Geneva Convention regulation strengthened my will to resist.

During rest periods my misery continued. Slumped onto my side in the walkway, I couldn't find a comfortable position for my head, which was matted with blood and covered with welts. There wasn't one spot on my head that wasn't tender.

Early into my second day at the interrogation center, things took a terrifying turn. During one of my "rest" periods out in the corridor, someone stopped in front of me. He grabbed my hair and pushed on my forehead until I was flat on my back. While he held me down, another guy grabbed my boots and stretched my legs apart. Their actions set my heart beating wildly.

"No move!" someone shouted.

My flight suit was unzipped. Someone lifted up my T-shirt. The guy holding my feet reached inside my flight suit and pulled my shorts down. What unspeakable tortures were they performing in this corridor?

Colonel Doom's threat of hacking away my testicles flashed in my mind. "Shit!" I thought. "After what they've already done to me, now they're going for my balls!"

UN investigators of Iraq's treatment of POWs during the Iran/Iraq war had uncovered instances of sexual assaults, Iranian POWs becoming impotent as a result of torture, and alleged castrations. Tales abounded of heinous Iraqi torture techniques. Those tales were shrieking through my mind as I lay there, exposed to my audience and whatever sharp implements they might wield.

I felt a pin prick the head of my penis. Battling my fear, I told myself, "Don't panic. Stay in control." It became a chant.

I waited for a knife to slice into my flesh. I felt a curious piercing sensation. Were they infecting me with bacteria? Why on my penis? Being spread-eagled on the floor and managing not to move was the quintessence of self-control.

For days I had been completely helpless, with no idea what they would do to me next. I was defenseless except for my brains and my will. The only victory possible was to not let them know how much they had affected me.

Every fiber in my body screamed: *Run! Get the hell out of here!* I wanted to surrender to fear and panic. I couldn't. It's amazing how strong you can be when you have to.

A few moments later, the strange jabbing stopped. To not yell or scream or utter a word was a small triumph. I never broke down. I never cried one tear for those bastards. And I made it through the inspection with my genitals intact. Much later I learned the purpose of this bizarre inspection: The Iraqis were looking for pilots who were Jewish, unaware that many American males are circumcised regardless of their religious beliefs.

By the evening of my second day in captivity, I was in bad shape: covered with black-and-blue welts, dehydrated, weak from hunger. I was dizzy and disoriented. My ears were ringing. My whole body stung from the beatings. Tight handcuffs stretched my arms up and behind my back; my hands were hot and swollen.

Winter nights in Iraq are cold enough to dust the northern mountains with snow. Sitting outdoors on the cold slab of the concourse, I shook from the bone-chilling cold, my twitching and shivering uncontrollable. An Iraqi jammed a piece of cardboard under my head.

"It is very cold," someone next to me pleaded. "Can we have a blanket?" Hearing the nightly pounding of Coalition bombers didn't make our captors more sympathetic. The Iraqi crouched next to him. "You are a criminal in our country," he spat out. "You do not deserve a blanket."

I sensed that the war was going badly for these guys. I wasn't talking, and they were getting violently pissed off. The interrogators seemed to be on a time schedule to get something out of us. My tactical information was perishable; much can change on the battlefield over twenty-four to forty-eight hours. The war was progressing, and these cold-blooded guys were impatient.

Before I knew it, I was back in the interrogation room. Accustomed to being blindfolded, my sense of hearing was sharp. I could detect, a split second before it hit, the sound of a club or fist or foot slicing the air. At first I flinched. As their anger intensified, my interrogators struck me harder and harder. My body reacted from kinetic energy. A punch in the side snaps you to the opposite side; an uppercut to the chin snaps you up, straightens you vertically. They'd knock me out again and again, and I'd come to moaning and groaning. It went on and on. My captors were getting frantic and out of control.

I heard another blow coming. The others had cut through the air with a faint whistle. This one headed toward me like a freight train. It slammed my head and neck back and launched me out of the chair. My body catapulted up and back. Before unconsciousness overtook me, my only thought was "*This* is the blow that killed me."

Iraqi Interrogation Center, Baghdad
January 20, 1991

I'm out on the patio with Cindy. In the warm sunshine, I bounce a tennis ball high in the air for Cami to retrieve. We laugh at how quickly she snaps up the ball. No . . . I'm in my tent, waking up from a long sleep. Why am I on the floor? I can't move . . . I can't breathe. Something warm and wet drips onto my chest. I feel pain . . . horrible pain. I hear movement and strange voices, but it's black before my eyes.

Suddenly I remember. *I'm in the interrogation room.*

Before I blacked out, the interrogators had started hitting me with a club like a nightstick, thick and rubberized, with a solid top and a spring at the bottom. A blow accelerated just before it hit. After a couple of hours I got to the point where I quit flinching. My captors had broken my nose several times, and hard lumps were accumulating on my head, but I was not going to tell them any plans for the amphibious landing in Kuwait. Ninety-four thousand Marines deployed in the Gulf area—including 18,000 aboard amphibious assault ships—counted on me not to jeopardize their lives.

I had been knocked out many times. When I saw flashing stars, I recognized relief coming. I'd lose consciousness—until they roused me again. I drifted into the welcomed darkness of unconsciousness many times. Each time they roused me, I wished for that natural escape again. The body somehow adapts to release you from pain and you fall quicker into that blessed peace.

After that last blow, I must have been unconscious a long time. Before, they'd wake me quickly with a slap in the face or a kick in the ribs. "Stand up!" they'd yell. Shaking and gasping, I would come back to life hearing the same voices and remembering the last blow. But this time my tormentors poked and prodded me as if wondering, "Did we kill him?" I was alive, but with a shattered nose and a fractured skull.

Someone hauled me back into a chair. The questions began again: "*When* will the amphibious landing take place on Kuwaiti shores?" the interrogator demanded. "*Where* will it take place?"

Iraq believed a Marine landing was certain. The Iraqis had positioned eight of their best divisions along the southern Kuwaiti coast. My interrogators were hell-bent on finding out about numbers of people, ships, aircraft, artillery, supplies, and when and where the forced-entry amphibious landing would take place. My captors wanted that information from me.

I couldn't give them what they wanted under Article IV of the Code of Conduct: ". . . I will give no information or take part in any action which might be harmful to my comrades . . ." It took every ounce of my willpower to control my fears and honor the Marine Corps motto—*Semper Fidelis,* "Always Faithful."

I heard the interrogator speak heatedly in Arabic with another Iraqi. Then his voice returned to me. "Where are the aircraft carriers? . . . How many planes does each carrier have? . . . Do the aircraft carriers have nuclear weapons?"

I shook my head. "I don't know."

"We know you've practiced. You know where the landing will be. You know how many Marine forces will attack."

The Iraqis' claims were true. In October 1990, part of my squadron had participated in Operation Imminent Thunder, a Marine amphibious landing practice widely publicized in the media. Two days before the war, I attended classified briefings. I learned the two locations in Kuwait being considered for the amphibious landing and details about locations, troop strength, priorities, and targets.

"Colonel Ah-*cree,* we are getting very tired of you not cooperating. You are going to tell us everything you know."

I remained silent. I would accept death before I divulged information that would hurt Coalition forces—especially Marines. How much longer could I last? My captors had intermittently interrogated me twenty-four hours a day for the past three days. The beatings had rubbed my skin raw. I had been given no opportunity to sleep and little to eat—only water, bread, a sip of tea, and a few spoonfuls of lentil soup.

I could no longer stand or sit without assistance. I would not have bet one nickel that I would live another week. Even if I survived interrogation, I thought they would turn me over to the public and let them dismember me.

"What can you tell us about the amphibious landing? . . . When and where will the Marines attack?"

"I don't know." I heard a weapon slicing through the air. Everything went black.

I awoke feeling calm. I was vaguely aware of something soft and warm cushioning my head. It felt oddly soothing, the closest thing to comfort I had felt in days. Was this all a bad dream? A terrifying nightmare? Slowly, I opened my eyes. Through a gap in my blindfold, I saw the green Persian rug. The soft object was my interrogator's brown leather boot. *Thump!* He kicked me in the head. By the end of this interrogation session, they had knocked me unconscious an unknown number of times and I still would not cooperate.

The Iraqis had eight years of practice processing, interrogating, and torturing Iranian prisoners. Studying karate, I'd been knocked around and banged up before and had learned to focus beyond the pain, but I was turning into a piece of human pulp. Handcuffed, I had to take their blows without defending myself. I was incensed at the way those bastards were treating me like a human piñata. Their cruel treatment only strengthened my resolve. Beneath my hunger and exhaustion burned a steady flame of anger. *No way am I giving in to them.*

In addition to demanding classified information, my captors tried relentlessly to force me to make propaganda statements against President Bush, the Marine Corps, and my country. Those words could never come out of my mouth. I couldn't do it. I couldn't give in. I set a standard of behavior for myself: to give away *no* classified information.

They knocked me unconscious countless times and I still didn't talk. That sent them a signal. My consistent resistance had established me as a problem prisoner they wanted to break.

It was a battle of wills, me versus them. I had lost track of time. I measured each interrogation session not in hours but in seconds, never knowing if my life would continue. I had no thoughts of Cindy or any of my family, only of surviving.

They dragged me out to the corridor. Every inch of me throbbed in pain. The interrogations had gone on for so long that death would be a welcome end to this hell. I considered one desperate possibility: I was probably in a three-story building. At some point I could stand up and roll over the ledge of the corridor. From even two stories up, I would at least be knocked unconscious, break some bones, or go into a coma. Maybe I wouldn't die, but I'd be of no use to them.

About fifteen minutes later I was half carried back to the interrogation room. My captors pushed me into a chair. Still blindfolded and handcuffed, I slumped over. The interrogation began—the topic: the amphibious landing. The interrogator was raging mad. He pulled my blindfold just high enough so I could see below it. A map of Iraq and Kuwait was spread on the table in front of me. "Where will the amphibious landing take place?" he demanded.

I was silent.

"Is it here?" He pointed to a location far from any planned operation.

I didn't answer.

The interrogator shouted, then his fist smashed into the side of my head. I saw stars as the blow threw me onto the floor. Someone heaved me back onto the chair. The interrogator was speaking quietly to others in the room. Someone walked out the door. The room was very still. I heard the Coalition aircraft bombings continuing outside. I couldn't imagine things getting much worse.

The door opened. The hushed deferential greetings as someone strode in told me this guy was most likely a senior officer in charge of the interrogation center. The visitor came near.

"Colonel Acree," he began, his voice agitated, "your aircraft are wrongly attacking civilian targets and destroying the country and people of Iraq. My wife has no electricity or running water, and little food to feed my children because of your attacks. I have a five-year-old son and a fourteen-month-old daughter. I have not seen them in over thirty days because of this unjust war against my country by your President Bush." He paused. "With my command, you could be taken from this room and shot." He paused again.

"How do you think I should consider this? How do you explain these attacks on the peaceful people of Iraq?"

I said nothing.

The interrogator yanked up my blindfold. Below and to my side, I saw an AK-47. That weapon can drop a guy flat in his tracks at a distance of two football fields. The interrogator thrust his hand beneath my eyes. Between his fingers he held a brass bullet. When he was sure I had seen it, he shoved my blindfold back down.

Click-clack. The bolt snapped shut as someone chambered the bullet into the AK-47.

The bolt just went home. He's loaded it.

Someone thrust the barrel into my chest, right over my heart.

"It is very easy for me to let these men shoot you," the interrogator warned. "You will *never* go home. You will die right here—right now. Is that what you want?"

I heard my heart pounding. Rivulets of sweat ran down my torso. "*When* will the amphibious landing take place?" the interrogator demanded, his wrath unleashed. "*Where* will it take place?"

"I don't know," I said, my voice halting.

A pen scratched on paper; someone wrote steadily. I was not going to tell them.

I listened to my breathing. My mind raced as I imagined the AK-47 firing. *Will my heart stop pounding immediately?* I wondered. *Or will I be conscious after the bullet hits me? Will it make a difference if I'm inhaling or exhaling?*

The head interrogator threatened me again. And again. After several threats, he barked an order. Everyone scurried out of the room—except the guy ramming the AK into my chest. The barrel shook, trembling in his grip as he waited for the order to shoot. *All he has to do is think about pulling that trigger.* For a moment I wished he would—at least that way I'd go fast.

"You tell me now or you will die," the interrogator said without a trace of emotion. "Your choice. Make up your mind."

He paused. "Where will the amphibious landing take place? If you do not answer, I will give the order to shoot."

I took a slow, deliberate breath. I thought of thousands of Marines afloat, preparing for the amphibious landing, oblivious to the choice on my hands—a choice that could cost many of their lives.

The barrel pushed deeper as the soldier tightened his grip.

"I don't know," I repeated. Waiting for the command to fire, I looked under my blindfold at a beautiful red wool Persian carpet. *Surely these guys wouldn't splash my guts all over this nice carpet?*

Silence ticked by for several seconds as I counted my breaths, wondering which would be my last. "Four . . . five . . ." I counted, to distract myself from the thought of dying. "Eight . . . nine . . . ten . . ."

I counted for two minutes.

The interrogator gave an order. The soldier jerked the rifle away. The game was over. I had won that round.

After a short period in the corridor, I was brought in for my next interrogation. This time, my captors asked about intelligence gathering: "Who is the senior intelligence officer? . . . Where are his headquarters? . . . How do you gather information on Iraqi forces? . . . What airplanes have sensors and equipment for gathering intelligence? . . . Where are these aircraft based?"

"I'm not high up enough to know about those things," I lied, and explained why. My lies were stacking up higher and higher like a house of cards. If they compared my answers with those of another POW, my lies might come tumbling down.

"You are lying," my interrogator told me.

I provided no information.

An Iraqi cocked a loaded pistol and shoved the cold barrel into my right temple. A mock execution is absolute terror, feeling the pistol shoved against your skull and knowing your tormentors are crazy enough to blast your head off.

I remained silent, certain each moment was my last. The barrel stayed against my skin so long the metal warmed.

I heard the click of the trigger.

It happened over and over again. By midday I had gotten through six mock executions without breaking. These were hard-bitten Iraqi veterans. They understand a hard line. I held the line, and I think they respected me for that. I had won with my mind and my resolve. Everything else had been taken away. If I'd made it this far, maybe I could make it out alive.

My initial Marine Corps discipline had developed in me a certain hardness that helped me deal with these difficulties. My martial arts training had taught me the self-discipline to control myself as if my body were made up of two parts: the outside shell, getting beaten; and on the inside, my brain. At least they couldn't reach that.

Coming to on the floor after a beating, I felt so ill I was sure they'd drag me straight out to the corridor. I had been knocked unconscious for the second or third time during a long and intense interrogation session. My body was wasted. I was no good to them anymore. Or so I thought.

A hand rubbed my right forearm, paused, then rubbed again. My arm felt icy cold. Rough hands held my arm tightly. I felt the sharp stab of a needle. "What the hell are they doing?" I thought. A strange sensation ran through my veins, then suddenly my arm felt hot. The whole right side of my body grew warm, hot, and finally numb. The feeling crept up to the right side of my head. The son of a bitch had injected me with a drug to break down my resistance. Going under, I silently cursed them. "You bastards; that's cheating!"

I was terrified they'd permanently damage me if I resisted again. I told myself, "Think, Cliff. If you stay coherent, you can find a way to protect the information somehow. You've got to come up with something fast—*immediately!*"

With the chemical flowing through my veins, I began to hallucinate. I went into the tunnel, a coping mechanism I somehow devised to prevent giving out classified information. In my mind I was standing in a dark tunnel with two bright lights on the ceiling halfway through the tunnel; one light was green, the other was red. Each time they asked me a question, a light would flash. Red meant the answer was classified, and I'd either remain silent, tell them I didn't know, or lie. If a green light flashed, I'd tell them stats from *Jane's All the World's Aircraft,* anything, to get through the interrogation.

In this experience, I was in a small compartment in the tunnel listening to a voice outside. I was coherent and focused, but things slowed down. I fought to concentrate and stay alert. When the questioning was finally through, they dragged me back out to the cold corridor.

I had no idea how long the effects of the injection would last. I was scared as hell the drug could permanently affect me.

Four to six hours later, I came out of it. My captors dragged me into another interrogation. After several hours, I was wrung out, my neck and upper body in torment. But running on adrenaline, painfully alert, I didn't even think of food or sleep.

After three days at the interrogation center, beatings and lack of food and sleep had pushed me to within a hairline of collapse. Just as I was running out of steam, my captors changed the rules again. Now they demanded I regurgitate a propaganda statement on camera. I remembered that during the Vietnam war the North Vietnamese had forced POWs to denounce the war. Now the Iraqis had the same goal.

That evening they repeatedly insisted, "You are going to get in front of the camera, and you are going to say, 'President Bush has unjustly started this war...'" Five sentences of pure crap.

I didn't have many options left. I had been knocked unconscious I don't know how many times. My brain was jarred, my flesh was bruised and torn. My captors hit me so hard, so often, and with so many instruments, I expected the next blow to kill or cripple me. I didn't know that my skull was cracked and my facial bones were broken. All I knew was I hurt like hell and wouldn't survive this much longer. I had no choice but to face that camera.

After hours of negotiations, bargaining, and refusals, I finally acquiesced to being filmed. "I will go before the camera," I conceded, "but I will only say my name and rank." I wanted to say as little on camera as possible. But the Iraqis had something else in mind—a two-page, one-and-a-half-minute segment denouncing President Bush and explaining why I felt this to be an unjust war against the "peaceful people of Iraq."

"I cannot say that," I told my captors. "I am a military officer. I am not a spokesperson. I am not authorized to say that."

"You are not cooperating!" the head interrogator roared. "You *must* appear before the camera and say these words!"

After several more hours, I negotiated down to a ten- or fifteen-second statement. "At least, if I have to get in front of the camera," I told myself, "I can verify I am alive and warn Coalition forces that the game in southern Kuwait has changed from antiaircraft fire to a surface-to-air missile threat."

By the time of the filming, late on my third day of captivity, my exhaustion was debilitating. Guards picked me up, dragged me into a brightly lit room, then pushed me into a chair. I had so little strength left I could barely remain seated.

I sat slumped over, with my head hanging toward my wrists, handcuffed in front. My spirits sagged as much as my body. My pride and principles told me, "Don't give in on *anything*." But to survive this ordeal I had to change.

My numb fingers groped a tall, canisterlike bucket between my legs. Was it to collect vomit or blood? A hand on my face pushed me back upright. Someone dipped a rag in the bucket and washed the dirt and blood off my face and neck. Someone pushed my hair to one side, straightened my collar, then removed my blindfold.

I blinked at the harsh lights. Until that moment, I hadn't been allowed to look around for more than a few seconds. Sitting against the white wall of an office, I faced a large video camera with a huge protruding lens and a microphone on a boom. A camera operator waited beside the camera. Beside him stood an Iraqi wearing dark glasses, his face obscured by the lights.

My audience will be forever carved in my memory. Five or six high-ranking Iraqi officers, probably generals, sat in a row of chairs across from me. The men looked hard-core. Each wore the ornate belt buckle of an Iraqi commander and carried an ivory- or gold-trimmed Browning high-power pistol in his holster. All but one held half-folded newspapers in front of their faces to disguise their identities in case I could identify them later.

"You stinking bunch of cowards!" I thought. I will never forget the lone officer who had not placed a newspaper in front of his face. He revealed himself, an overweight, younger version of Saddam Hussein, a punk in a uniform who looked like he would startle if you spoke too loudly.

The Iraqi working with me seemed frustrated as he tried to raise my head for a better camera shot. "Lift your head, lift your head!" the interpreter in dark glasses demanded. "Look up, look *up!*"

"I can't." I couldn't get my head high enough to even *see* the damn camera. My neck muscles had given up. It was all I could do to hold my head above my chest. I expected to pass out at any time.

"You *must* look into the camera," the interpreter ordered again. Someone finally leaned me back against the wall, and the operator lowered the camera so I'd look like I was sitting normally.

"We are going to ask you some questions," the interpreter instructed. "Look directly into the camera. Do not blink. Do not attempt to send any messages."

Their fear of blinking and sending messages was justified. In one celebrated case, Vietnam POW Jeremiah Denton had been filmed as he confessed to "crimes." He blinked his eyes repeatedly under the harsh glare of the camera lights—and was actually using Morse code to blink out a message about his torture that U.S. intelligence experts quickly deciphered.

We rehearsed the prepared questions and the answers I had agreed upon. They had trouble pronouncing my name. "Ah-eee? Ah-CAH-REE?" they kept asking. It always bothered me when people mispronounced my name, but this instance gave me precious time to maneuver.

Before the tape started, the interpreter told me I could send a message to my family.

"No," I told him. "I don't want to do that."

"Don't you want to say anything to your family?"

"No." I didn't want to say one word more than I had to. I was sure they were trying to trick me.

"Don't you want to let them know you're all right?" he insisted.

Maybe it was a good idea. If somehow Cindy saw me, she could tell my neck was injured and that I had been brutally coerced to appear on camera. By now she would have been notified I was missing.

The operator took his place behind the camera. The interrogator called out his first question:

"Would you tell us your rank and name?"

"Lieutenant Colonel Cliff . . ." I felt woozy.

"Acree," the interviewer cut in. The interpreter relayed each question in Arabic into the microphone, then asked me the question in English. He translated my answer into Arabic.

"What's your age?"

"Thirty-nine."

"What's your unit?"

"V-M-O-two."

"You are the commander of that unit?"

"Yes, I am."

"Your mission?"

"Observation and reconnaissance."

The interrogator ordered the camera turned off. He berated me to repeat a propaganda statement. I refused. Someone smacked me in the head. The camera was turned back on.

He continued. "How your aircraft has been shot down?"

"I was flying a mission in southern Kuwait and was shot down by a surface-to-air missile."

He ordered the camera turned off three times, and each time badgered me to make a statement. What I said on that tape and what my interrogators wanted me to say were completely different.

"Do you have a message to be sent?"

"I would like to tell my wife and family," I said, my voice catching, "that I am alive—and well."

"We cannot guarantee that will be broadcast in its original form," the interpreter said, referring to the last sentence about my family.

I had fought hard against appearing on camera and had defied their orders to repeat denunciations of the war, my president, and my country. Certain that the Iraqis would rebroadcast that sentence with a propaganda statement substituted for my own words, I felt defeated and deceived. I had won the battle but lost the war.

Being filmed by the Iraqis was demeaning, even though I had my chance to alert others flying in that region to the danger of SAMs. It might have given me solace to know that Guy Hunter and the other Coalition prisoners of war had also been videotaped. No matter how blameless or innocent the comments POWs made, we felt terrible about making the videotaped statements. Under sufficient torture, all men comply to a certain extent.

During Vietnam, the military Code of Conduct prohibited a soldier from giving captors anything beyond his name, rank, and serial number. Many POWs were tortured into making antiwar statements, and when they returned, they suffered from excessive guilt on top of their physical abuses. Recognizing that there is a limit to a person's ability to withstand cruel punishment, a military-civilian committee produced a new six-point code in 1977. Instead of authorizing military captives to give *only* name, rank, service number, and date of birth, they are now instructed that they *will* give name, rank, etc., then only "evade answering further questions to the utmost of my ability." The amended code, explained a Navy spokesman, gives a POW more latitude, so "if they are breaking his arm off, he need not carry the mental load along with the physical . . ."

The Gulf War POWs were the first users of the revised Code of Conduct, yet after being filmed by the Iraqis, each of us felt as if he had failed. And failure is a powerful demoralizer.

After filming the propaganda videotape, two people grasped me under the armpits and hauled me to my feet. My legs buckled. With a guard holding me under each arm, I was half carried, half dragged back to the open-air walkway.

Disoriented by horrific pain, I verged on unconsciousness. My head dangled wherever it happened to fall. My wrists and hands had no feeling left in them. My body was a mass of bruises and open sores. My nose and facial bones were shattered. But the greatest ache was in my heart, overwhelmed with guilt and regret. And now that they'd used me, they had no reason to keep me alive.

Our videotaped images would be broadcast around the world. I never imagined the worldwide sensation they would cause, nor Cindy's reaction when she saw mine.

4

Black Belts, Yellow Ribbons

Oceanside, California
January 18, 1991

Nothing. No answers, no information, no witnesses. Nothing.

I lay in bed the night of my notification, haunted by the only confirmed report we'd received: "The problem with Cliff's aircraft was *not* mechanical. . . . They were engaged."

Images flooded my mind, all of them frightening. I saw Cliff walking across the moonlit desert alone, stumbling onto a minefield, or being held at gunpoint. I imagined his OV-10 a crumpled heap in the desert, his lifeless body inside. "Please, God," I prayed over and over. "Let him be *alive*."

I wanted to argue with God that it wasn't fair. I imagined Cliff kneeling beside the bed praying, as he did every night. "Why Cliff?" I demanded. "Of all the people you could have chosen, why pick someone so honest and kind?" I had to trust that this was all part of God's plan. A plan I hated.

Never had I been so tired and less able to sleep. I lay awake all night. My only comfort was knowing that wherever Cliff was, he knew I loved him. From my bed, I tried to communicate with him—sending a telepathic message to wherever he might be. Feeling his love return gave me strength—strength I would need the following morning as I dealt with another consequence of Cliff's disappearance.

By Saturday mid-morning, Cliff's parents had been located and officially notified of Cliff's disappearance by a Marine casualty officer. Now that his next of kin had been notified, his name was released to the media. Within minutes, it seemed, someone alerted me that reporters and camera crews had descended upon our home.

TV vans lined the street. Thick cables snaked over the sidewalk. Reporters stalked the street ringing neighbors' doorbells in search of people to interview. One reporter was even caught traipsing through the bushes beside our house.

Our phone and doorbell began to ring. Friends answering the door responded with the statement we had posted above the phone: "Cindy would love to talk to you and is grateful for your concern. However, there is genuine concern that whatever is said may be used to hurt her husband or any other POW. The Department of Defense would prefer she make no comment. Thank you for calling." I had retreated upstairs to avoid the cameras that thrust through the door whenever it opened.

The more compassionate newspeople apologized for the intrusion. "I'm so sorry to bother you at this difficult time," they'd say, "but this is my job . . ." On the other end of the scale were those who tried to gain access by passing themselves off as family friends.

Guy Hunter's family was protected from the intrusion of the media since they lived aboard the Marine base, which allowed only reporters accompanied by a military escort. We were the only POW family physically approachable on the West Coast, and we were deluged with reporters from San Diego and Los Angeles, Seattle, and the national networks. The phone was ringing continuously as friends fielded call after call. Agitated by the commotion, Cami paced nervously.

I walked upstairs to the study, where memorabilia from Cliff's eighteen-year Marine Corps career decorated the walls. I peered between the blinds of the upstairs window at our once-quiet cul-de-sac. Fourteen news vehicles were lined up, end to end. Poles taller than our house supported network satellite dishes. Wires, cameras, tripods, and news teams crowded our sidewalk. Our street looked like a battle-staging area. I felt under siege.

"How your life can change in twenty-four hours," I typed into my journal. "From being an anonymous person—minding your own business, able to walk outside, drive to the grocery store—to suddenly being 'famous' for all the wrong reasons . . ."

Two doors down, a neighbor I barely knew stood on his front lawn surrounded by reporters. Of our neighbors, he was the only one who had never asked about Cliff or offered help during the five months since Cliff had deployed. "What on earth is he saying to them?" I watched him motion vigorously with his hands as he talked. The reporters scribbled on their notepads, assuming that everything he said was true.

Inside the house, the commotion had become nearly as great. Friends visited, flowers were delivered, and reporters requested interviews. It took three people to answer the door. Another person monitored CNN. Two others answered the phone, which rang the moment the receiver was replaced, and kept a detailed log of every call.

The volume of noise from telephone calls, conversations, television, and the doorbell ringing set my nerves on edge. When I was downstairs, I had to retreat to the rear-facing kitchen, adding to my feeling of being trapped in my own home. Even there, I kept looking over my shoulder for cameras. I jumped each time the doorbell chimed. Someone finally put a sign on the door: PLEASE DON'T RING THE DOORBELL. KNOCK SOFTLY INSTEAD.

Late Saturday afternoon, Mom, a gentle but tough-as-nails woman whom my friends immediately loved, arrived. No matter how old you are, a hug from Mom makes everything better. Accompanying Mom from Seattle was my closest friend from high school. A tall, poised woman with shoulder-length blond hair, Karen had known Cliff nearly as long as I had.

Cliff and I had met more than twenty years earlier at a karate dojo in Seattle. In 1970 we were both long-haired high school teenagers. One night during karate partner drills, I had found myself with a new opponent: a tall, lanky young man, well over six feet tall. His tanned face was framed by brown hair and his green eyes had a teasing quality. Beyond his smile, I sensed a special intensity, a seriousness, a focus. His stance was confident, determined—that of a leader.

The instructor bellowed the next sequence of moves: "Next set: straight kick, roundhouse, backhand!" Cliff and I worked our way across the mat. When our eyes met, I felt an instant, undeniable attraction. Feeling self-conscious, I laughed nervously. His steady gaze had not lifted from my face. *"Rotate!"* the instructor barked. Saved by the bell, I bowed and moved to my left and a new partner.

During the next twenty years, it seemed as if fate were always calling out *"Rotate!"* For seventeen years we moved apart and together again. Falling in love was easy; staying together was the hard part. There always seemed to be something between us, getting in the way—my career, Cliff's overseas deployments, long-distance misunderstandings, and now the Gulf, where Cliff had seemingly disappeared.

That Saturday wore on. My impressions were a flurry of phone calls, flowers, and food. I remember feeling numb. I remember praying. Several people visited to pay their condolences, including Cliff's former squadron CO, Jim Treadwell. The brawny retired Marine with the call sign "Bear" greeted me with a huge hug and tears in his eyes. He sat holding my hand as we explored all the possibilities. On the downside: Cliff's plane might not be found for months or even years. After twenty-five years, some 2,000 service-men were still listed as MIA in Vietnam. On the up side: Saddam Hussein was offering a $50,000 bounty for each pilot, good incentive for someone to bring Cliff in.

Hope of such a deliverance flickered on Saturday night when several friends called to ask about rumors of Coalition pilots rescued or taken prisoner. The name "Clifford David" had even been mentioned. We heard that a signal beacon had been received, then shut off. People theorized that Cliff and his AO might have been picked up by Kuwaiti resistance. Rumors circulated of life rafts being spotted, signals being picked up at sea. Speculation ran rampant, but none of these rumors was verified by official sources. It was hard, waiting for confirmed, official reports. I wanted to grasp any shred of hope. But we waited, watching CNN like everyone else. Debbie offered to spend the night again.

With all rumors proving unfounded, I went to bed with increased doubts and fears. And because my brain was running at peak capacity with worry about Cliff, I was again unable to sleep. I took a hot bath, leafing through the latest issue of *People* magazine. After reading the same paragraph for five minutes I realized the meaning of the words came too slowly, as if written in a foreign language I barely knew. Reading about Oprah's weight loss woes wasn't going to distract me anyway. I threw the magazine to the floor, never dreaming Cliff's picture would appear in the next issue.

I tossed and turned all night, waiting for the sun to come up. Since Cliff's departure in August, I had been so busy working, chairing the wives support group, and supporting him long-distance that I never had enough time. Now I had time. Nothing but time.

I tried to visualize his face as I'd last seen it five months earlier, before his early morning departure. I missed his teasing grin, his clear green eyes, even "the Look," his trademark frown when something didn't meet his high standards. I wanted to lock those memories into time. Already fading, they might be all I had left.

Sunday, January 20—the third day

I crept out of bed early, determined to make myself look presentable—or as presentable as one could with a face swollen from crying in bed and what looked like two black eyes. "What outfit should I wear *today* that I'll hate forever?" I wondered, knowing I'd associate the clothes with my misery. Pushing aside hanger after hanger, I wondered if I was foolish to hold out any hope.

How could Cliff still be alive? He'd been missing since ten o'clock Thursday night our time—sixty hours. We had heard nothing. With every passing hour, the chances of finding him had dimmed and my resolve to maintain a positive outlook weakened.

By eight o'clock Sunday morning, my morale had reached a low point. Sitting alone in the living room, I glanced at the door where I had greeted him so many nights when he returned home from work. "He's not coming back,"

I thought, suddenly filled with despair. "He'll never set foot in this house again. I'll never see him or touch him or kiss him again."

Hot tears flowed down my face as my brave front crumbled under the weight of my fears. Cami padded into the living room and laid her big, warm head into my lap. I stroked her soft black ears, envying her innocence. She blinked her brown eyes at me, and then, as if she understood, placed a big paw on my arm. Not wanting to wake Debbie, Karen, or Mom, I tried to hold back my retching sobs, but they escaped anyway.

I felt an arm circling my shoulders. Debbie sat down and hugged me close, cradling my head against her chest. "I wish you didn't have to hurt so much!" she cried.

"I feel like the Indian wife in *Dances With Wolves*." I thought of the scene where Kevin Costner's wife rides slumped over on her horse, fearful she will never see him again. "I want him to come home alive, and I'm trying not to look back."

Near the end of the film, the lovers are reunited on a wintry day, then tumble to the ground on a snow-covered hill. I couldn't imagine any happy ending for our story.

At a loss to control my grief, I hated being an additional burden to Debbie. She was worried about her own husband flying in combat. Soon Karen was with me, too. "You were a person in shock, a wounded animal, so lost and in pain," she recalls. "By nature you're so strong and controlled, it was shocking to see you struggling with such despair."

I dried my tears and reminded myself to stay strong for Cliff. Soon Don and Kay Beaver arrived. "I want to make a statement for Cliff," I told them. Guy Hunter's wife, Mary, had already talked to the press, tearfully expressing her fears, and had even scheduled telephone interviews with Dan Rather and Larry King. I didn't want my silence to be misinterpreted.

I had resolved not to talk directly to the press. I knew the reporters' technique: Ask the grieving wife several personal, emotion-laden questions. When she cries, zoom in for a close-up of her tear-blotched face. I was too proud to give them that.

Early that morning I had typed in my journal:

It's no fun to be "famous." My feelings are far less important than their getting a scoop, a sensational story, emotional statements, pictures of me out of control, broadcasting my pain and sorrow for all to see. . . .

Instead, I decided to prepare a written statement to show my love and loyalty for Cliff.

Upstairs in the study, I wondered where to begin. I turned on the computer and read my latest letters to Cliff, which he had not yet received. What better way to reconfirm my commitment and love than to include a portion of one in my statement? I imagined my words broadcast heavenward like a prayer, then beamed down to Cliff, wherever he might be. I wrote:

> LtCol Cliff Acree joined the Marine Corps in February 1973. He flew the AH-1 Attack Cobra and OV-10 Bronco during his ten plus years as a naval aviator. He was selected and took command of VMO-2 on June 1, 1990.
>
> Cliff loves to fly and is proud of the men in his squadron. He has often told me that he couldn't have asked for a better group of men to work with.
>
> Having Cliff gone has been difficult. We are very close—best friends, actually—and I couldn't ask for a more loving and devoted husband.
>
> What has helped me and continues to give me strength is knowing that Cliff is dedicated to serving his country and he will persevere. My goal is to do everything I can to support Cliff and the families of the men in his squadron.
>
> I have the greatest admiration and respect for Cliff, as a Marine, a husband and a father. . . . Wherever he is, he knows that I love him more than anything in this world and I always will. I'd like to repeat to Cliff a message from a letter I wrote to him on January 14, which he has not yet received:
>
> "We have so many things left to do, so much to look forward to. I love you very much and always will. I'm behind you in everything you do, sweetheart.
>
> "You have some difficult times ahead of you. When you get tired and discouraged or overwhelmed, just think of the strong love I have for you and that I'm backing you up and will be here for you, regardless of what happens. You can count on me for the long term.
>
> "I think you're the greatest, and have so much respect and admiration for you. I wish I could be there to comfort you and hold you. Just know that I'll wait as long as necessary for you to come home safely to me. Stay strong, sweetheart. I love you."
>
> I ask that everyone support our military families, wherever they may be assigned. . . .

Kay proofread my statement. I thought it kind of her to change my past-tense mentions of Cliff into present tense—as if he were still alive. Busy typing, I scarcely noticed the footsteps coming up the stairs. But moments later, Mom's strange high-pitched outcry—a crescendo followed by a decrescendo—got my attention.

"Oh God, this is it," I thought dejectedly. "They've found the plane and he's in it." Don walked into the room and settled into a chair facing me. Over his shoulder, a mirror in the adjoining room reflected a pale, drawn face; my eyes looked bruised, as if someone had beaten me. For the second time in three days, I braced myself for bad news.

"We received word of something early this morning," Don began. "I didn't want to tell you until it was confirmed. We think Cliff is being held as a prisoner of war."

Shocked, I drew in my breath. "Hope," I thought. "I have *hope!*" I let out a deep breath, feeling instantly charged. With new reason for living, I felt myself coming back to life.

Don had more incredible news. Pictures of Cliff and other POWs held in Iraq were expected to be broadcast on CNN.

With newfound energy, I gave directions to Kay and Debbie, who were proofreading my statement. "Okay, you two finish that section, then I'll correct it and—"

Debbie interrupted. "The old Cindy's back." She laughed. "She's starting to boss us around!" Her smile was relieved. "You've got your spark back!" she said, hugging me. We laughed for the first time in days.

I remembered the joyous reunion in *Dances With Wolves.*

"Maybe we *will* roll in the snow!" I told Debbie. From that day, the lovers' "snow scene" became my symbol of hope.

Don went downstairs to monitor the television while I finished my statement. Thirty minutes later, Don hollered up the stairs, "Cindy! He's on!"

I dropped my papers. My stomach tightened, so afraid was I to see the broadcast. Bonnie and Ann, Cliff's sister, had called, practically hysterical after seeing Cliff's battered face on TV.

I sprinted downstairs for the first glimpse of my husband, a prisoner of war—in the deadly grip of President Saddam Hussein, "the Butcher of Baghdad."

Iraqi Interrogation Center, Baghdad
January 20, 1991

Blindfolded and handcuffed, I felt myself being dragged out of the corridor of the Iraqi interrogation center. After three days of torture and terror, unrelenting pain racked my body. My captors at the interrogation center had nearly beaten me to death. Added to my physical pain was the crushing psychological pain of knowing I had submitted to being filmed for Iraqi television. Though I knew I had given my captors absolutely nothing of value, I felt that I had failed.

Two Iraqis half carried me out of the building and shoved me into a small bus or van. Shivering from the cold, I groped for my seat with fingers swollen to the size of carrots. I leaned forward, bracing my shackled arms on the seat in front of me and letting my head flop helplessly onto my hands.

Others moved onto the vehicle behind me. Their nauseating stench told me they were prisoners. *Could Guy be here?* Though solid blood clots clogged my nostrils, the shallow breaths my mouth drew in reeked of bodies covered with dirt, blood, stale sweat, and excrement forced from their bodies during beatings.

A blanket was pushed down on my head. Where were they taking us? We waited. Someone mounted the stairs. The door closed and the bus jolted forward. After a long drive with frequent turns the bus stopped and we prisoners were yanked from our seats.

Two men lugged me off the bus and into the cold night. We passed over cobblestones, through a gateway, and into a building. We moved down a corridor and through a small doorway. The place stank of urine and decay. I stood in the cold, dark room, head bowed to my chest like a heavy weight.

Someone tugged off my blindfold and unlocked the handcuffs. It felt strange to move my hands apart after having them bound for four days. The flesh of my wrists was hideously swollen over the red gashes left by the metal cuffs.

Blinking, my eyes adjusted. I saw a dilapidated prison cell in a dimly lit building. An Iraqi beside me held a sputtering kerosene lantern, the only light in the cell. Several other guards stood silently watching, their shapes merging with the darkness.

The Iraqi with the lantern motioned toward me. Speaking in Arabic, he presented me to an Iraqi officer wearing a long black leather coat over his uniform. The flickering lantern painted shadows onto the officer's face as black as his coat, deepening his scowl. The captain walked within inches of me and extending his hand toward my lowered face, raised my chin to look into my eyes. I winced. The corners of his mouth turned up into a half smile. He nodded smugly—as if to say, "We own you now."

The scene in the cold shadowy cell felt ghostly and surreal. Helpless, tired, physically and emotionally wrecked, I saw my life from a detached, almost accepting point of view. My captivity would happen whether I wanted it to or not—that was the reality of captivity. The captain released my chin. My head flopped back to my chest.

Someone walked past me carrying a dirty piece of foam padding and two blankets. Two Iraqis dragged me to a corner and dumped me onto the pad. The door closed and I was alone. I collapsed on my back on the foam pad and dragged the blankets over me as best I could with numb, swollen hands.

Sounds faded in and out—doors slamming, voices talking, footsteps tapping, my own breathing, hard and labored. I sank into an exhausted sleep. A few hours later I awoke, shaking with spasms of shivering from the night cold. I repositioned the blankets over me and dropped off to sleep again.

The rest of the night, I slept intermittently. New sounds disturbed my sleep—the crunch of footsteps patrolling the gravel roof above me, the tramping of boots in the courtyard, the occasional rumble of vehicles in the distance—interspersed with the intermittent rumbling of Coalition bombs besieging Baghdad.

As the sun rose that morning, I inspected my new dwelling, a nine-foot-by-nine-foot prison cell. I appeared to be in an old prison, probably built in the fifties and poorly maintained since then. The granite block floor looked like it had been spread with two shovelsful of dirt. A thick steel door with a skeleton-type lock closed the cell of crumbling plaster walls.

I stayed prone on my mat. I throbbed all over from cuts, bruises, and welts. My neck felt stiff and painful. Shattered bones collapsed my sinus passages and prevented me from breathing through my nose. I felt desperately hungry and thirsty. I hadn't eaten a decent meal in the five days since I was shot down.

I prayed my captors would leave me alone a few days. I couldn't risk another interrogation—not yet. But risk and uncertainty go with the territory of being a Marine. It's an accepted fact that when our nation elects to go to war, Marines are usually the first to go in and provide the forwardmost element of the attack as "the pointy end of the spear." Back when I joined the Marine Corps, the expression used was "First to fight." That was part of what intrigued me about the Marine Corps when I considered joining nearly twenty years earlier.

That fall of 1972 had been a transition period for both Cindy and me. Enrolled in her first quarter of community college, she also worked part-time in accounting for a department store. I was newly enrolled as a junior at the University of Washington in Seattle. Along with earning my business degree, I worked close to full-time for a car-rental agency downtown.

After a few weeks of classes, I realized I didn't fit into the university with its huge campus and lecture halls filled with hundreds of students. Nor did I fit in at home. Each day seemed to bring another verbal arm-wrestling match with my father that ended in cold silence. My need for change would be as inevitable as the arrival of winter.

One mild day that October, I walked with Cindy in a park near Lake Washington. Chasing her over a crisp carpet of leaves, I tagged her fit, slender body. We tumbled into a pile of fallen leaves, scattering them in a shower of autumn colors. I breathed in the earth-rich scent of fall as I pulled Cindy on top of me under a giant oak. She planted a wet kiss on my lips.

I enjoyed our time together. A good friend, Cindy was affectionate, goal oriented, and had a radiant smile. Framed by golden leaves, her heart-shaped face radiated contentment—with her job, her college studies, and our relationship.

I, however, was far from content. That afternoon Cindy had accompanied me to return my math and accounting books. After attending a few weeks of classes, I had dropped out. "Now you'll have more time for me," Cindy had said cheerfully. Between attending classes and working to pay for them, I had little free time. Listening to the few remaining leaves rustling in the wind, I felt my goals changing as surely as the seasons.

Cindy's happiness faded two weeks later when I made my announcement: "I'm joining the Marine Corps." I had been accepted into the Marine Corps Officer Candidate School Scholarship Program. Since I was a young boy I had been awed by the strong reputation of Marines and intrigued by their recruiting posters.

With the most rigorous selection requirements and initial training of all the services, the Marine Corps was the perfect place to prove myself. My father, recognizing the rigors of Marine Corps life, had advised me to join any service *but* the Marine Corps. That cemented my decision: It was the Marine Corps or nothing else.

With my departure set for February 1973, I felt distant, preoccupied. Mentally and physically, I was preparing to leave. While I worked full-time and stepped up my exercise schedule, Cindy kept up her usual frantic pace. Mornings, she attended college classes, and afternoons, she worked part-time in an accounting department. Evenings and weekends, she taught karate classes and competed in several tournaments. To promote the statewide tournament, she appeared on local television shows. Intensely focused, she could never just relax. "No wonder you're so tired all the time," I told her one night on a date.

Her fatigue worsened. Two weeks later, blood tests showed she had mononucleosis, the highly contagious "kissing disease." I was unwilling to allow anything to jeopardize my plan to join the Marine Corps. Even though my departure was only weeks away, I told Cindy we would not be seeing each other until she was well. From now on, the Marine Corps had to come first.

In the 1970s, our country was divided over the war in Vietnam. Most young people considered it old-fashioned to be patriotic and proud of the American flag. Not many of them were interested in joining the military—especially the Marine Corps. But there was nothing I wanted more. That's why the Navy doctor so devastated me on my second day of Officer Candidate School (OCS) in Quantico, Virginia.

I had spent my first day undergoing an initial examination and screening, including a battery of physical exams, vaccinations, and X rays. As I sat at the doctor's desk, his words horrified me: "The minimum recovery period is six months. I will be unable to approve your training here."

Seeing my reaction, he tapped my medical questionnaire. "You *did* have mononucleosis, didn't you?"

Before my moratorium on seeing Cindy, I had already unknowingly contracted the energy-sapping disease. "Yes, I did," I said glumly.

"And only six weeks ago?"

I nodded again.

As the doctor set my questionnaire on the table, I saw my grand plan going up in flames. He was right, I was still weakened from my illness. But I couldn't abandon my dream. I hungered for the challenges the Corps offered. And I had to fulfill the vow I had made when I was accepted: "I'll prove to my dad I'm better than he ever thinks I can be."

I looked at the Navy doctor, my back straightened. "I didn't travel all the way here to turn around and go home."

"Remember," the doctor said, "you have eleven weeks of rigorous physical training and little sleep ahead. In your condition . . ." He paused.

I saw my chance and launched into a detailed explanation of my recent routine of long work hours and strenuous exercise. "I can do it," I said. "I know I can."

After pondering my argument, the doctor picked up his pen and signed his approval. "Good luck. This isn't going to be easy."

Soon I learned firsthand what he meant by "rigorous training." At four each morning our drill sergeant kicked open the barracks door. We had ten seconds to be out of our "racks" and standing at attention. Our schedule continued at high speed until we climbed back into bed around midnight. Actually, I never slept *in* my bed. It took too long to make my bed to specifications each morning, so I slept on top, covered by my field jacket. During "free" time, 8:30 to 10 P.M., I studied military academics and readied my uniform for the following day. Polishing my brass or "spit shining" my boots for inspection took more than an hour each night.

Along with strict academics, my training included grueling obstacle courses, forced marches, and relentless pressure—all part of what the Marine Corps refers to as "controlled stress." The demands on my mind and body fostered two characteristics essential to a Marine officer: self-discipline and confidence. In a small but significant way, this indoctrination began the hardening I needed to face and survive the dangers and difficulties ahead.

During the first several weeks of training, officer candidates aren't allowed to call or write anyone. Later in OCS, time was a precious commodity, and writing letters skimmed the bottom of my priorities. When our drill sergeant finally allowed us to write home, my infrequent letters, short and cryptic, always went to my parents. Cindy wrote nearly every day.

March 15, 1973

Dear Cliff:

. . . I think about you at night and can never get to sleep! I called the post office and they said airmail is definitely quicker, up to two days faster. So how about sending airmail letters? Not that I wouldn't accept the eight-cent ones!

I requested Cindy mail her letters in white envelopes only—no flowery designs or bright colors to attract the attention of drill instructors. "And please don't send me anything but a letter," I added. "No cookies, no fudge, *nothing* to eat." One unfortunate candidate in my platoon received a huge box of rich fudge brownies from his mother. The drill instructor pointed out that the brownies wouldn't feed all sixty candidates in our platoon. We watched in horror as the candidate was forced to consume the entire box.

By my graduation on May 3, 1973, nearly a third of my classmates had washed out of OCS. Those who survived learned about self-discipline, sacrifice, and putting the group before the individual. They had earned every ounce of their gold bars.

A few days later, I arrived home a newly commissioned second lieutenant, remarkably changed after eleven weeks of officer candidate training—a total immersion course in being a Marine. But my toned muscles and Marine "high and tight" haircut were the least dramatic of the changes. I had also undergone a mental transformation.

Through the rigors and deprivations of OCS, I had developed the warrior mentality: focus on the task at hand, withstand physical pain, conceal fear, lead, endure. My sole focus was being a Marine.

Now, in my second week in captivity in Iraq, I needed every iota of that warrior mentality. Injured and exhausted, I felt gray and lifeless as the dirty foam pad beneath me. Motionless, hunched in the fetal position, I kept even my eyes still, trained on the door of my cell. I always lay facing the door. If a guard was coming for me, I wanted to know it before he got there. And sooner or later, they would come.

Oceanside, California
January 20, 1991

I raced to the television as Cliff's picture disappeared. A wave of disappointment washed over me. Then the newscaster said, "Lieutenant Colonel Clifford Acree." He pronounced "Acree" correctly, with a long *a* and the accent on the first syllable. Most strangers mispronounce our name.

This was all the proof I needed. I sobbed uncontrollably, gulping in air so fast my knees buckled and I could barely breathe. But these were tears of joy and relief. I never dreamed I'd be so thrilled to learn my husband was a prisoner of war!

I felt a high. "Okay," I thought. "We've crossed the big hurdle. We can go on from here." Our group by the television screamed, cried, and hugged, overwhelmed with relief and exhaustion. Behind me, Don was talking on the phone and chuckling.

"Yep, they've got him," he drawled. "And we're peeling Cindy off the ceiling!" Don never failed to break the tension with his quick wit and glib way with words. Between Don's friendly, down-home Texas humor and Kay's sincere, kindhearted manner, they offered the perfect combination of comfort and humor to ease my fears.

Don joined me in front of the television and tried to ease my concern. "This is good. Now the Iraqis will be accountable for him." Having seen Cliff's picture himself, he added, "Of course, he doesn't *look* that great ... he hasn't brushed his teeth, and he sure needs a shave!" Don forewarned me of the downside of Cliff's showing up on national television. "Now that the word is out, those turkey buzzards are going to hound you even more."

He was right. The phone was soon ringing off the hook again. Acrees from all over the country called. "Are we related?" they all asked. Friends called back to change their condolences to congratulations. Adding to the more than a hundred media requests came calls from agents for television shows I never dreamed would be interested in me: "Larry King Live," "Sally Jesse Raphael," "Nightline," network morning shows, and others. "If Mrs. Acree will grant an interview," they said, "we'll send a crew out on the next plane." Connie Chung called and guaranteed a sensitive interview. "I'll fly out the instant she agrees to an interview!" she promised. But now more than ever, I was determined to stay out of the limelight. With worldwide, instantaneous news coverage, I had to assume the Iraqis had access to my words and might use them against Cliff.

The media was looking for any angle. It was amazing the research they did to find one. Someone called from a newsroom in Erie, Pennsylvania, asking, "Is anyone in your family from here? Has anyone ever lived here or had any connection?" I was *born* in Erie. A Seattle newspaper researched the name of the Catholic priest who had performed our wedding ceremony and called him for an interview. Reporters researched phone books and public records and showed up on the doorsteps of Cliff's parents' neighbors in Seattle. They called his high school classmates. They even appeared on the playground of Stephany's school. It seemed everyone who knew us was being dragged along with us into an international media storm.

With my life being researched and dissected, I grew increasingly paranoid. Who else might be researching my whereabouts? In 1989, Sharon Rogers had narrowly escaped death when her family van was burned to a crisp. Allegedly, a bomb had been set by Iranian terrorists in retaliation for her husband's actions aboard the U.S. Navy's Aegis cruiser *Vincennes*. In 1988, while in the Persian Gulf, the cruiser accidentally shot down an Iranian civilian jetliner with 290 people aboard.

It was common knowledge my husband was a POW in Iraq. Seeing our house on the TV screen—with the address plainly displayed—I felt vulnerable and frightened. The Oceanside police department offered to monitor the house and make routine drivebys.

Many military families feared being prime targets for terrorists. According to *Newsweek* magazine, "Pilots who had given their full names and exploits to reporters during the first few days of the air war started using only first names or initials . . . worried that Iraqi agents would get their home addresses and organize terrorist attacks on their families."

A Navy chief warrant officer in San Diego, Michael Clark, pleaded with news organizations not to track down the families and neighbors of POWs and MIAs. The information could be used by Baghdad to coerce information—and wreak emotional punishment on the captured airmen. Later, the Pentagon announced it would not report the names and hometowns of individual soldiers, but lifted the restriction after news organizations vigorously protested.

Amid the frustrations came the bolstering calls from private citizens. Before the war began, I wondered if people cared about the sacrifices military families were making. Now the answer became clear with calls from people like fifteen-year-old Rebecca in Houston. With a trembling voice, she explained how each member of her family had selected a POW to pray for. She had chosen Cliff. Then, overcome with emotion, she gave the phone to her mother, who explained that since their family had little money to spare, Rebecca was using her allowance to pay for the phone call.

Callers identified themselves as "another military wife," "someone with two sons over there," "nobody important." An amazing number of people went to the trouble of locating our telephone number so they could express their love of country and support for our troops and their families. Cliff's friends called to assure me he was a fighter. At a time when my morale could have scraped bottom, these people proved that Cliff and the others were far from forgotten.

Still, that Sunday morning, hearing the constantly ringing phone and doorbell felt like listening to a car alarm blare while being trapped inside. I hadn't set foot outside our house since Thursday morning and was desperate to escape the pitiless scrutiny of the media.

"If you're going to get out of here," Don warned, "you'd better get moving."

Lois and Marty had invited me to their home, set on the cliffs above the Pacific Ocean. But I had to make my escape before 12:30. Kay had told media representatives that copies of my statement would be available on the porch by then. I handed thirty copies of my statement to Kay along with copies of Cliff's picture from our 1990 Christmas card—a picture that was eventually published worldwide.

Kay later read the statement over the phone to at least fifty news agencies. Some of the stations broadcast her reading the statement and intimated that it was me speaking. Friends must have wondered where I picked up that Texas accent.

I slipped on a light jacket, then peeked through the front blinds. A camera crew was setting up on the sidewalk. Trapped again! Don heard my groan. "We'll get you out," he pledged. Since my face was unfamiliar, even to local journalists, Don suggested I masquerade as his wife.

It was hard to believe I had barely known Don and Kay two days ago when they arrived at my door. Returning home only to eat and sleep, they had become a lifeline of support.

Don put his arm around my waist. "Ready to go?" he asked. He guided me toward the front door. Visualizing cameras flashing and microphones shoved into my face, I was terrified to step out on my own front walk. Mom, Karen, and Cami piled into my car in the garage and waited for the signal.

"Okay, here we go," Don said, giving me a little push. He held my arm tightly as if accompanying me down a dark city alley. The mob of reporters didn't have time to approach the couple who left the house and quickly climbed into a red sports car parked in the driveway. I put my arm around Don and he grinned as we sped off.

As Don's red sports car disappeared down the street, our garage door opened. Karen quickly backed my car down the driveway, past the startled reporters. Several of them jogged in vain after the car as it zoomed down the street. Karen heard one grumble, "Oh, shit."

As the car hummed on the highway, I felt elated to be out of that bustle of activity. We had foiled them! It was wonderful to be outside again. The sun shone so bright and intense. I only wished Cliff had the same opportunity. We rendezvoused, switched cars, and drove to our friends' home. CNN had been tantalizing us all afternoon with promises to broadcast the full video-tape of the POWs' interviews. We checked but nothing new had appeared.

Karen and I took Cami for a long, solitary walk on the beach. The fresh, salty breeze on my face felt wonderful, almost as wonderful as being left alone. I was still on a wonderful high from learning that Cliff was alive. It was a gift from God—more than I had ever hoped for.

Two hours later, we trudged back up the beachfront stairs. As we reached the top, I felt desperately tired. I had paused in my battle to stay strong. When I did, the fatigue I had ignored hit me like a heavy sedative. Lois, a versatile good cook, served me a bowl of steaming chicken soup, which I devoured.

We waited until dark to sneak back home. It wouldn't be until later that news vans would camp overnight in front of our house, hoping to be the first to scoop a story.

At seven P.M., we gathered around the television to watch the promised interviews with the POWs. CNN broadcast the audio portion only, a scratchy jumble of interviews. "How—your—aircraft—has—been—shot—down?" asked a heavily accented Iraqi voice. "What do you think about this aggression against Iraq?" One by one, the airmen answered the questions, their voices flat and their cadence unnatural, as if reading a script. I listened intently for Cliff's voice. Finally it came.

"Would you tell us your rank and name?" the Iraqi interrogator asked. "Lieutenant—Colonel—Cliff . . ." a voice answered, then trailed off. My stomach churned. His voice, unmistakably his, sounded so weak, so tired, so strained. I wanted to answer him back and tell him not to worry about me. I wanted to help him, to hold him. But he was far away, and I could do nothing.

The next day, I watched in anguish the full broadcast of what *Time* magazine referred to as "Iraq's Horror Picture Show." Cliff's usual erect posture was hunched over, his head lowered and his neck held stiffly. Staring straight ahead, his eyes had a haunting, glazed look, and his nose looked broken. He spoke slowly and deliberately, as if using every ounce of his concentration. He ended by saying, "I would like to tell my wife and family that I am alive . . . and well." His inflection made it sound like a question as his voice trailed off.

What had they *done* to him? I turned away from the TV. "He's *okay*," I said to the others watching with me. "He's in control. I can see it in his eyes." Though worried about his condition, I thought, "He looked *pissed!*" A Seattle television station even referred to "the glare of Cliff Acree."

Colonel Kuhn, who since Cliff's departure had been assigned to the Pentagon, wrote from Virginia, "There is no doubt in my mind, that the strength he so clearly showed to the world was the result of a stubborn conviction to do what is morally right—stubbornness that is deeply reinforced by his love for you."

Countless letters from strangers described their reactions to Cliff's appearance on CNN. John Brittain, from Myrtle Beach, South Carolina, sent an especially moving one:

> My oldest son, Christopher, asked, "Dad, what's wrong with that man, why won't he talk?" I told him that the Iraqis probably beat the prisoners to get them to say what they wanted and filmed them to show the world the Americans could be conquered. He said, "They didn't beat him, did they, Dad?"
>
> I told him you weren't buying what they were selling, you were too strong for them. It makes me proud, as it probably does anyone who realized what I did—that they didn't break your will, to read *their* statements in front of the world.
>
> My father was a Bataan Death March survivor from WW II, and a Japanese POW for three and a half years. He made it through what they dished out. He was the last man I saw as a tried & true hero until I saw your tape. . . .

I, too, was proud of Cliff's resistance to the Iraqis' propaganda scheme, but dreadfully afraid his rock-hard loyalty would get him killed. "Just this once," I silently scolded him, "can't you give in just a little?" Cliff had always been uncompromising about things important to him, especially loyalty to his friends.

After the night we met during karate partner drills, Cliff and I quickly became friends. Though my karate friends had dubbed me "Sinbad," Cliff simply called me "C."

In the spring of 1971 Mom had remarried. Cliff helped me adjust to the new father figure in my life. A quiet and reserved man, my new stepfather, Vince, was nothing like our outgoing dad had been. The one thing the two men had in common was their love and respect for Mom. I couldn't see past their differences and realize how much Mom had come to life since they met. Vince was a model of faith, kindness, and patience in putting up with Bonnie and me. In time, we came to recognize the inner qualities and strengths beneath a surface so different from our dad's.

One night Cliff approached me after class with a devilish look in his green eyes. I knew what was coming. He faked a punch above my head. I looked up to block. He swept his long leg under mine, pitching me backward. Before I could hit the floor, he scooped me up and threw me over his shoulder like a caveman. Though protesting loudly, I loved his attention.

"You've got a crush on Cliff," my friend Karen insisted. I had to admit it was true, but never considered dating him. I already had a steady boyfriend, a fellow karate student.

One day, my boyfriend shocked me with news that he had enlisted in the Army. When he left for boot camp, I hoped this would end a relationship that had gone on too long. I didn't know that before he left, he'd asked Cliff to watch over me "like a big brother." Cliff told him the idea spelled trouble, but hesitantly agreed.

That spring I graduated from high school and Cliff and I earned our black belts. The more time we spent together, the more dissatisfied I became with the big brother arrangement and Cliff's pecks on my forehead when he dropped me off after class. I sensed he felt the same way but was too princi-pled to betray a friend's trust.

"If only there was some way to get Cliff to follow his instincts," I thought. The opportunity came on a sunny June day that nearly ended in disaster.

We had escaped the city for a picnic beside the Skykomish River in the Cascades. A huge fallen tree stump served as our table. It jutted into the roar-ing Skykomish river that had swollen with water melted from glaciers and snowpack during the previous week's heat wave.

I dipped my fingers into the clear, emerald-green water, then quickly pulled them out. "Brrr!"

Cliff grinned. "Ready for a swim?"

"You first!" I teased. I hugged my knees and breathed in the cold, clear, pine-sweetened air. I felt safe and cared for with Cliff.

"For once, I wish he'd forget about being so honorable," I grumbled to myself, smoothing the red shorts outfit I'd sewed for the occasion. Our mutual crush remained unspoken. No matter what, we'd always be friends.

As if reading my mind, Cliff said, "You know, C, it's easy to be friends with you. I not only like you; I trust you. You're a good combination of a friend, a sister, and the girl next door."

Sister and girl next door? . . . I scowled.

"Want to walk out to those rocks at the center of the river?" I asked. "Bet the water's really moving out there."

Cliff popped the last bite of chocolate chip cookie into his mouth and pulled me to my feet. "Let's go!"

I followed Cliff out to the rocks, trying to match his long-legged steps as the water swirled below us. Farther out, the rocks grew to truck-size boulders. The river's roar nearly drowned conversation.

A short time later the sun receded behind gray clouds. The wind picked up and I felt the first drops of rain chilling my bare arms. Cliff jumped onto the huge granite boulder beside me.

"We'd better head back," he said.

"I'll race you!"

He laughed mischievously and took a giant leap to the next boulder.

"Hey, no fair!" I yelled over the noise of the river. Hurriedly, I jumped to the next boulder. My foot slipped on a slick film of splashing water. I plunged into the river.

"Cliff!" I shrieked as icy water sent cold shocks through me.

"Keep your feet in front of you!" he yelled as the current swept me quickly downstream. "Grab anything you can!"

I aimed for an outcropping of huge rocks. My body slammed into them and the surging water pinned me against a boulder.

"Hang on, I'm coming!" Cliff bounded from boulder to boulder toward me. Panting, he kneeled on the boulder above me and leaned over as far as he dared. "Here you go, grab my hand," he said. With a hard tug and a grunt, he hoisted me onto the rock beside him.

"You okay?"

I nodded, my mouth too numb to get words out. The river seemed to hum as rain splattered the rocks around us.

"Whew," Cliff exhaled. "You had me scared for a minute there." He looked me over as if I were a fish he had landed. His concerned expression changed to a grin.

"W-what's s-so funny?" I shivered. Squeezing water from my long hair, I looked down and saw red rivulets of dye from my outfit running down my arms and legs. Cliff doubled over, laughing.

"Thanks a lot," I sulked, folding my arms in front of me.

"Let's get you back to the car before you freeze."

We trudged back to the car under a downpour of rain, arriving with our clothes soaked to the skin. Cliff noticed my shivering. "Your lips are turning blue," he said as he opened the trunk. "That *is* an attractive shade on you—but we'd better get you warm."

Pulling out a blanket, Cliff wrapped it around my shoulders. He gave my shoulders a few quick rubs, then stopped, gazing down at me with a look I had never seen. Cupping my face in his hands, he bent his head and kissed me lightly on the lips.

As we rode down the mountain pass, the wipers beat out a hurried rhythm against the driving rain. But I felt warm from my lips to the tips of my toes knowing that our friendship had finally melted into love. But if I thought that development would keep Cliff at my side, I was wrong. Twenty years old, he was restless, ready to take on the world and accomplish something. At a turning point, he sought a new direction to his life. It was time for him to pursue the path to adulthood—alone.

Now, nearly twenty years later, I admired the courageous adult Cliff had become. Even in his exhausted and debilitated state, his presence had an impact. He could never have imagined how his image and that of the other POWs would galvanize world opinion. The sight of the injured pilots brought home to millions of people the fact that our country was at war. A war in which *we* were suffering casualties. The *Los Angeles Times* reported, "The display of the POWs moved the public from the euphoria of the early days of the war to the reality phase." *People* magazine cautioned that the POWs' "haunting stares, hinting of fear, anger, confusion, and pain, are a blunt reminder that the Gulf conflict is not some game to be played out with high-tech computer-controlled missiles and supersonic jets. It is war. And war is ugly."

President Bush fumed at the "brutal parading of allied pilots" and vowed to hold Saddam Hussein accountable for his blatant violation of the Geneva Conventions. "If he [Saddam] thought this brutal treatment of pilots is the way to muster world support," the president declared, "he is dead wrong." Protests arose from heads of state around the world. British Prime Minister John Major condemned the display, claiming those responsible would be "made accountable when the war ends."

The public, equally infuriated, flooded newspapers and television stations with outraged telephone calls. As PR, the Iraqis' clumsy attempt backfired. Saddam Hussein was dealing with a different America, one he had shocked into action. The display of downcast Coalition pilots served as a wake-up call to the American public and was a turning point in solidarity for the Coalition.

"We want to stress to you that these men are being held prisoner by Iraqi officials," the news anchor said before the POW broadcast, "and if we can presume, they are not able to speak freely." All the men who spoke intelligibly had criticized the war—all of them but Cliff. Yet careless newspaper accounts the next day alluded that he did.

I fumed reading the front page of *USA Today*. I had never spoken to that paper or any other, yet it printed: "Even the POWs' comments critical of the U.S. role in the Gulf were welcomed. Said Cindy Acree, wife of Marine LtCol Cliff Acree: 'It's all we have to go on. He's alive.'"

The *Washington Post* printed under Cliff's picture: "I think our leaders and our people have wrongly attacked the peaceful people of Iraq"—the statement a captive Navy pilot made. Fuming mad, Cliff's friend of twenty years Marine Major John Borley called the *Post* to demand a retraction. They balked.

"It's a simple editorial mistake to you," John fired back. "But he would rather *die* than say those words." The next day the *Post* printed a retraction.

Given Iraq's reputation for abusing POWs, and Cliff's inflexibility to accept failure, I feared he faced a great deal of suffering in the days ahead.

Even amidst our worry, Don and Kay, and the friends who came to support me, found humor to distract us. The media provided plenty, such as the melodramatic newspaper article that referred to our neighborhood as "Anytown, U.S.A." Television reports speculated on my "escape" to the beach. One claimed the key wives of our squadron had moved me to a "safe house." Another said the Marine Corps had sequestered me in a secret place aboard Camp Pendleton. Even the neighbor who overnight had become a "close friend" provided comic relief. Area papers said he had "volunteered to serve as a spokesperson for the family." From then on we jokingly referred to him as our "family spokesperson."

I had been on a high since learning Cliff was alive. The news that he was being held by the Iraqis had been a shock, a jolt off the Richter scale. My spirits soared—until I faced a new reality: Cliff was alive, but in the hands of the enemy, an enemy who had declared of Coalition troops, "We will drink their blood" and "tear them apart." At least on that day of filming he was still fighting. I prayed he could survive the months—or years—ahead.

MP Prison, Baghdad
January 25, 1991

Footsteps resounded eerily down the concrete corridor toward my cell. After seven days of captivity I recognized threatening sounds from a considerable distance. The sharp click of these footsteps—impatient, deliberate, and purposeful—alerted me like pistol shots. I listened, trying to determine how many Iraqis were headed my way. Three at least. "I need more time," I thought, quaking with fear as the menacing footsteps tramped toward me.

Four pairs of black boots entered my cell. A guard remained at the door.

A neatly groomed Iraqi officer led two Iraqi enlisted soldiers wearing olive-drab uniforms into the room. The guards, who looked to be only in their early twenties, wore red berets with gold eagle crests atop their black hair. Black clubs hung from their hips. Their uniforms, designed after the British, even displayed the abbreviation "MP" on their armbands.

I tried to push myself up to a sitting position. "Don't get up," the officer said, seeing me struggle. "Lie down." He walked across the gritty granite floor. His erect carriage and air of authority told me he was a man of stature.

The officer scrutinized me. Behind him, an enlisted man held a large, circular, chrome container that glistened in the light like a chalice. Against the decaying gray walls, its bright polish dazzled me; I hadn't seen anything that clean in days. The officer motioned toward the container. The soldier removed the gleaming domed lid to reveal a tray crowded with medical instruments, syringes, and vials of medicine. My muscles tightened in fear. Were these instruments of torture?

Mark Twain said, "Courage is resistance of fear, mastering of fear, not absence of fear." Every moment since my capture, I had been consumed with fear, but I had to overcome my natural instinct to let fear dictate my actions. An entire Marine Expeditionary Force plus 18,000 Marines afloat counted on me not to betray them. Loyalty to them concerned me more than dying. Whatever the Iraqis did to me, I had to resist.

"Do you have medical problems?" the man asked in accented English.

"Yes." My swollen face slurred my words. His dark eyes swept from my face to my feet, then rested on my crippled neck. I searched his face. Could I trust him? Our eyes met. His expression lacked the hatred shown by my captors at the interrogation center. My anxiety eased.

"I am here to look at you—to see what is wrong with you," the officer said as he appraised my hunched-over position. "I am a doctor. I'll see if I can help you. But you need to answer my questions."

I tried to nod but my neck was frozen.

"Do you have pain?" he asked.

"From my head to my toes," I thought. "Yes," I told him, watching his face, unwilling to trust any Iraqi. I remembered how my interrogators had focused the beatings on my injuries once I revealed them.

I told him about my head and neck injuries and indicated my arms, swollen and dark purple from the elbows down. My bloated wrists oozed blood and pus. "I can't feel much of anything below my wrists," I told him, pointing to my bulging wrists that looked as though they had been cinched with a red rubber band where handcuffs had bound them for four days.

"How did this happen?" He bent to get a closer look at my neck. I didn't want to anger him. If he was a doctor I needed him. "It happened after I was captured," I said. He looked up at me. "During my interrogation," I added.

He straightened. "No. That is not possible," he said. "Don't you think these injuries happened when you ejected from your aircraft?" In the reassuring tones of a salesman, quickly he added, "They must have happened then."

He examined the knots on my head, then tugged hard on something behind my ear. Youch, that hurt. What was he pulling on? My hair? Whatever it was, his continued jerking motions hurt my neck. I was about to speak when another hard tug broke something away from behind my ear. The doctor held up a filthy wad of gauze and tape caked with dirt and dried blood. I hadn't even realized it was there—for a week.

The doctor spoke in Arabic to his assistant, who handed him a pair of surgical tweezers. The doctor probed the flesh in the same spot as if looking for a deeply imbedded sliver. Each push felt like he nudged a nail embedded in my skull.

The doctor tightened his grip on the tweezers and yanked hard. I felt an instant sense of relief, as if a dentist had relieved a throbbing toothache. The doctor held up his tweezers and revealed a crescent-shaped metal fragment the size of a coin. He looked at me, then at the object, and back at me. With eyebrows raised, he asked, "Surface-to-air missile?"

"Yes," I replied.

His English was quite good. I told him so.

"Oh, no, it's not really," he said modestly.

I suspected he had been schooled in the United States. "Where did you go to medical school?" I asked.

"This is not something you need to know," he said stiffly. He was obviously a loyal "company man." He loaded a long hypodermic needle with clear liquid. A spasm of fear shot through me as I remembered the hallucinogenic injection at the interrogation center, but I was incapable of mustering any resistance.

"This is a muscle relaxer," he explained. "It will help your neck heal." I hurt too much to protest as he plunged the needle into my right hip. The stab of the needle disappeared into my other pain.

"I would give you other medicines," he said as he put away the syringe. "But because of your sanctions, we have a shortage of medicines. And your American bombings have destroyed our water supply and electrical sources." He looked at me accusingly. "Our children are dying."

I said nothing.

The doctor put away his equipment, then departed with his two assistants. The guard walked away, too, shutting the thick steel door behind him. I lay staring at the door cut into a dirty front wall facing the corridor. Turning my gaze to the right of the cell door, I saw a high window cut into the wall. This barred window, seven feet above the prison floor, was placed almost at the corner of the cell. Through that front-wall window I detected light from a much larger window cut into the outside wall of the corridor. I wondered if I could see outside through that window. I wouldn't know until I was strong enough to stand and walk across the cell.

A few minutes later, a guard delivered the afternoon meal, filling my metal bowl and setting it just inside the cell door. I rolled onto all fours and crawled across the rough granite block floor. Reaching for the bowl, I hooked my bloated fingers around its rim. After resting a moment, I backed up, pulling it back to my mat.

Unlike the interrogation center, meals here arrived twice a day. Each morning we received a breakfast of thick grain gruel and Iraqi brown bread; in the afternoon, a meal of rice and cabbage. The day I arrived, I ate more food than I had during the previous week.

Warming my fingers on the outside of the bowl, I thanked God for keeping me alive another day. I felt some of the taut muscles in my neck and back begin to ease. Though my body still felt like it had survived a painful car wreck, I'd been seen by a doctor and had food. Things could be worse—I could still be lying in the outdoor corridor at the interrogation center. I hoped my captors wouldn't send me back there once I healed.

I sucked down the rice, then attacked the cabbage. As I ate, I wondered how my squadron was faring. I hoped our early loss hadn't affected their morale. Had anyone witnessed our shootdown? Did anyone know Guy and I were alive?

"There was remorse," Sergeant Major Warner recalled, when our plane failed to return. "Of all the people, why the CO? There was anger. He took it upon himself to go above and beyond. We missed his presence. The smiles went off the faces. The whole atmosphere changed, but everyone pulled together. On the flight line the war was continuing."

A world away from my squadron Marines, I finished my last piece of cabbage and lay down, wrapping the blankets around my aching body. With my stomach satisfied, I felt drowsy, but I never slept during the day. Even at night, I remained painfully alert, jerking at the slightest noise. I listened to every voice, hoping to hear a word of English to ease my feeling of isolation.

Two Iraqis entered my cell that afternoon. One of them carried a stack of faded yellow cloth. "Take off clothes." He set the mound of canvas clothing, crudely sewn with black thread, beside me, along with white briefs. I didn't move. When the men realized I couldn't sit up they crouched over me and yanked off my black flight boots and wool socks. After lowering the zipper, they tugged off my tan flight suit by rolling me from side to side. They gathered up my dirty, bloodstained clothing. "I need my socks," I pleaded. "My feet are very cold." They looked at me, then walked away with everything.

Dressed in only my cotton Jockey shorts and a thin green T-shirt, I shivered hard, my bare feet already numbing. I had to dress. With stiff, wooden hands I pawed off my blue underwear. Though they provided warmth, I didn't want the filthy, smelly things. Shaking from the cold, I clumsily pulled on the white briefs, then wriggled into the stiff, baggy, yellow trousers. Panting from exertion, I gingerly pulled the long-sleeved yellow canvas shirt over my head and fumbled with the buttons. Black letters stamped like a cattleman's brand on the front and back blazoned my official status: "PW." Having expended every bit of my energy, I laid back down on my mat, my neck and head throbbing.

My eyes traced the boundaries of my cell. *Who wore this yellow uniform in the cell beyond mine?* The walls separating us seemed as thick as the walls of the Grand Canyon. Isolated, alone, and vulnerable, I craved an opportunity for contact with the other trapped souls. My chance would come sooner than I expected.

Oceanside, California
January 23, 1991

After his appearance on Iraqi television, no word came on Cliff's condition. As the days passed, my euphoria over learning that he was alive faded. I began the long wait, filled with rumors of death and endless questions: Had the Iraqis kept him alive after the filming? Was he being starved or tortured?

The International Committee of the Red Cross (ICRC), in charge of inspecting conditions of prisoners of war, had tried repeatedly—and unsuccessfully—to visit the POWs. Iraq's refusals made us even more fearful about the POWs' health and location. On January 21, Radio Baghdad had reported that Iraq intended to locate POWs in and around likely Coalition bombing targets. The day before, Iraqi radio claimed several U.S. pilots held as human shields had been wounded in air strikes.

I could do nothing to help Cliff, but at least I could avoid hurting him by my actions. Was it still unwise to be photographed? Could my words give the Iraqis ammunition against Cliff? My instincts told me yes. I wondered what the military "experts" would say. They had provided plenty of guidelines to military families *before* the war.

I called the Department of Defense, Marine Corps Intelligence, and Marine Corps Public Affairs. "Go with your gut-level reaction," one military officer said.

"My husband's life is at stake here," I told him. "I have no knowledge or experience in this area. Surely there is someone more qualified than I am to make this judgment call!"

In the days following, I spent hours on the phone looking for guidance, taking careful notes of my progress. Marine friends directed me to the

Casualty Branch of the Pentagon, the special assistant for POW/MIA affairs, the Office of the Secretary of Defense, International Security Affairs, POW/MIA Affairs of the Marine Corps, and the non-profit National League of Families.

But I was about to discover an unfortunate truth. On the POW/MIA issue, military experts were hard to come by.

Staffers in the services' top POW/MIA positions are rotated every two years. Only the Air Force had a top casualty officer with more than a year's experience.

As one POW/MIA advocate explained, "They know the form numbers, but they have little or no background in the issues." In his book, *Separated by War: An Oral History of Desert Storm Fighters and Their Families,* Edward Herlik offers an honest summation. "The home front POW/MIA issues were handled poorly. Individual casualty assistance officers and NCOs gave their all, but there was very little consistency or direction from the top. We spent months preparing for the war, but no discernible time preparing for that inevitable consequence."

Devoted Marine wife Jane DeHart, mother of a two-year-old boy and pregnant with her second child, offered to help me track down information. The wife of a Cobra pilot who had flown with Cliff for years, Jane had definite opinions and was not afraid to voice them. Her January 14 letter to the editor of the *Oceanside Blade-Citizen* pointed out the paper's bias in featuring military families who were not coping well:

> You insist on printing stories of families who whine and complain, when in reality, most of us are strong. Our attitudes are positive. We support our Marines, and we support each other. And while long separations are not unusual for military families, we recognize the increased tensions of this deployment, and we are surviving—very well.

Perhaps no protocol existed for POW family members, we conjectured, since our country hadn't had military captives since 1973. Would the guidelines for families of abducted CIA agents somewhat apply? Jane consulted a longtime family friend who was affiliated with the CIA. "If *you* were to disappear," she asked him with her usual candor, "what is the CIA's protocol on what your family should do or not do in your best interest?"

"A body of knowledge *does* exist about how families should respond to hostage situations," the CIA member told her. "But the information is not available to the public or even next of kin—it's classified."

"Well, isn't that the CIA all over!" Jane grumbled.

She turned to another friend, Ben Schemmer, owner and editor of *Armed Forces Journal International* and author of a book about the daring Son Tay Raid, the U.S. Army Special Forces attempt to free American POWs in North Vietnam. "Go cautiously for now," Mr. Schemmer advised me. "It's only been twelve days; wait till some other options have been tried. Read as much as you can on POWs, and trust that people are working to get Cliff out."

I sought out former POWs for advice and solace. Rose Buecher, wife of former Navy commander Lloyd Buecher, skipper of the USS *Pueblo,* captured by North Korea in 1968, offered her support. Sybil Stockdale, wife of Vietnam POW James Stockdale, called to share her wisdom. Assistant Secretary of Labor Tom Collins and his wife, Donnie, encouraged me. A seven-year Vietnam POW, Secretary Collins told me of Cliff, "I've seen a lot of scared faces, and his was not one of them." Former POW Senator John McCain told me he "talked to Bush, Cheney, Powell, and Scowcroft and they will not allow any settlement without POWs."

Navy commander Gary Thornton, a six-year Vietnam POW, was originally declared killed in action (KIA)—until, three years later, his mother received a letter with a Vietnamese postmark. "What will help him survive is his commitment to the uniform he wears and the country he is defending," Gary told me. "It's a conscious decision." Gary was calm, helpful, and funny—even talking about his own captivity. He sounded so healthy and robust that I thought, "If he could survive six years of torture and sound so 'normal,' Cliff can, too."

Mutual friends introduced me to retired Navy captain Bill Stark, another Vietnam-era POW, a tall, blond, ruggedly handsome man who seldom spoke about his captivity at the "Hanoi Hilton." In his home in the San Diego neighborhood of Coronado Island, where several Vietnam POWs had settled, he told me what surprising inner strength a person can summon when needed. "He can take whatever they're doing to him," he reassured me in his quiet but resonant voice.

Talking to prisoners of another war of twenty-five years ago gave me insight into what Cliff might be doing, thinking, and feeling, and was surprisingly comforting. I later learned that coping strategies devised by captives are amazingly similar for all people, of all wars, across all time. The ex-Vietnam POWs advised me to dig in my heels for the long road ahead.

Calls from friends in the Gulf cheered me. Scooter, calling from Abu Dhabi, where the *Tripoli* was in port, told me he had been dressing in his room when he heard Cliff's voice on TV. He ran to the set, but as I had the first time, missed seeing Cliff. Another Marine aboard confirmed his worst fears. Though shocked to learn that Cliff had been shot down and captured by the Iraqis, Scooter was reassured that he must now be accounted for by his captors.

Cliff's flight surgeon, Dr. Joel Lees, called from Saudi Arabia. "Your husband thinks of everything," he told me. As Cliff had requested before the war, Joel had personally inventoried and boxed Cliff's personal effects, taking particular care to secure the pictures and other personal items I had sent

Cliff. Joel told me that Cliff's and Guy's capture had spurred the squadron to end the war quickly. "VMO-2 loves the CO," he told me. "The squadron went through hard times before the CO took over, but he rebuilt not only the aircraft but the morale of the Marines."

Letters from Cliff's Marine friends bolstered my confidence in Cliff's ability to survive. Major Mark Gibson described his reaction to Cliff's TV appearance: "I could read the defiance—no matter how painful—in his expression. He is determined to endure, and *he will!*..." From Buzz Mills, Debbie's husband: "Cliff has more self-discipline than any man I know, it will pay off in this situation..." From Jane DeHart's husband, Peyton: "I regret that I do not know where he is, except for the small portion of him that lives in my heart."

Letters arrived from the Marines of Cliff's squadron; displaying his Marines' love and respect, their letters touched my heart. From Captain John Gamboa, the aerial observer who was Guy Hunter's alternate: "I'm sure you more than all of us know what a great man your husband is. The entire squadron loves him like a father. His kind and gentle nature has earned him the respect and admiration of all who know him. He has given us the leadership and support to form us into a tight knit group of Marines. I don't know of anyone who could have done that as well as your husband...."

From Major Steve Antosh, acting CO in Cliff's absence: "It is under his guidance that we continue to operate today. Cindy, to me that is the finest testimony to his leadership. He may not be here physically, but his leadership is burning brightly, and I can only hope to keep the flame going...we are doing everything we can to make our CO proud and not let him down."

From Sergeant Pat Korsmo, Cliff's intelligence chief: "He really listened, understood, and trusted us." From a corporal attached to VMO-2 in Saudi Arabia: "I will never forget the encouragement he gave me...I felt sick to know they [the Iraqis] had him. I just want to go up there and get them both back myself." From a twenty-two-year-old corporal: "It's hard for me to tell you what kind of man I think your husband is, because most of it is feeling.... P.S. When he comes back don't show him this letter."

The Marine wives boosted my morale as they closed ranks around me. My Marine Corps family, they brought food and took turns answering the phone, logging the calls, and walking Cami. Weeks earlier these same wives had rallied around Rosana when her infant daughter died.

Now, as if to repay the favor, Rosana selflessly supported me—she returned phone calls, read mail and recorded addresses, and cheered me when my optimism faded. She seemed to forget her own pain in helping me. "The only way I can make sense of Loren's death," she said, her expressive brown eyes glistening, "is to believe that she's a guardian angel watching over Cliff." She was at my side nearly every day, and her strength, dedication, and sense of humor sustained me.

My house filled with flowers, cards, flags, and yellow ribbons. The refrigerator was stuffed and the kitchen counters were laden with food brought by family, friends, and neighbors—a flat of strawberries, soup, blueberry muffins, cookies, fruit baskets, lasagna, cheesecake, entire dinners. But my usually hearty appetite had disappeared. Thinking of Cliff, I felt guilty eating at all.

I was certain the pounds were dropping off him now. "What is the Red Cross doing to get in to see the POWs?" I wondered. Not having heard from anyone in that organization, I started at the top and called American Red Cross Headquarters in Washington, D.C., and asked to speak to the newly named chairwoman, Elizabeth Dole. "She hasn't started work yet," I was told. "Call your local Red Cross office."

A few days later I met with the Red Cross representative at Camp Pendleton. "The ICRC is in Baghdad," she said. "They're 'knocking' once, even twice, a day, trying to get in to see the POWs." She also told me that even though Iraq was stonewalling any contact with prisoners, the ICRC recommended we prepare a message for our loved ones using the official Red Cross forms. Messages would be sent to New York, then Geneva, and delivered by the ICRC to Baghdad. It was odd to think that my personal letters would be handled by "the bad guys" in Baghdad.

In this first message, family members were to write only the same non-confrontational, noninformational message: "Anxious for news." We were to write ten or fifteen additional letters on the short forms, so when communication was allowed, the volume of letters would indicate a high level of concern about our prisoners.

That night, I stayed up late, drafting messages in the required seven-line format that would be cryptic to the Iraqis but would trigger happy memories for Cliff. "I'm glad our efforts studying EPs [emergency procedures] paid off," I wrote in the first form.

I had many happy remembrances of our twenty-one years of friendship. Our reunion in 1973 after Cliff's graduation from Officer Candidate School (OCS) was not one of them. After completing OCS, Cliff came home to Seattle on leave. Though I could hardly wait to feel his arms around me again, I respected his decision to spend his first day of leave with his parents. He had reserved his second day for me. Eagerly, I awaited our reunion and solidifying my plans to visit him in Virginia. Nineteen and in love, I had overlooked the separations we would face and assumed our relationship would continue, albeit long-distance.

The next afternoon, relaxing in the comfort of his arms, I brought up my visit. "When do you think I could come visit you in Virginia?" I asked.

Cliff's arms seemed to tense. He took a deep breath. "C, I don't think that's a good idea.... You'll be in Seattle, I'll be in Virginia, and I have no idea where I'll be stationed after that." He pulled away. "This isn't going to work."

He was right. A relationship between two young people living on separate coasts *was* impractical. "It doesn't have to be!" I wanted to insist. The firm look on his face told me there would be no dissuading him.

He shook his head. "I think it's best if we don't see each other anymore. . . . It wouldn't be fair to either of us."

I hated the sound of those words and the tears they brought to my eyes. I turned away, speechless. His love affair with the Marine Corps—and later, flying—had begun.

As we parted, he promised to visit before he reported back to Quantico to attend the Basic School. I nodded, choking back tears of hurt and disappointment. By the time he arrived for his farewell a week later, I had buried my hurt. His usual friendly self, Cliff was not the least bit apologetic about his very logical decision. Then, saying our good-byes, he dealt the final blow to my ego. "C, I hope you find a nice guy someday. When you do, I'd like to meet him."

Cliff was honest, perhaps to a fault, but his comment singed my wounded pride. "Even if he begs me," I vowed, "I'll never take him back!"

We continued to correspond, sending friendly, chatty letters or cassette tapes every few weeks. About six months after our breakup, a letter arrived from Cliff, its tone unlike the others. Sitting in a bar one night with his buddies, he realized he felt empty inside. "I should never have let you go," he wrote.

I stuffed the letter back into its envelope. "You had your chance!" My reply—ignoring his revelation—described my latest hiking and sailing trips with my new boyfriend. Cliff and I continued to correspond, but time gradually grew longer between our letters.

After earning a two-year degree, I transferred to the University of Washington to earn my bachelor's degree in psychology. In 1976 I graduated magna cum laude and continued on to earn my master's in kinesiology, focusing on the area of human performance and learning. As a graduate teaching assistant I taught an undergraduate course and assisted my faculty adviser in hers.

Two nights a week I worked as the drive-through teller in a bank. Because I worked alone, late at night, the branch manager allowed me to bring my two big dogs—Bandit, a protective German shepherd mix and Ajax, a friendly black Lab/Saint Bernard. Drive-through customers loved the novelty of being greeted by giant Ajax standing with his front paws on the teller counter.

On alternate weeknights, I taught a fitness course at the university. On weekends I drove to malls between Bellingham and Olympia, posing as an undercover "shopper" to evaluate employees' sales skills for a clothing chain. Determined to buy my first house, I lived frugally.

Meanwhile, Cliff pursued his Marine Corps career, and once again we were on the same coast. Since completing OCS he had held several positions and participated in the Saigon evacuations as a tactical air control officer.

After living in five states and three countries, in 1976 he returned stateside, to Camp Pendleton, California, to assist in developing a new ground-controlled radar bombing system.

Though I had no shortage of dates, I missed our friendship and often wondered about Cliff. We hadn't corresponded in several months, but I knew he lived near San Diego. When I accepted my aunt and uncle's offer to visit them in Southern California that December, I decided to look Cliff up.

As I dialed his parents' phone number in Seattle, I remembered our early years of friendship. I imagined his delight at hearing I'd be in town for a visit. I even pictured what it might be like to rekindle our relationship. That might be why I never caught the hesitation in his mother's voice when she read me his phone number.

A few weeks later Cliff and I dined at Naval Training Center San Diego's Admiral Kidd Club. Though three years had passed, being together again felt natural. Over a candlelit dinner, we talked easily about our careers, mutual friends, and families. We teased each other, laughed often, and when we danced, I remembered how right it felt to be in his arms. Cliff was flying home to Seattle for the holidays, and I imagined spending our first Christmas together in four years.

Laughing, we returned to our table after a long set of dancing. Cliff scooted my chair in for me, then seated himself across from me. Sipping my wine at the candlelit table, I wondered what might have happened if I'd reacted differently to his letter and change of heart three years earlier.

"C"—Cliff's uneasy voice pulled me out of my musings—"there's something I have to tell you." The laughter had faded from his voice.

I slowly put down my glass. What could make him so uncomfortable on such a fun evening?

Cliff cleared his throat. "I need to tell you . . . I'm engaged . . . the wedding is in three months."

Wedding . . . three months? My wine tasted as bitter as my thoughts. "Why didn't you tell me when I first called? . . . Or even earlier tonight?"

Cliff leaned forward, looking directly into my eyes. "I wanted to see you, to have fun like old times . . . if only for one night."

I looked away, my eyes burning. Fair enough. I had snubbed him; I had no claim. Swallowing my pride, I met his gaze.

"So, what's she like?" I dreaded hearing him brag.

He didn't. He talked about how so many of his Marine Corps peers, other twenty-five-year-old captains, had already gotten married. Feeling like the odd man out, he had decided it was time to settle down, too.

But the more he explained, the more I realized his decision had been based on finding the right time, not the right person. Aside from my desire for him to be available again, I saw the danger signs. The night before I returned to Seattle, I told him so.

Cliff's tone was serious. "Cindy, I've thought hard about not getting married, but I can't break this commitment to our families. I don't want to hurt anybody, especially you." He paused. "But I have to try to make it work. I have to go through with this marriage. It's the right thing for me to do. I'm sorry."

When I stepped off the plane in Seattle, the cold, damp weather suited my dreary mood. Cliff and I had drifted apart years earlier. Seeing him again had made me think we could pick up our relationship where it had left off. But the timing was all wrong. And I knew Cliff. When he made a commitment, there was no going back.

Once again, fate had ordered *"Rotate!"*

Oceanside, California
January 25, 1991

"Every day that passes, I know you're getting weaker," I told Cliff on the cassette tape I hoped he would someday hear. "I'm trying to be brave and live my life as a strong person . . . it's difficult feeling so helpless. I want to break down doors, make loud phone calls, get attention!"

Since my karate days in high school, I had pursued my goals with intensity, never letting go once I had locked onto them. In 1980 I achieved my long-held goal of buying a house. This "fixer-upper" on Stone Avenue had been rented for years and needed major cleaning and refurbishing. A work party of friends hauled away more than a ton of junk and trash from the backyard and uncovered a patio hidden for years under a layer of branches and leaves. My industrious mom worked miracles to clean the house and garage. And Vince patiently taught me how to do yard work.

The Stone Avenue house included a spacious walk-out basement that I converted into a rental unit. I resorted to bribery of my friends with mechanical knowledge who replaced the plumbing, furnace, and electrical service of the aging house. I learned that chocolate chip cookies could be used to bribe anyone—especially men.

The do-it-yourself jobs were mine. The men at the hardware store who knew me by name probably cringed each time I arrived with yet another home improvement project. I learned to tape and mud wallboard, repair toilets, install tile, and hang wallpaper. For months, tripping over paint cans and living with a thick layer of dust was a way of life. My two dogs added to the general confusion, stepping in paint and retrieving and burying small parts I needed. Though I enjoyed the independence of owning my own house, I valued the support of my new neighbor, Mary Pat, the mother of two grown girls.

My social life took a backseat as I devoted countless evenings and weekends to creating the downstairs apartment and modernizing the house. After five months of work, I proudly hosted my first family celebration. The quickly painted walls were still drying as my guests arrived.

One night I crawled into bed after midnight following a long night of painting, knowing I'd be dragging at work the next day. After graduating with my master's degree in 1979, I had traded in my backpack for a briefcase and accepted a position as a training officer with the same bank where I had worked throughout college. I loved my job developing and delivering training programs to employees across the state. Each day brought something new. How true that was, I learned the following day.

I awoke late and dressed quickly. After pulling my hair back and tying it with a ribbon, I dashed out the door to my office in downtown Seattle. Though the long sleeves of my business suit covered the paint splatters, I didn't feel my most polished. "No one will see me," I assured myself. I had no meetings or seminars to present that day.

All morning I hibernated in my office working on a budget plan. Around lunchtime something caused me to pause—a presence, the uncomfortable impression that someone was watching me. I heard a familiar, cocky male voice.

"Are you the person I see for a job application?"

I looked up at the tall, rangy figure standing in the doorway. It was Cliff. We had not spoken since he told me of his decision to marry, four years earlier. "Of all days!" I thought, brushing a strand of hair off my face.

With his thin, drawn face, Cliff didn't look that well himself. Learning of the challenges he had faced over the previous four years, I understood why. Though his marriage had been tenuous from the start, his Marine Corps career had progressed smoothly. Initially qualified as an air traffic controller, he later was accepted into flight school. With his high training grades, he was able to select the aircraft of his choosing, the A-4 Skyhawk jet.

Three weeks before he committed to the Skyhawk, he arrived home from work to an empty house and a note from his wife. She was moving back home with her parents, taking their baby with her. With an impending divorce and soon to be a noncustodial father, Cliff gave up his dream of flying the Skyhawk. Instead he opted for a shorter training course in the AH-1 Cobra attack helicopter.

His first flying assignment to a helicopter squadron at Camp Pendleton brought him closer to his daughter, Stephany. After training there for a year, he deployed to Okinawa, Japan, for six months and was now home in Seattle on leave. He needed a friend, and looked me up, knowing our talks would lift his spirits.

Having spent so much energy trying to forget Cliff, I was reluctant to see him. But in minutes his openness and earnestness melted away my reservations.

That weekend I accepted his invitation to dinner and a Seattle Seahawks football game. Afterward, we rode a ferry across Puget Sound. Once again our heartfelt talks came easily. It seemed that no matter how much time slipped by, we quickly renewed our closeness.

Cliff had intended only to rekindle our friendship. But soon we both admitted that the sparks of attraction still flickered. Cliff provided the unique combination I needed—he was caring and protective, yet respectful of my abilities and supportive of my ambitions. I was happy, but afraid to begin another relationship with Cliff that would end painfully.

"I'll prove my good intentions to you," he promised, as we began our long-distance relationship.

On my first visit to San Diego, I met his two-year-old daughter, Stephany, a shy toddler with blond curls framing her angelic face. I knew instantly those clear green eyes were Cliff's. She spent every other Sunday with Cliff, and when he arrived to pick her up, invariably she wore frilly dresses with lace stockings and shiny shoes. Determined she not grow up overly protected, he planned rough-and-tumble activities for her and taught her to swim.

The visits Cliff and I shared every three months or so were bittersweet. As soon as one of us stepped off the plane, the clock ticked toward the time we'd part. Our budgets didn't allow frequent visits. Twice he drove straight through from Oceanside to Seattle—1,300 miles in twenty hours.

Though I missed Cliff terribly, I was an ambitious twenty-seven-year-old with a fulfilling career. I hadn't even begun to think about marriage and children. I cherished my independence and was reluctant to give it up for any man, even Cliff. I had my dream to realize and Cliff had his—in the Marine Corps, a foreign life that held no appeal to me.

In September 1981, after we'd been together again for one year, Cliff prepared to deploy to Okinawa. Between his six months overseas and training obligations, we would be apart for nearly nine months this time—our relationship sustained only by letters and an occasional phone call across the globe from Okinawa. Our upcoming separation loomed like a jail sentence.

On our last phone call I poured out my distress to Cliff. I had plenty of friends, but most Saturday nights I spent alone. I wanted the freedom to go to dinner or a movie with male friends. "But *only* as friends," I emphasized through my tears. I had no intention of getting involved with another man.

Cliff flew to Japan. I wrote faithfully, but as time passed, his return letters became cool and formal. I puzzled over the change. He signed his Christmas card "Sincerely, Cliff." Eventually his letters stopped. "What happened?" I often wondered, but I was too proud to write and ask.

The summer of our previously planned reunion, my curiosity overruled my pride. Working up my courage, I called Cliff at his home. His cool, businesslike voice chilled me through the telephone line. He had been promoted to major, he told me—and was involved with another woman.

That was Cliff, never sparing the truth. "Of all the nerve!" I thought, rankled at how easily he had replaced me. I wanted to ask why his feelings had changed but didn't want to give him the satisfaction of knowing I cared. "Never again," I vowed. Once again, fate had called out *"Rotate!"*

In the years following, I kept myself busy with work, friends, and hobbies. I had forgotten all about Cliff—or so I convinced myself—though each time I saw a copper-colored Datsun 240Z, I did a double take.

Seattle, Washington
September 1987

I dropped my briefcase at the front door and scurried up the stairs to catch the ringing phone. Reaching for it, I wondered if it was a tenant calling with a problem. I now lived in a newer, bigger house in North Seattle. I had rented the Stone Avenue house as a duplex to two families.

I had refurbished my new house, creating a spacious apartment in the walk-out basement, which I rented to a girlfriend. My latest project had been to expand my master bedroom into a bed-bath suite with a balcony overlooking the wooded backyard. With three rental units to maintain plus my own house, household repairs kept me busy. I had a steady boyfriend but no desire to marry. Between singing in two choral performing groups, exercising, gardening, decorating, and traveling extensively for my job, my life was full. Still, I felt as if something was missing. Something I couldn't identify.

I picked up the phone. "Hello?"

"Cindy?" asked a voice from my past—five years in the past, to be exact. "This is Cliff Acree."

"Hello," I said coolly, remembering my hurt after our last phone call. Cliff told me he was in Seattle for a week of training at a local Navy base. "Would you like to join me for dinner?" he asked.

I hesitated. I had promised myself "Never again." Yet I was curious. Had he married again? Besides, why not take this opportunity to show him life was fine without him? "When would you like to meet?"

Over seafood, we chatted about our jobs, families, and mutual friends. Despite my plan to remain aloof, I began to relax and enjoy his company. Conversation came easily; we had known each other for more than seventeen years. Cliff was surprised to learn that I had been promoted to assistant vice president at the bank and that, at thirty-three years of age, I was still single. He, too, was unattached. His hardworking days left little room for recreation and romance, much less commitment. When we parted that night, we agreed to have dinner again before he returned to California.

Four days later, he arrived at exactly six o'clock to take me to dinner. Driving to Ivar's Salmon House, on Seattle's Portage Bay, we talked nonstop. I teased him about always trying to do everything perfectly and never making mistakes.

Later, seated at a candlelit table overlooking the water, Cliff reached across for my hand. He looked as if he had something important to say. I waited, breathing in the smell of alder-cooked salmon that wafted up to the high-beamed ceiling. Beyond a wall of windows, lights glimmered over the dark expanse of water.

"You know, C," Cliff began, his clear green eyes intent, "I realized several years ago I made a mistake . . . a big one." He went on to explain why he had stopped responding to my letters in Okinawa. "Prior to deploying overseas, squadron life is a busy, nerve-racking time. You need all the stability and support you can get. When your girlfriend says she wants to date other guys . . . Well, it's the kiss of death."

Convinced that my phone call was the verbal equivalent of a "Dear John" letter, he had decided to bow out of my life and save me from having to break off with him.

"It finally dawned on me that my judgment was too hasty and I made a mistake." He looked at me with a wistful expression. "I've regretted it ever since."

"He'd given up so easily!" I thought. But then, so had I—like Cliff, afraid to expose my feelings. I saw his actions in a new light. In that instant the barrier tumbled. I squeezed his hand in a gesture of reconciliation, then, half smiling, shook my head. "What might have happened without that misunderstanding?"

He paused only momentarily. "I think we'd have gotten married." His answer startled me. Maybe it was true.

As we were leaving the restaurant, he drew my arm through his, holding me close as we walked to the car. I had to admit it felt magical being with him again.

Three weeks later, he called to invite me to be his guest at the annual Marine Corps Birthday Ball. The Marine Corps's birthday, November 10, is a special evening of tradition and camaraderie for Marines and their families. All over the world, wherever there are Marines, a Birthday Ball is held.

"Tell me when you can fly down, and I'll make all the arrangements," he said, in typical take-charge fashion.

He had mentioned how much fun it would be to attend the ball together, but I hadn't taken his comment seriously. I was dating another man. I couldn't disappear to California for three days. I sent Cliff a letter explaining why I couldn't come.

When Cliff heard my answer, he couldn't mask his disappointment. "Well, if I can't go with quality," he said, "I won't go with anyone." I doubted that, knowing his friends had been trying to arrange dates for him.

For days after our phone call, a relentless pressure tugged at me like a magnet, a feeling of lost opportunity, of something valuable slipping away. The tension inside me grew. The weekend before the ball, I broke off my relationship with the other man.

After two days I could wait no longer. I picked up the phone to call Cliff. My hand hovered over the receiver. "I'm really going to feel stupid if he's asked someone else."

Cliff answered the phone. I blurted out, "Is your offer still open to attend the Birthday Ball?"

He whooped with joy, then chuckled for nearly a minute before he could speak. "I told you. If I couldn't go with quality, I wouldn't go with anyone at all!"

I hung up the phone wondering if I'd done the right thing. No matter— I was committed now.

Four days later, Cliff offered me his elbow, then placed his long, warm fingers over mine and tucked my hand to his waist. We stepped into the candlelit ballroom on San Diego's Mission Bay. The full skirts of my red evening gown whispered over his black shoes, polished like mirrors. The scent of my perfume mingled with his clean, manly scent.

I felt like a fairy-tale princess, wholly feminine in my flowing satin gown that left my shoulders bare below the shimmering jewels encircling my neck. Cliff looked handsome in his evening dress uniform, modeled after eighteenth-century British naval officers' uniforms. The waist-length coat worn over a white, pleated shirt emphasized his square shoulders. A stripe of gold braiding accentuated his long legs, and the red cummerbund highlighted his trim waist.

At dinner, his curious friends watched my affectionate bantering with normally solo Cliff. "Where have you been hiding *her*?" one of them asked Cliff.

I knew little about military life; everything about the Marine Corps seemed foreign. The life of the military wife has been described as "roses and thorns." Until that night I had imagined only the thorns—moves every two years, career interruptions, and lonely nights. Celebrating the 212th Marine Corps birthday, I experienced the rich sense of tradition and esprit de corps that makes Marines special. Never had I been so warmly welcomed. I discovered a thread of similarity in all the Marines I met. Strong and capable, they were consistently sincere and considerate of others. I enjoyed their subtle military politeness and stopped looking over my shoulder when Marines who worked for Cliff called me "ma'am."

That night I gained insight into the unique culture and history of the Marine Corps, and I began to understand the roses it offered loved ones. My three-day visit turned into a week's stay. Sometime during that week, it hit me: This is the man I've been looking for all these years.

On the last day of my visit, we strolled hand in hand around San Diego's Mission Bay, talking continuously. By the end of the four-mile loop, we'd discussed our values and compared our preferences on all the important issues: finances, children, religion, and of course, dogs. By the time I boarded the flight to Seattle, we knew that whatever the future might bring, we would share it together.

The following spring, Cliff flew to Seattle to celebrate my April birthday. We had dinner at my favorite Seattle restaurant, Henry's Off Broadway, where Cliff had reserved a secluded booth. Next to us, a mirrored wall reflected flecks of candlelight dotting the room's white-linen-covered tables.

A colorful bouquet of my favorite spring flowers caught my eye. I picked up a cream-colored place card resting against the dark vase and read the message inside: "Say yes!"

I did.

After returning to California, Cliff was apprehensive about telling nine-year-old Stephany about her new stepmom. They enjoyed a close relationship, and he worried that Stephany might react with jealousy or resistance. On one of their weekend "dates," Cliff carefully explained how we met, why he wanted to marry me, and when we'd marry. She listened intently, and when he finished, her big green eyes lit with excitement. "Does she have a ring?" Stephany asked. She seemed as thrilled about the upcoming marriage as we were.

After attending countless wedding showers and singing in friends' weddings, finally it was my turn. Late on the Friday night before our wedding, I awoke to a tapping on my bedroom window. I opened the drapes and saw Cliff crouched outside.

"Enjoy your last night as Cindy Blanchard," he whispered. "Tomorrow you'll become Cindy Blanchard Acree." He was proud I had decided to change my name to Acree, especially after he had asked me at least fifty times if I was sure I wanted to.

In a candlelight ceremony in September 1988, I became a Marine Corps wife. Waiting for the processional music to begin, I looked around me at two hundred gathered friends and family. "Am I really getting married?" I asked myself. "And to Cliff, after all these years?"

My beaded wedding gown trailed behind me as I walked down the white-runner-covered aisle toward Cliff, who waited at the altar in his dress-white uniform. I felt strangely calm—not from the glass of wine before the ceremony but from knowing this marriage was meant to be. We had chosen for the theme of our wedding "The Promise," based on a song whose lyrics stress never again saying good-bye.

After exchanging vows and rings, we read letters we had privately composed to each other. Cliff began:

Dear Cindy: You and I have traveled through many years together, and despite life's hardships, we have always remained friends. Our engagement began a renewal in my life that I could not have achieved without your love, understanding, and loyalty. You created in me the ability to love and to be loved, to share with you my strengths and doubts. . . . I trust you with my life and I will protect, love, and care for you forever. . . . I have an intense desire to love you, keep you happy, and keep us together—always. Together, we can do anything. . . .

Cliff finished with tears in his eyes. Guests sniffled as they fumbled for tissues. It was my turn:

Dear Cliff: I've got a crush on you! I've had one ever since I was sixteen years old. It was only fate that after all these years I'm finally marrying the man of my dreams. . . . Cliff, today I commit myself to you as your partner and as your best friend. I promise to always be there for you and I will do everything in my power to keep us together. Though miles may separate us, my love will remain constant and true. . . .

Our lively reception at the Corinthian Yacht Club, on Puget Sound, featured fresh salmon, limitless champagne, and a great dance band that played Cliff's request for our first dance: "Stand By Me." Sometime after midnight, we changed clothes, loaded our car, and headed to Camano Island.

After our seven-day honeymoon in Washington State and British Columbia, Cliff returned to California. Over the next six weeks I resigned from my job, rented out my house, shipped my belongings to California, and said my good-byes.

In October 1988 I stepped off the plane and searched the crowd for Cliff's face, eager to enact the happy ending to the tale of separation we had started eighteen years before. Being greeted by another Marine, not my new husband, should have been my first clue: marriage doesn't necessarily mean togetherness—not if you're a military wife.

Ten thousand miles to the east a storm was brewing.

We never saw the gathering clouds, never heard the voice of fate yell out one more time, *"Rotate!"*

5

No Time for Tears

MP Prison, Baghdad
January 27, 1991

I heard hushed voices coming from an adjoining cell. Was I hearing things? I'd have sworn they were speaking English. I cocked my head toward the faint sounds filtering into my cell through the barred window in the corridor. The quiet conversation floated toward me like soft strains of music.

After several minutes, I deciphered the words "F-16" and "pitch up," spoken with an American accent. Hope rose within me. I wasn't alone.

The voices faded. I reviewed their words, turning them over in my mind like clues to a puzzle. One of the men had to be an F-16 pilot. When was he shot down and what did he know? A second voice, too muffled to understand, seemed to have a British accent. My questions would have to wait until I could walk across the cell. For now just standing was excruciatingly painful. It left me dizzy, weak, and gasping for breath.

The next night, the quiet voices continued their subdued chat. Each night after finishing duty, the guards locked the corridor and moved out of earshot. Though the POWs occasionally risked talking during the day when no guards were around, they held their longest conversations at night.

I strained to catch a word here and a phrase there. The American, a major in the Air Force, was an F-16 pilot named Jeff Tice. I knew no details of the Brit except his name, John. Listening to their whispered conferences, I felt part of them, bonded to these other prisoners who didn't even know I existed. Their voices easily carried to me lying on my pad against the far wall of my cell. We had never been given any rules at the MP prison, but it was understood we weren't to talk. I hoped they wouldn't get caught.

By the end of my first week at the MP prison, I began to revive and the pain lessened to a steady, throbbing ache. Two guards still assisted me when I used the head twice a day, but I wanted to try standing on my own. With aching arms, and the ligaments in my neck crunching and grating, I pushed myself into a crouch, then straightened my stiff limbs to stand. My head pounded. The room swirled around me. With sharp pains throughout my torso, I tried to steady my wobbly legs, but they buckled underneath me. I would have to wait.

Someone stopped outside my cell, jingling keys. A guard opened my door and peered into my cell. "WC? WC?" he asked. Guards shuttled POWs one at a time down the hall past my cell to the bathroom, rushing as if worried one might try to make a break for it. "Move! Move!" they'd scold. The prisoners scurried in response; one even sprinted.

The guard, accompanied by a second, hauled me out of the cell and down the hall to the head. It smelled like a sewer and was just as cold and damp. Two porcelain footpads flanked a hole raised eighteen inches above a pit in the floor. Above the toilet, a small window allowed me a glimpse of the world.

A high, green cinder block fence enclosed the building. A row of shaggy date trees fringed the fence, their bowed fronds swaying in the cold morning breeze against the bright blue sky. It was an incongruously beautiful day to be locked inside a prison.

The next morning I tried standing again. My head pounded and I wavered like a flagpole in the wind, but this time I stabilized my balance. With one arm raised to brace myself, I dragged my clumsy feet in small wobbly steps toward the "talking wall." My outstretched hand finally touched the wall. I leaned against it, dizzy from the exertion, but standing. I waited. Silence.

How many other prisoners, from wars over the last forty years, had tried to communicate through this wall? Their agonizingly beautiful drawings decorated the wall. A dove with chains encircling its legs on one side. A small country farmhouse with fences outlining fields of crops and a corral filled with goats. I imagined an Iranian prisoner sketching the pastoral scene as he longed for home.

Minutes passed with not a sound. I shuffled back to the corner and collapsed on my mat, worn out. After eating my afternoon meal, I gathered my strength and made my way to the wall again. This time I heard talking. I wanted to join their conversation but didn't have the nerve to speak out, not yet.

A small, barred window partially covered by dirty, scratched plastic was cut into the back wall eight feet above the floor. Foam rubber sheathed much of it. I noticed that the upper half of the window contained a hinged push-out assembly, but I had no plans of escape. Even if I had the strength, rumors that an F-18 pilot had been tortured and stabbed to death by Iraqi citizens kept me inside. I wondered if this building looked like a prison from the air. Did the Coalition intelligence network know we were inside?

The next morning, I gathered my courage and shuffled to the door. Stretching to my full height, I could almost see the floor. The corridor looked empty. For a long time I listened. Straining to hear any sound, I heard only the throbbing of my pulse in my temples and neck.

I made my way to the "talking wall." Placing my lips on its surface, I moved my mouth and lips to speak. No words came. The fear in my gut sent a stern message to my vocal cords: "Don't talk! If you get caught, you'll regret it." I glanced toward the door one last time.

"Tice, can you hear me?" I croaked.

"What?" he said. "Who's there?"

"Acree," I said hoarsely. "My name is Acree."

"What?"

"My name is Acree," I said a little louder. "Cliff Acree. I'm a lieutenant colonel in the Marine Corps."

"Oh, *sir*," he said. "I thought I was the senior guy here."

"I'm an OV-10 pilot...hit by a SAM in south Kuwait. My AO, Guy Hunter, ejected with me," I rasped. "Have you heard Hunter's name?"

"No. I've got a British flight lieutenant on my right by the name of John Peters. Can you hear him?"

"Yes. But I can't make out much of what he says." I leaned against the wall, out of breath from the strain of speaking, keeping my eyes toward the door. We exchanged the names of everyone we knew who had been captured. I committed each name to memory.

With that exchange, my spirits rose. As the days at the MP prison passed, my body continued to heal. Life was different now, and I settled into a routine. You can get used to almost anything, I realized, even the loss of freedom.

One morning, I heard cell doors opening and closing, one at a time, a few minutes apart. POWs were being taken somewhere for about ten minutes, then brought back to their cells. I shuffled to the front window and looked out the corridor window to the courtyard. An incongruous picture: two Iraqi guards, armed with Browning high-power nine-millimeter pistols kicking a deflated soccer ball with their enemy in a POW uniform. The makeshift game of soccer briefly transcended their warring worlds.

A few minutes later a guard appeared at my door. "We're taking you outside," he said. I didn't move; walking still hurt. He opened the door and came in. "It will be good for you to go outside."

I gathered the blanket around my hunched shoulders and followed him down the corridor, hobbling like an arthritic old man. "You have ten minutes," he said as we entered the cool air of the courtyard. I sat down on a bench near a rusty, dilapidated pull-up bar. A young guard who appeared to be in his twenties leaped up to grasp a horizontal bar near my bench. After performing several pull-ups he jumped down. "You, you!" He pointed to me.

"No, I can't." I rested my chin on my hands and propped my elbows on my knees. Two uniformed Iraqis approached, pistols swinging from their belts. One of them held in his hand a clipboard, papers, and a pen. My muscles stiffened. If this was my next interrogation, why out here in the courtyard? I tightened the blanket draped over my neck and shoulders and looked straight ahead.

One soldier stood behind me while the one with the clipboard squatted beside me. "We are delivering papers at the request of the Red Cross." He pushed the clipboard in front of me. I glanced skeptically at the form. It contained several printed lines below the words "Name, Address, City."

His story raised a hundred red flags. This was bullshit. A military person is never authorized to represent the Red Cross, only a civilian with proper identification.

"We need you to give us the name and address of your mother, father, and wife." He held out the pen.

"Don't you want your family to know you're alive? Don't you know your wife, mother, and father are worried about you? Wouldn't they feel better if they knew you were alive?" He nudged me with the clipboard.

"Yes." I couldn't argue with him there. I often wondered if the Iraqis had released the names of those captured or if we had seemed to vanish, as completely as a plane disappearing over the Bermuda triangle.

"Do you have children?" he asked. "Wouldn't you want your children to know you are alive?"

"Yes, I would. But I cannot sign that paper."

"Where is your family now?"

"The United States." My voice shook.

"What city?"

I didn't answer.

"We need you to sign these papers so we can let your parents know you are here."

Just regaining my strength, I hated to antagonize them again.

"No," I said.

"If you want your family to be informed, you must sign this form. You are required to tell us your address," he insisted.

Of course I wanted my family to know I was alive. But the Iraqis wanted my address so they could mail something to the house or circulate it among Iraqi agents in the United States who could harm or intimidate my family.

I shook my head. "No. I can't." I emphasized the word "can't." In captivity, "can't" implies that you are not allowed to. "Won't" implies that you as an individual will not cooperate. In my two weeks of captivity, I had learned it was dangerous to openly resist and went from saying "No" to "Won't" to "Can't." It's all resistance. It's just a matter of degree.

He persisted, but I wouldn't budge. After our stalemate continued for several minutes, he stood up, clamping the board to his side. "I can't help you anymore." Shaking his head, he left with the other Iraqi.

As I watched them walk briskly away, I considered his proposition. My family probably didn't know I was alive. Had they somehow seen the videotape made at the interrogation center? I had no choice but to refuse. Walking back to my cell, I felt certain they would come back later to beat the information out of me. And I was just coming back to life.

Throughout the night, I twitched at every sound, expecting guards to arrive to beat me into submission. But no one came to rough me up. I couldn't believe they had given up that easily.

I counted my blessings to be at the MP prison. Here there were no beatings, no interrogations, and living conditions were tolerable. We didn't have the Baath Party or the Iraqi secret police breathing down our necks. Here, we shared with our captors an understanding of the military brotherhood— an understanding Saddam Hussein couldn't relate to. He never had any military training, only wore the uniform.

At the MP prison, despite our vast political differences, our guards generally treated us with the decorum of one military person relating to another. The Iraqi regulars taking care of us weren't kind, but they also weren't vindictive. However, late that night, I learned that it still didn't pay to become too relaxed.

I awoke as the voices of the two pilots parted the stillness. Soon, a door opened and quick footsteps sounded down the corridor toward us. Startled, I realized a guard had sneaked back into the cell block. I held my breath, eyes aimed at the door. The guard's shadow passed my cell.

"Tice!" he shouted into the next cell. "Why you speak? You know you should no speak!" He moved down to the next cell, shouting like someone scolding a barking dog. "Peters!" he yelled, his voice rising. "You no speak! *No* speak!" His footsteps faded down the corridor. Knowing the talking had ended for the night, I closed my eyes and fell back into a restless sleep.

An hour later I awoke with a startle as the door of the corridor banged open. Footsteps slapped the corridor and keys jangled. Bobbing lanterns illuminated the corridor. The door of Tice's cell crashed open with a deafening reverberation. Peters's door flew open next. Feet scuffled, and bodies grunted and scraped the floor as they were forcibly dragged away. Shaking with fear, I listened to their cries recede down the corridor. I knew damn well what would happen to them. Hours later their cell doors scraped shut and the heavy bolts slid home with a final awful echo. Long after the last of the sounds left the air, a frightening silence prevailed, breaking the tenuous link between us.

Oceanside, California
January 28, 1991

Gingerly, I slipped a knife into the upper right corner of the long white envelope, directly above the words "free mail" that had brought a smile of relief to my face in the months before.

Letters Cliff had written to me before his capture had continued to arrive from Saudi Arabia. I scrutinized every word, searching for clues to his physical and mental state before his shootdown. Did he seem overly tired? Had he been eating well? Was he assured of my love for him? It was eerie reading his thoughts while knowing his future, which he did not.

This letter, written on January 17, the first day of Desert Storm, was the last I would receive:

> Hi, Honey. Love you a lot. Flew into Kuwait's southern border today and controlled air strikes against targets that were actively engaging friendly targets . . . A sobering yet exciting morning . . .
>
> I took two of your oatmeal cookies airborne with me today. When our mission was complete and we were safely south into friendly airspace, I gave one to Guy and I had the other to celebrate. I spent the rest of the flight home thinking of how wonderful you are and how much I love you—Forever, Babe

As the days passed with no word about Cliff's condition, the press focused on new people and new stories. Early one morning I decided to venture out on a walk. My world had been my house, safe and secure but stifling. I peeked through the blinds. The street was empty of news vehicles, with only a white van parked up the street. Hurray! Three days with no media hanging around.

While the reporters camped out on our street, I had been unable to walk out the front door or drive. Mary, my neighbor three doors down, had helped me elude the press and escape. At a prearranged time, I scaled the three backyard fences between my house and Mary's. She let me into her garage, where I climbed into the back of her car and hid on the floor. She threw a blanket over me, then drove me down our street past all the reporters and news vehicles. How ironic it would be to learn that, in captivity, Cliff traveled the same way.

But after living under a microscope for so many days, I could finally come and go as I pleased. I snapped the leash onto Cami's collar. "I'm going for a walk, Mom!" I called. When I opened the front door, I gasped. Four feet from the front door, two strangers were setting up a camera and tripod.

I whirled around and slammed the door behind me. I screamed in anger. "*When* will they leave me alone?" Then the doorbell rang. Over and over again it shrilled as Cami barked and whined. Mom came running down the stairs to see what all the commotion was about. "Someone's got a camera up to the window!" she said, pointing to the door.

I hurried into the downstairs bedroom, all the feelings of invasion coming back. I sank to the floor with my arms folded over my head and sobbed. I felt vulnerable, exposed. It was too much—the shock of Cliff's capture, the worrying, the loss of my freedom. When would it all end?

For a few minutes I was unable to move. Then suddenly I felt a surge of anger. I was not going to spend Cliff's captivity as a hopeless, helpless victim.

I brushed my hands over my eyes, then called the watch captain of the Oceanside police. I dashed up the stairs and peered between the blinds. The camera crew was breaking down their equipment. They loaded it in the white van. As they started to drive away, a police car arrived. The crew tried to pull around the cruiser, but the officer parked it sideways across the street, blocking them in.

Weeks later, the pair—a Japanese film crew—would send a handwritten letter of apology. They were doing a story about Cliff being gone, they explained, and how his dog missed him.

The crew's reasons might have been innocent, but their visit convinced me I had a lot of hills to climb, and I was tired of sitting helplessly at the bottom and waiting. If people have high blood pressure, should they only pray for good health? No, they should pray for guidance while dieting, exercising, and helping themselves. I could no longer depend on prayer alone. I had no option but to try to help Cliff myself.

"But how?" I kept asking myself. It was up to me to pursue the answer. I read voraciously about POWs, including the book *In Love and War*, which chronicles the experiences of Admiral Stockdale and his wife, Sybil. He was a POW in Vietnam for seven and a half years. After reading Mrs. Stockdale's chapters, I truly appreciated my situation.

Vietnam-era POW/MIA wives had little government support and were intimidated into not mentioning their husbands' captures to anyone outside their immediate families. I skipped the admiral's chapters, but one night, flipping past, my eye caught sight of a gruesome drawing. A POW sat on the floor with legs outstretched in front of him. His head was being forced down between his knees by his Vietnamese captor. What searing pain he must have felt. Could Cliff's captors be that cruel?

I searched out and obtained a copy of the articles of the Geneva Convention, the international standards established for treatment of POWs. Iraq signed this agreement in 1956, which states that prisoners must be provided with adequate housing, sanitation, and food, and within a week be made available to international authorities for inspection. But getting Iraq to follow the Geneva accords was like trying to get every driver in the United States to obey the speed limit. Baghdad even reported that a downed allied pilot had been stoned to death by Iraqi citizens.

Later that week, letters arrived from military friends that suggested a possible approach to helping Cliff.

From Ken, a Navy friend: "... I've enclosed a copy of a letter that I have sent on his behalf to the Iraqi Ambassador. I intend to continue writing and to encourage others to write until we secure his release. Lacking a release, we will insist that he be treated humanely and with dignity. I'm a long way off in Korea, but will do what I can. I recommend you write to the Iraqi Ambassador also. If we show these people we care, I believe we can make a difference... God bless and keep the faith!"

Paul, a Marine Corps friend, made a similar suggestion: "Dear Cindy... I am convinced Cliff will be all right. He is strong physically, mentally, and spiritually.... Your strong and loving message to Cliff is a testament to your own strong character.... Persevere and never give up hope or feel you are alone or abandoned, for people far away are thinking and praying for you.... This is what I would like Deb to do if I were in the same situation...."

Paul, too, recommended sending telegrams to the Iraqi ambassador requesting that our POWs be treated according to the articles of the Geneva Convention. Iraq obviously cared about Western public opinion or it wouldn't have aired the POW propaganda statements.

That same week, a letter arrived from a Catholic nun. "We have quite a few Iraqis in San Diego.... Many left Iraq because Catholics face discrimination and their situation is tenuous in a largely Moslem nation," she began. Her fascinating letter described how we might communicate with Coalition POWs via the Catholic Church in Baghdad, but cautioned: "We would not want to jeopardize their families or the Church in this process and should know the political risks.... Be brave and hope against hope that Cliff and the others will be treated well...."

Should I follow our friends' advice, or could Cliff suffer as a result? Later that week, two Marine counterintelligence officers from Washington, D.C., answered my question.

I greeted the Marines armed with a prepared list of questions and dressed in a business suit. I was determined they not dismiss me as a distraught POW wife. I wanted them to trust me with as much information as possible, not pull any punches.

"Ma'am, we'd like to ask you a few questions first," one of them began. "When you saw Cliff's videotaped interview with the Iraqis, was there any indication he was trying to signal information or send you a message? Did you notice any subtle signs or communications?" I recalled hearing about Vietnam POW Jeremiah Denton blinking Morse code with his eyes.

"All I noticed was that he looked beaten. I think he had a hurt neck and possibly a broken nose."

They told me I would possibly receive mail from Cliff. "If you do, we'd like you to follow a special procedure," one of them said. "Handle it only with gloves, open it with a french cut [opening the end of the envelope, not the flap], then place it under glass to read it." I nodded, doubting the Iraqis would ever allow Cliff to correspond.

"When you're done reading the letter, put it in a plastic bag," he continued. "And if you don't mind, we'd like to come by and pick it up," he added. "We can learn a lot by analyzing the type of paper and pen used, the fingerprints, and any particles on the paper. Even the saliva used to lick the envelope could give us clues to your husband's location."

Days ago, things as bizarre as sending secret signals and analyzing saliva had seemed like scenes from a Tom Clancy novel. Yet seeing Cliff interrogated on national television was about as far out as any spy novel I'd read. I wondered if our intelligence sources knew where the POWs might be.

Our human intelligence sources (undercover spies) were limited since we had been friends with Iraq in the recent past, they told me. "We do have ways to keep track of him to a certain extent," an officer added. I hoped so. On January 29, Iraq announced that a POW of unknown nationality had been killed when an allied air strike bombed the site where he was being held as a human shield.

The Marine intelligence officers confirmed my decision to remain out of the limelight. "Because of modern technology, the enemy can have access to what you say the moment you say it." The media, a free source of information to the enemy, was better than intelligence operatives or equipment. The Defense Department advised against providing "any personal details regarding your missing relative in response to inquiries from unknown callers, media or otherwise. This will preclude giving the Iraqi government information for exploitation. . . ." Provided with a picture of me, the Iraqis could alter my face to look disfigured and tell Cliff they'd do worse if he didn't cooperate. Given a tape of my voice, they could use the voice pattern to make their own tape of me saying different words.

Dreading their answer, I asked about Cliff's Iraqi interrogators. Even allied forces relied upon information gained from enemy prisoners of war (EPWs). According to *Time* magazine, captured Iraqis were as good as any spy satellite when it came to providing information about enemy plans, equipment, and troop morale. Prisoners were rated A through C for the value of their knowledge, and 1 through 3 for their willingness to talk.

The officers told me that Cliff's captors would "build a book" on him, comparing his answers to those of other captives. They would be especially hard on him during his first days of captivity. My stomach churned. I felt bad when Cliff stubbed his toe; knowing he was enduring all this was heartbreaking.

He had never attended SERE school, a seven-to-ten-day simulated POW experience that teaches U.S. pilots the basics of survival, evasion, resistance, and escape. Participants experience sleep deprivation, interrogation, and brainwashing in order to learn to evade capture and survive in captivity. Cliff had read books on the topic, but I knew he was surviving by the force of sheer willpower and courage—traits no book had taught him.

For days I had worried that Cliff would hold out so long they'd eventually kill him. I swallowed hard. "I'm speaking as a wife now," I told the officers, hoping they'd understand. "I'm concerned he'll resist so hard that they'll . . ." I paused. "Go too far. If they . . . pressure him, will he know when to draw the line?"

"He'll know."

I relaxed a little. That would help, but it wasn't enough.

I asked the officers about the Catholic nun's suggestions. One of them read her letter then handed it back to me with comments written in the margins next to her ideas. "Be careful," "Too risky," "NO," they read. "These plans might endanger Cliff," the officer explained.

"I'm anxious to do something . . . *anything,*" I told the Marine officers. "Do you have any suggestions?"

One of them handed me an unclassified message: "General Guidelines for Next of Kin of Desert Storm Missing or Captured Service Members."

After the two Marines left, I eagerly read the three-page document, which listed recommended actions for family members, including:

- Avoid the potential for being victimized by what may appear to be well-intentioned individuals, those seeking permission to use your missing relative's name on a POW/MIA bracelet or to represent your interests. . . .

- Do not provide any personal details regarding your missing relative or family members in response to inquiries from unknown callers, media or otherwise. This will preclude giving the Iraqi government information for exploitation. . . .

- Do not wait by the telephone for minute-by-minute updates on your loved one's status. The casualty officer will notify you immediately upon receipt of any information which becomes available to the U.S. government. The U.S. government has a full and open disclosure policy.

- Do not avoid all contact with the outside world. Exposed and vulnerable as you may feel, you probably will not be subject to exploitation or curiosity unless you have made yourself a target.

- Using your discretion, request such support as you feel appropriate from your church and other responsible organizations. Suggestions include prayer . . . and a public letter-writing campaign to: His Excellency Abdul Amir Al-Anbari, Iraqi Ambassador to the UN . . . asking for humane treatment for American and Coalition captives in accordance with the Geneva Conventions. . . .

Reading the final suggestion, my heart quickened. Finally, something concrete I could act upon!

The next morning I headed to the gym, glad to be able to drive myself, and forgo the circuitous route jumping backyard fences.

After two weeks of worry and sleepless nights, just stepping up on the treadmill seemed like an effort, but I needed an outlet for my frustrations. Earlier that day, Iraq had condemned the POWs as "war criminals" who would be treated as such. As I began walking on the treadmill, I projected Cliff's image on the blank wall in front of me. Beyond his swollen, stricken face, I saw the inner strength I had always admired, his dark-circled eyes angry at being captured.

I walked faster. "Go get 'em, honey," I silently rooted. "You can do it. Give 'em hell!" Feeling stronger, I broke into a jog. He could feel my strength. We'd win this battle together. I ran like our lives depended on it, sprinting four miles across the Saudi desert to save him myself.

Wiping my wet brow, I stepped off the treadmill and knew what I had to do. I would talk to friends, relatives, neighbors—everyone I knew—and ask them to write letters to the Iraqi ambassador. I would enlist the help of organizations, schools, and churches. If I publicized our efforts, I had faith people would help when called upon.

I vividly imagined the results of a successful letter-writing campaign. Picturing a "CNN Live" broadcast from New York City, I saw a huge dump truck backed up to the curb in front of the Iraqi ambassador's office. The truck's tailgate lifted. "What an incredible outpouring of concern!" a newscaster commented as several tons of envelopes cascaded onto the sidewalk. I had my goal: one million letters of protest delivered to the Iraqi ambassador.

MP Prison, Baghdad
January 30, 1991

Three days passed without incident. I was allowed to take a cold shower and was given black Romanian-made socks and white high-top tennis shoes. Adequate food arrived twice a day and sometimes included hot, sweet tea.

One day I received the unexpected treat of a succulent tangerine. I devoured the fruit, then dropped the peelings into my water to extract the vitamin C. As my strength flowed back, so did my fighting spirit. I felt optimistic that I could manage this routine for an extended time.

The next night another tangerine arrived with my meal. I felt lucky to have received fresh fruit two days in a row. Maybe the truly hard times were behind me and I would only have to bide my time here until the war ended.

After finishing my rice, I picked up the tangerine to peel it. A chilling premonition warned me not to eat it. I sensed a change coming to my life as a POW—a change for the worse. I saved the tangerine.

Late that night, I heard doors opening in the distance, rustling, and guards talking as they crossed the courtyard. An alarm went off inside me. Several more guards entered the corridor. Their lanterns swayed rhythmically down the hall creating an eerie bobbing glow on the dimly lit walls. Hearing the clash of metal upon metal, I groped in the dark for the tangerine and stuffed it into the breast pocket of my shirt. I was leaving the relative safety of the MP prison.

Around midnight on January 31, my journey began. A guard entered my cell and applied a blindfold and handcuffs. The cold metal raked the tender scar tissue on my wrists. He pushed me ahead of him into the corridor. I walked hesitantly, like a soldier entering a minefield. I took a couple of steps and the guard shoved me forward. I stumbled, and each time I regained my balance, he shoved me ahead, hurrying, as if we had a train to catch.

With the guard prodding from behind, we walked out into the cold night air, crossing the cobblestone courtyard and onto a smooth surface. A few steps later, I bumped into a large metal object, gashing my shin. Groaning, I tripped and fell onto the pavement.

Still on my knees, I groped ahead of me with both hands and felt stairs, then a handrail. As I reached the top of the stairs, someone kicked me like a slow-moving mule, pitching me forward. A hand on my shoulder forced me into a seat. I leaned back against my manacled hands, sideways on the seat, facing the center aisle. I listened to others being herded onto the bus—by the shuffling of feet, I guessed there were ten to twelve of them.

Where were they taking us? Back to the interrogation center? I felt a stab of fear. The unknown in captivity usually translates into something worse. At the MP prison, I had gained needed strength and felt almost secure. I had learned the routines and knew what to expect from the guards. That was all about to change.

Footsteps shuffled down the aisle as someone threw blankets over our heads. The driver revved the engine and the bus lurched forward. We drove for nearly an hour, crossing railroad tracks, making frequent turns. The bus eventually stopped. Bright lights flooded through the windows and even my blindfold. The bus idled and a heavy metal gate creaked open. Two men boarded the bus and we moved on, slowly now. The drone of the motor echoed as we entered a large structure. The bus vibrated down a steep incline. As the grade pitched me forward, I had a terrible sinking feeling in the pit of my stomach.

The bus shuddered to a stop and the driver turned off the engine. I absorbed every sound around me with acute perception. Someone outside the bus barked commands into a vast emptiness; his voice echoed on walls far away. At each order, people scurried to obey, their rapid footfalls beating a hard surface. I heard no conversation. "This is not the interrogation center," I realized. I sensed heavy security. This was a fortified, well-protected structure, a place of awesome power. My heart beat out a warning: "To walk here is to know terror."

A hand pulled me out of the seat by the scruff of my neck. I was man-handled off the bus, walked a short distance, and turned over to someone who grunted an acknowledgment. I tried to orient myself to prepare for whatever might happen next. With my sight restricted, my other senses were so acute even the tiniest sound was magnified.

This place was tense, organized—and cold and quiet as a mausoleum. Footsteps resonated eerily on the concrete a long distance away. Fear and oppression hung in the air like a dense winter fog. No one made idle conversation. Unlike every other Iraqi structure, this one did not smell like tobacco. Obviously no one smoked here.

Anyone who moved was clearly inspired to immediately make shit happen. The Iraqis' urgent, almost panicky responses to commands told me someone of exceptional authority gave orders here.

"This is where the bad boys are," I thought, quaking with fear. These were serious, highly trained professionals. I knew with brutal certainty things were about to get worse.

Someone reached into my bulging breast pocket. Why would an Iraqi try to pick my pocket? I had no belongings—except for my tangerine. Instead of extricating the tangerine, the pickpocket tapped my chest with quick, repeated thrusts. My pulse pounded harder, faster—almost, it seemed, in rhythm with the painful stabbing tap, tap, taps of the pickpocket. His repeated attempts to wrench the fruit free felt like the violent chest thrusts of someone performing emergency CPR. This was no Iraqi thief but the rapid, chaotic clubbing of my own heart—hammering hard, racing out of control, feeling like it was about to burst.

A guard delivered me to someone who slammed me into a cement wall. I hit my face hard, unable to brace myself with my hands clenched behind my back. As my heart continued to rattle, hands grabbed me roughly on either side and pushed me forward. I walked the gauntlet, keeping my head down, waiting for the blows. I had always been escorted by one person shoving me from behind. Now I walked up cement stairs and through a creaking metal doorway with two Iraqis gripping me under the arms. Though blindfolded, I could see my toes and perhaps a foot ahead if I looked straight down. The doorway closed with a whooshing sound and the floor rose, rumbling beneath me. I had moved up from an old broken-down prison to one with an elevator.

The doors split noisily and we left the elevator, passing down a hallway and into a room where I was pushed onto a wet floor. The air smelled damp and musty, and was miserably cold. I felt a puddle of liquid seeping into my pants—a gift of urine from my new captors. The door closed and the key turned in the lock. I waited in suspense, blindfolded and handcuffed, my heart beating erratically. Fifteen minutes later someone returned. By then I was shivering uncontrollably from cold and fear.

Someone yanked me to my feet and tore off my blindfold. He gripped my arm tightly, mumbling angrily as he tried repeatedly to insert the key into the lock of the handcuffs, which shook along with my arms. I tried to hold still but was shaking too violently. After several tries, he turned the key, removed the cuffs, and left, locking the door.

A thin strip of dim light seeped in under the doorway. Why had they left me blindfolded for so long when it was this dark? And they had locked the cell even when I remained handcuffed. It made no sense.

The cell felt as cold as a meat locker, and my face started to numb. I rubbed my arms and stamped my feet to warm them but they felt like blocks of ice. I banged on the door. When a guard opened the small window in the door, I said, "Cold, cold!" He looked in the window with a grim expression that relayed, "We know you're there. You're a war criminal." He closed the hatch. A short time later, the hatch opened and someone stuffed a blanket through the rectangular opening.

Shaking violently, I wrapped myself in the blanket, then pressed my body against the door to absorb what little heat filtered through the crack under the door. The last thing I remembered before passing out was the sound of my teeth chattering. That night set the tone for the next twenty-three days I would spend in the prison the POWs called the "Baghdad Biltmore."

Baghdad Biltmore Prison
February 1, 1991

"Hunger hurts worse than a beating," I thought, feeling stomach acid rise to my throat. I had devoured my first meal at the Biltmore, a full bowl of rice served the midday following my late-night arrival, a meager portion by normal standards. I ate it gratefully, hoping it would stave off my hunger pains until the evening meal arrived.

But nighttime arrived with no more food and no water, although I had received a second blanket. "They're not used to us being here," I told myself as I slowly ate the tangerine I had saved in my pocket. That night, I tried to ignore the hunger pains and fall asleep. "They just forgot and they'll feed us in the morning," I reasoned.

Late that night bombs exploded in the distance, reassuring me that Coalition aircraft were still destroying targets in Baghdad—with brutal effectiveness, I hoped. As far as I was concerned, the more bombs the better.

The next morning—my second at the Biltmore—passed and they "forgot" to feed us again. That night, a full day after the rice meal, I was given a bowl of broth. To distract myself from my hunger, I watched several three-inch cockroaches scuttling around my cell. With no cracks or crevices in the airtight cell, I was amazed they had gotten in. I wondered why they'd want to; there was nothing for them to eat except the muck around the toilet.

The third day passed with only a second bowl of broth to sustain me. My hunger compounded. That night my intestines churned so loudly they woke me. I sat up on one of my blankets, weak and lightheaded. "They forgot again," I kept saying, trying to convince myself it was a mistake. "They can't be feeding us only once a day."

I winced as I changed position on the thin blanket below me. Sores covered my body from sleeping on concrete slabs for the two weeks since my capture. The cold and damp from the floor penetrated through the bottom blanket as if it were thrown over a block of melting ice. I never imagined it being so darned cold in the desert regions of southwestern Asia. But with its northern exposure and high altitude near snow-clad mountains, this region produced frigid weather with nighttime temperatures below freezing. The cold made my sore neck even stiffer.

The top blanket covering me fell short of my six-foot-three-inch frame, forcing me to choose between freezing feet and a freezing head. I chose freezing feet, exposing them to the intense cold and damp. My constant shivering burned much of what little energy I had. Taking in two or three hundred calories a day, I didn't have much.

Footsteps approached. I kept my eyes fixed on the steel rod that bolted the door to the floor. If the rod stayed in place, only the small window would open. If the rod moved up, that meant the handle was turning to open the door, and I was in trouble. I expected the first interrogation any time.

The rod stayed in place and the hatched window slammed open. A guard shouted something at me in Arabic. I drew in a deep breath and stood up, the crackling of my knees echoing against the walls. Grasping a blanket over my head, I cautiously approached the door, exhaling white puffs of air.

"Are you veddy cold?" the guard asked.

I watched him warily as I shuffled toward the door.

"How about an extra blanket?" he asked.

"Yes," I said. For once I wished I was shorter. Small rations and short blankets don't go far on a tall body. "I am *very* cold."

He put his face closer to the window. "No blanket! Sit down!" And then he slammed the window shut.

The regime of Saddam Hussein had trained these men to be indifferent to the suffering of others and fostered deep-rooted hatred and coldhearted cruelty. Given the chance to live in a free society, they might have been friendly, respectable people. I had to view them with pity, not contempt. If I survived, after the war I'd be going home to my family and a free country. They'd still be here.

I wandered back to my "bed" and plopped down. Drawing my knees to my chest, I pulled the blankets over me, carefully tucking them around me. If I left any opening, I'd wake up with violent shivers. At night cockroaches crawled over me. I let them be, unwilling to disturb my heat-conserving arrangement of blankets.

On my fourth morning at the Biltmore, I woke up famished. Daily rations had continued to be only a few ladles of broth and one or two pieces of hard bread. "No, no, this can't be happening." My panic grew. "They can't expect us to live on so little food." My gut felt like an empty pit, and mealtime was hours away.

Agitated by hunger, I walked restlessly around the four cinder block walls covered with red clay tiles. The walls of the gloomy cell seemed to close in on me. I rapped softly on one of them. They were steel reinforced. "Nothing's going to penetrate these walls."

My eyes darted about the cell. The only light entering my eight-by-twelve-foot cell came under the slit in the door and through one window cut into the back wall nearly to the ceiling. Covered with scratched and cloudy plastic, the barred window allowed in only enough light to determine whether the sky was white, blue, or black. Not being able to see outside added to my claustrophobia. I had no hope of escaping through a window, barricaded with a quarter-inch steel grid. "I'm tired and hungry, I don't speak the language, and I'm going for a walk?" A tall, light-skinned man wearing yellow pajamas and laceless high-top tennis shoes wouldn't exactly blend into the crowd. As one of my captors had reminded me, "You're in Baghdad now."

I paced the gloomy cell like an animal the first time it's caged. Even if I could escape, my captors had guaranteed I'd be torn to pieces, limb by limb. "The wives, sisters, and mothers of those killed by your bombs would be glad to seek revenge for their loved ones," they promised. I visualized a horde of hysterical women in black Arabic dress, their faces veiled around dark eyes filled with hatred, eager to inflict pain on the murderers of their loved ones.

Desperate to end my aching hunger and thirst, I hunted for a scrap of food or a drop of water. Toward the back of the cell a shoulder-high wall concealed a filthy Western-style toilet, empty of water but full of excrement. Opposite the toilet sat the bottom pan of a plumbed fiberglass shower stall. I twisted the hot and cold water faucets but nothing came out.

I looked around the cell. It felt cold, damp, and silent as a deep, dark well.

Beneath the toilet, a light-colored object mottled with dark spots caught my eye. I picked the item out of the dirt. It was a piece of bread about the size of a small child's fist and flecked with mold. I held it up to my face and swallowed hard, nauseated by its stale urine smell. My hands and forehead grew damp with sweat. Could I? Could I ever? Shuddering, I threw the moldy bread to the floor as a sickening realization came over me. The infrequent meals and scant portions were no mistake. Those bastards were deliberately starving us.

The Geneva Conventions can't prevent inhumane treatment any more than laws can prevent all crimes. And unlike the military protocol practiced by the young guards at the MP prison, the guards here took delight in scaring us. The older, hardened Biltmore guards woke us up at midnight, at three in the morning—any time we slept—to insult, threaten, torment, and terrorize us. "You deserve this!" they'd often shout at me. Guards especially loved to recite examples of the brutality I had inflicted upon the "peaceful people of Iraq."

I heard footsteps. The window in my door slid open. "Would you like more food?" a guard called in. As I sat up, he shoved something dark and slender through the opening. It was the barrel of an AK-47. I cringed, ducking my head while expecting him to hose the room down. He slammed the window shut, laughing hysterically at his sadistic assault.

My location, a few doors down from the guard station, was unfortunately convenient for random retaliation. At times the guards allowed outsiders into the prison to avenge the hardships they had suffered and the loved ones they had lost.

Hypervigilant, I startled at every noise, then would listen, holding my breath, describing to myself the sounds I heard like a play-by-play announcer at a ball game. "He's coming this way...he's stopping...he's jingling keys..." Each time I heard footsteps, I expected someone to drag me away for my first interrogation. But so far, I had never seen a soul except through the hatched window of the cell door.

Later that day, I heard footsteps in the corridor. Watching the steel rod, I heard the window slam open. I looked up to see the huge face of an Iraqi dressed in a military uniform peering in. He looked big and vicious enough to wrestle a grizzly. A white kerchief covered the lower half of his dark face like a surgeon's mask. "Are we getting medical help, or is he afraid we'll contaminate him?" I wondered. His dark eyes glared above his disguise with the hatred of someone whose entire family had been wiped out by an American bomb. I suspected the guards had let him in because of his power or personal connections. Shaking, I reported to the huge steel door, which faced a center corridor.

"What is your name?" the guard asked, his eyes narrowing.

"Acree."

"What is your nationality?" he demanded.

"American."

"Are you a pilot?"

"Yes."

He pulled down his mask and fired a huge glob of spit at me. His venom splattered onto my face, trickling down over my mouth. Grimacing, I turned away from the window and wiped the foam off on the back of my hand. Being spit upon is universally demeaning, and for a moment, my anger exceeded my fear. "Welcome," he said.

I had no strength or focus to retaliate, and if I had, surely this son-of-a-bitch would kill me. Never had I felt so powerless; I could only control my reaction. After the spitting incident I learned not to be such an easy target for guards appearing at my door.

"You think you will leave here?" a guard yelled through my window one day. "You will stay here forever! Even when the war is over, you will *never* leave."

As I remembered his threat, the walls of my darkened cell seemed to shrink around me. Other countries had played the cruel hostage game. After years, Terry Waite, Terry Anderson, and Thomas Sutherland still remained imprisoned in Lebanon with no sign of release.

The monotony of my solitary days and the darkness of the cell distorted my sensation of time passing. The days and nights blended together. Even on a clear day the winter sun cast only a diluted patch of light into my world like sunlight filtered underwater. When the pale sunlight receded, I felt even more isolated. Here no interior windows offered a chance to communicate with other prisoners. Guards constantly patrolled the corridor and monitored prisoners' positions. No one dared talk—except once each morning.

Morning arrived with footsteps beating the corridor. Doors slammed open, one by one, signaling roll call. I waited for my turn, pressing my ear against the door as the guards worked down the cell block questioning prisoners. Occasionally, I heard a faint reply. When my turn came, the window slid open to reveal three Iraqis standing in the corridor, one holding a clipboard.

"Name," one of them stated.

"Acree," I answered.

"Nationality."

"American." The guard holding the clipboard checked me off, then slammed the window shut.

In the five days since I had arrived, my cell door had never opened. Meals, blankets, insults, everything came through the small hatched window in the door. Maybe I'd spend the duration of my captivity locked in this cell. I hoped by now my captors assumed my knowledge was too outdated to be of use. It seemed too good to be true, but I felt grateful that they had left me alone.

I adapted to my new reality as best I could. Searching my cell for anything to make my survival easier, I found a few grains of powdered soap and mixed it with my saliva to wash the deep handcuff wounds on my wrists. Like a person living on the street, I hoarded everything, even the lint balls I found in the corner. I kept the hot and cold faucets on, and checked them ten or twenty times a day, hoping to catch a dribble in my mouth.

With each roll call, I learned to speak my name louder and louder, hoping a fellow prisoner would hear my name and know he was not alone. Others spoke louder, too, and I heard the names Zaun, Andrews, Eberly, and Maurizio.

The diluted light that fell through the cloudy window provided a welcome link with the outside world. If I positioned myself on the floor just right, the patch of light bathed my face in its life-giving warmth. With my head tilted upward like a plant toward the sun, the thirty minutes of filtered rays lifted my spirits.

I relied upon the narrow patch of light rising and falling to supply a cycle and predictability to my days—and a means to track them. When the sun patch reached the bottom of the cell floor, I made a tally on my makeshift calendar. Removing my left shoe, I positioned a protruding aluminum prong from one of the shoelace eyelets against the wall tile and etched a line alongside the others. I wondered when I would etch the last mark. The constant sense of uncertainty—of what would happen next and how long I'd be held captive—was a torture all its own.

As time passed, I found it easier and easier to lose myself in my mind. I retreated there to pray, be with my family, and talk with God. I took many excursions into my mind. Some days I went home; other days I visited my squadron.

I perfected my "burrito wrap" arrangement of my top two blankets. Carefully tucking in the sides underneath me, I left an inch at the bottom that I stuffed between my feet. I made a tunnel at the top and breathed warm air down to my chest. Even in my cocoon, my fingers and toes quickly numbed from the bitter cold. With my reduced muscle mass, and almost no subcutaneous fat to insulate me, the cold felt especially cruel.

The only thing as constant as the cold was my gnawing hunger. Nothing could take that away. I thought about food all the time—spicy Mexican food, chicken with mashed potatoes and gravy, a hot fudge sundae topped with Spanish peanuts. My hunger nearly overpowered me each afternoon when feeding time was near.

By now, I knew the sequence of sounds by heart: the elevator opening, utensils clanking, and guards greeting each other. Ivan Pavlov had been right: stimulated by sounds alone, I salivated.

Next came the sound I lived for: squeak, shuffle, squeak, shuffle. A guard shuffled down the corridor behind the food cart with one squeaky wheel. I anticipated being fed. My heart beat faster; my palms began to sweat. I was near panic in anticipation of receiving food as shuffling footsteps alternated with the opening and closing of cell windows. Intermittently a plastic bag rustled as he reloaded the cart with bread.

A few moments later the squeaky wheel started up the hall again. It drew nearer. My heart pounded in my rapidly rising and falling chest. I fought to control my impatience. I remembered my restlessness while waiting for my food to be served on airplanes and in restaurants. This hunger and impatience felt a thousand times more intense.

The cart arrived at a T in the corridor. A left turn meant my meal would arrive within minutes. A right turn meant another hour wait. More prisoners lived down that wing. I strained to hear in which direction the wheels turned. Yes! Thank you, God. The cart turned left.

Finally, the cart stopped at the cell next to mine. He filled my neighbor's bowl with broth. Each day, we received two small pieces of stale bread and a cup of tomato or blood-based broth. On a lucky day, I found small chunks of potato in the bottom of my faded plastic bowl. On other days I smelled urine or found a puddle of saliva. I listened intently for the sound of my neighbor's door closing, trying to quiet my anxious breathing. I counted off the seconds. One . . . two . . . three . . . four . . . five . . . *slam!* Eight seconds. Only one scoop of broth, I guessed. It was my turn. I waited in front of the door, drooling, swallowing, licking my lips.

The food cart approached. I stood at the ready, bowl in hand. I heard the guard spit, then snicker. The window opened and my hand shot the bowl to the window like the quick draw of a sharpshooter—but an eager, shaking one. A dark, hairy arm passed my filled bowl back through the window. A plastic bag rustled and the same thick arm reappeared with two pieces of unleavened brown bread.

"Thank you. *Shokrun,*" I told the guard. I wanted him to know I appreciated being fed, even if it was this bowl with only two scoops of broth garnished with a glob of spit. I walked back to my corner to eat, resisting the urge to gulp the warm broth like an animal. After saying a prayer, I drained my bowl. Then I ate my thin bread in small bites, chewing them as slowly as I could, wanting to gobble it all at once. I tucked a small piece into my pocket for something to eat in the morning.

Heaving a big sigh, I set down my empty bowl. After each meal, I felt a letdown like the day after a holiday. That was it for another twenty-four hours. By early evening my hunger raged, and I would spend the rest of the night preoccupied with how much I'd be served the following day.

On the morning of my fifth day at the Biltmore, I awoke with hunger grinding my gut. I opened my eyes. In front of my face, two long brown water bugs scuttled across my line of sight. They headed toward the toilet and the discarded piece of moldy bread. "If I get desperate enough I can eat the bugs *and* the bread," I told myself.

I sat up and pulled from my pocket the piece of bread I had saved. Warmed overnight by body heat, this "breakfast" helped soothe my ravenous hunger. I held it in my hand for a moment before chewing it in tiny bites. As my stomach acids attacked the bread, I thought about home and imagined walking on the Carlsbad beach with Cindy and Cami. After the worst blow at the interrogation center (which I later learned cracked my skull), I'd had a clear picture in my mind of throwing the tennis ball for Cami and her bounding happily to retrieve it. My memories of her centered around events and activities, pure pleasure. My thoughts of my mom and Cindy were tainted with worry about the heartache I was putting them through. How are they holding up? I wondered. God, I have to make it back to them. I have to see Stephany grow up.

Life at the Biltmore had exceeded my worst fears. Like the interrogation center, this prison exuded power and intimidation. But here I experienced tortures more subtle than the brutal, bone-jarring beatings of the interrogation center. Sleep deprivation, hunger, and constant fear of death were among the most unrelenting of tortures. I couldn't imagine being so cold, hungry, and tired and then being interrogated, too.

A faint noise pulled me into the present. I froze. Footsteps. My neck and shoulders tensed. Someone at the door. For the first time in five days. A noise sent my heart into a gallop: "He's stopping. . . . He's jingling keys. . . . He's putting a key into the lock. . . ." I held my breath.

My eyes stayed riveted to the steel rod that bolted the door. I pleaded silently, "Please don't move!" The hairs on the back of my neck prickled. Before the rod moved an eighth of an inch, I knew. The door swung open, and a guard yanked me to my feet and wrenched my arms behind my back. My reprieve had ended.

Oceanside, California
February 7, 1991

Aboard Camp Pendleton, our Marine driver maneuvered the white government sedan amid heavy security. The car carrying my sister, Bonnie, and me was headed toward VMO-2, passing through several checkpoints to deliver us to our meeting with Vice President Dan Quayle. The car reached the huge hangar of Cliff's squadron. The sight of the building—festooned with American flags and yellow ribbons and draped with a POW flag—brought tears to our eyes. We still didn't know if Cliff had been kept alive since his appearance on Iraqi TV.

My worries about Cliff were ever present. I had tried not to let them consume me. Writing in my daily journal, surrounding myself with supportive people, talking to family and friends on the phone, and keeping a routine helped. Most of all, I concentrated on my goal of publicizing our letter-writing campaign.

Convinced it could make a difference in the treatment of Desert Storm POWs, I had pursued the campaign with a vengeance. Former Vietnam POW Bill Stark recalled how dramatically his treatment had improved after a worldwide outcry in 1969. "Even the commander of the camp might feel the pressure and tell people to ease up on them," he said. Secretary of Defense Dick Cheney had sent a message to all commands suggesting military members write, using their discretion. Ironically, Iraq had used a letter-writing campaign in 1989 in the Iran/Iraq war to protest treatment of Iraqi prisoners of war that, Iraq claimed, was "clearly violating the Third Geneva Convention of August 12, 1949."

In Geneva, officials of the International Committee of the Red Cross (ICRC) gave the same bad news. Iraq still had not responded to repeated requests by its delegation of eight to visit and interview the allied prisoners.

I had drafted a letter to the Iraqi ambassador to the UN, His Excellency Abdul Amir Al-Anbari, which I hoped sounded firm but not offensive, then drove to the CPA office of friends Dee and Ken Barackman. Ken, a solidly built man of six-feet-four-inches with dark hair and mustache, and his vivacious, dark-haired wife, Dee, helped me refine the letter and print it in several type styles.

Dear Mr. Ambassador:

I am writing to express my concerns for the humane treatment of the Coalition captives.... Since the Republic of Iraq was a signatory of the Geneva Accords, I would expect Iraq to follow them as agreed upon.

I beseech the Iraqi government to treat Coalition captives in the same humane manner as Coalition forces are treating Iraqi prisoners of war. Substandard treatment of helpless captives will only enrage the world and lower international opinion of the government and people of the Republic of Iraq.

More than 100 letters arrived each day at the post office box opened by the Marine Corps for Mary Hunter's and my mail. I drafted a "Dear Friends" letter thanking those who had written, and suggested they write to the Iraqi ambassador, enclosing the sample letter I had written. Every day, Marine wives brought us food, ran errands, answered the phone, opened mail, and helped address and stuff envelopes.

My calendar pages had gone from being blank to being crowded with appointments and projects. Each day I kept busy with phone calls, letter writing, and meetings. There were always motivated, hardworking people to help me. Every night, I went to bed tired but satisfied with my progress and anxious to do more. Knowing Cliff was probably being starved or worse, I had no time to waste.

By now, Mom had returned to Seattle, and Bonnie, a versatile musician who thrived on her overly busy schedule, had arrived for a one-week visit. With her help, my plans accelerated.

Bonnie joined me to meet with the Marine Joint Public Affairs officer at Camp Pendleton to inform him of our campaign. "If you're serious about this letter-writing campaign," he said, "you need to think big, worldwide, and establish an organization with not-for-profit status."

We took our campaign to the next level, researching how to set up a non-profit organization and making phone calls to recruit the founding members. It felt good to finally have a focus and a tangible way to help our Coalition POWs and MIAs. I wrote in my journal:

> I'm achieving, organizing. I have to keep moving. It gives me perspective. I can't wallow in "what-ifs." You can't look at the big picture when you're drowning in your tears. The time when you can do nothing at all but cry for help is the worst. Like a drowning person going down for the third time, fighting, struggling, knowing it will all be for naught.

Since there had been no word of Cliff's condition since his appearance on the Iraqi television broadcast three weeks earlier, the Camp Pendleton Public Affairs Officer suggested I make a final statement to the media—my "swan song," as he called it.

My statement thanked the public for their show of support and apologized for my phone's being continually busy: "Calls vanish quickly, but letters endure. . . . I will be proud to show your messages to Cliff when he returns." I closed by saying, "To protect our POWs, the Department of Defense has advised POW families to make no further statements. I know we have all appreciated the world support that has poured forth. I wish to thank everyone who has kept us in their thoughts and prayers. You have given us strength."

Until the end of Cliff's ordeal (whatever form that would take) was near, I would remain silent. From now on, I had to work behind the scenes.

I made many phone calls to receive government approval of every step I took to set up the POW/MIA organization and the letter-writing campaign. The two counterintelligence officers I had met with gave their blessing. With their guidance, I received approval for the letter-writing campaign from the director of intelligence for the Marine Corps, the Department of Defense POW/MIA Policy Office officials, the National Security Council staff member in charge of POWs and MIAs, and the commandant of the Marine Corps.

And now I would have my first opportunity to publicize our campaign in my meeting with Vice President Dan Quayle and his military adviser. Bonnie and I entered the hangar through a special door, then were ushered upstairs to a conference room where we joined Mary Hunter and Don Beaver.

Security was tight in the building. Men in suits with radios and earpieces patrolled the halls with uniformed Marines. After giving his speech downstairs, the vice president would meet with the families of three young men killed in action (KIA) and then the POW families. The KIA families waited in a room across the hall. "You're lucky to be in *this* room," I told myself. I still had hope.

The cheers of Dan Quayle's audience downstairs brought my thoughts to my mission. Minutes later, I was briefed by the military adviser to the vice president. When I told him about our organization and letter-writing campaign, he was already aware of my actions. The information had been "moved up the channels," he said. I showed him the "Dear Friends" and Iraqi ambassador letters, and he said I could give copies to the vice president. Before the adviser left, he gave me his card, with the following address: "THE WHITE HOUSE."

"Call me if you need help," he said.

"We will!"

Vice President Dan Quayle arrived and presented me with a framed and signed picture taken when he "inspected" Cliff's OV-10 in Saudi Arabia in December. "We will not let this be another Vietnam," he said. "We will get these guys out."

I looked him straight in the eye. "So you will continue to give us your support?"

"Yes. The president and I both feel the same way. We're not going to forget these people." I thanked him, then told him about the organization and handed him an envelope containing the two letters.

Three days later I held my first meeting with the twenty founding members. I had a prepared agenda, plenty of food, and had placed on each person's chair writing materials and a framed picture of Cliff. The day before, like a nugget of gold, a roll of undeveloped film had arrived in Cliff's final letter. I enlarged my favorite, a picture of a grinning Cliff standing on the stern of a shuttle boat with the churning blue waters of the Persian Gulf and the battleship USS *Wisconsin* in the background.

Where was Cliff now—was he still alive? Our worst fear was that Saddam Hussein would make good on his January 21 threat to use the POWs as human shields at strategic sites. In a Radio Baghdad broadcast, Iraq said captured airmen would be treated as common criminals, not as prisoners of war, because they had "deliberately attacked civilians in extreme cold blood, even machine-gunning pedestrians."

"The behavior of those pilots is very far away from the honor and moralities of the military code," the Radio Baghdad broadcast added. "It is the behavior of ordinary criminals like that seen in American and European films...they should be dealt with on the basis of their being killers of defenseless children, women, and old people...every one of them will receive the punishment he deserves."

But looking around the group assembled in our living room, I felt more encouraged than I had in weeks. They were a hardworking bunch. We wrote our organization's mission statement: the identification, humane treatment, and release of all Coalition POWs; and chose our name: the POW/MIA Liberty Alliance for Operation Desert Storm. We selected our officers. Pat Antosh, a human dynamo and mother of five, was selected as president and spokesperson. A public affairs officer in the California Army National Guard, Pat had journeyed to Saudi Arabia three times during Desert Shield, escorting media representatives into areas occupied by National Guard units. Her husband, Major Steve Antosh, was the acting CO of VMO-2 in Cliff's absence.

CPA Ken Barackman, a Vietnam veteran with a deep, resonant voice, was chosen as vice president and treasurer. Rosana Martinez was voted in as secretary. The room was charged with excitement as we divided up tasks for fund-raising, public relations, volunteers, and other committees. As advised, I would stay in the background to avoid Cliff's being singled out.

Over the next week, more than 100 people would volunteer to serve on our committees. A San Diego attorney offered his services pro bono and worked with Dee and Ken Barackman to submit our articles of incorporation and bylaws for tax-exempt status. Owners of an advertising firm offered publicity. A friend in the finance business took over bookkeeping duties. Graphic artists in both San Diego and Seattle offered free design of our logo and letterhead. An Oceanside printer donated paper and printing for our "Dear Friends" and "Iraqi ambassador" letters. The owner of the office suites where I had worked offered a mailbox for our return address and mail collection. A San Diego radio talk show host offered a one-hour spot on his show and an article in his monthly newsletter.

As my guests departed that night after our first Liberty Alliance planning meeting, I became suddenly aware of my fatigue. From the time I started making East Coast phone calls at six in the morning, I hated to stop. Every day in captivity must seem like a lifetime to Cliff, I thought. But my work on the Liberty Alliance and its letter-writing campaign might help bring him and the others home sooner.

At the door, Ken Barackman's wife, Dee, turned to me. "You are *anything* but the downtrodden POW wife," she said in her usual ebullient voice. "Your leadership and inner strength are infectious."

"Thanks, Dee. I hope you're right." The following day my ability to inspire others would be tested before Hollywood's biggest stars.

Baghdad Biltmore Prison
February 12, 1991

"What do you know about strategic targeting?" a voice asked.

"I'm just an OV-10 pilot," I answered slowly, hoping my voice sounded steady. They wanted information about where Coalition bombers would strike next. I knew the answer. Coalition targeteers planned to relentlessly attack command and control capabilities, power plants, weapons assembly or storage areas, Scud missiles, or any weapons of mass destruction capabilities. "I have nothing to do with targeting." I shook my head. "All I do is observe and report."

From the moment they hauled us into the building, our captors aimed to deprive us, frighten us, force us to submit. Every minute, the overwhelming fear of death hung over us. At no time did I feel it more intensely than during interrogation sessions. Many times I expected it to be only a matter of time before my captors killed me for resisting.

Early on in my captivity I had decided that, no matter what my captors did to me or how bad I felt, I would not give them one piece of usable information. I would not reveal the location and capabilities of tactical units, the names of my commanders, or especially any details of the amphibious landing. If it cost me more pain or meant another gamble of my life with a gun held against my head, then so be it.

Sitting alone in my cell, anticipating the next interrogation was almost as terrifying as the event. When another prisoner was hauled off, I knew that sometime soon the victim would be me.

The interrogation sequence began with the metallic thud of my cell door crashing open. After being blindfolded and handcuffed, I was led out of my cell and down the now familiar route: turn left, walk down the corridor to the end, turn right into the interrogation room.

My captors at the interrogation center had focused on physical violence. My current tormentors were masterful mind benders who played on my innermost fears about my family and my future. They terrified me without laying a hand on me.

"Colonel Acree," the interrogator said. "We're getting tired of you not cooperating with us. You have not provided us any useful information and we think you are lying. We have no more patience for your attitude." He paused. "You must realize. We have been very lenient with you so far. Your future is totally dependent on our decisions."

With the war under way three weeks, interrogation questions had shifted from operational, perishable information to strategic intelligence needed to defend Iraq against the onslaught of allied airpower. Determined to extract whatever information they could, they were especially desperate for information about the amphibious landing. Believing the Marine Corps planned a World War II–style frontal assault on Iraqi positions in Kuwait, Iraq had placed more than 1,000 sea mines in waters near its heavily defended coastal areas.

"Colonel Acree. You must tell us everything you know." The interrogator's voice pressed, betraying his concern.

"Are they doing *that* bad?" I wondered. Cut off from communication with the outside world, I could only guess how Coalition forces were progressing. I sensed that the war was not going well for the Iraqis.

But my interrogator made wild claims of their success in the war. Fifty thousand American troops have been killed in the trenches of Kuwait," he declared. "We have captured thousands of prisoners."

I stared at the back side of my blindfold, listening intently. Could they have pulled off such a tactical surprise? Before the war the Iraqis barricaded Kuwait with minefields, barbed wire, and trenches we suspected might be filled with flaming oil to stop Coalition forces. Could that many troops have perished in them?

"An unprecedented ground war is taking place in southern Kuwait," he continued. "Iraqi armored forces are annihilating United States troops and personnel of other nations who have wrongfully taken sides against the people of Iraq."

I tried to justify his claims but realized they couldn't possibly be true. I could believe 1,000 casualties, not 50,000—that was 10 percent of our fighting force. Their ridiculous assertions broadcast their fears. Instead of demoralizing me, they confirmed to me their dire straits—and their awareness, I suspected, of an inevitable defeat.

As time went on they had become more desperate for information about the planned amphibious operation and other Coalition ground war plans. Article I of the Code of Conduct reminded me of my military commitment: "I am an American, fighting in the forces which guard my country and our way of life. I am prepared to give my life in their defense." And I had my own personal code of conduct: to make doggone sure what I knew in my head didn't come out of my mouth.

I had coped with more fear, stress, and pain than I ever imagined I could. Each day I wasn't killed was a victory, but I felt my physical strength diminishing. I moved slowly to conserve energy, but as the days passed, the pounds continued to drop off. I could not endure this deprivation indefinitely.

That night, a short time after I fell asleep, I snapped awake feeling Cindy's presence. "She's busy . . . she's doing something to help me." Her strength and determination gave me a profound sense of assurance. How she could help me, I couldn't imagine.

The next morning, from down the corridor in the interrogation room, I heard the painful cries of a prisoner being beaten. The awful struggle, muffled by the thick concrete walls, was unmistakable. Feeling powerless and angry, I listened to try to recognize the voice. Each person has a distinct way of responding to pain. Could this be Guy? Even in such pain, I'd be glad to know he was alive. Almost four weeks had passed since I had lost track of him at the interrogation center.

Hearing the prisoner grunt with each blow was almost worse than being beaten myself. "Uhh! Umm!" he moaned. Americans and British had more of an openmouthed "Oh!" or "Ow!" cry. The Iraqis were beating a Kuwaiti, I guessed. Then I heard a sharp, final-sounding thud and suspected that the prisoner's suffering was over. I prayed Guy was still alive. He was one of the finest Marines I'd ever met.

I tried to calm myself by visualizing Cindy's face. By now, she had received my last letter. Imagining her reading it, I felt terribly sad. What had I put her through?

Footsteps approached my cell. A key turned the lock and the bolt opened. An Iraqi guard swung the heavy metal door open. He entered my cell and twisted my arms behind my back to lock on the handcuffs. After blindfolding me, he gave me a hard shove that pitched me forward. I shuffled toward the door, my heart pounding with dread. It was interrogation time.

We entered a stuffy room that reeked of tobacco smoke at the end of the corridor. I thought, "There's something weird about this room." A strange sensation enveloped my body. Heat.

I was led into the room and left standing blindfolded. A minute later someone removed my handcuffs. They'd never done that before an interrogation.

"Lower your trousers," a voice commanded.

In dread and panic, I hesitated. My mind raced through a dozen grisly scenarios that might soon take place. This could be worse than any beating I'd had. Slowly, I tugged at the waist of my loose-fitting yellow pants. They slid easily to my ankles, exposing my underwear. My mind was going crazy wondering what they were going to do.

"Remove your underwear," the voice demanded.

I didn't know what to expect—gang rape or worse. I had no choice but to obey and take whatever fate was about to be given me. I pushed my underwear down to my ankles and stood naked from the waist down. My captors had stripped me of my freedom, my possessions, now even my clothing. I clung to the only thing I had left—the power of my own mind.

Fighting panic, I waited for some painful retaliation. Several Iraqis conversed in Arabic. You feel so vulnerable when you're blindfolded. Everyone has fears, but my Marine Corps training disciplined me not to reveal them. I relied on that discipline now.

A voice called from across the room. "Have you had any sexual diseases?"

"No, I have not." I stood half naked in front of an undetermined number of spectators.

"You are an Israeli agent," another voice said. "You are a spy, aren't you?"

"No, I'm not."

"Admit it. You are an Israeli agent who was sent to destroy the Iraqi government," the voice accused.

"That's not true," I said firmly. "I am a United States Marine."

"No. You are Jewish," the voice insisted. "You are a spy who conspired with Israel. Tell us now and you will avoid much pain and discomfort."

Someone approached and stopped in front of me, so close I felt his body heat. He leaned forward until I could feel his breath on my face. I felt a sharp prickling sensation on my penis. I stopped moving. I stopped breathing.

With a savage act of will, I stayed motionless. I could not allow my fear to gain control. Two other Iraqis approached, and the three conversed in Arabic. After a moment, one of them told me to dress. Relieved, I quickly pulled my underwear and baggy pants over my shrunken hips.

Someone reapplied my handcuffs and pushed me across the room into a chair.

"There has been an assassination attempt on your President Bush," a voice said. "He has been mortally wounded."

I sucked in my breath. Could it be true?

"Vice President Quayle will be the new president," the voice continued. "Do you think President Quayle will use nuclear weapons against Iraq?"

"I don't know."

"What is your opinion?" he insisted.

Cold and weakened by hunger, I forced my sluggish mind to think quickly.

"If Iraq uses chemical or biological weapons," I said, speaking slowly, "he may consider the use of nuclear weapons." I heard furious scribbling on paper as the Iraqis conferred among themselves.

"Where will the American army land paratroopers?" the voice asked. The Iraqis must be getting the piss popped out of them, I thought. They feared wave after wave of C-141s dropping thousands of airborne troops into Kuwait or Iraq. The Iraqis weren't trained or equipped to counter a massive paratroop insertion. Maybe they feared special operations forces attempting a POW rescue. In any case, I had no idea if the 101st Airborne Division planned these operations. I told my interrogators so. They moved on to questions about bridges.

I found out weeks later that the air campaign had destroyed Iraq's power plants, communications centers, and all but one operational bridge over the rivers surrounding Baghdad, preventing the delivery of needed food, water, and ammunition. All the Euphrates River bridges linking Baghdad to the Kuwaiti war zone had been demolished.

"How do you camouflage a bridge from radar?" my interrogators asked.

"Paint the bridge a different color," I suggested. The pen scratched my silly answer on paper. "You could hang a camouflage net from it," I added, knowing that a net would give the bridge even more radar resolution and make it a better target.

Then the questions got tough. "What can you tell us about the Marine amphibious landing?"

I didn't answer.

"When and where will Marines attack?"

I had been briefed on this information, and knew many lives could be lost if I revealed it.

Unbeknownst to me, strategies had changed from what I had been briefed on before the war. General Schwarzkopf had feared high casualties would result if the two Marine brigades aboard ship in the Gulf landed in an amphibious assault amid Iraqi minefields and heavy fire. And with three Iraqi divisions effectively tied down on the coast anyway in anticipation of the landing, he doubted that an amphibious assault would really be necessary. He asked General Boomer whether the Marines could invade Kuwait successfully from Saudi Arabia without the amphibious landing. Boomer said they could, but that the deception of a landing should be a high priority. So, long before my interrogation, Schwarzkopf had canceled the landing. The operation I had been tortured to give information about no longer existed.

After another long interrogation, guards led me out of the room. I felt a small measure of accomplishment, knowing I had resisted one more time. On the way back to my cell, I reviewed their questions and my answers. Had they believed my lies? Could I have done better? Then I heard the cart with the squeaky wheel.

My heart beat faster. The serving of meals had already begun. *I hope I'm not too late!* "Please, God," I prayed. "Don't let them pass me by." When my blindfold was removed in my cell, I said a prayer of thanks. On the floor was my orange dog bowl, half full of cold, greasy broth, and two pieces of bread. God was looking out for me.

Though I had attended church only sporadically, I had prayed every day. Prayer became even more important to me now. It gave me a feeling of peace and comfort. I prayed often each day and night. Every time I prayed, something got better. Sometimes I got a bigger morsel of bread, other times a piece of potato in the bottom of my broth.

As I ate my meal, my mind crowded with questions. When will I be interrogated next? Can I continue resisting without their killing me? How long can I survive on so little food? My weight was dropping fast. My only hope was the exchange of prisoners after the war. I was confident that my country and my president would bring me home someday, maybe in a body bag, but I knew President Bush would hold Iraq accountable for every POW.

Evenings in the cell block were dead silent, except for sounds coming from the guard station a few doors down. Occasionally, a cheap, worn-out radio broadcast martial music on Radio Baghdad. Muslim guards preferred broadcasts of prayer sessions. Twice as they changed the channel I caught a few lines of American tunes: "Duke of Earl" and "Georgy Girl." Recognizing Western music, the guards quickly tuned to another radio station.

At night I remained on alert, listening, attentive to every sound. Sleep came only in twenty- or thirty-minute increments. These short sessions were too little to shed my heavy-eyed fatigue but long enough to suffer my recurring nightmare about Guy Hunter.

That night, I fell asleep only to be visited once more by the dream that bedeviled me. The nightmare began with the staccato roar of a machine gun firing—a sound I heard outside my cell window nearly every day. I visualized the sound coming from an execution squad for prisoners, like me, who refused to cooperate.

As my dream continued, I was led to a courtyard, then stopped a few feet away from a dirty, bloodstained wall. Cuffed to a vertical steel pole in front of that cinder block wall was Guy Hunter—his head sagging, his knees buckled, his chest freshly stained with blood.

The scene shifted. Now I was the one tied to the pole. A firing squad, rifles at the ready, closed in. To my side I saw a ditch filled with the rigid remains of earlier victims. On the top of the heap of corpses lay Guy Hunter's. I recoiled at the sight of his ghastly bluish white face, then waited for bullets to slam into me.

As always, I woke up in a cold sweat. Shivering, I sat up on my blanket. "Is Guy really dead?"

I wondered how the rest of the squadron was doing. Knowing how they had responded to our capture would have lightened my heart. Later, I would learn that my squadron intelligence chief had said, "This is our worst nightmare. The CO was everything to us. He was a dad and we just lost our dad." The base chaplain said the squadron "reeled at the loss of its dynamic and powerful commanding officer... as they groped through their grief and the massive shift in leadership."

But the experiences and reactions of my fellow Marines were far from my awareness as I sat shivering in my cell that night. I wondered if the air strikes would continue obliterating targets in Baghdad for another day or another month. The sooner the air bombardment phase ended, the sooner the ground war would begin. Then it would be only a matter of time before a Coalition victory was most likely assured.

I reasoned the ground war would start sometime in February—certainly before Ramadan, which would begin on March 17 that year and would include prayer, reflection, and dawn-to-dusk fasting, all incompatible with fighting a war with Muslim allies. Not knowing when the ground war would start, I tried to pad my expectations and not be let down.

As I tried to fall back asleep, the ground shuddered beneath me. Coalition jets were back. The fearsome pounding of Baghdad by Coalition jets occurred soon after sunset, around midnight, and again just before dawn. As I listened to the explosions rip through the city, I felt another step closer to freedom.

My stomach growled as I listened for the second foray of bombs to hit. Radar-dodging F-117 Stealth fighters usually dropped two bombs per target. If one of these incredibly powerful weapons dropped, you knew another would soon be on its way.

Stealth aircraft had revolutionized air warfare. During World War II, to ensure a "good hit" on a power plant or another strategic target, Allied planes dropped about 650 bombs. Gulf War–era technology accomplished the same results with one cruise missile or laser-guided bomb. And instead of bombing entire cities, the aircraft could pick out an airshaft in an Iraqi building with high-tech precision. But not all of these "smart bombs" were dropped accurately on their targets.

Even with its greatly improved accuracy, the batlike F-117 Stealth sometimes missed its mark. From my cell, every few days I detected a bomb falling long or short of its target. If the plane released the bomb early, it landed short; if released late, it landed long, or beyond the target. More than once when a bomb fell close by the prison, the ground rocked beneath me with malicious force.

Earlier that week the Iraqis had claimed that Coalition bombs had killed many civilians. "You have bombed our city. You have bombed our people," they had said angrily during my interrogations.

Could it be true? Had Coalition planners mistakenly selected one or more civilian targets for destruction? How accurate was intelligence information about structures in Iraq? The Biltmore was a huge, well-reinforced building, but I figured it looked more like a hospital complex than a prison. Did Coalition intelligence suspect we were there?

Though I had no idea, by now American intelligence sources had identified three possible detention sites of Allied POWs. A classified drawing had been made of the most likely one. Though President Bush had secretly authorized plans for a possible rescue attempt, it was quickly concluded that even special operations forces could not free POWs held in downtown Baghdad.

The second foray of bombs exploded, sending flashes of light into the distant sky and destroying whatever was on the receiving end. Bursts of anti-aircraft artillery thundered as the Iraqis shot blindly into the night sky. Coalition planes flew largely unobserved by Iraqi radar. Hoping to get a lucky hit on aircraft they could not see, the Iraqis scattered bright spots of triple-A fire across the black sky.

Another flash of light illuminated the dark strip of sky through the high window. A low, howling sound rose in pitch to a loud, high-pitched wail.

The siren signaled pending air attacks to Baghdad citizens. "Great early warning system," I thought. The sirens usually went off just prior to—if not after—each bombing raid.

The cacophony finally died down, and I tried to fall asleep again. My intestines continued their protest, rumbling loudly in the deathly quiet cell block. My mind was equally active. Who was here with us who so frightened everyone? Was it high-level military or Baath Party leadership? Saddam Hussein himself?

I later learned that the POWs were imprisoned in a building on Fifty-second Street in Baghdad along with the regime's political prisoners. The building also housed the Baath Party and Saddam Hussein's regional intelligence headquarters.

Had I any inkling of these facts at the time, I would have known that we had been placed there as human shields.

Cliff and Cindy Acree met as
karate students in 1972.
High school sweethearts,
they drifted apart but
married eighteen years later.

Cliff in the cockpit of an OV-10 "Bronco" observation and light-attack plane.

Cliff and his squadron's advance party before leaving Camp Pendleton, California, for war. Cliff is directly under the center of the OV-10's wing. To his left, in camouflage, is air group commanding officer Col. Dan Kuhn.

Photo of an OV-10 taken by Cliff as his squadron flew over Labrador en route to Saudi Arabia.

To Cliff:
From one survivor to another. Thanks for your inspiration and leadership. Best Regards Always. Guy Hunter

Top: The remains of Cliff and Guy Hunter's OV-10 where it was downed in Kuwait. The inscription to Cliff reads: "From one survivor to another. Thanks for your inspiration and leadership. Best Regards Always, Guy Hunter."

Inset: A battered Cliff appears before Iraqi cameras. Afterward he was beaten yet again for refusing to denounce the war and President Bush. Despite torture, he withheld secret war information throughout his captivity.

During Cliff's imprisonment, Cindy worked tirelessly to keep the POW issue before the public. Here she *(back to camera)* and her friend Pat Antosh talk to Cindy and Kevin Costner and Ali McGraw at the Voices That Care recording session.

Finally released and back in Saudi Arabia, an emotional Cliff is greeted by his friend and his squadron's flight surgeon, Joel Lees. Comdr. Lees was one of the few people to know the full extent of his injuries.

Cliff and Cindy's reunion at Andrews Air Force Base, Maryland.

At the reception in a hangar at Andrews. *From left:* Col. Don Beaver, who with his wife, Kay, was one of many people, in and out of the service, who helped Cindy during Cliff's captivity; Marine POW Maj. Joe Small; Cliff; Guy Hunter.

On the bus just after their reunion, Cliff and Cindy have a rare moment alone together.

At the Bethesda Naval Hospital, Chief of Naval Operations Adm. Frank B. Kelso II and Secretary of the Navy H. Lawrence Garrett, III, flank the Navy and Marine POWs. *Front row from left:* Jeff Zaun, Bob Wetzel, Larry Slade, Cliff. *Back row:* Kelso, Craig Berryman, Joe Small, Guy Hunter, Russ Sanborn, and Garrett.

Left: Cliff, Cindy, and the Hunters arrive at the Camp Pendleton homecoming.

Below: Cliff is formally reunited with his squadron during the homecoming at Camp Pendleton. Guy Hunter is at the right.

Guy and Cliff field questions from the media.

Cliff and Cindy respond to the enthusiastic welcome at Pendleton.

Cliff; Cindy; Cliff's daughter, Stephany; and Bob Hope, one of many celebrities and ordinary citizens who supported the American POWs and their families during the war.

In 1997 with Muhammed "Big Mo" Mubarak, the Kuwaiti fighter pilot who inter-preted for and advised his fellow Allied POWs during captivity in Iraq.

Cliff and Cindy at home in Georgia in 1997 with Mark Edward and Stephen Freedom.

6

A Dual Battle

Burbank, California
February 10, 1991

"Ready to go, ladies?" The chauffeur gestured toward the open door of the black Mercedes. I hugged my sister, Bonnie, good-bye and climbed into the sedan with Pat Antosh. Bonnie was flying home that morning, and she had promised to spearhead the Seattle branch of the POW/MIA Liberty Alliance.

Pat and I settled into the smooth leather seats of the limo. It pulled out of the driveway and headed to Los Angeles and the all-star recording session of a musical tribute to America's troops in the Gulf. Proceeds from the single and video of "Voices That Care" would go to the USO and the American Red Cross Gulf crisis fund. (Eventually, 700,000 copies would be sold.)

As the car sped north, Pat and I planned our strategy. We wrote "POW/MIA Liberty Alliance for Operation Desert Storm," the organization's short mission statement, and an information number on index cards. At the two-hour reception before the taping, we would talk to as many celebrities as possible and hand each a card. If even one or two stars got involved as a result, we would have achieved our goal.

The sedan stopped before the guarded gate of Warner Bros. studios in Burbank, and I gathered my pile of index cards. An escort guided us into a one-story building crowded with people. As I walked through the door, I felt as though I had entered a Hollywood wax museum come to life. "Everyone's acting so normal," I thought as I passed a woman casually conversing with Richard Gere.

Clutching my stack of cards, I took a deep breath and walked into the crowd. I was greeted by Linda Thompson Jenner, who conceived the project and wrote the lyrics for "Voices That Care," and by her fiancé, David Foster, who composed the music with Peter Cetera. Moving through the crowd, I talked to Jane Seymour, Mike Tyson, Whoopi Goldberg, Helen Reddy, Brooke Shields and her mother, Teri, and Fred Savage, young star of *The Wonder Years*. Later, Fred's father took me aside. "Of all the people Fred met today, you made the greatest impression," he said. Most of the stars seemed genuinely interested in the alliance and gladly accepted an information card.

While chatting with Ali McGraw, a tall figure near the doorway drew my attention. Wearing blue jeans, a white T-shirt, and a navy sport coat, Kevin Costner entered from the adjoining room. I remembered how the wife's experiences in *Dances With Wolves* had paralleled my own and given me hope. I had to tell him. Minutes later, one of the organizers introduced me to him.

Kevin shook my hand warmly, his expression concerned. A pretty, dark-haired woman came from behind him. "Hi," she said, smiling sweetly and taking my hand. It was Cindy, Kevin's wife. I smiled, then focused my attention back to Kevin.

"Your film *Dances With Wolves* gave me hope when my husband was declared missing," I began. Cindy and Kevin listened with genuine interest as I spoke about the symbolism of the movie. "Folks! It's time to move to the studio for taping!" a voice barked. The Costners didn't budge.

I finished my story, both of them smiling, tears filling their eyes. I told them about the alliance, and Cindy offered her help. They both hugged me, and Kevin kissed me gently on the cheek. "Thank you," he said, his voice husky with emotion.

Much later, after Cliff's return, a large box would arrive with the return address "Dances With Wolves Productions." Cliff and I had only recently seen the film together. Watching the "snow scene" with Cliff at my side, I recalled how it had served as the symbol of hope for his safe return from captivity.

"Kevin must have sent me an eight-by-ten glossy," I joked to Cliff. I opened the box. The card inside read: "For Cindy and Cliff, with warm affection. Love, Cindy & Kevin." I opened the wrapping and found a beautifully framed print of the "snow scene" from *Dances With Wolves*.

After meeting Kevin Costner that morning at "Voices That Care" I should have felt faint, but I couldn't let my awe get in the way of the task I was there to accomplish. It was time for the taping!

We entered the cavernous soundstage that hummed with voices. Dim canister lights illuminated the center of the darkened room where sound and camera equipment flanked several rows of risers in front of black acoustic paneling. Technicians in headsets scurried around testing equipment. Stars milled around, talking and laughing. It was hard not to stare.

The stars piled up on the bleachers, and the audience members slowly filled several rows of folding chairs facing the risers. As Pat and I waited in semidarkness, a man approached. "If you would like to address the whole group," he said, "I can guarantee you will not be photographed."

My heart quickened. I nodded. "Yes, I would." As I rose from my seat, a shot of adrenaline coursed through me.

I walked toward the nearly 100 celebrities assembled on the bleachers for the "Voices That Care" taping. Gathering my courage, I remembered my mission: to bring world attention to the plight of our Desert Storm POWs.

"Everyone, please. I want all cameras to stop," the director requested. He looked left, then right. "There should be *no* cameras rolling." He turned and motioned for me to step forward.

Excited and nervous, I looked up at row after row of Hollywood stars waiting and watching me. The director introduced me, then stepped off to the side. Everyone was perfectly quiet, waiting for me to speak.

I took a deep breath, smiled up at the faces on the bleachers, and began. "We all saw the battered faces of the POWs," I said, my voice surprisingly steady and strong. "I'm sure you felt frustrated, as I did, that there was nothing we could do." People watched intently, many of them nodding and crying. I continued. "But now there is something we can *all* do. . . ." I described the letter-writing campaign and how those in the audience could get involved. As I turned to walk back to my seat, I heard an explosion of applause and cheering; they were giving me a standing ovation.

I felt weak in the knees as I took my seat in the darkened studio. As the group on the bleachers began practicing the chorus, my heart filled with emotion. I thought of Cliff, so far away. I had expected separations as a Marine aviator's wife, but I had never imagined such a gulf between our worlds of Burbank and Baghdad. The celebrity choir broke into the song's chorus:

Stand tall; stand proud!
Voices that care are crying out loud.
And when you close your eyes tonight,
Feel in your heart how our love burns bright . . .

At lunchtime, everyone walked to Brownstone Street, the faux New York block Warner Studios had used in *Funny Girl* and myriad TV shows. Pat Antosh and I ate lunch at one of the tables scattered around the back lot, then began walking back to the studio. Partway there I heard a male voice calling, "Cindy Acree!"

I turned to see a tall man in a baseball cap walking toward me. His long, lean build reminded me of Cliff's. "Are you Cindy Acree?" Chevy Chase caught up with me. I nodded. "I think what you're doing for your husband is great."

By the end of the daylong taping, I had met Richard Gere, Kenny G, Blair Underwood, Lindsay Wagner, Orel Hershiser, Billy Dee Williams, Henry

Winkler, Kenny Rogers, Harry Hamlin, Dudley Moore, Gerald McRaney, Wayne Gretzky, Michael Tucker, Nicolette Sheridan, and many others, and told them about our organization.

Michael King, producer of *Jeopardy, Wheel of Fortune, Inside Edition, Oprah,* and other shows, and his wife, Barbara, offered to send letters to everyone on their personal mailing list and to arrange television appearances. I hoped others we had spoken to would also come forward to help.

When the "Voices That Care" taping was over, Pat and I headed outside to find our driver waiting beside the limousine. We continued our planning until the car pulled into my driveway. The driver helped us out of the limo, then reached into his pocket.

"I'd like you to use this for your foundation," he said as he pressed a ten-dollar bill into my hand.

Our first donation! We were on our way.

Baghdad Biltmore Prison
February 6, 1991

Down the hall from my cell, cupboards opened and closed. Plastic and paper rustled. Footsteps headed toward the nearby guard station, and guards greeted each other good-naturedly. My nightly suffering was about to begin.

Metal utensils clattered as guards served their evening meal. The mouth-watering smell of beef cooked with onions wafted into my cell. The scent was as torturing as it was tantalizing. Lying in the dark cell, I pictured big chunks of hot, steamy beef covered with thick brown gravy. Guards conversed in Arabic sprinkled with a few words of English—"Boosh!" "Donkey!" "Dog!" "America!" Then silence except for the rapping of forks on plates.

The aroma of cooked beef filled my cell, mocking my hunger. My next meal was nearly a day away. I was so hungry it hurt. How many others was this bastard starving in Iraq?

As starvation continued its steady, heinous work, I could almost hear Cindy scolding me about skipping meals and warning that eventually my body would feed on its own tissues to maintain metabolism. I felt my body consuming itself.

Hunger has to be the most excruciating and thorough of all tortures. Unlike wounds that heal over time, the pain of starvation accumulates. As my body deteriorated, my survival instinct became overpowering.

Shivering under my blankets, I vowed to try to do something about the food situation. Not having heard of any captives above the rank of major, I assumed that I was the senior POW. As such it was my duty to speak up for the rest. If food rations had not increased by March 1, I decided I would request to speak with the officer in charge and plead for more food for the malnourished prisoners. The thought of the punishment I would receive because of my request scared me spitless.

It must have been two or three the following morning when I awoke to the sound of a fist pounding on metal. Half awake, I knew I must report to the door or risk getting throttled. With aching arms, I pushed myself up from the cold stone floor. The carefully arranged blankets parted and cold, raw air pierced my skin. As I straightened to stand, dizziness pitched me forward. The smallest physical effort took my breath away.

With all the energy I could muster, I shuffled like a sleepwalker on feet numbed with cold. The persistent banging stopped and the window slammed open. A guard peered through the viewing hole, his dark head wrapped in the red-checked Arab *gutra* headdress. He shouted angrily. Willing my legs to walk toward him, I moved zombielike, then bumped into a wall. Reeling around, I staggered off in the opposite direction, away from the steel door.

The heavy bolt raised, then the massive door crashed into the wall with a deafening echo. I froze, ears ringing, eyes blinking, body shaking. I tried desperately to comply, but my emaciated body refused.

The guard stormed up to me. "Lie down!"

He pushed me down to the floor, then stomped out of the cell. Wide awake now, I crawled back to my blanket and collapsed. Adrenaline surged, my heart raced, my temples pounded.

Breathing heavily, I drew my legs up to my chest and shifted position, searching for an angle without a bone protruding like a steel rod through my skin, rubbed raw after five weeks of sleeping on the concrete floor. I carefully rearranged the blankets, then drew in my withered arms. I had started out with little surplus fat, and now my skin hung slack where hardened muscles once had been.

I tried not to think about my hunger. Instead I thought about Cami. But in my distressed state, the craziest things came into my mind. I tried to recall all the characters' names in the television comedy *WKRP in Cincinnati*. I even pictured myself as my friends' dogs, roaming around in their backyards, finding a place to dig under the fence and escape. No matter how I tried to escape the pain of hunger with my mind, my body took over and kicked my ass with the agony of starvation.

I let myself slide into my fantasy world. That night I relived a Thanksgiving feast. I felt the warmth of the heated dining room through my cozy winter clothes, and Cindy's hand on mine. I heard voices and laughter. I smelled the savory odors of steaming turkey, buttery vegetables, and Cindy's fresh dinner rolls as they were passed around the laden table. Gratefully, I scooped a large serving of each food onto my plate. I squeezed

Cindy's hand, and she turned to me and smiled. Just as I dipped into a huge mound of whipped potatoes, the rumble of hunger in my belly screamed at me, and my eyes snapped open. There I was again, surrounded by the blood-and-urine-stained walls of my stinking cell.

I placed my hand over my aching gut, wanting to relieve the emptiness. My mouth burned with bitter acid, and mealtime was twelve hours away. Across from me, in the corner, lay the moldy, smelly bread. I grabbed it. For a split second I hesitated, then shoved it into my mouth, swallowing as fast as I could. Though its sharp, bitter taste lingered on my tongue, it helped ease the empty, gnawing feeling in my gut.

Around sunset, a prison guard dressed in Arabic clothes opened the door to my cell. He beckoned me with an index finger.

"What does he want with me?" I wondered, my stomach doing a flip-flop. Weak from hunger, I felt half dead as he tied a blindfold over my eyes and cinched my wrists behind me. My arm was increasingly weak each day when I raised it to receive my bowl of food. The last few days I had found it difficult to stand up. It was then that my captors had stepped up the pace of my interrogations. In the past week I had been interrogated not once but three times. They focused on me, I assumed, because of my rank—and especially because I was a squadron CO.

The guard led me out of the cell, ten steps down the hall to the right, then turned left into a room. "We must be in the guard station," I thought. "Is he bringing me here so the guards can get in their hits?" He removed my blindfold. He removed the handcuffs and motioned to several items on a table in front of me—a small metal bowl containing grimy, gray water; an ancient pair of scissors; and a dirty, worn disposable razor. He handed me the scissors and motioned for me to shave. I hacked away at my five-week growth of beard, but the dull scissors were useless.

"Just use razor," he said. I scraped the cruddy razor a few times over my cheeks, pulling and tearing at my whiskers. I left the mustache since it provided warmth. Besides, the Iraqis seemed partial to those. He reapplied the blindfold and handcuffs and led me back to my cell.

"This is strange," I thought. "Why are they trying to improve my appearance?" After five weeks of captivity, my filthy body looked about as attractive as an old stray dog's. My personal hygiene had dropped to a new low—dirt coated my body and my teeth felt like they were wearing big hairy mittens. Blood and dirt matted my hair, which itched constantly. What was this all about? I found out the next morning.

I had just eaten my morning bread when a guard came for me. He led me, blindfolded and handcuffed, down the corridor. I expected another interrogation. But we took a new and different route.

He led me into the elevator this time, and we rode down one or two floors. After walking down a hall and passing through two doors, we entered a quiet, carpeted room.

I blinked. For the first time, my blindfold and handcuffs were removed before an interrogation. A huge picture of a smiling Saddam Hussein dominated the room. I shifted my gaze then cringed at what I saw: a television studio. In front of me sat a burgundy couch shaped like a horseshoe. Two civilian Iraqis dressed in suits sat on the couch, their knees touching a small wooden coffee table. A tripod held a television camera facing one end of the couch. My heart beat faster. I remembered the tremendous beatings I had endured after refusing to repeat Iraqi propaganda on videotape at the interrogation center.

One of these goons handed me a filthy green Marine Corps flight suit. "Change clothes," he said. My hands were shaking as I took the flight suit. Several Iraqis watched as I pulled off my "PW" shirt and trousers. An Iraqi enlisted soldier was positioned behind the camera. He stared at me with eyes like cold black stones. He hated me, absolutely. With him stood a pudgy man who looked to be in his mid-thirties. He had a scraggly brown beard and long straggly hair touching the collar of his dark blue suit. Two uniformed Iraqis who were likely in their thirties stood nearby.

I tried to keep my hands steady as I pulled the zipper of the flight suit up to my neck. The suit sagged on me like a graduation robe; its arms and legs were way too short. I didn't know that it belonged to Guy Hunter.

The older civilian on the couch was a portly man who was probably in his mid to late fifties. He was dressed in a well-tailored gray suit, white shirt, and matching gray tie. His full-bodied hair fell over the tips of his ears, but every silver-gray hair was combed neatly in place. Sitting on the upper section of the velour couch, he motioned for me to sit on the short end facing the camera. I sat down opposite a dark-haired man who looked to be in his forties who wore a neatly pressed suit in tones of dark brown and green.

"Would you like a drink of water?" the silver-haired man asked in perfect English. He spoke in the smooth, modulated tones of a newscaster. He motioned to an octagonally shaped glass on the end table. My mouth was even drier than usual from fear. I wouldn't have put it past them to lace the water. I raised the glass to my nose, fighting to keep my hand steady. I took a sip. When I lowered the glass, the silver-haired man spoke.

"We are going to ask you a few questions." He signaled to the cameraman. I knew what they were up to: a public "confession" of my "crimes" to show to Iraqi civilians. I was on trial, with the newscasters acting as prosecutors. I swore to myself that I would not provide any classified information. I would not make derogatory statements about President Bush or the United States. No way would I compromise my values.

"Why do American pilots bomb baby milk factories?" the silver-haired man asked, in the way a lawyer cross-examines a witness.

I didn't want to piss them off or supply an answer fit for broadcast. "American pilots would never intentionally harm innocent civilians, non-military targets, or places of worship, to include a baby milk factory," I said. "We are very respectful of hospitals, places of worship, or known civilian communities." Neither newscaster spoke. But behind the television camera, someone spoke—to translate and comment on my answers, I assumed.

The newscaster frowned impatiently. The younger, black-haired, newscaster took over. "President Bush knows he is killing innocent women and children with his bombs," he said in fluent English. "You are a tool of President Bush. Why are American pilots dropping bombs on civilian targets?"

The questions were tricky, but at least they weren't tactical. "Americans would never knowingly attack a civilian target such as a hospital, a church, or a school," I said firmly. "We are specifically trained to never attack civilian targets."

He looked at me steadily for a few seconds. "Your country did," he said, his voice full of indignation.

I stiffened my back. "If an American aircraft ever had one bomb fall on a civilian target it would only be because of a system failure in the aircraft." My voice approached being forceful.

"Why does the United States do this? How can you justify American pilots killing Iraqi civilians who are not involved in the war?"

"Americans would never knowingly bomb civilian targets," I repeated.

"Why do United States pilots bomb Baghdad when there are no Iraqi military forces in downtown Baghdad?"

"I am not aware of where your forces are. I am an observation pilot who only saw the very southern part of Kuwait. I have no idea of the posturing of major Iraqi units in the field."

"What do you have to say to the people of Iraq whose families have been killed by American pilots?"

"American pilots would never, *ever* bomb known civilian targets, to include schools, churches, or hospitals."

"Do you agree with this war?" the younger newscaster asked tersely.

"It is my duty as a military person to execute orders given to me." That was not the answer he wanted to hear. His hateful stare said "You are a pain in the ass."

"Repeat after me." His tone indicated impatience. "Boosh is donkey."

"I cannot say that. He is my president."

He shook his head, and with a disgusted look turned to the silver-haired newscaster. Then, facing me again, he said, "We do not like your answers, Colonel Acree. I will ask you the question one more time." This verbal volleying continued for several minutes. Apparently, this time I wasn't going to get the snot kicked out of me—at least not immediately.

The newscasters debated in low tones. The camera was turned off. The black-haired newscaster shook his head, then waved his hand in a way that clearly said "You're worthless." The two younger Iraqis came out from behind the camera. "Get up! Put on clothes!" the soldier scolded. He came toward me like he was looking for a fight. He watched me pull off the flight suit. His angry gaze raked across my face.

As I dragged my arms into my "PW" shirt, he kicked me in the back with his black boot and sent me in a headlong sprawl onto the carpet. Another Iraqi joined in on the beating. I clenched my teeth and tried to keep my knees together. The silver-haired newscaster watched, a smirk on his face. Hearing my grunts, the younger newscaster looked over. When he saw they were beating me, he averted his eyes, his face expressionless.

I pulled on my pants as fast as I could. It was hard to keep from pitching forward. As I straightened, one of the goons busted me in the kidneys. It caught me by surprise and knocked the wind out of me. Wheezing, I hunched over—unable to stand, unable to fall. "You bastards!" I shouted in my mind. "When is this going to end?"

I bent over to pick up my canvas tennis shoes. I hurt so bad I could hardly get them on. When they reapplied the blindfold, I felt even more vulnerable. I wouldn't know who was going to take the next shot. Beneath my blindfold, I saw the feet of the two young soldiers on either side of me. The pricks got in a few more hits, working me over pretty bad.

Someone shoved me, real hard. I lurched forward. As soon as I regained my balance, he gave me another one. Now they were in a big hurry to get me out of there. One guy on each arm, they led me out of the room. I gripped my laceless shoes with my toes, scared to death I'd lose them. The guards threw me back into my cell.

The next day, when mealtime arrived, the hairy arm served me my bowl of broth. I waited expectantly for bread. Instead, he pushed a nearly empty plastic bag through the window. It fell to the floor. I snatched it up like a beggar who has spotted a fifty-dollar bill.

With cold fingers, I carefully picked out and ate all the little pieces I could. A spoonful of dustlike crumbs remained. As I drank my broth, I eyed the nearly empty bag stamped with the design of a palm tree and a man leading a camel. "Made in Jordan" it said. "These crumbs will be great to thicken tomorrow night's broth," I thought. But there might be no tomorrow.

I could use the bag to catch water. The one bowl of water I received each day barely quenched my thirst and left me none to wash my hands. Sometimes they "forgot" my water two or three days in a row. With the plastic bag, I could catch trickles of water from the faucet, wet my parched mouth, and wash my hands.

I gripped the bag tightly, torn between my two choices. Save the crumbs or collect the water? I looked at the water pipes, licking my lips. I was so thirsty. But the crumbs would supply extra nourishment. Crumbs tomorrow or water today? My heart beat faster. I paced the cell with faltering steps. A bag I would have thrown away at home now seemed vital to my survival.

"This is insane!" I thought. I sat down, exhausted, and forced myself to choose. I turned the bag upside down, and like tiny flakes of gold, the crumbs floated to the grimy floor. I carried the bag to the shower and spread it open beneath the pipes. That's when I saw the huge tear. Dammit! I couldn't believe the bag I had placed so much hope into was worthless. I sat on the floor, my shoulders drooping. Further strength drained from me as if I had a hole in me, too. I was exhausted, still hungry, and now I had no bread to save for the morning.

The days passed. My weight continued to drop off at an alarming rate. Feeling my body feed on itself was an eerie, disgusting sensation. Hunger overpowered my mind; I was desperate for something to eat, something to chew. During my daily meal, I chewed each piece of dry bread until it was almost soup.

Thick red scabs had formed on my wrists, healing the ugly gashes where handcuffs had dug into them. Gingerly, I tore off the scabs from the tender skin and dropped them into my broth. I downed the mixture that was as disgusting as the events that had created the scars. Weeks before I would have felt like a cannibal eating human flesh. Now self-preservation overrode my revulsion.

Settling back on my blanket, I prayed. "God, give me the strength and courage to survive this." God provided the comforting companion I needed on my frightful journey. He was always there if only I sought Him out. Our intimate, ongoing communication provided a sense of inner peace, renewing my courage and strengthening my faith.

During interrogations, hunger and exhaustion undermined my ability to resist. How could I continue to defy them in this condition? Then I thought of my fellow Marines and Coalition members, and knew I would die before I endangered them. To fail would be a lifelong disgrace more painful than torture.

Admiral Stockdale, a heroic POW during the Vietnam War, said, "Prisoners of war grow to live on honor and self-respect. Their reputation is one of the few things they have left in their world, and they value it as they would a life ring in a raging sea."

In my mind I visited my high school algebra class. I tried to recall the names of my classmates and where they sat. Earlier in my captivity, I had retrieved these dormant memories with amazing detail. Even as cold and hunger impaired my body, my brain had still projected clear images of my past. But now, I noticed the images dulling, blurring together.

That night I lay awake in my cell as allied bombing raids shook the prison. The thundering vibrations of the nightly bombings—hundreds per night—were like music, each blast bringing the war—and, I hoped, my captivity—closer to completion.

I wondered about the progress of the war. By now, the air campaign should have trashed the infrastructure of Iraq and significantly damaged its warfighting capabilities. It would be only a matter of time before the ground war commenced and Kuwait would finally be free. Then maybe we'd soon be free, too. Cheering the aircraft bombing Iraq, I never saw them as a threat.

My cell door opened again and I was blindfolded and handcuffed, then hauled roughly down the corridor. This time we took the standard route to the interrogation room. Someone shoved me into a hard chair.

They asked me several strategic questions. I refused to supply any information.

"I don't know," I repeated.

After weeks of being interrogated, I waited, expecting to hear the first blow cutting through the air. But I was about to experience a more terrifying torture. They began working on my mind.

"Why make this harder on yourself?" the interrogator asked. He spoke in a chilling monotone.

"Colonel Acree, you have committed war crimes against the peaceful people of Iraq. If you do not cooperate and answer our questions, we are going to kill you."

I heard him pace to the end of the table, then speak, his voice turned directly to me. "We are *tired* of you not cooperating," the interrogator said. "We shall have to get this out of you another way." His cold, calculated voice reminded me of the David Niven look-alike I had faced on the first day of my capture.

After a long pause, he said, "We want you to think about this. If you do not cooperate with us tomorrow, the torture will begin with the loss of a finger. With each lie or answer you refuse to give, we will cut off another finger."

My body stiffened. My eyes blinked behind my blindfold.

"Tomorrow there will be ten questions. If you have ten good answers, you will have ten fingers. And if there are ten bad answers, you will have *no* fingers."

His grisly prediction cut through me like a knife. He continued, his voice hard-edged. "The torture will continue, and we will send your body home in pieces to your wife."

I didn't doubt for a moment that he would act on his threat. I had read that Saddam Hussein, unquestionably one of the world's most ruthless leaders, had shot one of his own ministers, then had his body chopped up and delivered to his wife.

"What is your home address?" the interrogator demanded.

I could hardly speak. Would they try to harm Cindy? I would do anything in the world to keep her safe.

The conflict agonized me. Were they bluffing? Or would they carry out their threat? My voice shook when I answered, "I cannot tell you that."

"If you ever want to see your wife and daughter again," he said, "you must tell us."

A lump formed in my throat. I hated telling them anything about my family, imagining Iraqi agents in the United States blowing up houses. Was remaining silent worth dying for? I thought hard. By now, it had been five weeks since I hadn't returned to the squadron. If the Marine Corps hadn't seen the videotape from the interrogation center, they would assume I'd been killed or captured. By now Cindy would be in Seattle or be protected at the house. I hoped to God she was. She'll forgive me.

My voice uneven, I recited our address. Remorse ravaged through my body.

My interrogator's lips formed something approaching a smile. "Good. If you do not cooperate tomorrow, that is the address where we'll send your body pieces to your wife." His words added to my sense of betrayal.

"Cindy will never see me that way," I told myself. "A bag full of body parts will be intercepted."

"Think carefully of what I have said today," he said. "Tomorrow we will have your decision." They walked me back toward my cell. On the way, we stopped at the guard station. With my hands tied behind my back, four guards kicked and hit me, knocking me down repeatedly. Ten minutes later, I was returned to my cell, throbbing and bloody.

Fighting my Iraqi captors had been a horrible, terrifying test of my endurance, a war, albeit on a smaller battlefield than the one my Marines faced. I had fought my private war blindfolded, handcuffed, and starving, often inches away from the enemy.

But struggling against the demands of my Iraqi captors was not the only battle I had faced. At the same time, I had waged a fierce inner battle, a savage tug-of-war between my commitments and survival. And as my body deteriorated, my survival instincts were taking over. God, what was I becoming?

The interrogator's last words reverberated in my mind: *Tomorrow we will have your decision.* My battle had reached its apex.

Since my capture five weeks earlier, my only freedom had been my freedom to choose. Each time they threatened to kill me, I had wrestled with moral decisions, looking deeply within myself, questioning the values I'd always lived by. *What do you stand for? What are you willing to die for?*

Lying in my cell in the darkness, I remembered trembling during mock executions, the cold barrel of a nine-millimeter pistol or an AK-47 against my head or chest, thinking, "This is it. My last breath. If they pull the trigger now, I'll die quickly." My body wanted to give in, to do anything to stop the fear and pain.

But I had learned a lesson long ago in Officer Candidate School: Choose the difficult right over the easy wrong. Tomorrow's decision would be a difficult one. But I would rather die with my honor than betray my loyalty to my fellow Marines and my country.

The ground rumbled beneath me as the nightly bombing began, assuring me that the allies hadn't forgotten us. "Hurry up, guys, get us out of this stinking place."

I lay awake in my darkened cell contemplating death. My death. Not since an AK-47 had been pressed into my chest at the interrogation center had I been so terrified. "I'll have one more night to sleep and pray," I thought. If only I could say good-bye to Cindy. She had fought this battle with me. I regretted the pain and sorrow she and the rest of my family had endured. I felt great sorrow at knowing I would never see our families again. I asked God to be with me when tomorrow dawned.

But God had another plan in mind. Iraq had rejected an ultimatum to withdraw from Kuwait. President Bush had authorized General Schwarzkopf to begin the ground offensive. On that clear night of February twenty-third, the eve of the ground war, Coalition air strikes would escalate to a climax of nearly 3,000 sorties. Joining in the air strikes were five F-117 Stealth aircraft speeding unerringly toward their target, identified as "Regional Headquarters, Iraqi Intelligence Service"; it was known to me as the Biltmore.

Phoenix, Arizona
February 22, 1991

Waiting in the conference room with my Aunt Ethel and Cliff's parents, my hands tightened on the long white envelope I clutched. It contained a thank-you note to President Bush and information about our POW/MIA Liberty Alliance organization.

Though we'd still had no word on Cliff's condition, my heart felt lighter than it had in weeks. Iraq was taking a beating from Coalition forces, and that morning, standing in the Rose Garden, a grim-faced President Bush had given Iraq a final ultimatum: "The Coalition will give Saddam Hussein until noon on Saturday to do what he must do . . ." he said. If Iraq did not begin a massive unconditional withdrawal from Kuwait by noon on Saturday, February 23, the ground war would start.

When President Bush outlined conditions of Iraqi withdrawal, I wanted to hug him for the priority he placed on the release of prisoners of war. Instead

I would deliver a handwritten thank-you note to him via his wife, Barbara, whom I had traveled to Phoenix, Arizona, to meet. "Dear Mr. President: On behalf of the POWs/MIAs and their families, I want to thank you for keeping the POW issue at the forefront of world attention," the note began.

Our grassroots letter-writing campaign had snowballed. Organizations, schools, businesses, and church groups across the country mailed and faxed letters. Aided daily by a crew of Marine wives, I had sent nearly 1,000 letters encouraging people to send letters of protest. Within three weeks, the Iraqi ambassador had received an estimated 50,000 copies.

It amazed me what one or two people alone could accomplish. Using donated mailing labels and printing, Seattle Liberty Alliance members Jim and Mary Osborne had sent letters to 1,700 dental practices across the United States, Canada, and Europe. Hundreds of offices honored their request to send 100 letters of protest to the Iraqi ambassador. "I'm honored to participate," many called to say.

While thousands of people were trying to help our POWs and MIAs, others seemed to be using them as marketing opportunities. In the local paper, a couple was pictured holding Desert Storm T-shirts they had printed. They claimed that a portion of their profits was going to POW/MIA families. A singer who enjoyed renewed popularity from revival of his song during the Gulf War claimed in a public presentation that proceeds from a new song would be distributed among POW/MIA families. When Rosana called his office for details, his assistant explained that he had been mistaken.

POW bracelet sales were booming across the country. Wearing a bracelet to remember a POW had become popular during the Vietnam War. The narrow aluminum bands, stamped with the name and date of casualty of missing servicemen, were to be worn until they returned. Traditionally, wearers sent former POWs the bracelets when they returned. That would be a mail delivery I'd welcome.

Unfortunately, the flourishing bracelet business was unregulated. Many groups didn't take the time to contact families for permission or even verify information. Bracelets identified Cliff as being shot down in Kuwait, Iraq, and even Saudi Arabia. Anyone could print bracelets and sell them, even if they had no intention of using the proceeds to help the people whose names were printed on them. When friends called to ask where they should buy theirs, I told them, "Ask where their profits are going." I wasn't always so wise.

About two weeks after Cliff's capture, the local founder of a POW/MIA organization presented me with my first bracelet engraved with Cliff's name. The man had wanted me to accept the bracelet in a public ceremony in downtown Oceanside, with media present. "It will be good for Cliff," he had urged. I explained that my advisers had suggested I not be photographed. "Don't trust anyone," he told me. "Especially the government." Convinced that I wouldn't go public for any reason, he finally agreed to a private presentation in my home. With my mom and a few friends present, the man presented me with five dark-blue bracelets bearing Cliff's name. As we posed for pictures, I hardly felt like smiling. The metal bands stamped with Cliff's name and date of shootdown eerily reminded me of a tombstone. But the bracelets seemed to have an energizing effect on this man. "My phone is ringing off the hook with orders," he said more than once. "I may have to hire a full-time secretary to keep up."

After the man's visit, I had felt vaguely uncomfortable. It wasn't until days later that I realized why. He had left me with some POW memorabilia, including a flag, pins, and a T-shirt. Jane DeHart looked at the black shirt then quickly refolded it. "You don't need to see this," she said, shaking her head. A few days later, I decided to find out why. "To a POW this is a gourmet meal," the shirt read. On the back was printed a large cockroach. As I put away the shirt, I realized the reason for my discomfort. The man had never said he was sorry that Cliff had been taken prisoner.

Later, I told him I was establishing my own not-for-profit organization. He tried to dissuade me. We should join forces, he said, and merge our fundraising efforts. A member of the alliance visited his home operation and advised against it.

By mid-February, this entrepreneur was "swamped with orders," according to a San Diego newspaper. His orders were topping 500 a day for the aluminum bracelets that he sold for $5 each plus a $1 shipping fee. Before long, the man reported that he had sold more than 10,000. I was pleased that so many people had shown their support of our POWs and MIAs by buying bracelets but annoyed at his claim that "proceeds from bracelet sales will go to establishing a trust fund for the education of POW/MIA families and toward an ongoing public awareness program."

Then the industrious "bracelet man," as we had begun to call him, teamed up with a local radio station to sell bumper stickers of the U.S. flag. After his "administrative costs," he told listeners of the radio program and stated in his member newsletter, profits would be used to set up "a trust fund for the Desert Storm POW/MIA families in San Diego County," meaning the Acrees and Hunters. After 25,000 stickers were sold locally, he said, a second trust fund would be established for POW/MIA families across the country.

I was furious. I never asked him to collect money for my family. It seemed as if the plight of our POWs had simply become a money-making operation. And generous, hardworking people were being led to believe that Mary and I were gaining financially from our husbands' misfortune. Ken Barackman drafted a letter to the bracelet man, which he and I signed along with Pat Antosh and Rosana Martinez as officers of the Liberty Alliance:

". . . while we are aware of your organization's activities and certainly appreciate any funds raised on behalf of the Acrees, we must request that you refrain from any further unauthorized use of the names of LtCol or Mrs. Acree, the Acree family, or the POW/MIA Liberty Alliance. . . . The Acree family and their friends appreciate any funds which you have already raised on behalf of the family and ask that such funds be donated to the POW/MIA Liberty Alliance for Operation Desert Storm. . . ."

To my knowledge, no Gulf War POW or MIA family received any of these "trust funds" collected on our behalf. I doubted the other POW/MIA families wanted to be treated as charity cases. Like me, as each day passed, they felt more desperate to do something to help our loved ones who were missing or captured—or at least to find out if they were alive. I knew I had done my best toward that end.

One day Cliff's "personal effects" from his desk and locker arrived from the squadron. Though it would be hard to open the box and see his things, I wanted part of him, that connection. "Thank God I know he's a POW," I told myself, comforted by his favorite jeans and loafers.

Military procedure requires that all personal effects of persons classified as MIA/POW/KIA must be packed within twenty-four hours. A Marine wife whose first husband had been killed in the Beirut bombing told me she received all her husband's clothes back—laundered. The practice seemed so clinical. "Officials don't realize how important smells are," she said. "Along with pictures, that's about all you really have."

Cami understood smells. After I emptied the box, she went crazy with excitement and ripped the box into a million pieces. Maybe she hoped Cliff was hiding in there somewhere.

I dreamed even more vividly than I had in the months before the war. In my dreams before Desert Storm, I searched for Cliff and found him, but before I could hug him and kiss him, he would disappear.

Now that Cliff was a POW, I searched for him in my dreams to no avail. I dreamed of being a passenger on a commuter plane. I was proud of its smooth landing, knowing Cliff was one of the two pilots. Anxious to reunite with Cliff, I slowly worked my way up the long aisle to the cockpit area, where the two pilots worked on a wide instrument panel. After what seemed like forever, I finally reached them. The two men turned to face me, and neither one was Cliff.

In another dream Cliff was an auto mechanic. I spotted him working in the service bay of a quick-lube shop. Though his back was turned to me, I recognized the lanky body in the blue mechanic's jumpsuit. I waited impatiently for him to finish. Finally he finished and walked toward me—a black-haired man wearing an earring.

Night after night I searched for Cliff in my dreams. He was lost and I needed to rescue him. No luck so far—in dreams or real life.

There had been many false alarms and false hopes. In a daring rescue, a downed American airman who had ejected behind enemy lines was picked up by a U.S. helicopter that swooped down and flew him back to safety. An A-10 destroyed an Iraqi jeep headed for the airman. If only Cliff had been so lucky. Everyone wondered, "Is Cliff still alive? Is he being tortured, starved?" News reports claimed that a British prisoner of war had been killed under torture.

On the advice of my friends who were former POWs, I did my best to maintain an even keel and avoid an emotional roller coaster. To protect myself, I had a strict rule not to stay glued to the television and not to believe everything I heard.

Most of all, I continued to focus on Cliff's strength. We were fighting this battle as a team. I wanted him to be proud of me. That guided me in everything I did.

And now, as I waited for my meeting with Mrs. Bush, I felt almost optimistic, especially when I compared my situation with a Marine wife I had met that morning. Leigh Berryman was the wife of Harrier pilot Captain Craig Berryman, declared missing in action on January 28. The news had reported the story of a downed Harrier at seven A.M. that day, yet she had not been notified until about nine-thirty. Word of the crash was on the news even before the commandant of the Marine Corps heard about it.

My heart went out to her. I only had to wait two days before learning Cliff had been captured alive. She had been waiting for weeks. Authorities had little information about the crash of her husband's single-seat Harrier. His wingmen reported having seen the aircraft hit by a heat-seeking or "IR" missile. Her husband's aircraft had exploded and hit the ground, with no sign of a parachute. "It doesn't look good," officials had told Leigh.

"The *exact* words they used to describe Cliff's crash," I told her. "But Cliff ejected and two days later he was on TV as a POW. . . . You never know."

"I have to block out what they're telling me," she said, "go with something I feel inside—and hope and pray." Enthusiastic about the letter-writing campaign, Leigh was grateful for something constructive to do that would ease her sense of helplessness.

The day after Bonnie left for Seattle, Aunt Ethel had flown in from Florida. A wise, resilient woman, Aunt Ethel had accompanied me to meet Barbara Bush. Cliff's parents, Dee and Bill, had also driven to the base for the meeting with Mrs. Bush. Dee greeted me in the waiting room with a big hug, and I was happy to see that Bill had more color and more hope in his face than when they had visited me in January, days after Cliff's capture.

We waited for Mrs. Bush's arrival. When the door opened we all stood up. The first lady was introduced all around and hugged and kissed me. I kissed her back and put a raspberry lipstick print on her cheek. "Oh, that's all right!" she said in her down-to-earth manner.

We settled in our seats, with Mrs. Bush sitting next to me on the couch across from the Acrees. "You go ahead and cry," she said to Dee. "I cry all the time—when I'm happy and when I'm sad, and my family has to figure out which one it is."

"I appreciate how President Bush truly cares about our troops," I told her.

"I hope this will be over soon," Mrs. Bush said as she reached for and squeezed my hand. Her friendliness and natural charm put everyone at ease.

I briefly described our organization and its goals, then handed her the envelope with my thank-you note and the two letter-writing campaign letters. In her 1994 memoir, she recalls our meeting: "I was so proud of the wife. She had organized a POW/MIA support group and seemed to be doing well. They all spoke well of George and it was a very moving visit. The darling mother was teary and I couldn't blame her."

After Mrs. Bush's staff photographer took several pictures, it was time to go, and she shook hands all around. Mrs. Bush walked toward the doorway. Reaching it, she paused and turned. Smiling, her eyes crinkled at the corners and she waved the envelope above her head. "I'll give this to George tonight!"

I drove back to California with renewed confidence that Cliff would be coming home safely. Little did I know that he was trapped in a prison cell, facing possible annihilation.

Baghdad Biltmore Prison
February 23, 1991

A thunderous explosion jerked me awake. The wall of the prison cell flexed like an accordion as a pressure wave rocked the cell block. Bewildered, I sat up straight on my blanket, feeling the floor shaking beneath me. Like a giant pair of hands, air pressure squeezed my back and ribs so hard I thought my lungs would burst. With the rapid decrease in pressure, I exhaled hard. I turned around to look through the narrow window at the darkened sky as if I could see the giant beastlike bomb that had caused the tremendous blast.

"That was a *bad* hit," I thought. Night after night I felt the aftershocks of allied bombs, but none had ever landed so close. "What target were they after?" I wondered as the building continued to rock. "Could it be our prison?" I heard the clamor of high-pitched voices and dozens of footsteps beating down the corridor. The guards' voices quickly faded as they rushed to their bomb shelters.

The F-117 Stealth fighter drops bombs in pairs, so at least one more was on its way. The reality overwhelmed me—these precision guided munitions could slice through concrete ten feet thick. My adrenaline surged. I wanted to run around in a panic, yelling in the senseless hope that someone would hear and stop the bombing. That would only waste what little energy I had. My body ached from the beatings of earlier that day. I took deep breaths to steady myself.

Before I had a chance to think, a jet aircraft screamed overhead, this one unbelievably low. The electrical crackle of a laser-guided bomb filled the air. With a huge ripping sound, a second bomb tore into the roof of our prison, crashing through the reinforced concrete floors as easily as plywood. I heard an earsplitting *cra-a-ack!* as the delayed warhead exploded in a blinding flash.

With the violence of a volcanic eruption, the blast numbed my hearing and threw me against the wall of my cell. The whole building shook, and the floor rippled beneath me. Tiles dislodged from the wall, and plaster fell from the ceiling. Half the steel fasteners of the barred window broke free. With a loud crash, parts of the ceiling in the corridor collapsed. The Biltmore was being systematically destroyed. I covered my head with shaking hands as the cell disintegrated around me. Oh shit! We *were* the target!

Unbeknownst to me, the Biltmore was not only a prison but also the regional headquarters of Iraqi intelligence in Baghdad. Fifty yards away, underground bunkers housed Baath Party members. Not knowing that allied captives were held inside, Coalition mission planners had sent eight F-117 strike planes to destroy the Baath Party building and its bunkers.

I sat locked in my cell, alone, trapped. I was helpless as the prey of a stalking attacker. Another tense minute passed. The building still rattled, then I heard a sinister "SSSST..." Another bomb, the size of a sport utility truck, sliced through the air toward our prison at a rate of 200 feet per second.

These bombs were equipped with delayed fuses. Once the bomb ceased movement, or after a predetermined time had elapsed since initial impact, the bomb would explode. How it destroyed its target depended on the type of fuse. The bombs equipped with time-delayed fuses were designed to destroy hardened, reinforced, or underground targets. Bombs equipped with impact fuses would hit the outer shell of the target, crushing everything below.

"That was *too* close!" I heard a muffled roar as the bomb hit the complex at bunker level. The Iraqis seeking safety there had chosen the wrong hideout. The walls of the building quaked. Dirt, tiles, and bricks fell, burying the plastic bag I had treasured. The room began to fill up with smoke and debris. The Biltmore was taking a murderous beating. I grabbed my blankets and stuffed myself in a corner of my cell.

I had faced the new day with dread—it was the day when I would endure the slow, torturous death my captors had promised if I didn't cooperate. My principles were my moral compass. I knew I couldn't give in to my need for self-preservation.

"So *this* is how my life will end," I thought, oddly calm. Being instantly killed by a bomb didn't seem as frightening as being slowly hacked to pieces.

I huddled under my blankets, every muscle tensed, still quaking from the first pair of bombs. "If we're the target there's at least two more," I thought. I dragged in a shaky breath. Particles of dust swirled all around me and grains of dirt coated my mouth.

Into the silence roared a third 2,000-pound bomb. It bit into the rear of the building so close it felt like it hit the wall next to me. The blast sucked the wind right out of my lungs and hurled me to the far side of the cell. The concussion of the blast shattered more tiles. It partially blew out the window, including the quarter-inch steel grid covering it. More pieces of the roof fell. I heard the sound of breaking glass as light fixtures were torn from the walls. Aged water pipes groaned as they flexed and cracked before exploding. Glass and debris littered the floor. I smelled explosives, and the whole building crumbled and shook.

Prisoners pounded frantically on their cell doors. "Let us out! Get us out of here!" they yelled. But there was no one to hear their desperate cries. We had been abandoned by the guards, who had fled to an underground bunker, leaving us to die.

A third bomb had hit, so a fourth was on its way. Crouching on all fours in the middle of my cell, I waited under my blankets. My cell was at least three stories up. The damaged floor was so mobile and disintegrated that I figured when the last bomb came in the floor would collapse under me. "If it's going down, I'll ride that sucker down as far as I can. This is it. It will hit any second." I waited a minute. Then another minute. The cell block was in pandemonium. Prisoners yelled out names. "Is anybody out of their cell?" someone shouted.

I waited, scarcely breathing. Had they recalled the fourth bomb?

An aircraft screamed overhead.

"One more, incoming!" someone yelled from across the corridor. "Stand by, stand by!"

I braced myself for the final attack. Tile and plaster showered over me. My pulse pounded loudly between my ears but I could still hear the eerie *clack, clack* . . . clack, clack of the bomb's fins as they made their final directional corrections. The 2,000-pound bomb was like a huge monster turning its head toward its prey as it followed a laser beam to the target. It would explode on top of us, destroying the building and everyone beneath it. I waited for the explosion.

For weeks I'd had no control over whether I would live or die. I'd only had control over my decisions. Because of them, I had expected my life to end many times. Now, in the ultimate irony, I was about to die not at the hands of the Iraqis but at the wrong end of a Coalition bomb.

I waited. This was my last minute, my last second. I thought I'd be terrified facing life's end. Instead I felt an unusual calm, a deep sense of satisfaction. I had done the best that I could.

Oceanside, California
February 24, 1991

Each day we waited anxiously for news as rumors that pilots had been rescued sparked, then faded, along with our hopes. On Sunday morning,
February 24, the ground war began. "Our strategy in going after this army
is very simple," Chairman of the Joint Chiefs of Staff General Colin Powell
had told the American people. "First we are going to cut it off, and then we
are going to *kill* it." His blunt message was chilling. My stomach churned
with mixed emotions. Yes, kill the bad guys—but not Cliff! How could I
root for the devastation of Iraq's military power when Cliff might be held at
a site the allies intended to destroy?

In a fiery speech hours after the start of what he called "the mother of all
battles," Saddam Hussein reissued his orders on Baghdad radio: "Fight them
and show no mercy toward them." Between patriotic songs, Baghdad radio
broadcast a grim message for Coalition forces: "By God, we will send you
back to your kinfolk as lifeless corpses. Your deaths will be by our hands."

Baghdad had endured five weeks of aerial bombardment. Disease was
spreading there because of lack of water, supplies, and medicine. With each
day, every person in Iraq had less chance of survival. My little support group
silently wondered: Is Cliff still alive? But on the surface we maintained a positive attitude. People around me deliberately said, "*When* Cliff comes
back..."

I coped by maintaining my daily routine: rising at six, starting two batches
of the bread requested by the previous day's letter-writing campaign work
crew. Then I wrote personal messages on "Dear Friends" letters, and thank-
you notes, and made calls to the East Coast. The day's crew of volunteers
arrived at 8:30 to a house filled with the aroma of steaming coffee and fresh-
baked bread or cinnamon rolls. I grew closer to this supportive group of
people more quickly than under ordinary circumstances. Their companionship and laughter bolstered me.

My sister called every morning to get the latest news, then relayed the
information to the Seattle phone network. Bonnie had established a Seattle
branch of the Liberty Alliance, and had held several meetings with its twenty
members to plan their letter-writing campaign. I was blessed to have such a
close network of family and friends.

Mary Pat wrote every day with humorous anecdotes. Along with the letters I got from friends and relatives, each week I received notes from former
coworkers, neighbors, and grade school through college classmates and
teachers. The nostalgia their names alone evoked felt like an appearance on
This Is Your Life.

Public support remained strong. Hundreds of individuals—along with corporations, churches, schools, and community organizations—offered their support to our letter-writing campaign. Thousands of people wrote letters to the Iraqi ambassador and spearheaded efforts in their communities by recruiting friends, neighbors, and business associates to attend meetings and write letters.

Mail from the public had steadily increased. Our volunteers could hardly keep up with requests for sample letters to the Iraqi ambassador. We'd sent out more than 1,000 "Dear Friends" letters, and I tried to write personal notes on at least half of them. Every day brought more letters of encouragement. Some of the letters—like the one from a child who wrote, "Dear Kernel Acree, Sorry you are in a rock"—made me laugh; others—like the one from a woman in Ontario, Canada—made me cry. "I have a timer in my pocket which goes off all day long," she wrote. "When it sounds I stop to talk with God and ask His care for Cliff and the others."

The postal service did a wonderful job of forwarding letters with incomplete addresses. One, written by a woman who saw my letter to Cliff in *USA Today*, was addressed simply: "To Mrs. Cindy Acree, wife of Marine Lt. Col. Clifford Acree—USA." It arrived all the way from Switzerland.

Wives who opened the growing stack of mail found not one negative letter. Many of these letter writers included their phone numbers, adding, "If there is *anything* I can do, just call." Thoughtful, generous people sent unique gifts—handmade flags, framed Bible verses, bracelets engraved with Cliff's name, and original poems. The acts of kindness of these people I didn't know took me away from my own problems.

Feeling indebted, I was obsessive about immediately writing thank-you notes. But Barbara Bush was even more prompt. Three days after our meeting in Arizona, I received a handwritten note from her: "I am very proud of you and the action you are taking for the MIAs/POWs. I know your darling husband would be proud of you...." Mrs. Bush and I corresponded several more times.

An employee of the California Youth Authority who worked at a Youth Training School in Chino told us of the letter-writing campaign she had initiated:

> The young men we have are 18 to 25 and in maximum security for committing some pretty wicked crimes, but not a day went by that my students didn't ask about Cliff.... One of my gang member murderers got your picture from the paper and made a frame and gave it to me.... if you understood the backgrounds of these kids, to hear them being really concerned about the good guys was very touching.... I made 500 copies of the letter and many inmates signed them and I sent them in.... It was great to have gang members that really hate each other, like Crips, Bloods, etc., all working together for one good cause.

At his own expense, former Vietnam POW Bill Stark sent letters to the 546 members of NamPOWs, the organization of former Vietnam POWs, asking for their support of our letter-writing campaign: "She has determined to form an organization comprised of POW families and other caring people dedicated to the proposition well-learned in the Vietnam War, that 'Silence on the POW issue is *not* golden!' . . . I am relying upon you guys to back me up—and so is Cliff Acree."

A fraternity at UCLA organized a letter-writing campaign among the other UCLA fraternities and sororities, and planted a tree in Cliff's and Guy's names as a permanent reminder of the students' concern for Desert Storm POWs and MIAs. As a living tribute, the mayor of Seattle dedicated a tree in the name of "Lieutenant Colonel Cliff Acree."

Classes of schoolchildren wrote letters to me, and some wrote letters to Cliff. One such class was Stephany's sixth grade. Her letter read: "My class is writing to you because my teacher felt it was the right thing to do. I cannot tell you how much proudness I have in my heart that you are risking your life for our country. . . Report cards come out this Wednesday and if there is any way, I will tell you how I did . . . I hope you get this letter soon because that means you have a doctor. . . Love always, Stephany."

My impromptu speech at the "Voices That Care" taping and other recruiting efforts continued to pay dividends. Producers of the *Joan Rivers Show* offered a seven-to-eight-minute spot. Cindy Costner and Dr. Jay Gordon, of ABC's *Home Show,* offered to recruit other Hollywood celebrities. Blair Underwood of *LA Law* called to offer his support. Husband and wife Michael Tucker and Jill Eikenberry from *LA Law* volunteered to be celebrity spokespersons. Actress Shanna Reed of *Major Dad* volunteered as a third spokesperson.

But my biggest ally by far had become Navy Chief Warrant Officer Michael Clark, the same person who earlier had pleaded with news organizations not to pursue POW and MIA families. A POW historian and advocate, he had founded the largest POW museum in the United States at Recruit Training Command's POW/MIA Museum in San Diego. "I have three goals," he had said when we met. "To make sure you aren't lied to. To keep you informed. And to get your husband home."

Michael had long been an advocate of POW/MIA families. He remembered the better treatment of captives that had resulted from a Vietnam-era letter-writing campaign. After the first POWs were captured, Michael had quickly drafted a letter to the Iraqi ambassador—surprisingly similar to the one I had created.

After talking on a San Diego radio program in early February, within three hours, he received 280 requests for his sample letter. An article in a San

Diego paper generated hundreds more. Within two weeks he had faxed and mailed nearly 4,000 copies of his letter.

"What's his angle?" I had wondered when I first read the newspaper article about Michael Clark speaking out for POWs. I had learned to be wary of any person or organization claiming to help the POWs. For the same reason, Michael had been wary of our organization when Jane DeHart first contacted him. He grilled her with questions: "What are the organization's goals? . . . Is there any money to be made?" She sounded so genuine that he agreed to attend one of our planning meetings—the first of many. He became impressed with our organization's goals and structure. "You've surrounded yourself with talented people," he said, surprised at what our nine committees had accomplished in such a short time.

I immediately trusted Michael, a soft-spoken man with deep brown eyes that radiated warmth and sincerity. With his handsome, tanned face, and empathetic manner, he could have played the trusted surgeon in an emergency room drama.

Experienced in the government's handling of POW issues, Michael cautioned me on what to expect in the weeks ahead. During a Liberty Alliance meeting the day the ground war began, he told me something I will never forget: "You will be the last to know." Michael pointed to Ken Barackman, sitting on the couch across from me. "*He* will find out the fate of your husband before you will," he said. He explained that the military has to verify all sources before it can release official word. With the tremendously long chain of command, the information appears on the news before the military officially notifies family members.

Somehow Michael had found a way to shortcut the chain. "Information is available if you go through the proper channels," he said.

In the weeks ahead he would repeatedly supply me with information—hours before I received it from official channels. Astonished at his accuracy, I would wonder, Who are his sources? Top-ranking military brass? Highly placed government officials? An informant in Baghdad?

He never could reveal the answer.

7

Miracles Can Happen

Baghdad Biltmore Prison
February 23, 1991

"One more! Incoming!" a prisoner screamed. Huddled under my blankets on all fours, I waited in terror for the fourth 2,000-pound bomb to pierce the prison. Tiles and bricks fell from the walls as the building continued to disintegrate from the previous three blasts. I prayed we would be spared.

A low shaking rumble was followed by a massive roar as the bomb hit the concrete building dead-on. The concussion threw me to the opposite side of my cell. With a loud crash, bricks, tiles, and mortar disintegrated; the lights went out. Blinded by the smoke, I closed my eyes. When I blinked them open, my room had literally gone crooked: The detonation had bent the frame of the steel door and caved in the window.

Much of the prison compound had been destroyed, but miraculously, not the section in which the POWs were being held. All survived without serious injury. Years later, I learned why.

At a military function in 1995, I met Brigadier General Buster Glosson. A white-haired, outspoken man, he had been one of the top planners of the lethal air assault against Iraq. Operating in offices at the headquarters of the Royal Saudi Air Force, he prepared the daily computerized tasking order of thousands of sorties flown against Iraq by an armada of more than 2,500 warplanes.

In his North Carolina drawl, General Glosson told me that the nighttime attack I survived had been intended to level the Biltmore. Five F-117 Stealth fighters had been scheduled to carry out the strike. Thanks to serendipity—or divine intervention—only two of the original flight of five made it to the target. Three were diverted to destroy an unscheduled, higher-priority target.

(One of these "went down in the chocks"—never took off—due to mechanical problems.) The two remaining fighters aimed for the headquarters of the complex, where Baath Party members were most likely housed. If all five aircraft had come in as planned, none of us would have survived.

Years later, while assigned to the faculty of the Marine Corps Command and Staff College in Quantico, I met one of the Air Force students in the class, an F-117 pilot, Major Paul Dolson. One day midway through the school year, I stopped to talk with him.

"By chance were you flying on the twenty-third of February?" I asked.

"Yes, I was," Paul answered, his expression quizzical.

"Was your target in Baghdad?"

"Yes."

"Do you remember your specific target that night?"

"The Baath Party regional intelligence headquarters."

"I was in the compound that night as a POW."

His eyes widened in surprise as he realized I had been in his target. Later that year, Major Dolson gave me a copy of the FLIR video from his cockpit that showed the attack on our prison—and another memento. He had saved the arming cable lanyards of every precision guided bomb he'd dropped during the war. The arming cable lanyard, a long cable, tethers the bomb to the aircraft. After the bomb drops a safe distance from the aircraft, the lanyard becomes tight, arming the bomb. After the bomb is released, the bomb bay doors close, and a short length of arming cable remains attached to the airplane. Major Dolson gave me a lanyard from one of the two bombs he dropped on our prison that night.

He also told me an interesting story. Before Desert Storm, his uncle suggested that he carry a dozen small American flags with him in the cockpit during the war. "Tuck them into your G suit before every combat mission."

"Why?" Major Dolson asked his uncle.

"After the war, you'll know why."

Major Dolson returned home from Desert Storm, and one by one, he gave the small flags away to relatives and friends—all but one, which he felt an unexplainable urge to keep.

"Why am I hanging on to this last flag?" he had often wondered. After our conversation, he knew why.

Major Dolson gave that last flag to me.

But now, on a February evening in Baghdad, I was reeling from the effects of the four 2,000-pound bombs that had hit our prison, the Baghdad Biltmore. *I'm alive!* Gasping for air, I felt half dead.

Too many times I should have died—ejecting from my burning aircraft, missing the lethal power lines, surviving interrogations and beatings. Being spared from the bombing was one more example of God's watching over me—it wasn't my time to go.

The night air was a swill of smoke and dirt, smelling of cordite, the bomb's explosive powder. After the deafening blast, it was eerily quiet. I groped for my tennis shoes. Before the bombing, I had been using them as a pillow. I hastily put them on and moved closer to the door. My old "neighbor" at the MP prison began talking rapidly and loudly.

"This is Flight Lieutenant John Peters—RAF!" he yelled. "Is Simon Burgess out there? . . . Is there a Lieutenant Colonel Acree here?"

I coughed hoarsely to clear debris from my throat. "Lieutenant Colonel Acree here! Has anybody seen Hunter?" No answer. "Has anybody seen Hunter?" From the end of the dark hall, a voice called, "Yes, Hunter is down here!"

Excitedly, prisoners yelled out their names and units. Our voices intermixed as everyone talked at once. We took roll call up and down the hall.

I heard John Peters talking to an American who spoke in a smooth, modulated voice. "You're John Peters?" he asked.

"Yes. Who are you?"

"I'm Bob Simon of CBS News."

"Hey, CBS News is here!" an American voice yelled. "Open the doors, get us out!"

"CBS News is filming here?" I thought. I was amazed they had gotten in so quickly. Why were they allowed into this place?

"Bob!" an American yelled. "Put my name on TV; make sure my wife knows I'm okay!"

"I can't," Simon answered. "I'm a prisoner just like you."

The American's response echoed everyone's reaction.

"Shit," he said.

Prisoners called out more names and greetings, and banged on their cell doors, trying to get out. Each time I yelled, I inhaled air dense with grit, debris, and cordite, then coughed up soot.

Another prisoner called out amid sounds of plaster and debris crumbling, "We're gonna make it. If we can survive something like this, we're gonna make it!"

But for the grace of God, I could have been so many grains of dust. Such had been the fate, I later learned, of most of the guards who fled to the bottom floor, which collapsed and buried them. The underground bunker for Baath Party members had been the target. The bunker was toast.

We continued talking to each other from our cells, getting everyone's names. I heard someone tell John Peters the ground war had not started yet.

"Bloody hell!" Peters replied. "What's taking them so long?"

Sirens began to blare. Boots crunched on broken glass in the corridor. Guards carrying flashlights were returning with army reinforcements armed with AK-47s and rifles. The sirens warning us that a bombing was expected soon ceased.

I heard keys turning in locks and shouts and curses in Arabic. Our damaged cell doors wouldn't open. Using sledgehammers and crowbars, the guards pried and beat open the doors, their anger mounting with each blow. Three of them pounded and pried the lock on my door until it broke. Then they pounded more to wedge the warped door open four or five inches. The thin beams of their flashlights pierced the grainy darkness, casting sinister shadows on their faces.

Two guards stood back two or three feet and then rammed the door with their shoulders. With several heave-ho pushes and loud grunts, they forced the door open enough to enter my cell and drag me out. "*Yallah, yallah*—Move, move," they demanded. I tried to carry a blanket out of the cell with me. A guard tore it from my grasp and threw it on the floor.

Three angry guards kicked and beat me, then dragged me into the hallway, littered with light fixtures, glass, tiles, and other debris. Other prisoners were yanked out of their cells, but a few were left trapped in them.

The sound of running water grew louder as guards dragged me down several ladder wells to the basement of the building, now cluttered with rubble and flooded with pools of water from ruptured lines. As I walked over broken glass and mortar, guards repeatedly hammered me, knocking me to the ground. With no laces in my shoes, the heels continually flopped up, and a jagged piece of glass flicked into one. The next time I stepped down, the glass pierced my heel. I ducked the blows and made my way through piles of rubble as best I could, while each step drove the piece of glass deeper into my foot.

As I walked through a pool of water mixed with gasoline from ruptured fuel tanks, the shoe came off. I reached into the puddle to search for it, but my fingers were still numb. The guards throttled me. In a daze of hunger, scared spitless, and weak, I struggled to keep my balance. Desperate to keep that shoe, I reached in again and found it. As we walked, the guards kept nervously looking up toward the sky, as if expecting another attack jet to come screaming overhead.

We climbed over a crumbled wall into the starlit night. Outside, I sucked in the cool, clear air. A row of white stone houses lined the silent city street, and beyond them lay a huge, populated city. I saw no people, no lights, only blackness everywhere, as if I had arrived at a deserted city on the moon. The only sound was the drone of the engine of a bus parked two blocks away.

I looked quickly back over my shoulder and in the dim light surveyed the damaged prison. Once a modern structure resembling a government or university building, the prison, like its prisoners, had badly deteriorated. Beneath the moonlit sky, the white building looked ghostly gray.

While one end of the massive structure remained intact, the other end was smashed as if a giant's hammer had broken it off. Truck-size chunks of concrete were strewn about as if unearthed by meteorites.

Moments before, the Biltmore had been an impregnable hunk of reinforced steel and concrete. Now it looked fragile. The four-bomb attack had taken less than five minutes. A fist smacked my face for surveying the damage. The boost my spirits had received from seeing the destruction of that prison was worth the punch.

I was handcuffed and dragged up the stairs of a bus, mashing my shin in the process. I worked my way toward the rear left exit door. This bus had no seats. In the darkness, I lowered myself to the floor and felt the head of someone lying to my right and groaning. I patted his head to remind him he wasn't alone. As we waited for the bus to leave, I tried to pull the shard of glass out of my heel; it broke.

Two guards took turns demanding the name, rank, and nationality of prisoners and asking whether they were pilots. Those answering yes when asked if they were pilots were slapped across the face. A guard roamed up and down the aisle of the bus, whacking prisoners with the butt of his AK-47, then sat down about an arm's length away from me. Guards covered us with blankets to keep us from seeing where we were going or each other.

"Where are they taking us now?" I worried. Not knowing our fate, I felt horribly insecure. Wherever we were going, I prayed we would make it there alive. Our bus was an easy moving target for allied forces ranging the night skies. I prayed we would make it to our destination safely.

God had answered my fervent prayers to survive the bombing. I was back in the world of the living. Now I had to worry about that damned ruthless interrogator who wanted to chop my body into pieces if I didn't cooperate.

It must have been the night for miracles. I never heard his voice again.

Abu Ghuraib Prison, outside Baghdad
February 24, 1991

At about two in the morning we arrived at a two-story civilian prison on the outskirts of Baghdad. Arabic voices shouted directions to the driver as he squeezed the bus through a narrow entryway.

The bus stopped and the blankets were lifted. We were in a mammoth complex, an old, ugly prison much like the one John Belushi is released from in *The Blues Brothers*—only darker and dirtier. The Coalition POWs later named this prison the "Joliet."

I later learned that this prison, Abu Ghuraib, was the largest in Iraq, housing more than 100,000 prisoners. Yet the huge yellow-gray facility wasn't prepared to receive 25 more. The guards crowded us into three old, narrow, filthy cells. I didn't know that Bob Simon and three other CBS newsmen had traveled with us and were taken to a different cell block. The guards crammed 11 POWs into one six-foot-by-ten-foot cell and 10 into the other.

After five weeks of solitary confinement, I was elated to see so many other aviators. But like the others, I remained quiet to avoid a beating. An Iraqi, someone of authority, entered our cell. He looked our group over as if surprised to see us, then retrieved a bag from his jacket. He reached into the bag and pulled out a handful of dates. We all thrust out our hands, and he put two dates in each hand. As he did, we each told him our nationality: "British"; "American." The sound of English-speaking voices was as invigorating as the fresh air outside the Biltmore. Knowing I was not alone in Baghdad boosted my morale as much as the dates boosted my blood sugar.

After the Iraqi left, we all began to speak—quietly at first, then louder as our conversation burst forth. Being able to talk to another human being, especially a fellow Marine, was a gift from God—second only to being reunited with Guy Hunter.

I felt a tap on my shoulder and turned around to see someone who looked like a wild man, a bushy-white-haired, definitely thinner, haggard, unshaven Guy Hunter. Bad as he looked, he was a sight for sore eyes. He reacted with surprise at my similar "wild man of Borneo" appearance of dark, matted hair and dirt-caked body.

Jeff Zaun came up to me. "Colonel Acree, you win the contest for the best-looking beard," he said. "You look like a ship's captain. You've got the nicest red beard."

All night long, the POWs sat on the dirty floor, which was covered with bird droppings for some reason, and debriefed each other. Accountability was our first priority: "Who do you know that has been captured? Who's alive?" We shared names and memorized them so Iraq would be held accountable for every last POW when it was time for repatriation.

A prisoner who had been captured much later in the war told Jeff Zaun, "You were on the cover of *Newsweek!*" We all chuckled. After weeks of little to eat, most of us looked like skeletons, with hollow cheeks and concave stomachs—except for Zaun, who had been fairly chunky when captured. When he pulled his shirt over his head, we all stared. "Wow, a stomach!" I thought, looking at his paunch.

"Did anybody check your private parts?" someone asked. "They did mine." "Mine, too." Everyone had undergone the "package check."

When Guy and I compared the stories we had told our interrogators, we discovered that our lies had been amazingly similar. Calmly and matter-of-factly, everyone swapped stories of their capture. We compared notes and discussed survival techniques and how to best resist interrogation.

I was relieved to hear that others had been filmed, too. Several admitted they had given information to our captors. When I heard that my video-taped interview and that of several others had been on national television, my spirits lifted. Cindy would have seen me and would at least know I had survived ejection and capture.

But I got an equally huge letdown when recently captured prisoners confirmed that the ground war I thought would be well under way had not even begun. I had expected it to have started at least a week or two earlier. Was something going wrong? Maybe the war wouldn't be over in the three to six months that everyone had predicted. Still, the news about the success of the air campaign and the comfort of being with other POWs gave me renewed hope of returning home alive.

We crowded on the bare cement, huddled shoulder to shoulder, legs intertwined, chattering like kids at a crowded slumber party. The energy we drew from one another rejuvenated our spirits and bolstered our courage to endure whatever might lie ahead. All night long I memorized prisoners' names, ranks, and branches of service.

In the gray light of the new day, sparrows chirped beyond the cell's one window. A guard brought us one bowl of rice-and-barley soup. We passed the bowl around our group, each taking a sip, then passed it around again. The guard returned with black tea, and we shared the strong, heavily sweetened drink with grateful delight. I couldn't remember enjoying any food more. If I had to remain in captivity, I hoped it would be here.

Later that morning, guards marched us out of the two-story, narrow building into a courtyard. We were ordered to put both hands on the shoulders of the person in front of us and to keep our heads down. We weren't blindfolded, and the sight of those yellow uniforms and the touch of another human being again lifted my spirits and eased my feeling of isolation.

They ordered us to sit facing a wall, ten feet apart. "Keep your heads down. Don't look up," guards commanded. I noticed pistols holstered on their belts. "They're going to shoot us right here in the courtyard? In daylight?" In the distance, a radio broadcast a forceful voice. I didn't know it was Saddam Hussein ordering "no mercy" for Coalition forces.

On that clear, cold day, we sat in the shade in the courtyard with no blankets, freezing. Dog tired, I slumped sideways to lower my head to the ground, but my neck hurt and I couldn't find a comfortable position without putting pressure on the swollen spots from the beatings I had received.

Early that evening, guards marched us back into the building, again with our hands on the shoulders of the prisoner in front. My neck was stiff from the cold. Keeping my movements small, I gave the person in front of me a gentle neck rub. Guards brought us to the second-floor cell block and put everyone into a solitary cell.

When I entered my cell in the old prison, I noticed what looked like a metal hook, high up on the left-side cinder block wall. "What is that thing doing there, and why am I in this cell?" I wondered, conjuring up images of gruesome torture. "This is where they truss up uncooperative guys while they're knocking the crap out of them." When the guards left, I worked the hook free, hoping to use it later to dig between the cinder blocks. I continued my search and noticed that most of the cracks between the cinder blocks were filled with easily removed green wax. I later found another useful tool hidden in a crack between two cinder blocks: half a razor blade.

That night, I lay against the door shivering. I was trying to get even a degree or two warmer than the cell, chilled by an outside window. I was too cold to fall asleep. Hours later I was given a thin blanket that provided enough warmth to stop my teeth from chattering.

The next morning I peered around the edges of the cardboard stuffed into my barred exterior window and saw an inner courtyard on the ground floor below my second-floor cell. At one time it had contained a volleyball court, but the two steel posts that had held the net were all that remained. Men in dirty, striped prisoner uniforms shuffled around the courtyard. Some washed clothing in plastic bowls or checked themselves for fleas and lice. Others picked dust balls off their blankets and slapped them to remove dirt. Some sat staring vacantly ahead, looking lost and hopeless. Guards walked among them, peering up into our cell block to ensure that we didn't talk or motion to the other prisoners.

The Biltmore prison had been deathly quiet. This packed-to-capacity prison was noisy, with footsteps in the corridors, male voices, and metal doors clanging. During my first trip to the bathroom, I glanced over the side of the three-foot walkway that ran alongside the upper cell block into the interior of the prison. We were on the second deck, which overlooked darkened lower-level cells packed with prisoners, including two civilian families—political prisoners, I guessed.

I devised a way to do reconnaissance of activity outside my cell: I walked clockwise in circles, slowing when I passed the door, making each circle larger than the last. On my last pass before stopping, I glanced to the right through the barred door and caught a guard, six to eight feet away, sneaking up on the cell, the look on his face that of someone hunting. He was checking to see if I was talking or using hand signals or other covert activity to communicate with other prisoners.

I discovered that the concrete mortar between the cinder blocks went up only five feet from the floor. Using the metal hook I had found, I enlarged a hole between the blocks on the wall separating my cell from the next. Scraping away minute amounts with each pass, I progressed as slowly as a mole burrowing into concrete.

On my third day at the Joliet, the cell door opened. In walked a burly, bearded, dark-skinned, dark-haired man wearing a POW uniform so ripped at the seams that portions of his legs were revealed. I had learned not to trust anyone outside the bars of my cell. I appraised this Iraqi-looking man wrapped in a blanket and carrying a bag of bread. "Here's my plant, an infiltrator, a spy," I thought.

The voice of the dark man sounded somehow familiar, much like that of a Kuwaiti pilot named Muhammed Mubarak, who, along with another Kuwaiti colonel, had briefed Marine aircrews at our base prior to Desert Storm with insights on the Iraqi military.

I asked my new cellmate specific questions and realized that now Muhammed Mubarak, or "Big Mo," as his friends called him, was a prisoner, too. He told me his Kuwaiti A-4 Skyhawk had been shot down on the first day of the war by Iraqi antiaircraft fire. The Iraqis had been hard on Mo; the legs of his snug-fitting uniform had nearly been torn off during beatings.

Mo and I talked about our experiences at the Joliet, including the day we were marched in from the courtyard and brought to individual prison cells. "The person behind me rubbed my shoulders," Mo said in his Arabic accent, his voice incredulous.

I smiled. "That was me."

Mo had lived in three different cells before being paired with me. He spent his first night at the Joliet with some Brits and an Italian Tornado pilot, Lieutenant Colonel Gianmarco Bellini. Suffering from amnesia after being shot down, Bellini had lost nearly three weeks of time. By the time he met Mo, he had regained his memory and worried about his copilot, Captain Maurizio Cocciolone, whom he hadn't seen since shortly after their capture.

On Mo's second day at the Joliet, the Iraqis split up his group of ten. When they ran out of individual cells they happened to pair him with Cocciolone. Mo was happy to tell Cocciolone that Bellini was alive and being held in the same prison.

On Mo's third day at the Joliet, he was brought to an empty cell. Later that day, the Iraqis brought in new prisoners—Egyptian laborers wearing farmers' clothing, some of the nearly three million Egyptians who had worked in Iraq before Egypt joined the Coalition. When the Gulf War began, Iraq rounded up hundreds of Egyptians. Iraqi guards filled Mo's cell with the newly captured Egyptians and brought him to mine.

Mo had brought with him an extra blanket made of goat's wool. Using the half razor blade I had found in my cell, we cut his blanket into serapes and insulation liners for our tennis shoes, working quickly while the guards ate lunch. We donned our serapes under our shirts so they wouldn't know we had destroyed their blanket. I collected threads from my blanket to make shoelaces, and for the first time in weeks, my feet were warm.

It was wonderful to have company after so many weeks alone. Because Mo spoke both Arabic and English, he was a lucrative source of information for the other POWs. The guards often played the radio: martial music—songs about Iraq and glorifying Saddam Hussein, Mo told me. When the radio broadcast information or the guards talked where he could hear, Mo passed on what he gleaned.

On February 24, the day after we arrived at the Joliet, Mo had clearly heard a radio broadcast of Saddam Hussein. "He called on the Iraqis to be brave and patriotic in fighting the imperialist enemy invading their homeland," Mo told me. Mo guessed that the broadcast—intended as a morale booster—had signaled the beginning of the ground war.

I passed Mo's information to other prisoners using the "tap code." First used by American POWs in the Korean War, the tap code provided the primary means of communication for POWs in Vietnam.

"You're a magician," Mo said as he watched me.

The tap code is based upon a 5x5 arrangement of the alphabet (the letter *C* is substituted for *K*) with the letters *A, B, C, D,* and *E* forming the top row.

A	B	C	D	E
F	G	H	I	J
L	M	N	O	P
Q	R	S	T	U
V	W	X	Y	Z

The first signal communicates the column of a letter; the second signal the row. For example, if I coughed or tapped *tap* (row one) . . . *tap, tap* (column two), that would indicate the letter *B.*

Transmitting information with the tap code is accurate but slow. I sent a message to the Italian POW, carefully counting the taps for each letter. "Aircraft?" I knocked. "Bread?" he answered.

Searching the same wall, Mo and I discovered a hole in the sixth block up that was plugged with a piece of blanket and green wax. I pushed on the plug and it fell through to the other side.

Guy Hunter was talking to his Italian roommate—Gianmarco Bellini—when he saw a small round object fall out of the cinder block wall. Through the hole a large eyeball peeked back—mine. We were neighbors. Mo relieved Bellini's fears about his comrade with news that Cocciolone was alive and well.

Searching on the opposite wall, nearly to the floor in the far corner, Mo found a three-inch opening in the concrete. Crouching, he shoved the metal hook into the hole and pushed it through to the other cell. He dragged it over the ground back and forth. Someone tugged on the other end. I had another Marine neighbor: Marine Harrier pilot Captain Craig Berryman. Eventually all the prisoners poked holes from cell to cell, creating a communications line. It was great to communicate in any way possible, and our morale strengthened because of it.

Unlike the Biltmore's single afternoon meal, here we were fed two times a day. That afternoon a guard came to our cell. "Would you like soup or tea?"

Silly question, I thought. How could anyone on a starvation diet pick black tea over much more nutritious soup? "Soup," I quickly answered.

"Tea," Mo said.

After eating my meal of soup and bread, I spread a few crumbs on the windowsill. A flock of birds dropped to my ledge in a flurry of wings, then chirped as they pecked at my offering. As they flew away, I got a wonderful taste of freedom and contact with the outside world.

One of our dilemmas was that we were left for long and unpredictable periods of time between trips to the bathroom. By midnight that night, Mo was desperate to relieve himself. "I learned my lesson," he told me. "When you're cold, don't drink tea at night."

"Use the plastic bag," I suggested. He immediately filled the empty bread bag. Now what? At midnight, on the second floor, we had no idea what was under our window—another row of cells, an entrance door, or a guard. Mo overturned the urine-filled bag out the window and we took our chances on where the contents would land. Fortunately, there was no response from below.

The next morning, I described a strange dream to Mo. In it, part of our group had been released. When it was our turn, Mo, Guy, I, and several others were taken out of our cells. After being handcuffed, we were loaded onto a bus. As we drove down a two-lane highway, south through Iraq and into Kuwait, I felt relieved to have both Guy and Mo safely with me. We neared the southern border of Kuwait. In the distance I saw rows and rows of barbed wire along the border separating us from Saudi Arabia.

One hundred yards before the border, the bus stopped and we got out. A long trench prevented us from crossing into Saudi Arabia. I walked closer and looked into the trench and saw that it was filled with something—sacks of garbage? It was a mass grave, filled with blood-splattered bodies, recently mowed down by a firing squad. We were to be marched to the pit and shot in full view of those on the other side of the border. I couldn't believe I'd made it through the ejection, the interrogations, and the bombing, only to get wasted 100 yards from freedom. The dream revealed my premonition that the end was near, but many obstacles stood between me and freedom.

"Tell me more about the Muslim religion," I asked Mo that morning. When we compared our spiritual beliefs, I realized we prayed to the same God and shared the same values. Only our rules were different.

Mo and I had both gone through the same soul-searching, wondering if being a POW was punishment for wrongdoings. Mo shared his conclusion: "Always we say, no matter what happens to you, good and bad, God wanted you to go through this, to learn from it." I agreed. The challenges of captivity had tested us and fostered a deeper belief in God and faith in ourselves.

I asked Mo how he felt about the Iraqi people.

"The Iraqis are a great civilization," he told me. "There are many nice, intelligent Iraqis. But during Saddam Hussein's regime things changed. There is a saying, 'Nations will follow their king's religion.'"

We compared our dreams and plans for what we would do after our release. We both wanted to spend more time with our families and further our education. We talked of someday attending a military school in the United States together.

As we talked, I noticed a strange prickling sensation on my chest. Unlike the annoying itching I experienced at the Biltmore, this was a constant knawing, crawling, almost pinching feeling. I walked toward the window for better light and lifted my clothing. Nothing was there. "What's going on?" I wondered. Then I felt the same crawling sensation in my hair and crotch. "I have lices, too," Mo told me. With the additional lice infested blankets at the Joliet, my infestation had multiplied from an occasional nuisance to a rampant invasion.

As we talked I kept rubbing my eyes. They burned and felt swollen and crusty.

"Mo, do my eyes look any different to you?"

When Mo described them to me, I realized that I had conjunctivitis. I was so preoccupied with survival, however, that those two annoyances didn't even register on my scale of concerns.

By our third day at the Joliet, an epidemic of dysentery began to spread among the POWs, caused by poor sanitation and the greasy, contaminated water we had been drinking. The dysentery had not yet affected me. That night Berryman awoke with agonizing intestinal cramps. I tried to comfort and encourage him. "We are going to get out of this alive. The worst is probably behind us. Other Marines are with you, and we'll get through this together."

"Your words enabled me to keep up my fight against our captors," he later told me.

When allied airmen rolled in that night, planting bombs on their targets, I felt comforted knowing they were doing their part to end the war and get us out. Throughout the night, jets screamed overhead, hammering Iraq, that night's air offensive dramatically greater than before. The building trembled as the bombs thundered closer to our prison, one far less solidly built than the Biltmore.

Carlsbad, California
February 26, 1991

On a rain-swept day, the POW/MIA Liberty Alliance held its first press conference to formally unveil the new organization and its goals. Once the ground war began, on February 24, everyone had been hopeful the war would end quickly.

But peace was not yet at hand. That morning President Bush had rejected Saddam's offer of a conditional withdrawal, calling it "an outrage." He said the Coalition would "continue to prosecute the war with undiminished intensity."

Regardless of the success of the ground offensive, the alliance's members voted to proceed with our press conference and letter-writing campaign. Even with a swift Coalition victory, the Iraqis might attempt to keep POWs even after the war was "won."

During the conference, I stayed hidden from the press. I listened from an adjoining hallway as Pat Antosh, dressed in a conservative civilian suit, addressed the gathering of reporters.

"Our initial goal . . . is to have a representative from the Red Cross or the Iraqi Red Crescent Society visit the POWs and obtain a complete listing," Pat said. So far there had been no contact with the thirteen members of the Coalition forces identified as POWs, and another twenty-nine allied troops were listed as missing in action.

Our press conference received good news coverage locally and nationwide. Press packets included pictures and statements from Jill Eikenberry, Michael Tucker, and Shanna Reed.

I remembered Michael Clark's advice about the press. "You need the press," he had told me. "But *you* run *them*. Rather than react, deliver prepared statements every time there is a development. Pacify them, or they'll stay here waiting."

Taking his advice, I issued a press statement:

> I feel encouraged and optimistic by the news that the war is in its final stages and victory is near. I am also heartened by President Bush's commitment to keep the POW/MIA issue at the forefront of peace negotiations.
>
> As we know, the war is *not* over and Iraq has still shown no evidence of abiding by any of the Geneva Conventions . . . [and given] no reassurances or information about our loved ones to families of prisoners and those missing in action. I am hopeful the world community will continue to put pressure on Iraq regarding the POW/MIA issue.

As the ground war continued, enemy troops surrendered in such mass quantities they couldn't be counted. Shell-shocked Iraqi troops even surrendered to Western journalists. *Time* magazine reported of the captured Iraqis:

"The POWs were starved, thirsty, often sick. Many had been terrorized by their own commanders, who used roving execution squads to shoot or hang troopers suspected of wanting to desert." Allied forces eventually captured more than 80,000 Iraqis.

Publicity for the alliance and its letter-writing campaign continued. Pat Antosh and Michael Clark appeared on a locally broadcast edition of the Michael Jackson radio program. I met with former president Ronald Reagan when he visited Camp Pendleton to address military families. After our private meeting, I slipped unobtrusively into the back of the crowded auditorium with Don Beaver to watch Mr. Reagan's speech. I thought I had attended incognito, but three days later, my picture appeared in the *Los Angeles Times*.

On the afternoon of February 27, General Schwarzkopf gave his now-famous "mother of all briefings." "When the decision makers come to the decision that there should be a cease-fire," he said, "nobody will be happier than me."

That night, President Bush announced that all U.S. and Coalition forces would "suspend offensive combat operations, to take effect on February 28 at eight o'clock in the morning, Riyadh time—exactly one hundred hours since ground operations commenced and six weeks since the start of Operation Desert Storm. . . ." His declaration was not officially a cease-fire, but the halt to offensive combat operations had the same effect. "Foremost in my heart is the question of our prisoners of war," President Bush added.

Journal entry:

> I'm trying not to get my hopes up too high or too soon. We have to wait a little longer to know Cliff is safe. Many families need to know if their loved ones are POWs or were KIA. I feel so sorry for them. The phone is ringing off the hook with reporters. I'm letting the calls go on the answering machine. I must spend my time in the best way to help Cliff and that is to continue getting the word out to as many people as possible.

In a news conference, General Schwarzkopf reported that the ground war had proved so successful that Allied forces could have continued on into Baghdad. "We were one hundred and fifty miles from Baghdad, and there was nobody between us and Baghdad," he said. "If it had been our intention to take Iraq, to overrun the country, we could have done it unopposed for all intents and purposes."

I wish you would have! I imagined Special Forces commandos storming into a prison, pulling Cliff up from the floor, untying his hands, and leading him to freedom.

That same day, Iraq accepted all twelve UN conditions, including immediate release of all hostages and POWs. This positive step gave me a modicum of relief. Until that moment I had been calm, wary, and skeptical. With the end in sight, for a moment I allowed myself to imagine meeting Cliff when he came home.

The next day, Abdul Amir Al-Anbari at the UN said he wanted immediate repatriation of the POWs. *Maybe our letters to him helped.* But we had heard nothing about the status of any POWs. Newspapers reported on February 28, "The last time allied prisoners of war were seen by anyone other than their captors, they were being displayed on television, some of their faces bruised and all of their voices stilted as they recited Iraqi-scripted propaganda." Still, I felt heartened by President Bush's vow that morning: "We are going to get back our POWs, and we are going to do it fast." The president and the American people would not tolerate repeating the mistakes of handling American POWs in Vietnam, a nationally recognized tragedy.

The next day, I was in the garage with the door open. Out of the corner of my eye, I saw a neighbor approach—our "family spokesperson." He had come to deliver a message reminiscent of the movie *Poltergeist.*

"I wanted you to know they're coming back," he said, referring to the press. "They'll be here any time to interview me." I wanted to tell him what I thought of him, but remembering Aunt Ethel's advice—"Do the right thing last"—I kept my mouth shut. Besides, if I told him off, I might read about it in the papers in the morning.

Within the hour, the first press vehicles arrived. From that day on, many camped overnight. The reporters who slept inside their TV news vans hoped to be the first to record my reaction to the news of Cliff's release. Around the clock, a uniformed Oceanside policeman monitored them from a patrol car parked at the curb. The papers reported (accurately) that every morning I supplied the officers with warm, freshly baked bread.

Calls from the media started flooding in. Many newspeople were persistent and called daily. Especially competitive, the network morning talk shows pressed for a promise that they be "on the record" as the first to have requested an interview with Cliff and me.

I issued a statement: "As we know, the war is not over until Iraq has complied with all four of President Bush's requirements . . . painful as these past six weeks have been, I have the comfort of knowing my husband is a recognized prisoner of war. We must not forget the many MIA families who wait not knowing whether their loved ones still live. The apparent end of the war is not a signal for us to let down our guard. Your letters are more important than ever. . . ."

To get his immediate attention, hundreds of people—businesspeople, church groups, individuals—faxed letters to the Iraqi ambassador. I imagined his fax machine spitting out page after page.

On March 1, the Red Crescent Society, Iraq's equivalent of the Red Cross, claimed to have seen the POWs. I called the local Red Cross to confirm the report.

"They have *not* seen the POWs," a representative said emphatically. "Those reports are unconfirmed."

Cease-fire talks were delayed at least one more day. Communications between Iraq and the United States had to go through Moscow.

Our worries mounted. Weeks earlier, an Iraqi enemy POW (EPW) had claimed that two British POWs had been killed by their captors. On March 2, newspapers added credence to his claim, reporting: "A senior allied officer revealed intelligence reports indicating two British airmen were tortured and killed by their Iraqi captors in January. . . ."

On Sunday, March 3, headlines announced BAGHDAD LETS NEWSMEN GO BUT HOLDS ON TO POWs. The four haggard-looking members of the captured CBS news crew told of blindfolds, beatings, and solitary confinement. Veteran war correspondent Bob Simon said, "I want to express the hope, the fervent hope, and my prayers that people we met along the way—Americans, British, Kuwaitis—will be following my footsteps within hours." That night, bearded and gaunt, he appeared on *60 Minutes.* Simon said he would have killed his captors if he'd had the chance "and would have felt no more remorse than I did when I stamped out the cockroaches in my cell."

That same day at a meeting tent in the desert of southern Iraq, General Schwarzkopf met with Iraqi Lieutenant General Ahmad to discuss the formal cease-fire agreement. His first request was to allow the ICRC immediate access to the POWs held by Iraq. After two hours of talks, the Iraqis agreed to all the allied demands, including information about persons listed as MIA and the "immediate" exchange of POWs.

"There was only one moment at which Ahmad showed any emotion," General Schwarzkopf recalls in his memoir, *It Doesn't Take a Hero.*

> He [Ahmad] presented an accounting of Coalition prisoners of war held by Iraq. "We have forty-one in all," he said. I made notes as he read them off: 17 Americans, 2 Italians, 12 British, 1 Kuwaiti, 9 Saudis. This left a number of people unaccounted for, and I quickly brought out our list of MIAs, but he stopped me. "And we would like to have the numbers of the POWs on our side as well."
>
> "As of last night, sixty thousand," I replied. "Or sixty thousand plus, because it is difficult to count them completely." His face went completely pale: he had had no concept of the magnitude of their defeat.

That same day Iraqi Ambassador Abdul Amir Al-Anbari claimed that ten POWs had already been released. I had heard nothing. Representatives at the International Committee of the Red Cross (ICRC) Headquarters in Geneva and at the Pentagon said the reports were unconfirmed. I kept myself involved in the alliance's work. It had been a lifesaver for me—and, I hoped, a lifesaver for Cliff.

Abu Ghuraib Prison, Baghdad
February 28, 1991

The allied bombing continued until dawn. When the sun rose, the barrage was over, the attack aircraft gone. A fierce wind was blowing, and somewhere a radio played martial music. Soon Iraqis in distant streets began firing their antiaircraft artillery guns into the sky. One or two hundred yards away, within the compound, I heard small arms fire. Tremendous bursts from their weaponry continued intermittently all morning. "What's going on?" I wondered as I listened to what sounded like a gun battle. My mind raced through many possibilities.

Throughout the day, the sporadic barrage continued. A guard told one prisoner the Iraqis were celebrating their "victorious victory." Mo suspected a cease-fire or the end of the war. Neither of us knew that, after seven months of occupation, Kuwait had been liberated.

Iraq had begun a massive, disorganized retreat from Kuwait. Panicked, demoralized Iraqi soldiers were fleeing from Kuwait to the Iraqi city of Basra on a four-lane highway. Reporters began calling it the Highway of Death as it grew littered with vehicles destroyed by allied forces. According to Secretary of Defense Dick Cheney, the mother of all battles had turned into the mother of all retreats.

In Kuwait City, allied forces discovered an auditorium filled with an enormous sand-table map. The twenty-by-thirty-foot model of Kuwait displayed guns pointed seaward, toward where four sweeping arrows marked the locations where the Iraqis had anticipated the feared Marine amphibious landing.

Around midday an Iraqi voice came over the radio. Mo had trouble making out the words of the distant radio broadcast. We didn't know it was Saddam saying Iraq had won an enormous victory over the entire world, especially the United States. Though he had ordered his troops to withdraw from Kuwait, he said, Iraq had wiped the allies' noses in the dirt.

That night, the power went out in our prison. Even without any lights, the interior of this prison contained more light than the Biltmore. The guards built a bonfire on the ground floor—for warmth, I'm sure, as well as light. As I watched the flickering fingers of light dancing over the dark walls, I realized that the constant din of the nightly allied air strikes was absent.

The next morning, an unwelcome sight appeared at my door: the Baath Party crew who had taken morning muster at the Biltmore. *Damn! They've finally caught up with us.* So they weren't killed during the Biltmore bombing.

Working their way down the row of cells, the three men recorded into their ledger detailed information on each prisoner.

That afternoon I was allowed to use the bathroom. While I was there I washed my filthy socks. Walking back from the vile, urine-stained bathroom, I was stopped by the tallest Iraqi I'd ever seen. Dressed in a tweed sport coat and tie, the six-foot-seven-inch, 250-pound giant towered over me. With a strange look in his eyes, he brought one huge hand down as if to strike me. I flinched, expecting another beating. His hand landed firmly on my shoulder.

"Do you have children?"

"Yes," I said warily, "I have a daughter."

"Would you like to see her again?"

"Yes. Of course." I hoped this wasn't another threat against my family.

"It won't be long. You will go home in three days."

"I hope you're right." I could never trust anything an Iraqi told me.

On March 1, I heard rustling, cell doors opening then slamming shut, and footsteps departing. A group of prisoners was being led away. Were Guy and Marco among them? We tapped on their wall. No response. We looked through the hole. They were gone.

"Is this good or bad? Good for them, bad for us?" I wondered uncertainly. "What does this mean?" My mind was constantly running through scenarios. We thought we'd be next, then nothing.

Craig Berryman and his cellmate had been left behind, too. All we could do was wait our turn. We waited. And waited. Night fell, and still no one had come for us.

When a guard came with our evening meal, Mo asked, "If they're gone, can we have their blankets?" The guard brought us the other prisoners' bowl and their two dirty, lice-infested blankets. We used them to make a bed in the middle of the cell. That night, sleeping back-to-back with Mo, I experienced the strange sensation that my bruised hips, knees, and spine were being cushioned from the hard concrete. Mo's added body heat and companionship warmed my body and soul.

I didn't know that seven of us, those in the last four cells, had been left behind. The order in which we would eventually be released would have nothing to do with name, rank, nationality, or day of shootdown. The guards transporting us had room for only ten prisoners in their vehicle. The rest of us had to wait.

At dusk on March 2, we remaining POWs were taken out of our cells, then blindfolded and handcuffed, this time with the more modern, one-time-use plastic handcuffs. We were led outside the prison facility to a large vehicle that had no steps.

I backed into the opening of the vehicle, felt for the seat, then rolled onto it, leaning on my side as the next person moved in beside me. I didn't know if

Mo was being transported with me. When the bus stopped, our names were called and one by one we were led off. We were hit and kicked as we moved to our new destination. Whenever the Iraqis moved us, I braced myself for my situation to get worse.

My blindfold was removed; I was in a courtyard with Mo and about five other prisoners. I lifted my eyes. Gray coils of barbed wire crisscrossed overhead. We were led into an adjacent house that was smaller than the typical American single-family home. Guards marched the seven of us into the building. We moved down a progressively darker hallway that turned at a right angle and led to the doorway of a small room. With the door of the ten-foot-by-ten-foot room open, there was just enough light curving down the hall from the entryway to see. We later named this room "the Bat Cave."

Near the floor, a pipe ran the perimeter of the room, six inches above the floor and away from the wall. I had visions of being chained to that pipe for unknown atrocities to follow. The steel door closed, and we were engulfed in darkness.

We sat on the damp floor of the windowless room with no lights. Though he didn't mention his fears to us, Mo knew this was an Iraqi hideaway house used as a secretive jail. "The Iraqis are very good at making people disappear," he explained to me years later, when 623 abducted Kuwaiti citizens remained missing in Iraq. "Looking in Iraq for prisoners, no one can find them; no one suspects they would be in a neighborhood like this."

A few minutes later, the door opened and dim light stabbed the darkness. A guard arrived carrying food. As senior officer of our small group, I set guidelines for sharing food equally, but some POWs didn't want their fair share. Unbelievable, I thought, devouring bread, cream cheese, and dates. Sitting in the darkness, I ate ravenously, not knowing my turn was coming.

After eating, I made sure we knew the name of everyone in the room, and we took stock of each person's injuries. Bob Wetzel and Maurizio Cocciolone seemed the worst off. They had sustained broken bones in their shoulders and arms during ejection.

The door opened again and a short, overweight Iraqi colonel greeted our group. He had to open three doors along the angled hallway to get to us. I was sitting closest to him when he entered the room with his two henchmen. The balding commander with long gray sideburns spoke to Mo in Arabic, pointing to us. Mo listened intently. "Don't dare change any words that you interpret from Arabic to English. I will know," the colonel had warned Mo.

Mo nodded, then turned to me. "What is your nationality?" he reluctantly translated.

"American," I answered. Before the colonel could ask the next question, I added, "I am a United States Marine."

"Are you a pilot?" Mo asked, translating.

"Yes."

The colonel spat on me, then shouted in Arabic. Mo summarized in minimal words: "Tell him he is a dog. A filthy dog." My anger burned.

Then Mo translated more of the colonel's words: "George Bush is a donkey and dumb, a bastard. Tell him to repeat."

I shook my head.

"Just say it," Mo urged me. "Say something. . . . If you don't, he'll keep on asking."

I had never said anything bad about George Bush—not anytime in my captivity—and I wasn't going to start there. I just gritted my teeth as he waited.

Finally the colonel focused his attention on another issue.

"Ask them if there are too many in this room," he ordered Mo.

"No," Mo quickly answered. "We are happy together."

"Don't answer for them," the colonel said. "You ask *them*."

We agreed with Mo; staying together and being able to talk were wonderful treats. Mo pleaded with the colonel to give us enough light so we could see to eat, and to allow a doctor to visit.

The colonel answered in a forceful one-way conversation. Mo translated: "You people came here to destroy our country and our nation. . . . By the generosity of the peace-loving people of Iraq, we have decided you should have better treatment. But you do not deserve such improved treatment because you are war criminals."

The colonel left us in our dark, damp, musty Bat Cave.

More food came later that day—bread, cheese, tomatoes, lettuce leaves, boiled eggs, and dates—a ten-course meal to us, and an obvious last-ditch attempt to fatten us up was obvious. Mo was the server. In total darkness, he called each person's name, then held out the food while the person groped for his hand.

Living in continual blackness, with no day or night, distorted our sense of the passage of time. We sat in the dark, each in his own spot, unable to see each other or anything in the room. After we had been in the Bat Cave nearly a day, someone in our group called out, "Hey! I found a toilet!" He directed us to its concealed location. "Feel the wall; come around the corner. It's like a closet with a hole in the center. Make sure you don't step in it."

When it was my turn to use the inground toilet, I braced myself on the wall behind it and discovered a plumbing tank, five feet above the floor. I reached into my pocket for a couple pieces of stale bread I had carried with me from the Joliet. I left them on top of the tank. If they stopped feeding us again, I wanted a reserve stash.

But their efforts to treat us better continued. A guard arrived later that day. "Do you need anything?" he asked.

Mo answered in Arabic, "The Americans like *your* dates very much."

The guard left and returned with more plump, rich dates. "How about tea?" he asked.

"They like your tea, too," Mo answered. Soon we had more tea.

Our captors were feeding us better, but by now my appetite had vanished. I didn't want to eat; I wanted to roll over and die. I was racked with violent intestinal cramps from my stomach to my rectum. I staggered to our newly found head every thirty to sixty minutes. The pain made me scream aloud. Weak from cumulative hunger, thirst, and fatigue, each trip depleted my strength. I nearly blacked out each time.

By the fourth or fifth trip, I was groaning and bellowing, reeling over the toilet, semiconscious. Until that day, I hadn't had a bowel movement in five weeks. Now it felt like someone was repeatedly squeezing out my intestines. Dale Storr, a tall, lanky, Air Force A-10 pilot, helped me back to my spot and got me to lie down. I closed my eyes, on the verge of slipping into unconsciousness.

Sometime later a doctor visited our group—the first medical attention any of us had received in a month. When I told the doctor, who spoke fluent English, about my cramping and uncontrollable diarrhea, he gave me some pills. "I would give you more pills," he said. "But our country is out of medicine. Our water here is bad because you pilots have bombed our water supply. There are many sick people in Iraq."

Though weak and shivery, I tried to make conversation. "Where were you trained as a doctor?"

"The United States."

"Where in the United States?"

"Michigan."

He refused to talk anymore after that.

Late that night, a guard came to the door and called for Bob Wetzel and Maurizio Cocciolone. After they were led away, Mo asked the guard where they had been taken. "Somewhere to be taken care of," he answered. "You could be next. It could be tonight."

Twenty-four hours later, late on March 4 or in the wee hours of March 5, the door of the Bat Cave opened. We remaining five POWs were allowed into the hallway and saw the Iraqi colonel who had spit on me. In Arabic the Iraqi said to Mo, "I *hate* to see you leave." The colonel's tone of voice expressed his desire to keep us and torture us.

Blindfolded and handcuffed, we were led out of the building, then crawled into another vehicle. After a twenty-to-thirty-minute drive we arrived at a "halfway house," a single-story structure that might have once been an airport hangar. Other prisoners had been brought there a couple of days earlier. My damp, dark, closet-size cell was so small I could stand on one side and touch the opposite wall.

Exhausted, dehydrated, plagued with horrible stomach cramps and diarrhea, and in constant pain from the piece of glass that was still embedded in my foot, I felt frustrated and near my limit. My turbo-propelled bowels needed to move every hour.

Doubled over in pain, I knocked on the solid door of my cramped, drafty cell. Through the small barred window I tried to communicate with the two young guards.

"Shh . . . shh . . . No speak," they said. I used hand motions, clutching my gut. "Mo!" I screamed at the top of my lungs. "Tell them I have to go to the WC *right NOW!*"

They told Mo to mind his own business. I moaned and groaned in agony. Finally they let me limp to the toilet. I didn't even have a chance to yank my pants down before my bowels violently let loose. About every hour throughout the night I suffered brutal attacks of diarrhea.

After sunrise, in my solitary cell at the halfway house, I was brought a breakfast of bread, fruit, and hot tea. I didn't eat or drink a thing; I still couldn't tolerate food.

Early that morning, a civilian who looked to be in his twenties came into my cell. "Come with me," he instructed. Barely steady on my feet, I followed him out of the cell. He motioned down the hall, where, next to a chair, a table held a small bucket of water, a bar of soap, and a shaving razor.

I held up my palms. "I'll keep. No shave. No problem." The civilian took me back to my cell. Fifteen minutes later, an older guard, possibly in his fifties, about six-foot-four and 220 pounds, arrived. He beckoned me with his finger as if saying, "You're not getting away with that."

He led me down the hallway to the same chair and table. I feared I might be in for another television interview. "Wash, wash, swim, swim," a guard said, pointing at a bowl of cold, gray water loaded with whiskers. Another guard shaved my face with a dull razor. They left my reddish mustache.

Another guard threw me a new yellow PW uniform. I changed out of my grimy, grayed uniform into the bright, spotlessly clean one. Looking back, I wished I'd thought of wearing my new uniform over the old one—not only for warmth but so I could remove the new one and return looking as filthy as I had in captivity. On the way back to my cell, I saw Mo being brought in. I winked in silent greeting.

Mo later told me that when the Iraqis shaved him, he asked for a new uniform; his torn, ragged pants were almost falling off his body. "No, you're okay," they told him. He was returned to the cell he shared with ten POWs. His cellmates had spent their weeks of captivity at the MP prison: nine Saudi Arabian prisoners of war and Army Specialist Melissa Rathbun-Nealy, the first U.S. servicewoman since World War II to be reported missing in action.

The nine Saudis didn't trust Mo any more than I had when he walked into their cell at the halfway house. As I had, they feared that the dark-haired, dark-skinned prisoner in the torn uniform was an Iraqi spy. They wouldn't talk to or even get near Mo.

After breakfast, my cell door burst open. A guard stood in the doorway with a clipboard in his hand. "Are you Acree?"

"Yes."

"Wait here. You are going home now."

I readied myself for release by gathering my shoes, bread, and blanket. As ordered, I filed out of the building with my hands on the shoulders of the prisoner in front of me. I was on my way to freedom, but I felt no surge of joy, no elation, no excitement. I was still in Baghdad, a long way from the border and safety. I saw no one but Iraqi guards. Why should I believe their story?

As we approached the doorway, someone sprayed our lice-infested bodies with cheap cologne. I blinked in the dazzle of bright sunlight. A huge portrait of Saddam Hussein towered over us. I guessed one of my wishes hadn't come true.

8

From Darkness to Light

Oceanside, California
Sunday, March 3, 1991

Media representatives continued to press for an on-camera interview about my hopes for Cliff's release. Instead I released another statement:

> We have not heard any official word about Cliff's condition or confirmation of his release. Our last knowledge about Cliff was his original appearance on CNN in January. It is too early to speculate until we know more. I am anxiously awaiting news and remain grateful for the support of family, friends, and the Marine Corps. In this time of uncertainty they continue to provide me with encouragement and support.

Aunt Ethel was due to fly home, but I had begged her to stay until we knew Cliff was safe. Even Cami had become attached to Ethel's companionship and affection. Before her arrival, Cami had slept outside my second-floor bedroom, guarding the house from her high vantage point. Now that Aunt Ethel bunked in the downstairs guest bedroom, Cami curled guardlike on the landing, halfway between her two responsibilities.

Sunday afternoon, Michael Clark called. He knew I was going crazy with worry and anticipation. The Red Cross was still being denied access to POWs or even a list of their names. "Don't get too excited yet," he said. "But there has been movement." Sources had told him Cliff had been moved to a halfway house and his release was imminent.

That night I hosted another alliance meeting at my home. As we munched on pizza, our mood was cautiously optimistic. The media reported that a group of ten POWs was to be repatriated on Monday. We all predicted Cliff would be in that first group. It only made sense. Whether the

216

Iraqis released the POWs according to length of captivity, rank, or even alphabetically, Cliff should be among the first released. We laughed about whether he would walk out with long hair and a beard. My tension subsided a little. But I still didn't know if he was alive. Until I saw his face I couldn't get excited.

The following morning, Pat Antosh was scheduled to appear live on ABC's *Home Show.* I had planned to accompany her, but with Cliff's release seeming imminent, we decided I should stay home and wait for word.

Monday morning, I got up at 5:30 and turned on CNN. The next broadcast showed POWs in yellow uniforms boarding a bus. The newscaster said Iraq had released six American POWs and four others from Britain and Italy. Quickly, I scanned the screen for Cliff's face. One of the men—tall and very thin, with a mustache—looked similar to Cliff but yet not like him. Had Cliff changed so much that I didn't recognize him? I looked closer. No, it couldn't be him.

A minute later the phone rang. It was Pat Antosh. "It's not him," were her first words. Up early for her nine o'clock television appearance in Los Angeles, she had already watched the broadcast twice. Cliff was nowhere among the ten. My heart sank—but since I'd never allowed myself to believe he would be among the ten, it sank only halfway. I had faith in Cliff and in President Bush's pledge. Later that day, General Colin Powell reaffirmed that pledge, saying, "For those American families who still anxiously await word of a loved one missing in action or held prisoner, I make this pledge: This war won't be over until we get a full and immediate accounting of *all* POWs and MIAs."

That morning I spoke anonymously on the *Home Show* during Pat's segment.

"We will not use your name," the host assured me. "Is this cause for euphoria?" she asked.

"We're cautiously optimistic," I answered over the phone. "We're continuing to keep pressure on Iraq until everyone is repatriated."

Tension grew. I kept busy baking bread, writing letters to schoolchildren and their teachers, and sending out many notes of thanks. Leigh Berryman called that night. She demonstrated her inner strength and bravery when she tried to cheer me. "You're logical about these things the way I am," she said. "They released one black, one woman, and the Brits because it was said they had been killed. You said your husband was skinny anyway. They're probably keeping him to fatten him up."

I was amazed that she was considering my situation so closely when hers was so tenuous. The next few days would be torture while she waited to hear if Craig was among those released. She had already waited thirty-seven days since her husband was presumed killed in action. She was convinced he was coming home.

I wished I could tell her she was right. I kept remembering the nickname of the Harrier: "The Widowmaker." Neither of us would have imagined that Cliff had been comforting her husband in prison, both of them very much alive.

Michael Clark called that afternoon. Before bed, I listened—one more time—to the cryptic answering machine message he had left. "Keep your periscope level," Michael's calm voice said. "Have a good night's sleep, and tomorrow you should be a happy woman."

Tuesday morning, I got up at 4:30 and turned on CNN. "Baghdad Radio has announced Iraq has released all POWS," the announcer said. They reran footage of the previous night's press conference with the first group of POWs released. I knew not to put a lot of stock into anything Baghdad Radio reported. It had also announced that Iraq won the war. I wrote in my journal:

> Tuesday, March 5, 1991—4:45 am: This day is the embodiment of "so close but yet so far." I still don't want to set myself up for a fall. I want to hear that Cliff is alive and well. Then I can wait as long as necessary to see him. I'm getting pretty good at waiting now. The past few days so many things have happened, yet things seem to move so slowly. . . .

At 6:30 A.M. the phone rang. Knowing I needed my sleep, Michael Clark had waited four hours to call me. He told me he had received "positive information" about Cliff early that morning. He hinted that he knew Cliff had been released, but didn't say it directly. I read between the lines, knowing he didn't want to usurp official Marine Corps channels. He didn't tell me he knew of a problem with Guy Hunter.

By late morning, hyper with worry and anticipation, I needed to burn off energy. But reporters were camped out in vehicles on the street, waiting for me to emerge. Once again, my neighbor Mary helped me elude the press. Lugging my gym bag, I scaled the three fences between our houses, not knowing I had a spectator behind venetian blinds. Mary smuggled me out past the news vehicles in her car, and at the agreed-upon time retrieved me from the gym. Back over the fences I went.

I threw my gym bag over the last fence, then jumped down into our backyard, my shoes sinking into the moist dirt. A police officer greeted me. "Very athletic, Mrs. Acree," he said, grinning. A few days later a San Diego newspaper revealed that our "family spokesperson" had called and offered it a picture taken of me through his blinds. They had turned down his offer.

I walked in the door and saw Rosana. "Anything new on the news?"

"As a matter of fact, there is," she said coyly.

Within minutes Don Beaver called. Rosana and Debbie listened, their faces full of anticipation. Military officials had released the last list of freed POWs. "Cliff's name is on the list," Don said.

"Oh!" I gasped. "Was Craig Berryman's name on the list?"

I couldn't believe his words: "Berryman's name is on the list." He paused. "Guy Hunter's is not."

I gripped the phone, a lump in my throat. Guy had been displayed on television with Cliff, but that had been five weeks and thousands of allied bombs ago. How could I feel relieved, knowing something had happened to Guy? Poor Mary had been so certain he would return. She had already packed her bags, ready to go immediately to Wiesbaden, Germany, when Guy was freed.

"I'm checking to make sure it wasn't a mistake," Don said. "Intelligence sources have not indicated there have been any problems."

I could hardly talk.

"All the Red Crescent provided was a list. The ICRC has not yet had access," Don pointed out. "They're looking into a room with a bunch of scraggly-faced guys with bad haircuts. They don't know who is there."

"Oh . . . I feel so terrible for Mary," I lamented.

"Hey now, don't you feel guilty. Let's keep our fingers crossed."

I put down the phone and looked at my friends, my expression deadpan. I couldn't let go. Not if Cliff was safe and Guy was not.

Debbie touched my arm. "It's okay, Cindy. You can get excited now." She and Rosana screamed in unison, then locked me in a group hug.

We waited for word about Guy. Two hundred and ninety-four Iraqi POWs (EPWs), out of tens of thousands, were to be picked up in Saudi Arabia and flown to Baghdad. Thirty-five allied POWs would be brought out on the return flight. Would Guy get off that plane? It was unsettling. We wondered whether the Iraqis had done something barbaric at the last minute.

Later that afternoon, Michael Clark called. His sources told him Guy was alive; the Iraqis had not accurately reported the names. "And don't believe stories on the news about POWs being delayed one week," he said. "They will be delayed in Baghdad, but only for one day." A rare rainstorm and high winds were buffeting the North Arabian Desert. Two hours later, as soon as he was notified, Don called me with the same report.

I hated the thought of Cliff's staying in Baghdad even one more hour. "Hurry, get him out of there!" I prayed.

With word that Cliff had been released, the crowd of media vehicles camped in front of our house grew exponentially. I stayed hidden from view. Reporters approached Pat, Ken Barackman, and Rosana when they visited.

"We're not popping champagne corks yet," Pat said in front of the cameras. "We're tempering our emotions until we actually see them."

Our friend Jane, now noticeably rounded with her seventh month of pregnancy, took the whining, agitated Cami for a walk around the neighborhood.

"How pathetic!" Jane exclaimed when she walked back through the door. A photographer had approached her as she waddled after Cami. "Look!" he said to his colleague. "There's Cindy Acree's dog!"

That night several friends in Seattle called, all laughing. They had seen the network broadcast of Cami charging excitedly down the street towing Jane behind her. Before long, I hoped, the media would report more exciting news about the Acree family than Cami's walk.

Somewhere in Baghdad, Republic of Iraq
March 5, 1991

"Is it over?" I shifted in my seat on the bus, too frightened to yield to feelings of elation. For the first time we had been moved during daylight hours with no blankets covering us and wearing no handcuffs. Five or ten minutes into the bus ride, someone removed my blindfold.

"Do not look out the windows," the guards had warned, motioning to the windows with curtains tightly drawn. We'd never been allowed such freedom, I realized. Riding in the cleaner, bigger bus, I felt the first stirring of hope. But it was too early to allow myself to rejoice, I knew. We were still vulnerable, our group of mostly Westerners, riding through the streets of Baghdad clad in bright yellow uniforms.

I sneaked a fast glance around me. Six rows of seats on either side of the aisle held two prisoners per seat. I risked looking behind me and was relieved to see Guy Hunter. I noticed a prisoner of small stature with long scraggly hair and bandaged arms. "Must be a Delta Force guy," I figured, knowing that special operations troops often didn't have military haircuts. When the prisoner spoke, I couldn't believe my ears. It was a woman, Army Major Rhonda Cornum, the second American woman POW. Cornum had been captured by the Iraqis one week earlier when the helicopter she was riding in crashed during a mission to rescue Air Force Captain Bill Andrews.

When the blue-and-white-striped bus arrived at the Nove-otel, a hotel in downtown Baghdad, several people boarded. "You are now in the custody of the International Committee of the Red Cross," one of them said. "We will take care of you. You are going home today."

My eyes darted nervously around me. On alert, I still couldn't relax. Downtown Baghdad was a long way from safety. Outside the hotel, camera crews, soldiers, and Iraqi civilians milled around. Many of those Iraqis had relatives, friends, and neighbors who had been killed by Coalition bombs and would love to get their hands on us.

When we arrived in the hotel, Max Meyer, the bearded, gray-haired leader of the Swiss ICRC delegates, gave a welcoming speech, his English accented. "Where is the Kuwaiti POW?" a worker asked, wanting to make sure Mo got out.

"Here I am," Mo called as he came forward. The nine Saudis rushed up to him. Hugging and kissing him, they apologized for mistrusting him in their cell.

Several male and female Red Cross workers walked us up the stairs to the fourth-floor reception room. They divided us into groups by nationality for documentation. I could scarcely take in all the sights and movement around me.

Gathered in a room with the door closed, the former POWs talked quietly in excited tones. The Red Cross team was well organized and attentive, even though they had known nothing about our release until the morning before when the first group was handed over.

The Swiss workers asked us for the names of any Coalition prisoners we had seen and updated us on the war. They gave us tea, coffee, and Swiss chocolate bars—the item most requested by the first batch of released POWs. A doctor checked us for medical problems needing immediate attention.

I was awed at the amount of color, people, and spaciousness around me. So quickly I had gone from starving in a cold, stinking prison cell to eating Swiss chocolate in a luxury hotel. My darkness had become light; my solitude companionship; my terror...less terror.

Because we were still fearful of the many Iraqis around the hotel, our behavior remained subdued. "By international law you are free," an ICRC delegate told us. "The Iraqis will guard us; no one is allowed inside. Ignore everything outside." They were trying their best to get us out of Iraq that day.

The Red Cross laid out a small buffet of food they had brought into Baghdad—salmon, potatoes, cauliflower, noodles, and more Swiss chocolate bars. The Iraqi civilian "bodyguards" went to the head of the line and helped themselves to heaping plates of food. When Max, the head of the Red Cross, saw them finishing off their heaping plates, he severely chastised them. "This food is not for you! You have been hired to guard these people, not eat their food!"

As a senior POW, I stationed myself toward the end of the line. By the time the last four of us went through the line only a few spoonsful of noodles with vegetables and several pieces of chocolate remained. We split the food four ways and inhaled it.

Rhonda Cornum watched the famished POWs eat. "Your enzymes won't be able to process all this food," she cautioned. "You'll get the runs!" We were too busy stuffing our faces to take her warning seriously. An hour later, my food went right through me.

After eating, foremost on everyone's mind was getting out of Iraq. A plane was scheduled to fly us out that afternoon after delivering the Iraqi POWs. While we waited, we exchanged stories on the progress of the war. As one of those held longest, I was anxious to get caught up—and especially to hear news of VMO-2.

Then the Red Cross people gave us bad news. "We're sorry," they said. "It's too windy for the plane to fly into Iraq. You'll have to stay in Baghdad one more night." The aircraft had flown to Saudi Arabia to pick up the Iraqi POWs, but because of sand storms in northern Saudi Arabia, it couldn't return to Baghdad until the following morning.

Their announcement fueled my fears that someone could knock down our hotel room door, then kill us or take hostages in retaliation for the war. Though the hotel fire escapes had been boarded up and the bodyguards guarded the doorways with AK-47s, I prepared for that possibility. When the Red Cross gave us a ticket with an ICRC identification number, I wrote the number in pen on the rubber toe of my tennis shoes. If Iraqi civilians stormed the hotel and someone later found me with my head missing, I figured they could identify my body if my shoes were attached.

Each of the POWs was given his or her own room, but after being alone for so many weeks, no one wanted to be alone again. With us swapping war stories was a member of the British Special Air Service (SAS) special forces patrol, an elite group with the motto Who Dares, Wins. The man had dark curly brown hair, a long mustache, and a leg braced with steel pins piercing his flesh. After he was initially wounded, the Iraqis had ripped the bandages off his wounded leg and tortured him for information.

He later told a sobering story of his capture in another war, in another country. The Red Cross had taken custody of him in a hotel, and before he could walk to freedom, soldiers had stormed in and taken him hostage again.

The former POWs stayed together talking for hours, exchanging stories. Finally Guy and I moved to a room together, locking the dead bolt and security chain behind us.

I went into the bathroom to clean up. Startled, I caught sight of myself in the mirror. The image—of a haggard, thin, undeniably old-looking man—was frightening. Away from the prison's darkness and dirt, I realized how filthy I was. Stripping off my clothes, I noticed the pungent odor on my hands. I had become immune to my own stench. I turned on the warm water in the pink 1960s-style bathtub. The warm splash of water on my skin was soothing. I lathered every inch of me with soap, scrubbing away the dirt and smells of the past months. The water drained out the color of charcoal—

partly because of bombing residue—and left a thick, greasy ring in the tub. After a second shower, the water ran off brown.

Before going to bed, Guy and I pulled the drapes, then barricaded the locked and chained door with a chair. We were afraid that Iraqi armed guards or hostile civilians would storm in. We shoved the bed against the wall, then hopped in together—for body heat and protection. Normally, I would have shunned such intimacy with another man, but as with Mo, I welcomed such closeness.

The next morning, a murky, drizzly, gray day, we walked out of the hotel wearing dark woolen sweaters over our yellow uniforms. Walking single file, we boarded a bus while a crowd of photographers thrust their cameras toward the curtained windows. Another crowd, this one of Iraqis, their brows furrowed, their expressions suspicious, gathered around the bus. They hemmed it in until armed guards cleared the way.

We drove down the streets of Baghdad. It was a city much like any other modern city, except this one had charred piles of rubble where important targets during the war had once stood, witness to the deadly accuracy of Coalition bombing. "This was the main telephone-exchange building." The ICRC representative pointed to the scattered remains of a building that looked like a hurricane had ripped it apart. Its destruction had wiped out communications all over Baghdad. "This was a military headquarters. . . ." Buildings across the street or on either side of the blackened, scarred buildings were eerily intact, untouched save for a broken window or two. We drove around huge craters in the road and through several checkpoints.

On the streets, I saw only a few Iraqis going about their business. Wary looking, none of them smiled or chatted. They looked tense, cautious, and uncomfortable, as if they had emerged from caves or basements to a changed world. They appeared uncertain, as if wondering, Is this truly peacetime or only a temporary lull in the war?

Red signs in English and Arabic told me we were nearing our destination: Saddam International Airport. We waited in the bus at what was left of Baghdad International Airfield. Every hangar had been destroyed or left with minimal framework standing. Iraq had hidden its aircraft in concrete-reinforced hangars. Of 594 aircraft shelters, 375 had been destroyed. Here at the airport, only the passenger terminal, a target of no military value, had been left standing. Iraqi troops milled about it.

Two 727s landed on the dusty, wind-swept airfield and taxied toward us, the planes due to bring us out. A stairway was rolled up to the doorway of the first aircraft. Minutes later, a line of returning Iraqi prisoners (EPWs) walked down the ramp of the plane on their way to be repatriated. Each carried a brown plastic garbage sack filled with MREs, water, and toiletries. Grimfaced Republican guards in black berets looked at them in silence. Their eyes clearly conveyed a look of disgust and contempt, as if to say, "You're scum."

As the tragic column of EPWs filed toward shabby, old buses, no one shook their hands, talked to them, or smiled. They had served in a war and now, returning home, met no celebration, no family, no greeting. It was as if they were being blamed for losing the war. The Republican guards couldn't even welcome their own military brethren back. *What pricks.* The hunched-over former prisoners—nearly 400 in all—looked unhappy to be home and desperately afraid. We had no idea what would happen to them when turned over to their government. The Iraqis had suffered a crushing defeat and I suspected these men would be punished.

An ambulance pulled up near the airplanes. I later learned it carried not only the stretcher cases but also three British SAS troops whose identities were shielded.

After a two-hour wait that seemed to last forever, the former POWs boarded one of the Swiss Air 727s with high winds blowing sand into our faces. The jet engines began to whine. I looked out the window. Several triple-A sites remained on the airfield. What if an isolated military unit had missed word of the cease-fire? What if a disgruntled, infuriated squad or platoon with antiaircraft artillery or a handheld surface-to-air missile wanted to take a parting shot at the pilots who had destroyed their country? After dealing with unpredictability for so long, nothing would surprise me now.

As the airplane backed away from the terminal, several Iraqi soldiers ran onto the field to man their antiaircraft sites. They trained their guns on our plane, taunting us. As the plane taxied to the runway, the aim of their guns followed. We waited for clearance, then roared down the runway to takeoff speed.

The jet rumbled and shuddered as it lifted off. Everyone cheered. But our celebration was brief; no one felt it was time for true rejoicing. We weren't home yet. It got quiet as we each returned to our own thoughts. Skies were cloudy, with two miles of visibility. Many of us looked out the windows of the civilian plane, searching for a missile. A lot of prayers were being said.

The plane entered the clouds at 2,000 feet. "You couldn't see it coming anyway," I told myself, and turned away from the window. Unlike the jubilant atmosphere you might expect, throughout the trip the mood was hushed as people engaged in quiet conversation or contemplation. Our behavior was guided by a deep suspicion that this might be another false hope, easily dashed.

The second Swiss Air jet followed, flying in formation with ours, then crossing underneath. As the two jets separated, the Swiss Air staff handed out blankets, wool scarves, and candy, cookies, and coffee. I turned down the food, but was grateful for the blanket and scarf to warm my ever-cold-to-the-bone body.

The plane sped closer to the Saudi border. When we were still in Iraqi air-space, two Royal Air Force Tornado F-1s came up alongside us, close to the wing tips of our 727. The pilots waved and smiled, then finished their wel-come by conducting victory rolls close abeam our aircraft. Shortly after the Tornados arrived, two USAF F-15s joined up, with equally enthusiastic air-crews welcoming us back. One of the pilots took off his mask and punched the air with his fist as if saying "Way to go! Welcome back!"

After executing victory aileron rolls, the planes lit their afterburners, shot out a stream of bright infrared flares, and went straight up. All four fighters escorted us toward the Saudi border. A few minutes later, the pilot came over the loudspeaker: "Ladies and gentlemen, we have now left Iraq and entered Saudi Arabian airspace." The plane erupted in cheers and applause. *Now* we were safe.

I wondered when and how the Red Cross team would leave Iraq. Max Meyer would correspond with me in the coming years, asking in a future letter: "You ever intend to go back into Iraq? For me answer is no; I am on the black list and a 'persona non grata,' fortunately I could leave the country in a very well organized action via Saudi-Arabia in a small plane!"

Air Force Colonel David Eberly, the senior U.S. POW, spoke over the loudspeaker, telling us how he wanted to orchestrate everyone getting off the plane. He would step out of the plane first, salute, then drop back to get Mo. He and Mo would walk side by side down the ramp, followed by the rest of the POWs. The Americans were to remove their sweaters and leave the plane in order of rank.

I heard his voice, and thought, "We've just been released from hell. Now we're worried about social graces and how to walk off the plane?" How we got off the plane was not important. What was important was that we'd all gotten out of Iraq and we had freed Kuwait. If anyone should get off that plane first, it should be Mo. Moments later, Colonel Eberly's words didn't register; I was thinking about the person I most wanted to see when I stepped off that plane: Doc Lees.

I looked out the window and saw the outskirts of the city. "There's the airfield," someone said. As we began our descent, I grew strangely concerned about what would happen to me once we got to Riyadh. After weeks of having no control over my destiny, I worried that I would still have little say in who did what to me. Where would they take me after we landed? Had I been per-manently replaced as the CO of VMO-2?

As the Red Cross–chartered plane taxied into the air base at Riyadh, the capital of Saudi Arabia, I looked out the window and saw thousands of people. It looked like the whole world was outside waiting for us. We heard their clapping and cheering as the door opened. A reception group boarded the plane. They informed us of the plan for deplaning. General Norman Schwarzkopf and Saudi Arabian General Khaled bin Sultan, the Joint Forces commander, wanted the Kuwaiti pilot to deplane first, they said. He would be followed by the nine Saudis, then the rest of the POWs in order of rank.

Mo was overcome by the honor to be bestowed upon him. "You deserve it, Mo; go for it," we told him. Tears formed in his eyes as everyone congratulated him. Though embarrassed, he obeyed orders and walked off the plane first in his dirty, torn, revealing uniform.

My turn came. I stepped out of the plane into bright sunshine. I had begun my journey in captivity on the "trip to hell"; now I felt I was ending it in heaven. It seemed a lifetime—not just seven weeks—since I had told Guy "Drop your radio" and we had become prisoners of war. Still I did not trust even then that I was free.

I stepped onto the ramp and looked around me. A zealous crowd of Coalition military people and many photographers had assembled on the tarmac. "What's this all about?" I wondered, hearing thousands of people cheering. Walking down the ramp from the plane, I realized these were well-wishers here to welcome us home.

The first person waiting at the foot of the stairs to greet us was General Schwarzkopf. Tan and overpowering, he looked huge compared to us bags of bones. His eyes sparkled and he had a most heartwarming smile. *He* saluted *me.* I stood at attention.

"Sir, I am Lieutenant Colonel Cliff Acree, United States Marine Corps. I am reporting to you that all naval officers known to me in captivity are all present and accounted for." The general completed his salute and extended his hand. "Welcome home, Colonel," he said. "I'm proud of you."

I shook his hand. "Thank you, General. I will never forget that you took the time to welcome us back. Thank you so much, sir." Next I met the Saudi Arabian Joint Forces commander. I stepped onto the red carpet that had been rolled out for us and worked my way down the receiving line. I met high-ranking officials from Great Britain and Saudi Arabia. The other services had senior officers meeting their former captives; I did not see one Marine. At the end of the line, I looked across the parking lot. Other ex-POWs embraced their waiting comrades. "Now what do I do?" I wondered. I didn't know the escorts and medical personnel had been instructed to wait at a medical evacuation plane about 100 yards beyond. It was then I saw familiar faces: two VMO-2 pilots and Joel Lees.

"I saw a look of recognition come over your face like a light turning on," Joel recalls. "You looked hot, feverish from the intestinal infections, and hungry—not only for food but for reassurance, for the sight and touch of someone you loved. You were not the commanding officer I had seen seven weeks before."

Joel strode toward me, wide-eyed, as if seeing someone coming back from the dead. He raised his arm to salute me, then thought better of it. He held his arms out as I rushed to hug him, not as a military officer but as my friend. The sight of him brought tears at last to my eyes, and I fell into his arms. Back with squadron mates, *now* I was free.

Riyadh, Saudi Arabia
March 6, 1991

I saw the television cameras pointed in our direction, filming the POWs' first steps in freedom. "Joel, would you please help me walk?" I put my arm toward him. "I'm really weak right now—shaky."

Joel shored me up with my right arm over his shoulder. The VMO-2 pilots assisted, taking some of the weight off my painful foot.

Along with the other former POWs and our military escorts, we moved toward the C-141 transport plane being readied by the medevac crew. We waited outside while the crew readied meals and assigned seats.

"Hey, GW!" someone said. We turned around to see Guy walking toward us wearing a big grin. Joel burst out laughing in relief and amusement. "Your hair is not that of a Marine officer," he joked at the sight of Guy's head of woolly gray hair. "You look like a white Don King!"

In Riyadh, each POW was assigned an escort, or "shadow." Joel Lees was assigned as mine. We boarded the plane for the one-hour flight to the island emirate of Bahrain. This transport aircraft, rigged for carrying medevac and litter patients, was configured with a small section of passenger seats toward the back of the large, open interior. There were no wall coverings, but American flags hung over the cabin area.

Soon after boarding, someone handed me a small green camouflage bag containing a toothbrush, toothpaste, a comb, and other toiletry items. After clinging to threads and scraps of wire, it felt strange to have so many possessions handed to me.

While the rest of the POWs boarded the plane, I was first to be offered a new Marine uniform—an olive-green T-shirt, underwear, black boots, socks, and a flight suit with my squadron patch.

"Thanks." I dropped the pile of clothing on the seat cushion, then tore open the buttons of my yellow POW shirt. I yanked the shirt off, followed by my stained canvas shoes and smelly socks.

I ripped off my dirty, lice-infested pants and underwear. Joel said nothing. He watched in wide-eyed surprise as I symbolically freed myself from my ordeal. Without a second thought I stripped naked in front of everyone on the plane—including some of the aircrew who were women.

Meanwhile, the other POWs had received their uniforms. By the time I zipped up my flight suit, the women flight crew members had gone up to the front. Several male crew members had formed a human privacy curtain around the remaining POWs who were undressing. I stuffed my POW clothing into my green carry-on bag. "I'm going to save this garbage that was on my body," I told Joel. Someday I'd look at it again—for now I wanted it out of my sight.

A doctor was assigned to each POW to assess medical problems. Joel asked me questions and took lengthy notes on my injuries. I received a box lunch of chicken, sandwiches, chocolate, and cheese. Though my stomach still felt queasy, I was light-headed with hunger. Joel told me the food was probably too rich for me. But seeing me tear into the sandwich he said, "Go ahead," gratified to see me eat.

Being treated so well required some adjustment. People had cheered for me. Now others called me "sir" and gave me more food than I could possibly digest.

At seven o'clock that evening, the aircraft landed at the darkened Shaikh Isa airfield in Bahrain. Carrying my camouflage bag under my arm, I carefully negotiated my way down the steps toward the waiting dignitaries. After listening to several people make statements I barely comprehended, we were whisked by bus to the white hospital ship the USNS *Mercy*. Our every move was orchestrated. Sailors manned the rail of the gangplank, restricting access of the press, who gathered below the giant red cross painted on the ship's hull.

Limping aboard, I felt like a battery drained to the last volt. Weak, exhausted, and sick, I had nothing left. I worked my way up the gangplank as military photographers snapped photographs. Dutifully, I shook the many hands extended in welcome by the ship's crew.

I neared the top of the gangplank. Mechanically, I went through the motions of greeting the ship's commanding officer and his key staff. Still in a state of near shock at being released, I saluted the captain of the ship and his executive officer, then dropped my hand, feeling dazed and physically and emotionally depleted.

I turned away to enter the ship's hatch. "Hey, Colonel—what's shakin'?" I looked to my right and saw my Navy buddy Scooter, his lips turned up in an impish grin. How had he gotten here?

Scooter later told me that, shortly before the ground war kicked off, the *Tripoli* had struck a powerful contact mine floating unseen below the surface of the water. With his ship dry-docked at nearby Asry for repairs, he had talked his way past the tight security on the *Mercy*. I dropped my bags and pinned Scooter against the wall with my hug.

"Sir." A navy corpsman escorting the POWs pointed to the Navy medical people. "Please follow them," he tactfully urged. Then, looking at Scooter, "He needs to come with us."

"Hey, Cliff, you've got to go now," Scooter said gently. "I'll see you tomorrow."

Going up to the ward, it was all a blur. The huge berthing suite the size of a basketball court had been configured with fifty double-decker beds on racks that folded down from stanchions in the center of the room. The rows of bunk beds awaited casualties, but the repatriated POWs appeared to be the only patients. Except for the two POWs with orthopedic injuries, all the POWs would stay in this area. The two womens' bunks were curtained off for privacy. Vietnam experience proved that the camaraderie of the unit eases the repatriation process. Members of the medical staff were assigned to debrief POWs on their injuries and how they had sustained them.

Soon, Joel Lees accompanied me into an examining room. Sitting atop the examining table, with Joel on my left, it dawned on me once again that I was safe now. No longer battling my captors, I could relinquish the burden of taking care of myself to Joel and the medical staff of the *Mercy*.

For the first time since my shootdown, I had the luxury of time to think. In captivity I had repeatedly expected to die. Each time I had pushed my emotions—rage, anguish, fear, sorrow—aside. Now, with the strain of survival gone, those saved-up emotions refused to be ignored.

A tall, heavyset doctor arrived. "The first thing I'm going to do is examine you," the graying Navy captain said in his kindest bedside manner. "And I'll need to use a few instruments," he forewarned.

I nodded. Feeling my emotions on the brink, I tried to keep the atmosphere light with a joke. "You can do anything you want . . . as long as you don't break out a club."

My attempt at lightness failed. Like an explosive charge triggers an avalanche, my words detonated a barrage of stockpiled emotions. The feelings engulfed me. Covering my face with my hands, I cried uncontrollably, grateful to be alive, stunned that I had survived.

After the doctor's cursory examination, I was given a cell phone and escorted topside to the ship's helicopter pad. I felt amazed to be free of handcuffs, to feel the breeze on my face, to see the sky. It was equally amazing to use a handheld phone to call across the world to my wife and talk for as long as I wanted. Cindy's familiar voice comforted me and launched my emotions back to the surface. "Too many times I thought I'd never talk to—you—again." I choked up again. I wanted to tell her everything I had endured, but didn't want to worry her. "I'm alive."

I asked her to apologize to a squadron wife who had collected and mailed more than 100 Christmas cards for VMO-2 Marines. "Please tell her the day

I was shot down, I was going to write her a thank-you note. Tell her I deeply appreciate everything she's done for the squadron—it was a very unselfish thing for her to do. I swear the letter I was going to write that day, besides yours, was to her. I thought about that so many times in captivity. I felt terrible I didn't write her a thank-you note."

Aunt Ethel, still visiting from Florida, got on the phone.

"Did they treat you well?"

For the first time since my release, I felt a burst of anger.

After a pause, I blurted out, "If you call starvation and brutality good treatment, then I received good treatment." Uncomfortable with my surge of emotion, I changed the subject. "How's Cindy doing?"

"Cindy is a tower of strength. You'll be surprised at all the things she has done."

I called Cindy's family and my sister, Ann. "What a person has to go through to be a hero," she said. "Let's not do this again!"

After calling my parents and Colonel Kuhn, I asked permission to go belowdecks. Used to following orders from my captors, I asked permission before each move I made. After feeling powerless for weeks, it was amazing to have every request granted.

One of my first requests was for pediculicide soap and shampoo to treat my lice. Using it twice rid me of the pesky creatures. I had blood samples taken and underwent several medical tests and evaluations. After what I'd been through, almost anything was tolerable. I was so glad to be back I felt numb to it all. I felt like I had run on adrenaline for forty-eight days, and the day I got back, I crashed like someone taken off amphetamines. While Guy was up walking and talking, I felt wasted and spent every free minute in bed trying to rest.

Aboard ship, wherever I shuffled in my robe and slippers, a small crowd of medical people followed—a Navy captain, a lieutenant commander, two nurses, and two or three petty officers—the doctor and his team assigned to ensure my care and well-being. The image we created was almost comical, like that of a mother duck followed by her ducklings.

By the time we hit the rack around midnight, it had been a long day for everyone. Guy and I climbed in our beds, one above the other. Joel slept in a bed around the corner. I fell dead asleep.

But between the floor creaking from movement of medical personnel and fifty people turning over in their beds, the hospital ship ward was not the quietest place. The slightest sound woke me up. Tired as I was, I found myself wide awake, my mind operating at full speed.

I waited until 5:30 the next morning to get up. I tapped Joel lightly on the shoulder. "Joel, it's time to get up."

He blinked open his eyes. "What time is it?"

"Let's go," I urged. I wanted to talk, not sleep and be alone.

My impatience struck him as funny. "I thought you'd be zonked for a long time."

It would be weeks before I could sleep longer than three or four hours at a time.

The next morning, Scooter returned, bringing me a tape player and several cassette tapes. "With all the nurses hovering around, this is great eyeball liberty," he kidded.

I spent the next hour or more being debriefed by two intelligence officers in civilian clothes. I told the brief story of my shootdown and capture, and I recalled the names of every Allied prisoner I had seen or heard of.

Several Marine officers visited next. The first was my commanding officer of Marine Aircraft Group 13. Finally, I was able to ask him the question that had concerned me throughout my captivity.

"Am I still the CO of VMO-2?"

"Yes, of course," he said.

"Sir, that's the best news anyone could give me," I said. "I had nightmares about that."

"There was never any question," Colonel Bioty said. "The decision was made by the commanding general."

John Gamboa, a VMO-2 Marine, videotaped our visit. "Sir, would you say it just one more time for the camera?" he asked, grinning.

"You *are* the CO and you will remain."

The Marines cheered. "Ooh-rah!"

Oceanside, California
March 6, 1991

I broke my rule not to stay glued to the TV. At four A.M. I turned on CNN and waited for news that more POWs had been released. Two hours later I saw the report I had waited for, POWs walking down the stairway of a plane. Cliff emerged.

Wearing a yellow POW uniform with an orange scarf draping his neck, he hesitated in the doorway of the plane. Then he pushed his heels together and earnestly saluted the waiting dignitaries. Holding his scarf to his chest against the wind, he slowly stepped to the foot of the stairs with Guy behind him. He worked his way through the receiving line, then walked ahead slowly, looking lost. A moment later, his face held in his hands, he fell into the arms of Joel Lees, sobbing.

I watched several Marines hug Cliff and slap him on the back. The camera panned the airfield, where other POWs jumped and leaped and gave high fives to waiting comrades. With his right arm draped over Joel's shoulder, Cliff limped across the tarmac with two other Marines helping prop him up.

I screamed then sagged to my knees, head in my hands, sobbing. "Thank you, God, thank you."

"Every one of 'em's a hero!" General Schwarzkopf's booming voice told the crowd of reporters.

"How do they look to you?" one reporter asked.

"They looked happy to be home. Happy to be in freedom."

Overjoyed, I bounded up and down for five minutes.

Later that day, President Bush gave his "Victory Speech" before a joint session of Congress. "We went halfway around the world to do what is moral and just and right," he said. "And we fought hard and—with others—won the war."

I prepared my final statement: " I am thrilled by the news of Cliff's safe release. . . . I've always said our wedding day was the happiest day of my life, but today may top even that. . . ." I thanked friends around the world, and especially President Bush, for keeping the POW/MIA issue at the forefront of world attention.

Every time the phone rang that day, I hoped it would be Cliff. But each call was a friend or a reporter asking if I'd heard from Cliff. When I explained my suspense, they graciously cut their calls short.

Late that afternoon, the phone rang again. I picked it up and heard static on the line. "Cindy?" For the first time in two months, I heard Cliff's voice.

Calling from the hospital ship USNS *Mercy,* just three hours after leaving Baghdad, Cliff sounded tired, weak, and almost deliriously happy to be free. He was standing on the helicopter pad of the ship, which was docked at the tiny island nation of Bahrain. Two navy doctors, a nurse, and Doc Lees hovered over him. "I haven't been alone for one minute since we landed in Riyadh," Cliff said. Knowing Joel was watching over him lifted a heavy weight from my heart.

"I worried about you the entire time," he said earnestly. "And I missed the Marines of my squadron so much. I felt like they were my brothers, and I wanted to be with them."

He continued talking almost nonstop. "I'll always take care of you. I had a good family, my faith, and my country. That's all you've got when there's four walls and bars . . . I didn't know if I'd ever talk to you again. I'm okay. I'm alive . . ." He kept talking as if unable to staunch the flow of emotions now that they had begun. "Too many times I thought I'd never talk to you again," he kept repeating.

I said little, simply waiting for him to go on.

"Don't worry," he said in a high-pitched voice. "I'm not coming back a nutcase!"

Squeezing the phone, I struggled to keep my voice even. His emotions were frail, and I had to be strong for him. Over and over I reassured him of my love for him, that I hadn't gotten tired of waiting or given up.

I almost hated to ask about his treatment. When I did, there was a long silence. "They didn't treat me okay," he said haltingly. Coming from Cliff, that had to be a vast understatement. "I'm okay... I walked back alive," he added, his voice starting to break. "I didn't know if I would ever make this call."

I wondered about his captivity and the events leading up to it, but decided not to probe. We would save that conversation until we could talk face-to-face and he felt ready.

"The longest I slept was twenty or thirty minutes," Cliff went on. "It was the strangest thing. I would wake up out of a dead sleep and *know* that you were thinking about me, praying for me, or doing *something* for me. You gave me strength to survive."

Joel got on the phone and told me Cliff followed dutifully wherever he was led. He had been through a tremendous culture shock. "A positive culture shock, but nonetheless it couldn't have been more extreme. You change with the environment and accommodate as best you can to survive." He told me that Cliff acted compliant and, because he had been deprived of material possessions for so long, had formed an almost obsessive attachment to items he was given, including his disposable toothbrushes.

"He's worried that you might think he was captured because he made a mistake," Joel said. "Obviously some of his fears are not fully rational. People are jubilant that he's back, yet he doesn't perceive the depth of that sentiment. And he is sick. When you don't feel well physically, you're not yourself."

Medical personnel, still conducting extensive tests, had already detected a compressed spine, intestinal bugs, neck and shoulder injuries, nerve damage in his wrists and hands, nose and skull damage, and shrapnel wounds.

Joel forewarned me that Cliff had lost a lot of weight and looked thin.

"He looked thin before," I said.

"Now he looks *very* thin," Joel said. Cliff weighed 145 pounds instead of his usual 180. "All my hard work down the drain!" I teased Cliff when he got back on the phone. We talked for several minutes, then Aunt Ethel had a turn. When we ended our call, he sounded tired but promised to call again soon.

That night I typed an entry in my journal, trying to sort out the fugue of emotions swirling inside me:

Thursday, March 7, 1991: Yesterday was a day filled with emotion, yet I continue to hold back. I'm waiting for the moment I will feel that deep sense of relief and relaxation knowing that Cliff is okay. It didn't come Sunday night when Michael Clark told me an initial group of POWs would be released and Cliff's name was mentioned. It didn't come Tuesday when I received official word Cliff was alive and among the final 35 to be released. It came only partially when I saw him walk down the stairs of the plane, but not yet. Will I need my hands on him to do that? Or maybe I'm getting so skilled at holding it all in, it will take time to let it leak out slowly for fear it will all come rushing out uncontrollably.

Yesterday it seemed as though everyone was crying but me. I did get teary-eyed and shaky-voiced when people cried as I told them "Cliff is okay." And I did allow myself to momentarily cry in our "circle hug" with Rosana and Debbie, since they were sobbing. I don't want to sob until Cliff and I can rejoice and sob together.

On Friday, March 8, finally able to publicly identify myself, I spoke on ABC's *Home Show* via telephone from the office complex where the Liberty Alliance had held its press conference.

"I'd especially like to thank President Bush for keeping the POW/MIA issue at the forefront and always insisting on their return," I concluded. "And let's not forget there are some who have *not* returned. MIA families are waiting for word on their loved ones."

Thirty minutes later, Colonel Beaver escorted me downstairs into a courtyard crowded with people who were there to attend my press conference. It was hard to believe I had barely known Don and Kay seven weeks before, when I was first notified that Cliff was missing. Tireless, caring, and committed, they earned my eternal gratitude.

Dressed in a royal blue business suit and wearing a silver POW bracelet, I walked toward the outdoor lectern, past the row of reporters and photographers. After weeks of staying secluded while news vehicles lined my street, it felt odd not to be avoiding the media. The night before, I had typed up potential questions and answers and memorized them. Out in the crowd, I saw friends, neighbors, members of the alliance, and Michael Clark, his military status disguised by a business suit.

"I've been looking forward to the day when I could share my joy in Cliff's safe release," I began. "In the past, I've had trouble explaining to my family what I mean by 'the Marine Corps family,'" I said. "Now they've seen it with their own eyes. From the moment I was notified that my husband was missing, I've been treated with care and compassion."

I spoke briefly about the events of the previous seven weeks and thanked everyone who had helped with our letter-writing campaign. I recounted details of Cliff's phone call from the hospital ship. "He says he's been dreaming of my cooking for forty-eight days," I told them, "and I'm looking forward to fattening him up."

I told them Cliff slept only in twenty- or thirty-minute spurts and often woke from a deep sleep knowing I was thinking about him, praying for him, or doing something. "If he woke up every time I was doing one of those things, it's no wonder he didn't get much sleep," I added, laughing.

A reporter relayed a story from Mary Hunter. "Did your husband tell you Guy Hunter was knocked unconscious by the missile and it was he who ejected Hunter as the plane fell?"

"No, he didn't tell me that."

"When did you first find out your husband was released?" a reporter asked. I hesitated. What should I tell them? I shifted my gaze toward the back of the crowd, where Michael Clark stood with military bearing, hands clasped in front of him. His eyes caught mine and didn't move. Subtly, he shook his head. I turned back to the cameras. "When Marine Colonel Don Beaver told me."

Hospital Ship *Mercy*, Bahrain
March 7, 1991

A busload of VMO-2 Marines arrived for a visit, among them Sergeant Major Warner and my intelligence chief, Staff Sergeant Korsmo. Doc Lees briefed them before they came into the ward where the POWs were isolated. He told them about the injuries to my neck, head, and hands, and gave them a feel for my emotional frame of mind. "He's very weak, but will want to talk and find out information," Doc said. "Try not to get him too excited; keep it short. And don't squeeze his hands—he doesn't have much feeling in them."

Before the Marines arrived, I had felt tired, sore, weak. I did little—just sat or lay on my bed asleep, or wishing I was. My stomach was upset, my intestines were cramping, my foot hurt, and I worried about the numbness in my hands, fearing I would never fly again. I had no strength, no stamina.

When my visitors appeared, I felt a miraculous transformation, an infusion of energy. They found us in a church service. The chaplain said a few words, then a VMO-2 Marine sang a hymn. We prayed, and Colonel Eberly gave a short speech.

After the service, the Marines went back to the ward with us. "Being in this ward is like being on CNN," one of them remarked, seeing in person the POWs he had seen on TV so many times.

Even knowing of my captivity, the Marines seemed surprised at my ghostly white, weak appearance. Wearing my robe and pajamas, I embraced them and we all fought back tears. "You're the first Marine colonel I've ever hugged!" our intelligence chief told me.

Guy and I sat on a bench with the Marines sitting cross-legged on the floor in front of us. Guy immediately joked with the guys, telling the story of his capture. The oldest of the American POWs, Guy said he lay on the floor in his cell at one point and told himself: "You are too old for this stuff!"

"Good old GW, just like always," one of the Marines said.

I was anxious to find out how the squadron fared during the war. My first question was "How's the squadron doing?" I had missed so much. Like a man coming out of a coma, I wanted to make up for lost time.

"Sir, everyone is okay. We're flying," said Sergeant Major Warner. "Did we get the FROGs?" I asked, referring to the target we'd spotted just before the missile hit. "Who got them? . . . When?"

They told me we had spotted five FROG missiles hidden in a fire department building. Four Harrier aircraft later destroyed the missiles and the resultant explosion extended into the atmosphere nearly 10,000 feet.

One of the Marines handed me a letter written by Major Steve Antosh, who took over as acting CO in my absence. He wrote:

> Skipper, I cannot adequately express how your Marines feel today. . . . You can be proud of your squadron's accomplishments during Desert Storm. We met 100% of our assigned missions. . . . All told, with six aircraft we flew 286 sorties. . . . Every Marine and sailor assigned to VMO-2 is full up and ready to carry on. Sir, we hope we did not let you down. God speed, Sir. See you in the States.
>
> Semper Fi,
> Maj Antosh

I had so many questions about the number of sorties the squadron had flown, targets destroyed, and tactics employed. Woozy, I struggled with words, choosing them carefully. I repeated the visiting Marines' answers to help the information register. Our intelligence chief told me our Bronco crews had saved countless U.S. Marines and allies in the war from tragic "friendly fire" by averting air strikes on Coalition forces mistaken for enemy targets. "For the infantry, we were 'the Eyes of the Storm'!" he bragged. Later I would watch videotapes of laser-guided bombs scoring bull's-eyes on Iraqi bunkers and blowing up bridges without harming nearby travelers.

"Some Marines think you'll be coming back to VMO-2 in Saudi Arabia as the CO," the sergeant major told me. He'd explained to them that I needed medical treatment and would be going back to the States. "They wanted to see you, physically," he said. "You're our CO." Everyone had wanted to come, but Sergeant Major Warner had explained that my getting medical treatment was more important than their desire to visit me.

I talked a little about my experiences. The big question everyone had was "What happened?" All I could tell them was that I saw the missile just before impact, saw a flash, then felt the explosion. It had taken a *long* time for Guy to eject, and then me. I had waited, looked down, but the ejection seat seemed to fire late, and I had hurt my neck during ejection.

The Marines amazed me with news of Cindy's POW/MIA Liberty Alliance organization. "That's what she was working on," I thought. "The squadron jumped on the letter-writing campaign," Sergeant Major Warner told me. "The guys felt good there was something we could do, and made hundreds of copies of the letter to send to family and friends across the United States." He lifted both palms, feigning indignance. "By the time we really kicked it off, you were released!"

The men felt that visiting me was a proper ending to the war. "The war didn't end when there was a cease-fire," my intelligence chief said. "It truly ended when you were released."

Sergeant Major Warner later confided, "To see you again was like seeing a brother. I try not to feel that way about people, especially in a war environment, but you're our hero. Not because you were a POW. Because you're a different brand of man." His words confirmed the unspoken bond we shared.

I was worried about my squadron, but dog tired. The men had to get back to the squadron by dark since there was still fear of terrorism. When everyone left, I wilted. It was back to the struggle of recuperating.

That night, Joel left to check on some of my tests, and John Gamboa stopped by to see me where I lay in my hospital bed.

"How are you doing, CO?" he asked. I saw in his eyes he wanted to talk.

"I'm just flat exhausted. Really, really tired."

Earlier that day, I had learned that a close Marine Corps buddy, an exceptionally skilled pilot, had been killed during the war flying a Cobra escort mission. "Are you *sure?*" I asked. The news really set me back. I felt old, hunched over, and feeble. I hoped I didn't look as bad to others as I felt. "John, how do I look compared to the last time you saw me?" I knew Gamboa would be direct and honest with me.

"You look real tired and sick."

"I'm alive." I sank back onto my bed.

My second night on the *Mercy,* I walked up to the quarterdeck. The medical team stood tactfully to the side while I savored the huge starlit sky, and the velvet black water, dotted with reflected light from a nearby dock. *I'm out. I'm free.* Thousands of men, women, and children in Iraq still suffered.

No metal doors crashed, no feet rapped down the corridor. No angry voices cut through the night. I stood for a long time under the celestial light savoring the peace, the quiet, and my freedom. It's an eternal irony that sometimes we need to lose something before we can fully recognize its value. I recalled an anonymous quote on freedom I once read: "For those who have fought for it, freedom has a flavor the protected have never known." Lifting my eyes toward the stars, I composed my own ballad on freedom.

What Freedom Means to Me

    To walk without being blindfolded
    To raise my arms without handcuffs
    To see the sky and feel the warmth of the sun
    To speak my own thoughts
    To sleep without fear
    To know I'll eat today
    A day without terror and pain
    To stand in defense of freedom—and win.

9

The Gulf Narrows

Camp Pendleton, California
March 9, 1991

The powerful thrust of Lear jet engines pushed me into my seat as the C-21 lifted into the bright sunshine. The jet rose from the airfield and my heart lifted with it. I was on my way to Buckley Air Force Base in Colorado. There I would join families of other returning POWs for our flight to Andrews Air Force Base in Maryland as part of Operation Yellow Ribbon, the repatriation of POWs from Operation Desert Storm. It was exciting to take off from "Cliff's" airfield at Camp Pendleton in a plush aircraft, seeing the sights so familiar to him. *The next time I see this airfield, we'll be together.*

During the four days since Cliff had called from the hospital ship *Mercy,* pandemonium—the positive kind—had reigned at our house. Florists delivered flowers and balloon bouquets. More letters and telegrams arrived from strangers who had shared my sorrow and worry, and now my happiness and excitement. POW bracelets started to return, many with emotional letters and pictures attached. People sent newspaper and magazine clippings and videotapes of television news stories. One woman sent a scrapbook showing Cliff the efforts of people to bring him home. The air felt electric, like the atmosphere in a bride's home on her wedding day—charged with excitement, anticipation, and eagerness.

Within hours of my phone call with Cliff, even Cami's demeanor changed. "My God, look at that dog," Dee Barackman had remarked. She had been patrolling the house for weeks, but now she was off duty—on her back, hind legs splayed, front paws curled loosely on her chest, eyes half closed. You'd swear she was grinning.

The phone rang incessantly, with fifty or more calls a day from well-wishers and local and national news media. Written messages arrived from military officers. From the commandant of the Marine Corps, General Alfred M. Gray Jr.: "You can be proud of Cliff. He led VMO-2 with confidence and purpose, and they performed professionally and successfully in combat despite his absence—a true mark of his leadership. . . ." From the Marine Air Group commander, afloat: "Your handling of a most difficult situation has shown courage, stamina, and patriotism that has been inspirational." From Barbara Bush: "Dear Cindy, Please know that when the POWs appeared safe and sound on the television and your Cliff's face and name were shown—I shouted with joy. . ."

Jubilant letters of congratulation came for Cliff. From his friend retired Navy commander Tom Kelly, a Medal of Honor winner: "Welcome home, hero! When I first saw you on Iraqi TV on January 20, you had that look in your eye . . . I knew then you'd make it home safely. Those bastards were probably relieved to get rid of you. . . ."

The one person I didn't hear from again was Cliff. My joy was shadowed by concern over his condition and his mention of "brutality and starvation." What had they done to him?

TV news featured an interview with the wife of a POW in Germany during World War II. "The pain of remembering never goes away," she said, referring to the horrors of her husband's treatment. "It just buries itself a little. Be ready and be tolerant," she advised POW wives. "They're going to act strangely . . . I *bet* on it."

Thursday night Colonel Beaver came to the house to help me pack for Cliff. I needed Don's help not only with selecting the proper military uniforms and accessories but with thinking logically ahead. My emotions were surfacing, but I tried to hold them back. Searching through Cliff's closet was ridiculously thrilling and brought home what I was about to do. I stacked his favorite jeans, tennis shoes, and shirts, imagining him wearing them.

My travel plans and preparations had been made at the last minute. Don Beaver had called Headquarters Marine Corps a few days before the POWs were released. "Have plans been made to fly the spouses to meet their husbands and wives?" he had asked. Incredibly, headquarters staff said they hadn't thought about how to involve spouses in the reunion phase. When they did, I received less than forty-eight hours' notice of my travel plans—not to West Germany, as originally expected, but to Andrews Air Force Base in Maryland.

Stephany visited on Friday night, and in a long heart-to-heart talk, I told her how much we both loved her. She understood why she could not join me on this trip to see Cliff when he was still sick and weak. She knew he would want to be strong when she first saw him again.

After our talk, Stephany wrote him a letter that I promised to deliver. I assured her we would call her on Sunday night, and that when he returned and was feeling better, she would see him. Each spouse was allowed to take a companion, and I chose Melinda Bargreen, a friend who was also a journalist for the *Seattle Times*. An intelligent, self-assured person, Melinda's frequent advice over the phone had helped me immensely while Cliff was in captivity. After fending off the press for so many weeks, I didn't want to share my first minutes with Cliff with just anyone. If anyone could write about our private reunion and do it sensitively, Melinda could.

That afternoon I said good-bye to Kay Beaver. For the first time, I saw tears in her eyes. In the past weeks, she and the other Marine wives had demonstrated the true meaning of the Marine Corps family—humoring me when I needed brightening, comforting me when I needed support, bolstering me when I faltered. Kay had made not one but five official calls during Operation Desert Storm, two with sorrowful endings.

A resilient woman, Kay had kept her emotions in check. Now, like me, she could let them leak out a little. Her husband, Don, had received military orders to accompany Mary Hunter and me to Washington. I felt sorry that Kay, too, could not accompany us.

The plane hummed as I looked out the window to the snowcapped Rocky Mountains. I felt my excitement build. The flight crew of the C-121 gave the POW family members VIP treatment. Wherever he was, I hoped Cliff was being pampered, too. He'd given his all to the Marine Corps—long before becoming a POW. Nothing could make up for what he'd been through, but I hoped he would get the recognition he undoubtedly deserved.

As we stepped off the plane at Buckley Air Force Base, Colorado, an Army National Guard band saluted the families with "The Stars and Stripes Forever." The Corsairs Precision Flight Team made a ceremonial flyby and flags with yellow ribbons waved everywhere. Every detail—from the officers who greeted us, to the band members who had given up their weekend, to the proud people hoisting flags and POW banners—spelled caring, joy, and gratitude.

Families boarded the large Air National Guard jet as the band played a military march. Walking down the aisle of the plane, I noticed a dark-haired woman in front of me. It was Leigh Berryman, the brave MIA wife who had never given up hope for her husband's return. I tapped her on the shoulder. We both squealed and hugged, now both having reason to celebrate. I wished every family involved in the Gulf War had gotten such good news.

The sound of the jet's engines reving was a lullaby relaxing me further. Was it all over? Could I let go? By the time we landed at Andrews Air Force Base at 5:30 that evening, my emotions were a jumble of euphoria, anxiety, and nerves. The entire trip would soon be a series of hazy impressions if I hadn't described it in my journal.

Each POW/MIA wife was assigned a local military officer to serve as an escort. Mine was Air Force Major Tom Madigan. He drove me to my quarters on base, a VIP room in the Bachelor Officers Quarters. On the bed sat an enormous white teddy bear and beside it was a gift bag containing snacks, a $50 gift certificate, and earrings donated by the PX staff. I felt like a VIP.

That night, families of the repatriated POWs (RPOWs) attended a dinner at Andrews AFB. As I sipped wine with my meal, the knot in my stomach I had grown used to began to unravel. "I'll see him in less than twenty-four hours!" my heart sang out, and I allowed myself a small surge of excitement.

After dinner, medical and public affairs officers gave short presentations. The first speaker took the podium. "The battle is over," I thought. Tension flowed from my body. It was all downhill from there.

But the speaker's official, simplistic advice told the families little we didn't already know. They left us with many unanswered questions about the following week's schedule and how we might ease our loved ones' repatriation. Next a general reviewed the plan for reuniting the returnees and their families—a plan that had obviously been made without considering the human factor. Hearing the arrangements, I realized I had one more battle to fight.

The returnees' flight would arrive about noon. After proceeding through a brief VIP receiving line and listening to speeches by Secretary of Defense Cheney and the senior returned POW, the families would be reunited. After their reunion with millions of people watching, the RPOWs and families would be driven in a bus to a huge reception in a hangar to meet military and political dignitaries.

"Expect lots of reporters when you get off the bus," the speaker said, predicting "intense interest and the competitive nature" of the press. But that wasn't the bad part. He continued and I made notes on the outline we had been given. They described the reception as the place where the RPOWs and families would gather for "greetings and farewells," because after the reception, Navy and Marine Corps RPOWs would board a bus to be driven to the hospital where they would stay overnight. Families would not see them until after 8:30 the next morning.

I felt myself growing angry. What a plan. In one fell swoop I would greet the husband I hadn't seen for seven months, share him with hundreds of people at a reception, then after not a minute alone, have him snatched from my arms again.

The RPOWs would need time alone to readjust, officials explained. I couldn't speak for the other POW families—especially those that included more distant relatives who had not been invited—but I *knew* Cliff would not want me out of his sight. After weeks of fear and uncertainty, the arrangements added more stress to families who had already been through enough.

I wrote notes outlining two requests I planned to make of the medical staff. The first was to allow the RPOWs and spouses private time before the hospital check-in on Sunday night. The second request was to accommodate spouses at the hospital if overnight stays were required. I knew Cliff would recover faster with me at his side.

After the presentations, I spoke with military officials and Dr. Eisold, director of the medical program at the National Naval Medical Center in Bethesda, Maryland. I explained why I thought their plan was neither satisfactory nor realistic. Their initial compromise was to allow the spouses to ride with the RPOWs to the hospital before being separated until morning. "That's not good enough," I told Don Beaver, shaking my head and fighting back tears.

Don went to bat for me and spoke to Dr. Eisold in private. "They deserve some alone time together," he argued. "Even if it's just moments." He suggested the RPOWs arrive at the hospital by four P.M. for inprocessing, then remain with their wives that night—whether at the hotel or at the hospital. "Being together tonight is not about sex," Don told him. "It's about needing to hold each other."

Dr. Eisold nodded his understanding.

Walking back, Don gave me a thumbs-up sign. "You've got it wired," he said. That evening, returnees and wives would be allowed to remain together.

After the reception, I headed back to my room. By that time my defenses were up again. Still on West Coast time and keyed up, I forced myself to bed early. I wanted to have time in the morning to burn off my nervous energy with a run before the brunch.

I lay in bed in the dark, unable to sleep. Something made a swishing sound in the vicinity of the door. I switched on the light and found a note had been slipped into the room beneath the door.

Cindy—Good news! Bonnie saw *new* footage of Cliff on the *Mercy* "walking briskly" across the room and shaking hands. She said he looks "quite thin" but really great. Strong and happy—not at all sick.

And today you will hold him in your arms. . . .

Love, Melinda

I rushed to turn on the TV. A few minutes later, I saw the same news clip myself. Pilots in flight suits descended a ramp, saluting Navy officers. Cliff walked through a reception line carrying a bouquet of flowers. No mustache.

"How are you doing?" someone called to him.

"Great!" he answered, his smile saying so much more.

After months of worrying and hoping, it was now not *if* but *when* I would see him. Imagining Cliff's aircraft speeding toward me, I felt like a kid again, waiting for Santa Claus to arrive on Christmas Eve. "Better be in bed, girls," Dad would warn Bonnie and me. "He's coming!" Tingling with anticipation,

I'd had difficulty falling asleep then, and I had the same trouble now. The next twelve hours were unquestionably the longest in my life.

Bahrain
March 10, 1991

After four days on the hospital ship *Mercy,* undergoing preliminary physical and psychological examinations and debriefings, twenty of my group of twenty-one American prisoners of war began a sixteen-hour flight home on a plane festooned with balloons; yellow ribbons; and red, white, and blue crepe paper. Our ranks included eight Air Force, four Army, three Navy, and five Marine Corps personnel. Our span of captivity ranged from seven to forty-eight days. Twenty of us boarded a Boeing 707 on flight Freedom Zero-One. Army Sergeant Daniel Stamaris boarded a special C-141 medevac flight because he was stretcher-bound due to a broken leg suffered when the helicopter he and Rhonda Cornum were riding in was shot down. Both planes would converge at Andrews Air Force Base to reunite us with our families.

Each former POW had been assigned a military shadow, or escort. Mine was Dr. Joel Lees. We sat next to each other on the plane, and over the hum of the engines, we talked about our families. I told him I was damned glad to be alive and from now on I would do things differently. Time was valuable, and I wanted to spend it wisely. Work had consumed my youth. I realized I had been overdedicated to my work and made a conscious decision to cut back and spend more time with my family. I spoke to Joel of the faith that had sustained me. I wanted to learn more about the Bible and develop a closer relationship with God.

"You've just been through a near-death experience," Joel commented. "If anything can convince a person God is around, that can. I'm humbled by your faith."

Dr. Robert E. Mitchell, head of the Special Studies Department of the Naval Aerospace and Operational Medical Institute (NAMI) was aboard. He made himself available to the former captives to discuss our physical symptoms and the mental changes we might experience. Since 1974 Dr. Mitchell had overseen NAMI's ongoing repatriated prisoner of war medical program that included World War II, Korea, Vietnam, Iran hostages, and now Desert Storm prisoners of war. He explained, "The long-term goal of our studies is to determine whether captivity-related problems can be predicted and possibly handled differently in future prisoners of war. As we follow people from year to year, we also learn about the aging process and how it affects performance in the military and aviation environment."

John Gamboa, Guy Hunter's shadow, videotaped the POWs during our sixteen-hour flight to Andrews Air Force Base. When he asked for comments, the former POWs kidded him, saying "No speak!"

During the flight, the attentive staff roamed the aisles tending to our needs. But anytime someone approached, instinctively I felt apprehensive. My head snapped around if I sensed someone approaching from behind. I rubbed my arms, remembering the feel of cold metal around my wrists. When your captors take the handcuffs from your arms and the blindfold from your face, it doesn't automatically remove the scars from your memory. Cindy's love and care would help fade the bad memories and heal the wounds.

The first leg of our journey brought us to Sigonella, Italy. My squadron's "excellent adventure" had journeyed to the same Navy base seven months before. I hardly felt like the same person.

About two o'clock in the morning, I stepped from the plane to the sound of cheering and was astounded by the sight in front of me. At least 1,000 men, women, and children, waving flags and banners lined the flight line. They had gotten up in the middle of the night to greet us. The emotional outpouring from the exuberant crowd overwhelmed me.

Though it was hours before opening time, the base's Wendy's opened for us. I ordered a hamburger and a soft drink, then automatically reached for my wallet. Embarrassed, I said to the manager, "I'm sorry, I don't have any money. I haven't had a wallet for a while."

"Please," he said. "We are open just for you. We are honored and happy to serve you in any way." I was shocked that he would give me a free meal just because I had been a POW. The warm and gratifying response at Sigonella was another indication of the mass outpouring of affection the POWs were soon to receive in the United States.

Our next stop on the way to the States was Shannon Airport in Ireland. More throngs of well-wishers came out to greet us. It didn't sink in that these people were there because of us, symbols of the courage of all the Coalition's armed forces in the Gulf. Somehow, someday, I meant to repay them for their kind welcome. I never take anything without giving something in return.

As *Freedom One* sped through the skies, I munched on pizza and thought about food. I made a list of the foods I wanted to buy in the grocery store and of my requests for Cindy to make. Using a pen again felt strange; my hands largely still had no feeling in them. Would I ever fly again? I had missed flying more combat missions. But as POWs, we had fought a different kind of battle—a battle of fear and loneliness, and resistance. We had fought in closer combat than any pilot and did so blindfolded and handcuffed.

"What surprised you most during captivity?" someone asked me.

"That I got out of there alive."

"What was the hardest for you during captivity?"

"It would be hard to nail down the *most* difficult thing," I answered. "High on the list would be the constant fear of not knowing what would happen next." It surprised me that someone could treat another human being so badly. Our captors didn't care about us as individuals. They were going to get what they wanted no matter what they had to do.

Captivity had been an almost unbelievable challenge. "This is your test, Cliff, and you'd better pass," I had often thought. You have to resolve that although you might not come out of there alive, how you endure and survive captivity is up to you. The decision is yours, not your captors'. You can return home with your own dignity and your own honor, or not. I had fought and won my own war, a war nobody knew about.

Throughout the interrogation and torture, I never cried. I didn't want to give those bastards the satisfaction of knowing they had reduced me to crying. I didn't leave one tear in Baghdad. But after weeks of reflexively suppressing them, I knew the tears were coming. I allowed myself to imagine Cindy in my arms and the tremendous feeling of relief holding her would give me. I wanted to forget the past and focus on that moment.

I wondered if she would bring my wedding ring. She had designed it using stones from the engagement ring her father had given her mother. I had left it with her for safekeeping when I flew to Saudi Arabia. "I can't wait for you to put this back on me when I come home," I had said, trying to act positive. For so many long weeks the possibility of my doing that had seemed dismal.

Where would I link up with Cindy—at a hospital or an administrative headquarters? Laying my head back on my seat, I let my eyes sink shut. I imagined the moment when I would push open that last door and lay eyes on her face. Every minute in the air brought me closer.

Andrews Air Force Base, Maryland
March 10, 1991

Standing on the cold tarmac, I shivered as a bitter wind whipped against me. The fears, the anxieties, the anticipation that had been building inside me for months were all coming to a head. Since the August morning when I had said good-bye to Cliff in the dark, I had ridden an emotional roller coaster of great highs and deep lows. Now I neared the end of the ride, stomach churning, anticipating the grand finale, the final unknown: What would he be like when he returned?

The anticipation of the crowd multiplied as rapidly as its numbers. Thousands of people had converged at the flag-bedecked Andrews airfield to witness a historic event many had feared would never come to pass. At any moment *Freedom One* would land, delivering Desert Storm prisoners of war to their families.

The morning had passed with agonizing slowness. After my morning run, I had attended a brunch with the service secretaries, the commandant and the sergeant major of the Marine Corps, General Powell, and Secretary of Defense Dick Cheney.

After breakfast, with gathering impatience, I waited for the bus that would take us to the flight line. Finally we boarded. The bus seemed to crawl to its destination. "This is taking forever," I kept thinking. As we waited to disembark, I felt more jittery and on edge than at any time during Cliff's captivity. There was little to be nervous about now—Cliff was out of captivity, and his plane would soon taxi down the runway—but the accumulation of nervous energy from these last days felt almost unbearable.

I had imagined the POWs stepping off the plane into the waiting arms of their loved ones. Instead, we next of kin were herded off the bus into a VIP viewing area marked off by heavy ropes. Hundreds of people eddied around me, all talking excitedly, as if waiting for the clock to strike midnight on New Year's Eve. The best viewing spots were already taken. Standing several feet behind the restraining rope, I strained my ears for the sound of the jet. I stood on my tiptoes and craned my neck, but saw nothing but the backs of the tall military officers in front of me. Don Beaver moved the officers aside and parked me directly behind the rope. Melinda Bargreen was nearby, a few rows back.

One hundred yards to my right, behind a chain-link fence, thousands of spectators amassed around the airfield terminal. Hundreds more had climbed on top of the building to obtain a better view. As if gathering for a parade, the jubilant crowd multiplied and grew louder as I watched. Children, teenagers, parents, young, and old braced against the cold, anxious to greet their returning POWs. Even the chilly weather couldn't dampen their enthusiasm. Cheering, waving flags, carrying handmade banners and signs, and speckled with yellow ribbons, they were living, breathing examples of those who had helped me through Cliff's captivity. They had renewed my faith in the generous, caring nature of people.

In front of me to the left, a more subdued group chatted on the other side of the restraining rope near the podium: Secretary of Defense Dick Cheney; his wife, Lynne; and General Colin Powell and his wife, Alma, a colorful scarf adorning her black coat. These four had introduced themselves to me minutes earlier, but it wasn't until I saw a film clip seven years later that I would remember meeting them.

On a large viewing platform directly across from me, members of the media gathered amid gray and black speaker boxes towering over them and scores of thick cables snaking beneath their feet. Photographers on the four-foot-high platform brandished cameras, with extra lenses strapped around their waists and more cameras dangling from their necks. Others stood behind television cameras, their protruding lenses staring at the POW families, recording our every move. They were all jockeying for the best camera angle to get a poignant, award-winning shot.

I was relieved to see the mob of reporters, photographers, and technicians cordoned off under the watchful eye of uniformed police officers. Allowed free rein, newspeople would immediately descend upon the nearest POW family, demanding to know, "What are you *feeling* right now?"

An icy wind whipped the hem of my coat. I wrapped it tighter around me, trembling from the cold, and a bad case of jitters. I reached into my coat pocket and pulled out the gold wedding band I would soon place on Cliff's finger. I read the inscription: "C & C, Today and Forever, September 10, 1988." "We've been married two and a half years today," I reflected.

My attention jolted back to the flight line. Something was happening. The crowd was no longer cheering. Its screaming sounded like the roar of a Super Bowl crowd after a touchdown. The bodies behind me pressed forward. People pointed excitedly.

The sight of *Freedom One* made me catch my breath. As it steadily descended, landing gear lowered, nose angled downward, the blue letters above the row of passenger windows clarified: UNITED STATES OF AMERICA.

I felt the pressure of tears withheld. A lump choked my throat and I swallowed hard. My heart pounded harder and faster. "Don't cry. Don't cry!" I recited to myself. I could hardly hold back the feelings rushing over me.

As the plane taxied toward us, a member of the crew stuck a small American flag out of the cockpit. It finally came to a stop. The cheering, clapping, and whistling overwhelmed the decelerating whine of the jet's engines. A huge white passenger ramp with a red-carpeted stairway was pushed up to the main door of the plane. Mr. and Mrs. Cheney and General and Mrs. Powell positioned themselves at the foot of the stairs. We awaited the POWs and their walk to freedom.

I felt a wild surge of adrenaline. The dream I had longed for was finally coming true. "Stay calm, hold yourself together," I told myself. "You have to be strong for Cliff." The tension of anticipation mounted.

The heavy door swung open to reveal an interior decorated with a gigantic yellow ribbon rippling in the breeze. The crowd surged forward in a wave, pushing me against the restraining rope. Light-headed with anticipation and excitement, I tried to take in a full breath of the cold air. My chest felt heavy, my heart pounded. I clutched the rope as the crowd pressed hard against my back.

A powerful, unexpected fear suddenly gripped me. Was I ready to confront what they had done to Cliff? What if the ordeal had changed him? Would he ever be the same? The thought chilled me like the frigid wind blowing across the tarmac. I pushed my fears away and concentrated on the scene in front of me.

Air Force Colonel David Eberly was first off the gleaming aircraft. As the RPOWs stepped onto the red-carpeted stairs in order of rank, an announcer stated their names over a loudspeaker. The Air Force band, its tubas adorned with yellow ribbons, played "Tie a Yellow Ribbon 'Round the Old Oak Tree."

I braced myself for my first glimpse of Cliff and the aftermath of "brutality and starvation." Two men walked down the ramp, then Cliff emerged in the doorway, his much-thinner body dressed in a green flight suit and flight jacket. He blew out a breath of air, then started down the ramp. After he shook hands with Secretary Cheney, he spoke to him earnestly. I wondered what he was saying; he was holding up the line.

From where I stood, several yards away, I couldn't hear Cliff saying, "Sir, one thing I never worried about was that President Bush would bring us home." He pointed his finger at Secretary Cheney for emphasis. *"Never."* Cliff shook hands with General and Mrs. Powell as the military brass band played "God Bless America," then continued beyond the receiving line toward a row of brown folding chairs.

Watching Cliff scan faces in the crowd, I realized as one of the first off the plane, he would walk to a chair at the far end of the line, farthest away from where Don Beaver and I stood. To get within shouting distance, I had to move to my right through the crowd. With Don behind me, we plowed through the onlookers as Cliff made his way toward the second chair from the end. Friends and relatives watching on television around the country later asked me, "Who was that Marine you were dragging through the crowd?"

Don and I stationed ourselves behind the rope across from where we expected Cliff to pass. "We did it," I said with a smug smile.

"This was clearly not well thought out," Don grumbled. Then he grinned and shrugged. "But we can't argue, we're getting him home."

My sight riveted on Cliff as he passed the roped-off area where I stood. I couldn't wait to hang on to him and never let go.

"The family members looked ready to lurch over the row of chairs," Cliff recalls. "I felt obligated to keep everybody moving, to have some sense of order and structure. We were still military officers and the American public was watching.

"It was like waiting for someone at the airport," he remembers. "Seeing them walk down the ramp toward you, the last fifty feet is the hardest to wait. Your expression was almost one of shocked disbelief. You seemed to be holding your breath, as if you wanted to save that moment in your mind forever. I wanted to say, 'Cindy, take a breath!' and then hold you. After all I'd been through, it was hard not to touch. I found a good compromise: I looked into your eyes.

"As I came nearer your face grew lighter and lighter. The burden of worry was starting to ease. Your mouth formed a half smile that said, 'Is it true? . . . Yes, but I haven't hugged him yet.'"

Cliff neared his chair. The press of bodies against me became unbearable. I could wait no longer. I slipped beneath the rope and maneuvered around a chair into his arms. We locked in a tight embrace with hundreds of camera shutters clicking nearby. Other family members flooded past the rope to greet the POWs. But the media, the well-wishers, the other family members all ceased to exist as we connected. "I've got a lot of tears to cry," he whispered.

Then quickly, I let him go. He sat on a folding chair and I positioned myself behind him, my hands on his shoulders. He found my hand and grasped it below my silver POW bracelet, pressing it securely to his chest. Leaning his head back against me, he closed his eyes and relaxed his stiffened shoulders. Cliff and I later named the picture photographers snapped of that moment "The Mother Eagle Picture."

The brass band played the national anthem. Military personnel saluted; I placed my right hand over my heart. Former POW Sergeant Stamaris, wearing his uniform and red beret, saluted as he lay on a litter draped with an American flag.

With the simple phrase "Welcome home," Secretary Cheney greeted the returnees, then added, "Your country is opening its arms to greet you." The crowd broke into a roar again, waving flags, banners, and balloons. Military personnel stood at attention. "Nothing we say today can erase the loneliness and the dread that were your constant companion while prisoners of war . . . in solitary cells, alone, unarmed, and vulnerable," Secretary Cheney said. "Only you and those who have shared this special ordeal can understand how it feels to return to freedom."

Then the senior returnee, Colonel David Eberly, spoke for his fellow POWs: "'Someday' finally came and we're *glad* to be home."

Addressing Secretary Cheney, Colonel Eberly said, "I'm proud to report the conduct during captivity of the ladies and gentlemen beside me has been without question. Their sense of honor to duty and country has been beyond reproach."

He turned to the families. "I've saved the best for last. You need to know that those who waited also served," he said. "And, sir, if you'll excuse us now, we have some time to make up with our families."

During the blessedly brief but emotional tarmac ceremony, my hands stayed on Cliff's shoulders. Now the stampede was on in a rush of hugs and shouts of joy as the cameras whirred. Unlike the British POWs and their wives—who enjoyed quiet, private reunions—our first embraces were broadcast around the world.

Cliff stood up and pulled me into his arms. "It's been too damn long," he said. He gripped me so hard my feet lifted from the ground.

"I would have waited a lot longer," I whispered.

Voices and motion swirled around us. An island of quiet emotion amid the jubilant celebration, for those few seconds we lost touch with everything but each other.

Melinda recalls, "Looking at that much happiness up close is like gazing into bright light: It's hard to do without getting tears in your eyes."

That afternoon in Seattle, Bonnie and her husband, Don, welcomed a standing-room-only crowd of family and friends to their home. As the house filled with music, conversation, and wonderful smells from the kitchen, camera crews from three major TV networks set up, their long cables snaking through the house. "What a wonderful beginning," Bonnie said on the live broadcast. "Now we can be happy."

Don missed the whole party. He stayed in the downstairs music room, where he had set up a video camera to tape a message from each guest on a two-hour-long video "welcome home card." Their messages to Cliff, which ranged from lovingly compassionate to risqué, were sure to make him laugh and cry.

On the flight line at Andrews Air Force Base, I kissed Cliff, then backed off so others could have a turn at greeting him. It was then that we noticed a Marine colonel in an olive-drab trench coat standing nearby. It was Colonel Kuhn, Cliff's former commanding officer. He was the man who'd had so much faith in Cliff's ability to turn around VMO-2, lead six planes halfway across the globe, and ready the squadron for combat.

Cliff and Colonel Kuhn hugged fiercely, shedding unfettered tears. "You were always with me," Cliff said, his words choked with emotion. In the months that followed, Colonel Kuhn would demonstrate his friendship and concern for Cliff's recovery through phone calls, notes, and a visit.

Several military officers shook Cliff's hand and gave him congratulatory embraces, wiping their eyes unashamedly. Cliff pulled me close to him, slipping his arm around my waist, and we walked to a nearby bus. We passed by the chain-link fence separating the noisy crowd of onlookers from the airfield. I noticed a placard that read WELCOME HOME, CLIFF!

"Cliff! Cindy! Way to go!" someone yelled from the crowd. "Colonel Acree!" came another call. "We love you!" someone shouted. Their comments and the sea of faces blurred as we smiled through our tears. Riding the bus to the reception, Cliff and I held hands, half turned toward each other. I couldn't take my eyes from him.

Amid a crush of camera crews and print photographers, we walked from the cold into a warm, brightly lit hangar decorated with tall clusters of red, white, and blue balloons. Hundreds of people milled around, talking, in a sea of military gold braid, stars, insignias, ribbons, and other accoutrements of high-ranking political and military leaders. Reporters were cordoned off.

Cliff kept one arm around my waist as he introduced me to several Marine officers. One of them was a grinning Guy Hunter, full of good humor, tall tales, and hearty laughter. I liked him immediately.

"I have been told," General Gray said to Cliff that afternoon, "that they [the Iraqis] tried to get you to make a statement against President Bush, and that you refused. The president is going to hear about this, because I'm going to tell him."

People kept trying to drag Cliff away for more introductions and photos, but he tightened his hold on me. Finally he reluctantly released his arm from my waist. "Ten feet, max," he said, pointing authoritatively. I promised to move no farther away from him.

After the reception, the POWs were to enter the Walter Reed Army, Bethesda Naval, or Malcolm Grow Air Force Medical Centers in the Washington area. Joel Lees offered to chauffeur us to Cliff's inprocessing at Bethesda, just north of Washington, D.C.

Cuddled in the backseat, I showed Cliff my POW bracelet. I had so much to tell him, but held back my chattering. "It gave me so much strength to know you were waiting for me," he said. But his clear green eyes looked troubled. Then a confession he must have been holding back burst forth.

"I tried my best . . ." he said. "But . . . I gave them our address. I held out as long as I could. . . . I was certain they'd kill me. I feel terrible about it." He looked devastated. "I am *so* sorry."

My eyes teared up again, seeing his pain. I turned in my seat and put my hands on his shoulders. "Honey, please don't feel bad. It was no secret anyway. Pictures of our house were all over the news—anybody could have gotten our address." He looked as though a great weight had been lifted from him.

That had been his only concession. I told him how proud I had been when I saw his interview on CNN. "Except for one pilot who mumbled unintelligibly, you were the only one who didn't make a propaganda statement. I knew you really suffered for that."

He stared at me, his eyes wide in amazement. He couldn't believe it was true.

"Yes. You were the only one," I reported, squeezing his hand.

"We won," he said. "We *won*." His head fell to his hands and his tears flowed. "I didn't give them a thing," he choked out. He had fought so hard. Until that moment, he hadn't realized how hard.

Bethesda Naval Medical Center
March 10, 1991

"Our long journey has finally come to an end," I told the crowd of reporters and photographers. My eyes focused on Cliff. Several returning POWs had already made brief statements from the onstage podium in the Bethesda Naval Hospital auditorium. When the Marine public affairs officer asked if a family member would speak for the families, I volunteered. "The ultimate expression of support came today at Andrews Air Force Base," I continued. "There was no doubt in any POW's mind that *this* time, America supported them all the way."

Huge, white, multistory Bethesda Hospital stood sentry over its neatly trimmed parklike grounds. Inside, the ward reserved for RPOWs probably never looked less like a hospital. Signs made by schoolchildren brightened the plain white walls; balloons, flowers, and ribbons decorated nearly every room. An enormous banner extending down the hallway told the former POWs YOU ARE NOT AND WILL NEVER BE FORGOTTEN.

Cliff's private hospital room was stocked with fruit baskets, flowers, and snacks, and furnished with a table, several chairs, and rented bedroom furniture. On the same floor, a large four-bed ward had been turned into a hospitality suite with food and cozy rented furniture to give it a homelike atmosphere.

Dr. Eisold and his medical staff welcomed us warmly, putting my worries to rest for good. Cliff filled out paperwork to be admitted, and we were each given an identification badge and released for the night. It was after sunset when Joel drove us to our hotel, the Marriott Suites in Bethesda, where an entire floor had been reserved for POWs, family, and the POWs' "shadows," or escorts.

Cliff and I looked at each other in delight and amazement when we read the hotel manager's letter given to us upon check-in: "While you are with us, feel free to use our restaurant, room service, and other hotel services, compliments of Marriott." The staff did everything they could to make our stay comfortable and stress-free.

A military guard posted in the hallway of the fourth floor checked our identification badges as we stepped off the elevator before heading to our room. Almost giddy with joy, we swatted the door closed behind us. Alone at last. Cliff set our suitcases down and hooked an arm around my waist.

Pulling my arms around his neck, he smiled down lovingly. "C," he whispered, "I'm *hungry.*"

We ordered room service. Before eating, Cliff bowed his head and silently gave thanks for his meal. After nearly a minute of prayer, he wiped his eyes. "I'll never take food for granted again," he said. He winked at me and dug in. He ate with abandon—so did I. It was as if we had *both* been starving.

Cliff polished off enough dinner for two hungry farmhands, but saved one of his two apple dumplings for a middle-of-the-night snack. He would wake up hungry for several nights.

We sat on the bed and called Stephany, Cliff's parents, and other family and friends. Cliff thanked everyone profusely for taking care of me and participating in the letter-writing campaign. Our friend Mary Pat described the welcome-home party in Bonnie's North Seattle home. "The mood fed on itself like a fire," she said. "Everyone was charged up, outrageously happy and silly. Not only had we won the Super Bowl, but we were fifty-point underdogs and Cliff had run the winning touchdown. A hometown hero who belonged to us. Everyone became instant friends, united in our happiness over Cliff's release."

Having seen our reunion on CNN, our friend Debbie told us, "The sight of you two on TV, standing and wiping each others' tears away, was the climax. Then Cliff put on his mask to be his public self."

His public and private selves had always been a study in contrasts—the tenderness in his manner toward me versus the "take-command" mode he entered when dealing with military personnel. For now, those two sides seemed more closely merged than ever before. He didn't resist my taking care of him. As I soothed and reassured him, I touched both the husband and the Marine.

With a voracious appetite for information, Cliff craved news and kept asking questions. As we started unpacking our bags, he turned on CNN. Automatically I tensed, feeling the familiar pain in my chest, when I heard the accompanying music of "Headline News." I wanted to bury our suffering in the past, not think about what each of us had gone through. We briefly saw ourselves in the film clips of the reunion, but also watched reports on continuing problems in Kuwait and Iraq.

Later, I climbed into bed and propped myself on one elbow, facing the bathroom. The hiss of water in the shower ceased. Cliff grabbed a thick white towel slung over the glass-walled enclosure and limped out into the vanity area. I studied his familiar body as he dried himself off, long legs planted in a wide stance. Thick red calluses covered his ribs, hips, knees, and shoulders. Bruises and scabs in various stages of healing dotted his body. The healthy, robust face I remembered had been replaced by pale skin and cheeks as hollow as his belly. His strongly muscled legs now gave way to sharp angles everywhere. More than thin, he looked like a refugee from a famine.

In the mirror, Cliff saw me watching him. He rubbed his head with the towel. "Body by Baghdad," he joked.

He switched off the light and moved toward the bed through the pitch-black room. "How can you see?" I asked.

He let out a wry laugh. "I've been living with the sight of a mole. I'm used to darkness."

He climbed into bed next to me. It seemed like years since I had enjoyed his freshly washed smell in bed.

"Ahhh. This bed feels so soft." I heard the weariness in his words. He rolled toward me, and I stroked his head, neck, and shoulders. He sighed again, long and deep, savoring my gentle touch.

"It feels so good to have someone touching me who isn't trying to hurt me." His voice hinted at remembered pain. I sensed a vulnerability in Cliff I had never seen before and powerful emotions skimming just below the surface.

He was safe. He was near me again. We could stay together as long as we wanted. This was the dream I couldn't allow myself to imagine. But together now, my fantasy had come true. The constant ache I had grown accustomed to was already beginning to fade.

With a weary gust of breath, Cliff closed his eyes and his body relaxed against mine. The day's excitement had finally caught up with him.

No blindfolds, no beatings, no bombings.

No rumors, no reporters.

No worrying, no wondering.

I felt the thick scab of a gash on his shin. "Youch," I said. "How'd you get that?"

"A guard kicked me with his steel-toed boot," he said matter-of-factly. A shudder of apprehension went through me. Would their repeated cruelty rob us of the intimacy we had shared?

Lying in the warm curve of his body, the unaccustomed sensation of his long length against mine reminded me of our wedding night. But Cliff's fatigue told me we would culminate *this* long-anticipated day by falling asleep in each other's arms. Cliff's fingertip trailed down my shoulder. After seven months apart, he had other ideas.

The Gulf between us disappeared as everything we had shared over our twenty years—separations and reunions, friendship and love, obstacles over-come—reunited us again.

Later that night I walked toward the bed carrying Cliff's apple dumpling. He sat up with two pillows stacked behind his head, his legs stretched out and his arms resting at his sides. I handed him his snack. With his lips curved in a smile, he radiated contentment. "You look pleased with yourself," I teased.

His smile widened into the familiar dimpled grin I loved. He chuckled lightly. "I've had everything tucked up under me for so long—it's nice to know it still works!"

I had my beloved husband back—the Cliff I knew. The next several days, however, would reveal what his ordeal had cost him.

Bethesda Naval Medical Center
March 11, 1991

"How many times do you think you were knocked unconscious?" one of two Navy doctors asked Cliff. Sitting at a small round table in his hospital room, I braced myself for another detail of his brutal mistreatment.

"A dozen? . . . I lost track," Cliff answered.

"Multiple recurrent episodes of head trauma with resultant loss of consciousness of unknown duration," the doctor noted on Cliff's medical record.

On that first day at Bethesda, Cliff had begun to recount to a variety of Navy doctors the story of his imprisonment. He described his ordeal, without a hint of self-pity. I tried not to outwardly cringe at the horrifying details. "He made it through," I kept reminding myself. That night I wrote in my journal:

> It's hard to hear all the horrifying things he went through—but comforting to look over and see he *is* here, in one piece. He knows I'll be here whenever he needs me and can take whatever he has to say. I want to hear it, understand, and help.

For the next five joyful, worrisome days it seemed our every moment was scheduled. Cliff's time was packed with doctor appointments, treatments, counseling sessions, and medical tests. One morning I counted eight doctors crowded around him in his hospital room. By noon each day, Cliff was physically and mentally exhausted, and his days continued till six or seven each night.

It became clear to doctors that Cliff had not only been treated harshly in Iraq, he had almost certainly been more savagely beaten and tortured than any of the other POWs—because of his senior rank, his status as a pilot and a CO, the timing of his capture at the beginning of the war, and his maximum resistance to interrogation.

In physical terms, doctors reported that he had suffered a "chronic cervical strain from concussive trauma sustained while ejecting and during interrogative beatings . . . multiple recurrent episodes of head trauma with resultant loss of consciousness of unknown duration with associated post-traumatic periods of amnesia . . . nasal fractures . . . obvious flattening deformity and deviation of the nasal structures . . . airway obstruction caused by blunt trauma . . . olfactory nerve damage, smell ability impaired to all modalities... hearing loss... radial nerve injury and weakness of the interosseous, grip strength, and thumb extensors of both hands, right more than left, secondary to tightly bound handcuffs... expected complications of weight loss, malnutrition, and diarrheal disorders secondary to inadequate food intake and contaminated water sources..." He would need reconstructive surgery to restore his sense of smell and normal breathing.

In mental and emotional terms, the damage was harder to assess. He had endured "variable levels of stress-related psychological trauma consequent to incarceration and interrogation," doctors said. Marines are tough guys, and commanding officers in combat are supposedly the toughest of all. Cliff consistently underplayed the harrowing details of his ordeal in captivity, but I knew privately he was asking himself those questions so important to an aviator: Will I ever be healed? Will I ever fly again, or will my injuries clip my wings for good?

The skilled team did its best to repair his body, but wounds to his psyche would take longer to heal. Each night in bed, I stroked his head and massaged his shoulders. "It's nice to have a head without lumps," he said. "I was so tired of them beating on me."

Neurologists said Cliff's captors had beaten him so severely that his skull had fractured, nearly driving bone fragments from his nose into his brain. That he had survived was a miracle. Because he had been beaten into unconsciousness several times, irreversible brain damage was a real concern.

Unfortunately, the medical tests he had to undergo to determine the extent of the damage closely replicated his captivity experiences. The needles of frequent blood draws evoked memories of the injections he'd received in Baghdad. The hearing test, X rays, and CAT scan took place in small, dimly lit rooms with one tiny window or none at all. The MRI forced him to lie motionless in a dark, narrow cylinder for what seemed hours while staccato sounds so similar to those of a machine gun attacked him from all sides.

One night, after another grueling day of being poked, prodded, x-rayed, and tested, Cliff looked at me with tired eyes. "I'm looking forward to having *one* day without pain."

We met with a nutrition expert, the dietitian for the Naval Academy's athletes, who gave me suggestions on how to help Cliff regain his weight. As Cliff described the diet he had survived on for the past seven weeks, she began to cry.

Every morning he recounted his ordeal to different doctors. Every afternoon he spent three hours in closed-door meetings with intelligence debriefers, telling his story in minute detail. He walked out of each private debriefing moving like someone who had lost a lot of blood: slowly, shoulders drooping, head hanging, face a sickly white. Reliving the events seemed to allow his fatigue and ill health to overcome him. But he was willing to give this full accounting to help future POWs.

During those days of debriefings at the hospital, Cliff was trying to cope with the demands of the public to know more. At the same time the intelligence officers had warned the returned POWs not to reveal details of their treatment in captivity. Nine Americans missing in action might still be held by the Iraqis, and revealing the truth might bring reprisals upon them.

Members of the media waited outside the hospital, hoping to interview returnees leaving the building. "Are you POWs?" they asked pairs of thin-looking Marines or Navy officers. We avoided the reporters by walking straight from the hospital to the connected parking garage and back. On our first day at Bethesda, two reporters stopped us as we entered the parking garage elevator with Joel Lees.

"Can we ask you some questions?" one of them asked. After an exhausting day of medical and intelligence interviews, the last thing Cliff wanted to do was tell his story again. "I'm sorry, no," he said. We stepped past them into the elevator. The two reporters took the stairs. When the door opened, they were waiting for us. Cliff told them no again. They walked away—convinced, we thought. When we drove down the ramp, their car pulled alongside us. Joel sped up past them. After this third try, they left us alone.

On Tuesday afternoon, Secretary of the Navy H. Lawrence Garrett III and Admiral Frank Kelso II, chief of naval operations, visited the POWs. The returnees gathered in the lounge, all in uniform except Cliff, who was wearing pajamas, with his bandaged foot propped up on a stool. That morning a doctor had operated on his foot to remove the souvenir he'd picked up after the Biltmore bombing. The firmly imbedded piece of glass had been difficult to find.

"Facing a ruthless enemy, they were courageous, determined, and honorable. Despite brutality, privation, and fear, they persevered," said Admiral Kelso. "They are America's heroes. They made us all proud."

"I'm not a hero. I'm a survivor," Cliff told a Navy reporter.

On March 14, RPOWs participated in separate news conferences at Andrews Air Force Base and Bethesda to answer Americans' questions about being held captive. Five Marine and two Navy POWs at Bethesda were introduced to the anxiously awaiting press. With honor and humor, they recounted their days in Iraqi hands.

The conference began with a statement to the media from Bethesda medical staff about the condition of the returnees under their care: "Good spirits and basically sound mentally and physically, as evidenced by our ability to allow them to leave the hospital every night, including the first." I smiled, remembering the original plan. "We are emphasizing family time and casual clothes, which has been very therapeutic," Dr. Eisold said.

Cliff sat stiffly at a table with the others, and I could tell he was in significant pain. Although he had given the full, uncut version of his story to the intelligence debriefers and medical staff, in public he glossed over the brutality he had endured.

"There were times when things got very. . ." He paused. "Not so good. At those times I removed my mind from my body by focusing on my wife, Cindy, and imagining her training our dog, Cami. I just went away mentally. That got me through."

"Is it true you received harsher treatment than others because of your senior rank?" a reporter asked him.

"They were real glad to see a Marine aviator," Cliff answered. "They were real glad to see a commanding officer. I was never in the same location with the other people who were being interrogated and beaten, so I couldn't be sure. All POWs had it bad. Some worse than others."

Because most of his injuries weren't obvious—he wasn't in a cast or a wheelchair—people outside the immediate medical circle assumed that he was fairly healthy and hadn't been badly treated. That impression was reenforced not only by Cliff's take-charge military demeanor but also by his unwillingness to complain.

Some returning POWs had sustained more injuries before their capture than afterward. The Associated Press reported: "Army physician Colonel Russ Zajtchuk said today an examination of the five being cared for at Walter Reed 'didn't suggest any mistreatment of the prisoners.'" According to the *Los Angeles Times,* Brigadier General Richard Neal, chief spokesman for the U.S. Central Command, said initial reports indicated the injuries suffered by all released POWs came from plane crashes or ejections from aircraft. The public tended to see the POWs as "one person" who had experienced relatively the same treatment, same experience. I worried others would conclude that Cliff, too, had not received "any mistreatment."

Navy Lieutenant Jeffrey Zaun, whose bruised and cut face had shocked the public when his stilted statement appeared on the Iraqi-made videotape, reported that most of the wounds Americans agonized over were caused by "popping out of a plane at five hundred miles per hour." He also said he had "banged" himself "in the nose," hoping he could disfigure himself so he would not be shown on Iraqi television. "Maybe a little bit of it was getting slapped around," he added.

I found myself stunned to read that some captives—especially those captured late in the war—had received relatively benign treatment. Melissa Rathbun-Nealy, the first female American prisoner of war, declared her captors "the nicest people. They did all they could to make me comfortable. I'm probably the only POW who has ever gained weight."

Like the captured CBS journalists, she had been in the wrong place at the wrong time. "I'm not a hero," she admitted. "I just got stuck in the sand."

The military services moved quickly to honor the returnees by presenting them with medals. Such awards are important to military members as visible and continuous recognition of a job well done or a heroic act. Every person serving in the U.S. military during the Gulf War—at home or abroad—was awarded the National Defense Service Medal. All Desert Storm POWs were awarded the POW Medal. Those who were injured—whether from enemy-inflicted wounds or from plane crashes—were awarded the Purple Heart. Despite the fact that some prisoners had received dramatically different treatment, the same medals were automatically awarded.

I had heard that the Marine Corps, more than any other service, was frugal and conservative when awarding medals. But in my mind, Cliff deserved some sort of recognition for the valor he had demonstrated by his refusal to give in to his captors' demands to provide significant intelligence that would be harmful to his fellow Marines. But until the twelve hours of statements he'd recorded during intelligence debriefings were listened to, only the naval doctors and intelligence officers would know what Cliff had done.

On March 16, General Gray presented the Purple Heart, the Prisoner of War Medal, and the National Defense Service Medal to the five Marine RPOWs. "They stand before us today as special, special forever," General Gray commented in the awards ceremony. "They are proof that we don't have robots in the armed forces. We have individuals: intelligent, thoughtful, sensitive, tough physically, and more important, tough mentally."

I felt a radiant pride as Cliff moved from the front of the stage to the podium to speak on behalf of the other Marines. His erect bearing belied his pain. The epidural anesthesia used during his foot surgery had left him with a painful backache.

"During captivity, we had many things to worry about—day by day, minute by minute. But one thing I never worried about during my forty-eight days was coming home. I knew my country and my president would bring me home, whether in a body bag or walking across the border to freedom. I knew I was coming home."

After the awards ceremony, we returned to Cliff's hospital room, where phone messages and letters continued to pour in from friends and supporters. I will always remember those who took the time to locate us and welcome Cliff home. At the same time, we were deluged with requests for interviews—eighty-eight in the first three days—from network shows; Seattle, San Diego, and Los Angeles newspapers; and TV stations. Other POWs appeared on television shows, but Cliff wanted to devote his energy to healing.

After six days of extensive medical tests, debriefings, and treatments, we received the news that all of Cliff's tests had good results. Doctors said the CT and MRI scans of his brain were normal, showing only "extensive fibrotic-scar formation" from his nasal fractures . . . head, neck, and cranial nerve findings showed he had "no significant neurological residuals," only "impaired auditory spatial localization suggesting left temporal lobe injury," which they hoped would improve over time.

Cliff was given a day off to spend as he chose. We spent it with Joel and his wife, Kathy, also a naval doctor, who had flown to Washington from California. After attending a church service that Sunday morning, we headed to Washington, D.C., for some sightseeing.

It was a clear, cool day in our nation's capital, the air scented with the promise of spring, of renewal. We strolled across a large expanse of treed lawn near the Tidal Basin of the Potomac, savoring the peaceful beauty around us. Overhead, tiny buds of green and pink dotted the branches of Japanese cherry trees. After the flat, gray landscape of captivity, Cliff seemed to experience even the most common sights—blue sky, leaves moving in the wind, a bird winging by—as if for the first time.

He tilted his head back and inhaled deeply, drinking in the sweet, fresh air like one who is parched. "I really appreciate the freedom to walk at will without a blindfold and handcuffs, or a captor hovering over me. Life is a gift."

We walked beyond the 555-foot-tall Washington Monument down the grassy east-west mall toward the Reflecting Pool, past Frisbee players, kite fliers, and camera-hugging tourists conversing in many languages.

One hundred yards north of the pool, the dark Vietnam memorial seemed to emerge from among the trees. The 492-foot-long granite wall that sliced into the hillside was etched with nearly 60,000 names of those who died in Vietnam. Walking alongside the stark chevron-shaped wall—with the earth sloping up and the rows of engraved names rising beside me—felt like sinking into the war.

The visual impact of the staggering number of names triggered a range of emotions in me—relief that Cliff had returned alive, regret that so many others in past wars had not, and gratitude for the kindness of the American public, who had given me strength and welcomed Cliff back with open arms.

We continued walking along the somber wall of names. Thanks to the support of the world community, wide media attention, and President Bush's strong stance, neither Cliff nor I had to endure the isolation, pain, and loneliness experienced by the Vietnam POWs and their families.

Cliff turned to me. "Freedom is precious," he said, his eyes glistening. "You don't fully realize its value until it's taken away."

The wall gradually diminished in height, and we rose again into the open air with a renewed awareness of our good fortune.

After our day of sightseeing, our foursome dined at a busy, casual restaurant in Bethesda. The owner discreetly approached our table. He thanked Cliff for his service and offered us a bottle of wine on the house. Cliff humbly thanked him, surprised at being recognized.

We perused our menus and I felt my stomach rumble. "I'm starving!" I exclaimed. "Oops," I said sheepishly, glancing at Cliff.

"Me, too." He patted my leg and smiled.

From the day of our reunion, he had gradually come back to life. The six pounds he had gained helped fill out his cheeks and return the color to his skin. His energy level was improved and he retained only a slight limp. He had begun making remarks that made me laugh, and I found I could tease him again. Sometimes for a split second I would even forget what had happened.

A waiter brought our meals. Cliff clasped my hand and, closing his eyes, bowed his head in prayer. Everyone followed suit.

I prayed for a happy future—Cliff healthy, the two of us together as much as we wanted, starting the family we hoped for. Cliff, too, was anxious to put the past behind him and be fully healed. But doctors recommended he continue to take it easy for a while. Giardiasis still plagued his intestinal tract, nagging pain in his neck and back made some movements difficult, and his body remained weakened from malnutrition and abuse. Comparison of responses on his entry and exit psychiatric tests indicated great improvement since the beginning of his stay, though he had a "continued desire to avoid basements, trains, and tunnels." Psychologists predicted he would continue to experience occasional symptoms of Post-Traumatic Stress Disorder (PTSD).

Now that his debriefings were completed, Cliff wanted to leave his captivity behind. As each day passed, he placed more pressure on himself to lock up the horrors hidden inside. But sometimes they leaked out, much to his dismay.

Partway through dinner, Kathy knocked over her wineglass. The goblet crashed to the table, spilling its contents. At the sudden noise, Cliff sprang from his seat, a look of terror on his face. Embarrassed, self-conscious, he quickly sat down again. Breathing heavily, he apologized for his reaction. His face expressed the disappointment and annoyance of a scolding parent. He had expected his internal wounds to mend as quickly as his external ones. I did not know then that some scars are impossible to heal.

The next morning Cliff jumped out of bed. This was to be his last day of tests at Bethesda. He was keyed up and excited, eager to return to Camp Pendleton and his home, his daughter, his dog, and his Marines. Goal oriented, he checked his watch every thirty minutes. "I feel like I've been here three weeks," he said as we drove into the Bethesda parking lot for the last time.

After two hours of final consultations, Cliff was free to go. His medical care couldn't have been better. "He'll need to rest and take it easy," one of his doctors cautioned me—as if I would have any say in the matter. We said goodbye to Dr. Eisold and his medical staff at Bethesda—and our insular life away from the media and demands of the real world was over.

By the time we reached our hotel room I was noticing a definite change in Cliff. He zipped up his flight suit and checked his image in the hotel room mirror. "I almost feel like a Marine now," he said.

"You are a Marine, and you have been," I assured him. "Especially these past two months."

After donning his flight suit, he stood more erect. He was no longer the recuperating hospital patient but a United States Marine eager to resume his duties and put the past behind him. He wouldn't feel like a true Marine until he got back in the cockpit; he missed flying as much as he'd missed eating. But his medical problems had to be resolved first.

Before Cliff could receive an "up chit"—approval to fly again—he had to regain feeling in his hands and resolve his symptoms of Post-Traumatic Stress Disorder—the recurrent and intrusive "re-experiencing" of a trauma.

We drove to Andrews Air Force Base, where an Air Force C-21 jet awaited to fly Guy and Mary Hunter and Cliff and me back home to Camp Pendleton. A small group of military officers and wives—including my escort, Major Tom Madigan, and his wife, Phyllis—was there to see us off.

We said our good-byes and climbed the stairway into the plane. As the jet engines roared to a crescendo, I checked my lap belt, remembering the kind remark Mrs. Madigan had made as she hugged me good-bye: "All the officers' wives—we really do appreciate the way you speak up," she said.

My days of having to fight and speak up were over. Our battles, Cliff's and mine, though fought apart, had been won. Facing war and death, he had found courage and honor. Facing fear and helplessness, I had found strength and faith.

With our long-awaited reunion behind us, we could end this grim chapter in our lives and return to a normal life. As the jet gathered speed and lifted off the runway, I relaxed into my seat, naively believing it was true.

Marine Corps Air Station, Camp Pendleton, California
March 18, 1991

The Air Force passenger jet crested the Santa Margarita Mountains, bringing Cindy and me closer to our welcome-home celebration at Camp Pendleton. Scanning the mountainous terrain, I caught sight of the town of Temecula, Interstate 15, and other reference points I had used so often when I was flying Cobras and Broncos out of Camp Pendleton.

Though I wasn't at the controls this time, I felt a rush of joy at flying over familiar territory. After eight days at Bethesda in Washington, D.C., and a day of travel west, I was nearly home. It was a 10,000-mile trip from Baghdad to here—and the last few miles were the longest.

As the plane approached the Camp Pendleton airfield, I straightened in my seat to quickly review the notes for my speech. Minutes later, the plane taxied to a stop in front of columns of Marines standing at attention. Several hundred jubilant civilians crowded on bleachers cheered wildly and waved American flags, signs, ten-foot-long welcome home banners, and clusters of yellow balloons.

I placed my olive-drab "cover" on my head, then grasped Cindy's right hand; in her left she held a small American flag. Her reassuring smile and nod told me, "I'm proud of you; now we're in this together." But even when we were worlds apart, she had shared my ordeal.

I took a deep breath, then ducked through the doorway, pulling Cindy out after me. Squinting into the late-afternoon sunshine, we climbed off the stairway onto the red carpet where several Marine officers, including Colonel Don Beaver and his wife, Kay, waited. The crowd applauded and cheered as I saluted the Marine officers.

Before the Gulf War, I had read about the unprecedented support of the American people, but seeing and feeling such genuine affection still overwhelmed me. Thanks to citizens like these, our nation was stronger and more united than at any time during the last several decades. I felt indebted to them for their support of our armed forces.

Cindy, Guy, and Mary followed me onto the windswept runway as horns blared from nearby fire engines. A Marine band played "God Bless America." Two OV-10 Broncos were parked nearby on the tarmac, where 200 Marines of VMO-2 stood at attention. The rest of the squadron was still based in the hot sands of Saudi Arabia. Having my Marine Corps family there to greet me made my return home even more special. I raised my right arm to them in a sign of victory.

The four of us were greeted by the base commander, Brigadier General Michael Neil, and by Major General Harry Blot, commanding general of the 5th Marine Expeditionary Force. Kay stepped forward to hug me; Don slapped me on the back. With her colorful skirt billowing in the warm breeze, Kay handed Cindy and Mary bouquets of red roses.

I shook hands with Guy, then stepped up to the podium, which was adorned with a yellow ribbon. The crowd was silent. "Standing before this squadron is a dream come true for me. And let me assure you, the pleasure is all mine."

I pulled my folded speech from my pocket. Behind me, colorful flags snapped in the breeze. I drew a deep breath to compose myself. "Seeing all of you here today, it's hard to believe that two weeks ago I was living in a cold, dark, filthy prison cell in Baghdad. Standing once again on the flight line of Camp Pendleton among Marines is one of many dreams that have come true for me." The crowd cheered and whistled.

I thanked our military leadership and the American people for their support and our families for their prayers and perseverance throughout this ordeal. I glanced toward Cindy, standing to my side and slightly behind me. I wouldn't have survived captivity without her. "I would especially like to thank my wife, Cindy, for her unending devotion, love, and support, which gave me the greatest source of strength to return home." I turned to look at her. "I am proud of you for the aggressive action you took in a seemingly helpless situation."

I thanked Joel Lees, Pat Antosh, Colonel Beaver and Kay, and other friends for their support. Last, I thanked all those throughout the country who had supported the efforts of the POW/MIA Liberty Alliance, especially the local members who got the organization off the ground and kept the vigil going.

I breathed deeply of the warm air. "The brutality and the hardships of being a prisoner of war are behind us now. We look forward to returning to our families and our fellow Marines, and we will always remember those who gave their lives and made the greatest sacrifice of all." I paused. "It is absolutely *wonderful* to be back home."

I tucked my speech into my pocket, then turned away from the podium.

"Lieutenant Colonel Acree, your squadron awaits," a Marine announced.

I strode toward the formation of Marines standing at parade rest.

"Squadron, attention!" called the acting commander of the rear detachment at Camp Pendleton from his position in front of the formation. He executed an about-face, then saluted me. I returned his salute.

In a clipped voice he said, "Lieutenant Colonel Acree. *Now,* VMO-2 is all present and accounted for." The Marine Corps flag and the unit colors unfurled as the band began to play "The Star-Spangled Banner."

I dropped my salute, and with that brief ceremony I was reunited with my 350-member squadron. Even while in captivity, I had never relinquished command of the squadron. I rejoined Cindy, and with the formalities completed, we were mobbed by family members, friends, and well-wishers. Guy's three children and two nieces hugged his legs or snuggled in his arms. Several people brought POW bracelets to return to Guy and me. "I deeply appreciate your efforts to help me and the other POWs return to our country," I told those who had worn a bracelet bearing my name. "I'm going to take all the POW bracelets and make something with them as a permanent reminder of your support."

Cindy introduced the local members of the POW/MIA Liberty Alliance. It was incredibly gratifying to meet the people who had worked so hard to return me to my freedom. Then Guy, Mary, Cindy, and I left the crowd of well-wishers and walked toward a large group of reporters who remained cordoned behind yellow ropes.

"How does it feel to be home?" one of them asked.

"Returning home is an utter relief," Guy said.

"I know I'm home when I'm with Marines and my wife," I said.

"What was it like being shot down?"

"A very bad day!" I replied with a smile.

"What are your plans now?" someone asked.

"To spend quality time with my wife, and hit every good San Diego restaurant and *eat*," I said.

Guy said he looked forward to jogging and lifting weights. "I'm *still* a POW," he quipped, grinning at Mary. "But now it's prisoner of wife!"

"We're looking forward to spending some quality time together," Cindy told a newspaper reporter. "These past days have been so busy with tests, briefings, and treatments. Cliff needs some peace and quiet . . . and I'm going to make sure he gets it!" We were both eager to return home to the normal life we had dreamed of—drinking coffee and reading the newspaper on Sunday mornings, taking walks with Cami, spending time with Stephany.

After the ceremony, Cindy and I were driven in a white military sedan that was led by a police motorcycle escort to ensure a safe and uncomplicated last leg of my journey home. During the twenty-minute drive, people in cars waved and honked their horns. I almost looked over my shoulder to see who they were waving at; I felt honored and humbled by their attention. It was incredible to think that people I had never met felt so strongly about my return.

Shortly before dusk, the car climbed the hill toward our home. As it rounded the bend our house came into view. Balloons and welcome home banners draped the front entryway and the garage doors. The cul-de-sac was filled with a noisy assembly of friends, neighbors, reporters, and photographers. Three barking neighborhood dogs joined the din.

I stepped out of the car onto the sidewalk. Cami, yelping behind the front door, announced my arrival. She hadn't forgotten me. I couldn't wait to rush in and see her. First I needed to thank the crowd for their sincere gestures of friendship and support. I told them how deeply their presence had touched me. Then as more cameras flashed, the reporters began asking their questions.

Minutes later, the front door opened. Cami dashed out, her neck adorned with a patriotic red, white, and blue bandanna. Barking boisterously, she rushed toward me. "Cami!" I crouched on the walk, arms outstretched, calling her anxiously. She ran toward my open arms, then growling menacingly, charged right past me. Diving into the crowd, she pounced on one of the three visiting dogs.

"Cami!" I called. "Cami! Come!"

She ran back and hurled herself at me, slobbering my face with kisses. Then neighbors presented us with a card and a gift certificate for two nights' stay at San Diego's landmark Hotel del Coronado. "*Two* to a room here. . . .

You can have as many blankets as you want . . . the food's better here . . ." the card quipped.

I gave reporters a few more sound bites, then Cindy and I waved good-bye and walked into our house. After being away for seven months, it was like a dream to stand in my own house. So many times during my captivity I had doubted that I would ever see it again. Now, finally being home, I felt overwhelmed with how lucky I was to be alive.

Cami ran ecstatic circles around us, as if rejoicing that her family was whole again. I wandered around the familiar downstairs rooms, newly trimmed with welcome home banners, balloons, cards, and flowers. I walked up the stairs and set our bags in the master bedroom. Cindy lingered several steps behind while, in a trance of rediscovery, I toured each room. I felt the soft carpet under my feet, ran my fingers over the furniture, and looked out the windows with no bars to block the view.

I was no longer in a filthy concrete cell with blood- and urine-stained walls and guards walking by the door. I was home—a warm, wonderful, heavenly place.

Living in a tent in Saudi Arabia those months before the war, I had missed the comforts of home—a soft bed, good food, not having to stand in line for meals, showers, and phones. "Boy, this cot is uncomfortable," I'd think when I awoke each morning after four or five hours' sleep. "Life can't get much tougher than this." I went from that to no bed, no sink, no shower, almost no food.

I was home with the simple pleasures I had been denied, but my mind had not yet arrived. I didn't feel the rush of relief, the deep sense of relaxation I had anticipated. The strong feelings and apprehensions of being a POW overrode even the thrill of coming home. It would take time for the memories of brutality to go away and the good feelings to sink in.

The next morning we ate breakfast at a favorite spot I had dreamed about in captivity. While we were eating, a man walked by our window seat, smiled, nodded, and waved. It felt good to see a new face that was caring and friendly, not sent to harm me. But it surprised me that a stranger would recognize me. At the grocery store that afternoon, I was surprised again when several more people approached to shake my hand and welcome me home.

Two days later, I picked up Stephany for our first weekend together. When I went to the Gulf, she was only eleven, but she seemed to have matured to seventeen while I was away. After I knocked on her door, I cried like a kid. For me, she was emotionally as strong as an ox. She made me proud to be her father.

Now that I was home, I planned to make my family and my recovery first priority. I would stay out of the limelight. Let the other Desert Storm POWs appear on *Larry King Live,* be interviewed for *People* magazine, or tell their stories in supermarket tabloids.

My joy at being home was overshadowed by my fatigue. Above all other concerns, I wanted to regain my health and return to my duties as CO of my squadron. The demands of being a CO tire even a healthy person. Once I returned, I would want to give nothing less than 100 percent.

But it looked like the rest I needed to regain my health might be hard to come by. I had arrived home to a list of speaking requests—as thick as a phone book—compiled by the Marine Corps public affairs officer. There were requests to speak at the Navy Dental Technician Ball, to serve as grand marshal for several welcome home parades, to attend a ribbon-cutting ceremony unveiling a Rockwell International space shuttle, to speak on world peace at the Hollywood Bowl, to participate in fund-raisers for the Special Olympics and other charities, to appear on eight radio and TV shows, to attend a dedication and reception for a landmark flagpole, to preside at a ceremony to remove the yellow ribbon from the turret of the Hotel del Coronado. More requests—to appear at fund-raisers, publicity gatherings, media events, and homecoming celebrations—had accumulated on the answering machine and arrived in thick stacks of mail.

I had so many choices of how to spend my time. Though fatigued, I wanted to repay the love and caring that had flowed in my direction since I was taken captive. I had been brought back from the brink of death; the least I could do was share my time.

"Remember what the doctors said about taking it easy," Cindy cautioned. "The social obligations can wait." She insisted that getting away together would be the best thing for me. I preferred to stay home and hibernate, but maybe she was right. At home, I'd feel compelled to answer the hundreds of unopened letters, the packages of returned POW bracelets, and the scores of phone calls. After our weekend with Stephany and a four-day visit with my parents, Cindy and I escaped to Monterey, California.

Driving north up the coast on Highway 101 at sixty miles an hour felt like flying. I hadn't driven for two months, and before the war I'd only driven a pickup truck at slow speeds in dusty Saudi Arabia. But after a few minutes on the open road, I began to relax and enjoy the ocean scenery, the cool, moist morning air. I hoped that after a few days of relaxing I could put the past behind me, regain my strength, and feel like myself again.

We checked into the stately old multistoried Bachelor Officers Quarters (BOQ) at the Naval Postgraduate School in Monterey. The next morning, we went shopping at the base exchange. I'd never enjoyed shopping before, but for the first time I felt enthusiastic about buying clothes. I replaced the watch my captors had stolen, bought two new shirts and a pair of khaki pants, then headed to the shoe department. There I discovered that, for some reason, my right foot was now nearly one size bigger than my left.

On the second day of our visit to Monterey, we had lunch in the basement dining room of the BOQ. Though I didn't feel like eating, I ordered a sandwich and a bowl of soup. I wanted to please Cindy, who was impatient for me to recoup my weight loss. But my appetite had not returned.

The damage from the Iraqis' beatings had left my nose blocked and reduced my sense of smell. I missed being able to smell the sweetness of Cindy's perfume, the scent of pine trees, the fresh smell of clean clothes. Being unable to smell the food reduced its appeal, even when Cindy prepared the dishes I had longed for in captivity. On the rare occasions when I did have an appetite, I found it hard to eat half of what I used to. The medication to eliminate the giardia in my system kept me constantly bloated and queasy. Knowing she worried about me, I hadn't complained of these problems to Cindy.

After finishing her lunch, Cindy eyed my nearly full plate. She glanced up, frowning. "You'll never regain your weight eating like that."

"My stomach is still upset."

She looked back with regret in her eyes. "I didn't know."

"I just can't seem to get going. I can't get my batteries charged."

"You need to think of yourself as someone getting over the flu or pneumonia," she consoled. "It will take time. You've got to build a good, strong foundation now with food and rest."

I shook my head, discouraged. Each morning since being repatriated, I had hoped to awaken feeling revived, strong and healthy again. Ready to return to a normal life. But as the days passed, my recovery seemed at a standstill. Instead, I felt worn out. I tried not to let my captivity get to me, but my days in Baghdad affected me from the moment I awoke until I fell asleep at night.

Sudden noises—the crashing of cubes in the hotel ice maker, a car backfiring, a window slamming shut—startled me. Jet planes landing nearby reminded me of the bombings in Baghdad. Bread sticks and tomato-based soup at the Olive Garden restaurant evoked memories of my starvation diet.

My sleep habits had changed. I tossed and turned restlessly in my sleep. My hamstrings had shortened from too many weeks of lying in the fetal position, and my legs felt stiff. The calluses all over my body made lying down uncomfortable. If Cindy brushed against me, I awoke with a start. The night before, Cindy's leg had touched mine and I sprang out of bed yelling, "No! No!" "I thought someone was carrying me," I told her after I calmed down.

Caffeinated drinks made me too shaky; still on the edge, I found it difficult to relax. I had little feeling on the tops of my hands from wrists to fingertips. That morning in the hotel, I had hung up the shower head and walked away with my thumb still hooked to it. Cindy and I didn't hold hands anymore; knowing her hand rested on mine but being unable to feel it was creepy.

I used to be in control, able to achieve whatever I set my mind to. Now I felt powerless over my body and mind, struggling just to feel normal. I couldn't leave the experience of my captivity behind.

"We have to give it time," Cindy said again. She gently placed a hand on my arm. "We can't expect too much too soon."

She had done everything possible to ease my transition back to normal life. I don't know what I would have done without her—my friend, my wife, and now my lifeline.

We left our table and headed up the curved stone stairway to our floor. We had reached the midpoint of the dark, cavelike stairway when the rattle of a jackhammer vibrated loudly from below.

Bang-bang-bang!

I jumped. The roar of the jackhammer hit me like blows of a sledge-hammer, reverberating up my spine. The sound was familiar, too familiar.

As if escaping a hail of AK-47 fire, I rushed up the stairs, breathing fast, ears ringing, my heart ramming my chest walls. With shaking hands, I turned the key in the lock, then went directly into the bathroom. I began to brush my teeth, a deliberate attempt to distract myself from the terror that had taken hold of me.

Drawing in ragged breaths, I finally put the toothbrush down. I doubled forward, gripping the edge of the sink. Tears began to fall into the sink. Like the steam building up in a pressure cooker, my emotions demanded an outlet.

I felt Cindy's arms around my heaving shoulders. "I'm sorry," I told her, dismayed at my weakness. Like most men, I'd been conditioned to believe that crying and other demonstrations of vulnerability are "unmanly."

"This is healthy. It's part of the healing."

"I get scared walking up the stairs. . . . That's stupid!"

Her arm tightened around me. "*No,* it's not," she insisted. "That sound triggered the emotions and pain you felt in captivity."

She coaxed me to sit on the bed beside her. Safe within the intimacy of our twenty-year friendship, I let the painful memories pour forth. "Every morning I heard a sound like that. It sounded like a machine gun. I thought the Iraqis were killing prisoners who weren't cooperating.

"I didn't doubt they'd kill me. I visualized being brought into a square with tens of thousands of Iraqi citizens. I'd hear the rifles fire, and a second later I'd have bullets in me—at least it would be quick."

Cindy brushed away her tears. "They were cruel."

"They were just doing their job," I said, shaking my head. "The people who beat me were just carrying out orders." I had often reminded myself of that. If they didn't do as they were told, they would suffer the same treatment. That belief at least buffered my rage.

"That doesn't mean you can't feel angry," she offered gently, as if she knew I was pushing back my emotions. Cindy stroked my back, her touch gentle and soothing.

"I'd see stars before I blacked out...so many times." I gritted my teeth, feeling anger suddenly boil up. "Those bastards...they said they'd chop me up if I didn't cooperate...."

We sat in silence for a minute. Then I forced the ugly memories of Baghdad back to their dark hiding place. What a strange power they held over me, yanking me back when I least expected it. I could no longer deny the truth: I had only begun to travel the long, rocky road to normality. Until then, simply adjusting to everyday life would be triumph enough.

10

All I Want Is a Normal Life

Oceanside, California
April 27, 1991

The crowd in the amphitheater roared and rose to its feet, wildly waving flags. With more than 100,000 cheering spectators, Oceanside's Proud to Be an American Day was the West Coast's largest Gulf War homecoming celebration.

The long-standing ovation continued as Lieutenant General Walter Boomer, the highly respected commander of all Gulf War Marines, introduced Cliff and Guy Hunter. Cliff looked handsome and deceptively fit in his Marine Corps uniform. He turned his gaze from General Boomer toward the uproarious crowd. Sitting in the front row, I took off my sunglasses so Cliff could see my face. We locked eyes, and he winked. I was proud of the courageous actions that had brought him onto that stage. He had paid a price greater than most realized.

Most people could never detect Cliff's residual health problems—pain in his wrist scars, obstructed nasal passages, pain and stiffness in his neck and back, fatigue and nausea from the giardia that still plagued him, continued numbness in his hands, and eighteen pounds left to be gained.

The lingering effects of captivity discouraged Cliff. He wanted nothing more than to put his ordeal behind him, regain his health, and fly again. But it was no wonder his progress had been slow. During his thirty-day convalescent leave, only four days had been without multiple social engagements, leaving him little time to rest and recover.

Each week since Cliff's return, dozens of speaking requests from organizations had poured in through the Marine Corps public affairs office and in phone calls and letters we received at home. "We know you must be anxious to get back to normal," the letters invariably began, "however..."

It was hard to chose between requests from such worthwhile charities as the Disabled American Veterans, the Special Olympics, and the Community Service Center for the Disabled. Cliff found it difficult to turn any of them down, especially requests from schools and youth groups like the Boy Scouts. He wanted to spread his message to young people about the importance of core values.

But these social obligations—speaking at charity functions, celebrations, ceremonies, and parades—were physically and mentally taxing. After his presentations, well-meaning people closed in around him, offering their hands to be shaken, introducing themselves, asking for autographs, and plying him with questions. Their conversations were like interviews: "What kind of plane were you flying?" . . . "How were you captured?" . . . "How did they treat you?" Surrounded by well-wishers, he often stood for an hour or more greeting people after making his presentations.

I worried that he would exhaust himself trying to do the right thing. A journal entry expressed my private concern:

> I feel I need to continue to protect and guide Cliff until he is back on his feet again. He gives all his strength to the public eye, but when we are together privately, he needs to be renewed.

But the American people had been so supportive, Cliff couldn't say no, feeling he owed them a great debt of gratitude. When he wasn't making appearances or traveling to them, he spent much of his time at home returning phone calls, writing thank-you notes, and responding to the thousand or more of kind letters he'd received since his capture. Many letters included requests for him to send an autograph, picture, or personal note, or make a personal appearance. All of them communicated the love, support, and caring of the American people.

From Ella Smith of Dallas, Texas: "You'll always have a special place in my heart even though we will probably never meet. . . ." Many letters echoed her sentiment.

From Sherry Ann Clapper, Saugus, California: "To *Our* Dear Lt. Col. Acree: What a way to become famous, huh? How weird it must seem to you to suddenly belong to all of us. The day you were captured, we had our POW bracelets made . . . we didn't get just one—we got 50 with your name on it. . . ."

From Major B. F. Brady, USMC (Ret.), Mesa, Arizona: "We wish you a speedy return to a normal life and success in your future together. I'm glad I can part with this bracelet so soon. . . ."

From Linda Melimaki, Escondido, California: "I thank you for your service to our great country, for helping to preserve our freedom, for keeping my family safe from harm. My thanks goes also to your family, for sharing you with us. I know the public scrutiny was not easy. God bless you and your family. I hope your lives are able to be 'normal' again soon."

Many of the letters we received included POW bracelets in a variety of colors and materials—Cliff would receive them for years. Instead of a POW bracelet, one letter writer included a button printed with ALL I WANT IS A NORMAL LIFE. Cliff and I laughed, realizing how much truth that slogan contained.

In mid-April we had flown to Seattle to visit our families. While we were there, Cliff made two one-hour presentations at his former high school, met with students, signed autographs, and gave interviews.

We visited Christ the King Church and renewed our wedding vows. Afterward, Cliff spoke to the uniformed, banner-carrying students of the church school about the importance of telling the truth and doing the right thing.

We met with Seattle Mayor Norm Rice, who, during Cliff's captivity, had dedicated an evergreen tree in his name that was to remain potted until his release. After our meeting, we drove to Golden Gardens Park on Puget Sound for a ceremony and tree planting. Cliff finished his speech on freedom just before the rains came.

Cliff attended our friend Mary Pat's retirement party and drove her home after her final day of work. "*My* trip to freedom," she quipped. The next night Mom hosted a birthday party for several family birthdays, including mine. My best gift came in my card from Cliff. "If you're ready to have a baby," he had written, "so am I." The next morning we attended a service at Cliff's boyhood church. Afterward, Cliff greeted church members at a reception held for him. I was surprised by the sense of familiarity total strangers felt for him.

With Cliff able to attend in person, my sister, Bonnie, finally hosted the Mother of All Parties, an open house with 100 of our family and friends attending. Cliff was interviewed by reporters from the *Seattle Times* and local TV stations.

In between the scheduled events, Cliff made the rounds, visiting relatives and friends. I was beginning to realize how often I'd have to share him. I noted in my journal:

> I have Cliff back, but not really. Everyone wants a piece of him—including friends who suddenly surfaced, eager to be quoted in the paper, attend parties, and gain political endorsements.

But most long-forgotten friends had not reappeared to bask in reflected glory. Most meant well. Having vicariously lived through Cliff's captivity, even people who didn't know him felt like old friends.

We returned to California with both of us tired and Cliff fighting a heavy cold. The next morning, he got up early and dressed in his flight suit.

Though he was far from healed, Cliff's thirty-day convalescent leave was over and he was returning as the CO of VMO-2.

At 6:30, I handed him his lunch. "Are you sure you're doing the right thing?"

"I'm not a hundred percent," he said wearily. "But each day I'm not at the squadron is a day I'm not being as good a CO as I could be."

"I hope you're not rushing it." His sense of duty was so compelling, I could never convince him to stay home. He felt to do so would be letting down his Marines.

Cliff's schedule as CO was more taxing than ever. He left home each morning before 6:30 and didn't return till 7:00 that night—if he didn't have a social function. After work he often changed from his flight suit into a more formal Marine Corps uniform before heading to an event that could last until 10:00 or 11:00. Just attending a portion of the many events Cliff did wore me out.

Ten days after our return from Seattle, we hurried out of the house to board a white limousine with Stephany to attend the day-long Proud to Be an American Day celebration in Oceanside. John and Linda Lechner, owners of an Oceanside limousine service, had arrived promptly at 7:30 to drive us to the first event.

Each event brought its own pressure, and that morning I sensed Cliff's tension. As grand marshals, Cliff and Guy Hunter would lead the gigantic parade to honor the troops and all who supported them. Afterward, Cliff would speak onstage before a crowd of tens of thousands.

We arrived in downtown Oceanside to meet the organizers and other guests for a continental breakfast. Stephany and I loaded our plates with muffins and fruit, but Cliff, surrounded by well-wishers, never made it to the food table. On our way out the door, he grabbed a handful of strawberries. We boarded the limousine with Ricardo Montalban and headed for downtown Oceanside, where cheering spectators lined the streets. We climbed onto the back of a red Firebird convertible, and with Stephany seated between us, started down the parade route.

News reporters walked alongside the car, interviewing Cliff.

"What does this parade mean to you?" one asked. A photographer with a video camera on his shoulder zoomed in.

"How do you feel *now* about the war in the Gulf?" asked another.

"What pressure," I thought. "All I have to do is sit here and wave."

At the end of the parade route, we were dropped off at bleachers placed on the street and found our front-row seats on the reviewing stand. I sat in the stands between Cliff and Guy, who continually entertained us with his funny comments. Politicians rode by in convertibles. Sunshine baked the crowd as a tank, a howitzer, and amphibious vehicles rumbled by. High school bands and pom-pom girls performed. Rows of U.S. Marines, Medal of Honor winners, and Pearl Harbor survivors received tumultuous cheers and whistles.

A band of graying Vietnam veterans in decades-old uniforms walked past. A Marine officer suddenly bolted from the crowd and embraced the Vietnam veterans, bringing tears to many spectators' eyes. I was glad for the tribute to these veterans and hoped it would help heal old wounds.

Several news reporters from radio and television stations approached Cliff, wanting sound bites for their evening broadcasts. Newspaper reporters arrived, too, pen and paper in hand. As soon as one reporter stepped aside, another took his place.

A Los Angeles television station reporter approached to interview Cliff. Before he got there, another arrived.

By now Cliff and I had opposite problems. Reporters and the public inundated him with questions on everything from his captivity experience to his political views. I was rarely asked any questions at all. After fending off the media for weeks, now that I was free to talk, I was shunted aside.

But while waiting to speak to Cliff, the second reporter asked me what I thought of the day's celebration in contrast to the end of the Vietnam war. "Thanks to the Desert Storm victory, Vietnam veterans are finally getting the homecoming parades they deserved twenty years ago," I answered. A surprised look came over his face and he asked me a few more questions.

The last reporter moved on, and Cliff took his place beside me on the bleachers. "You got to talk!" he said, grinning. "I tried to stall so you could talk longer."

The parade's grand finale approached—eighty-five Marines carrying a 47-by-82-foot American flag horizontally down the street. Cliff wandered into the street to gaze disbelievingly. The enormous flag filled the street. "That flag was the prettiest sight I've seen since I've been a free man," he told reporters from the *Los Angeles Times.*

"Other than me!" I teased when he sat down.

After the parade, we walked with Stephany to a gym near the waterfront amphitheater. In a room filled with tables and chairs, a long luncheon buffet held an array of food. We went through the buffet line, then wandered about the gym with our plates, looking for a free table. But every seat was taken. One person after another stopped Cliff to ask him about his experiences.

"Of *all* the people in this room," I thought, "Cliff deserves to sit down and eat." He'd eaten only a bowl of hot cereal six hours before and had an onstage appearance upcoming. Even after we found a place to sit he couldn't finish his meal because of the well-wishers surrounding our table.

Soon it was time to take our seats in the front row of the outdoor amphitheater. Cliff and Guy had been told that they would each say a few words, but at the last minute, 1st Marine Division commander Lieutenant General Walter Boomer told Cliff he wanted him to give a speech. As a rock band entertained under the hot sun, Cliff scribbled notes on a scrap of paper. Soon someone retrieved him to go backstage.

I could see the top of Cliff's green cover as he stood offstage. In addition to the routine demands of being a squadron CO, the obligatory functions— telling his story over and over, skipping his own meals while others ate and listened, standing for long periods, thanking people, answering questions for an hour or more after his presentations—had taken a toll on his health.

Once he had returned as CO, Marines assumed he was fully healed. They couldn't help comparing him to Guy, who had quickly returned to his robust health, lifting weights and running.

At a recent fund-raiser brunch, the commanding general of Camp Pendleton grasped Cliff's right hand and shook it firmly. "Been out running much lately?" he asked, making small talk.

I felt a stab of sympathy for Cliff. He was still too weak to exercise. And with little feeling in his right hand, he had been shaking hands with his left. Cliff's flight surgeon and friend, Joel Lees, was the only one at Camp Pendleton who knew of Cliff's physical disabilities and how he had sustained them.

Cliff continued standing as the comic Yakov Smirnoff entertained the crowd, then local politicians and military generals spoke. The crowd listened to taped messages from President Bush and former president Reagan. Ricardo Montalban addressed the gathering. Then General Boomer came onstage to say a few words. Finally Cliff and Guy walked onstage to tumultuous cheers.

The volume of the crowd doubled as Cliff and Guy rested their arms around each other's shoulders, exchanging looks of mutual respect. General Boomer handed the microphone to Cliff.

Cliff raised the microphone to speak. An expectant hush fell over the crowded amphitheater. He hesitated. "I am honored . . ." he began. He spoke of his appreciation, then after a minute seemed to falter. Sooner than I had expected, he ended rather abruptly.

The crowd responded with resounding applause. General Boomer must have requested that Cliff cut his speech short, I thought. Still, it seemed odd. I waited politely during several award presentations, then made my exit with Stephany.

Knowing how the day's activities must have drained Cliff, I was anxious to head home soon after his speech. Remembering my plans for the following morning I realized they were a mistake. Not anticipating Cliff's continued fatigue, three weeks earlier I had scheduled a brunch for seventy of our friends to thank them for their support. I had already stuffed the freezer and refrigerator with food and had drawn up a list of chores for Cliff, among them moving furniture and setting up tables.

Stephany and I entered the noisy crowd outside the amphitheater and found John and Linda waiting with the limousine. We waited in its cool interior and finally Cliff emerged from the throng of people. He opened the car door and saw my worried look. "Reporters wanted to interview me," he apologized. "They took Guy and me off to another room."

Cliff climbed into the limousine beside me. As the car pulled smoothly away from the crowd, his body sagged into the leather seat like a pile of rags. I twisted in my seat to face him. "Honey, are you okay? Why did you stop your speech so suddenly?"

"I just couldn't say any more. I had to stop." He shook his head, ashamed of what he considered a substandard performance.

Cliff's eyes closed and his head dropped against the seat back. "We need to get you home and into bed," I said. His list of chores could wait.

When the car arrived at our house, Cliff blinked open his eyes, his gaze bleary. "I'm feeling a little lightheaded," he whispered hoarsely. "I just need to sit for a minute."

I waited outside Cliff's door, holding my purse and program. Suddenly Cliff's head drooped, and his sunglasses and cover fell from his hands. He slumped forward onto the red-carpeted floor.

I shoved my things into Stephany's hands, told her to wait on the front doorstep, then climbed back into the limousine, kneeling on the floor next to Cliff.

"I used to be a nurse," Linda told me. She helped me push him upright onto the seat. His body felt odd, a heavy, dead weight I'd never lifted before.

Thinking quickly, Linda rushed to the trunk and found some T-shirts she'd purchased at the day's celebration. She soaked the shirts in bottled water and laid the folded cloth over Cliff's forehead. He moaned and rolled his head to one side, reacting to the strip of cloth.

"Try not to cover his eyes," I asked.

Cliff started to come to. He blinked his eyes open and tried to lift his head. After a few moments, he insisted on standing. With Cliff's arms draped over our shoulders, John and I walked Cliff through the front door. We paused at the foot of the stairs. "Why don't you sit here for a few minutes?" I suggested.

"No, no, I can do it," he insisted in a ragged whisper. Mumbling apologies, he barely lifted his feet high enough to make each step. The sight brought me physical pain.

How normal he had looked. Few would suspect how unstable his health was and how easily he could fade. Even I was shocked at how weak Cliff had become, especially remembering how healthy he used to be. The Iraqis had taken a strong, vigorous man who ran four miles a day and returned one who collapsed in front of me.

And, I knew, the changes were more than physical.

Cliff still flinched at sudden noises and jumped if I surprised him with my presence. Persons suffering episodes of Post-Traumatic Stress Disorder are always on guard and hyper. During the Civil War, this condition was called "soldier's heart." In World War I, the term used was "shell shock," and in World War II, "battle fatigue." The trauma they have sustained has sensitized the part of the brain that processes fear, and a startle response is their first instinctive reaction to fear. I had trained myself to call softly when approaching him from behind.

His eating habits had changed in odd ways. He no longer wanted sandwiches for lunch. He ate only a baked potato, indulging himself with a whole one after praying in captivity for a couple of small pieces in his broth. Remembering the treat he'd received a few days before his release, he now loved eating plump Middle Eastern dates. He began a tea-making ritual on the Saturday mornings he was home, using cardamom seeds in the manner his cellmate Mo had taught him at the Joliet. He would not eat so much as a cracker before he bowed his head to thank God.

Cliff seemed to suffer when his hunger wasn't immediately satisfied. Before meal times, memories of salivating as he waited for the squeaky food cart leapt to life. He apologized for his impatience. "I'm just not a normal person when I'm hungry," he explained. I made sure dinner was ready when he walked in the door from work.

Sometimes an object—such as the yellow plastic bowl he came across in our cupboard—would carry him back. "This is just the size bowl we used at the Biltmore," he said, raising it with both hands. "We used it to eat, drink, and clean ourselves." He stared at the bowl, transfixed.

Despite the beatings he had received, his recall of the traumatic events of his captivity was almost photographic. The adrenaline his body had produced to give him the bursts of energy he needed in the dangerous, stressful situations of captivity was also nature's way of engraving those fearful memories into his brain.

Now, weakened and barely coherent, he sat on the bed apologizing, worried that he had scared Stephany. John and Linda said their good-byes. "I'm sorry for the trouble I put you through," Cliff apologized.

"You have nothing to apologize about," John said.

I thanked John and Linda, and with Stephany, we started for the door. Linda looked back over her shoulder. "You have a wonderful wife, Cliff."

"I know I do. She's what brought me home."

After seeing the couple to the door, I returned upstairs alone. "That must have felt terrible, to pass out," I said.

Cliff leaned back against his pillow, letting his eyes close. "It wasn't so bad . . . I wasn't getting beaten up first." He dropped onto his side, drawing his knees up to his chest.

I touched his warm forehead. "I'm going to call Joel."

"No, please don't bother him," Cliff pleaded. "I was just tired."

"Most people don't pass out when they're just tired."

I sat with him for a few minutes. So many times I wished I could wipe away Cliff's pain, share his struggles and suffering. But I couldn't create a protective bubble around him, and he wouldn't want me to.

"I'll leave so you can rest."

"Just give me a couple of minutes and I'll be ready to go."

"The only place you need to be is in *bed*."

"I should be helping you with the brunch," he felt compelled to insist.

"What I want you to do is rest. You are a terrible patient." I left him resting on the bed, and ten minutes later heard movement and rumbling around upstairs. I went up and found him dressed in his shirt and jeans, pulling on his shoes.

"I couldn't sleep," he said, "so I can help you now."

The following afternoon after our brunch guests had left and the dishes had been put away, I treated myself to reading the Sunday paper. In the garage, Cliff was reading the directions for installing a new garage door opener. The house was quiet, and with Cami and Murphy curled up at my feet, I relaxed, knowing we had no functions to attend that evening. The peaceful afternoon felt like one of those normal Sundays we used to take for granted.

Scanning the local news section of the paper, I spotted Cliff's picture in an article about the Proud to Be an American Day parade. Walking into the garage to show him the article, I approached the weight bench where he sat studying the instructions.

Seeing him working on a project in his garage brought to mind the "old days," the earlier months of our marriage. I forgot about the red pepper he sprinkled on his food to give it a flavor he could detect. I forgot the choked, clogged breathing sounds that kept me up at night, and the nightmares that appeared out of the darkness, waking him suddenly. I forgot about the handwriting I had to do for him because his fingers still lacked feeling and his hand muscles easily cramped. I forgot about the damage to his ears that kept him from hearing my voice from another room, about his mood changes and the lapses in conversation when he was lost in another world.

I forgot how captivity had changed him.

Without thinking, I approached him from behind, the folded newspaper in my hand. Reaching in front of him, I set the paper on top of the directions he was studying, catching him off guard.

His head snapped up. The directions fell from his hands as he sprang from the bench. "Goll! What was that?" he said in a high-pitched voice, and spun to face me as if he'd seen a ghost.

Shuddering convulsively, he grabbed his neck as if he had just been struck there. He wrapped his arms around himself, shaking like someone with typhoid fever. He looked and acted terrified.

I felt like someone had punched me in the stomach. "Honey, I'm so sorry... I forgot." I wanted to reach out and comfort him but knew it was too soon. When he relived a beating, he didn't want anyone's touch, not even my gentle one.

Cliff blew out a big puff of air, trying to calm himself. "I felt like I was back there again, sitting hunched over, cold... Sometimes when they beat me, my blindfold would slip and out of the corner of my eye I could see the shadow of something coming at me. They came at my neck from the same direction that newspaper just came." He paced around the garage, shaking and rubbing the back of his neck... and rubbing... and rubbing... trying to rub away the pain and terror of another time.

"My neck hurt so bad. I thought they'd paralyze me or kill me." He wrapped his arms around himself as if he were cold. Watching him pace and shiver, my chest ached with guilt at causing him more pain.

Had this been a TV movie, we would have returned from Bethesda to a happy, normal life. But in this world, even happy endings have their flaws. The joy of our reunion had been followed by frustrations, hindrances, and heartaches we had never anticipated.

I had been woefully unprepared to deal with the aftermath of Cliff's captivity—the ups and downs of his physical and mental recuperation and the pressure of the public requests made upon him. Hungry for knowledge on the adaptation of POWs after repatriation, I had scoured books and journals. But most discussed only captivity experience, not how to cope with its consequences.

Cliff massaged the back of his neck. "I'm sorry I jumped, babe."

"*I'm* the one who should be sorry," I said, biting my lip. "I promise I'll be more careful."

Our life together had resumed, but it was not a normal one. I had my husband back—but not the same one I had kissed good-bye eight months before.

The next morning I walked into the Jazzercize Center in Carlsbad for my first class since Cliff's return seven weeks before. I handed my membership card to the familiar woman at the counter.

She smiled brightly. "I expected you to walk in here beaming," she remarked. She punched my card and handed it back to me. "Is everything back to normal now?"

Politely I nodded, wondering if it would ever be.

Sacramento, California
May 3, 1991

Cliff's hand nudged me forward. I glanced down at my black cocktail dress, then entered the doorway of the large banquet room. "Walk straight, stand tall, smile, and give some eye contact," I reminded myself as I moved toward four hundred clapping, cheering people.

Cameras flashed as we passed between the linen-covered tables of the black-tie event in Sacramento. At the raised dais in front of the room, a crowd of people joined us, nudging me aside as they jockeyed for a spot at Cliff's elbow. Smiling, I stepped back. I knew the routine.

I accompanied Cliff to as many of the events on his busy schedule as possible. In one typical ten-day period, he gave a television interview at our house, was grand marshal of a parade, attended a fund-raiser in Hollywood, spoke to several Boy Scout troops, was guest of honor for the California Highway Patrol, spoke at the Young President's Club in La Jolla, lectured a class of eighty in a Navy Law of War course, and attended a Vietnam veterans ball and the Navy/Marine Corps Relief Ball.

Every experience of fame has its downside. Like it or not, overnight celebrity status had been thrust upon Cliff by the well-meaning public. Whether we were shopping at the mall, buying groceries, or eating at the local frozen yogurt shop, people recognized Cliff and stopped us to ask about his ordeal. At ceremonies, dinners, parades, conventions, military engagements, and fund-raisers, people sought out Cliff to talk, shake hands, and sign autographs.

After ten weeks of smiling and nodding, I had grown tired of my role as "Cliff Acree's wife," the proverbial "good woman" standing (literally) behind her man. The public saw Cliff as a heroic figure. I just wanted my husband back.

But Cliff's sense of duty to the public and the Marine Corps barred him from taking time off to recuperate, schedule his needed nose surgery, or spend time relaxing with me. I had even met privately with Doc Lees to express my concern. He left me a "prescription" slip for Cliff that read: "Just say no to social engagements. . . . Use for one month."

A Navy psychiatrist at Camp Pendleton, Lieutenant Commander Dr. J. T. Hardwig, had advised him the same. To get an up chit, Cliff was required to meet with this psychiatrist in sessions alone and with me. He was loath to revisit his unpleasant memories in the therapy sessions, but I welcomed the opportunity to discuss Cliff's burdensome schedule.

"If you weren't a POW, what would you be doing now?" Dr. Hardwig had asked Cliff during one of the sessions I attended.

"I'd be taking leave, spending time with my wife and daughter, doing chores around the house . . . maybe getting away for a week or two."

But we had turned down generous vacation offers from around the country—"a tranquil few days in spectacular scenery" at Sterling Vineyards in Napa Valley, California; one week at a time-share; seven days and nights at any of eleven Hilton hotels; one-week accommodations and meals at the Homestead Resort in Hot Springs, Virginia. Our weekends were already booked.

"You've already been self-sacrificing," Dr. Hardwig reminded Cliff. "You've given a lot for your country. Now you need to take care of yourself and say no to almost *all* of it. Tell them it's on doctor's orders."

Our busy schedule had offered many perks, with interesting events and people. But I would have happily given up the celebrity-filled events for time alone with Cliff. Out of our last fifteen months of marriage, we had spent ten apart. But whenever I felt frustrated and resentful about the drain on our personal time, I reminded myself to be thankful for what I *did* have—a husband who had returned home alive.

Fate seemed to have said, "You got him back . . . now you have to share him."

Cliff remained standing on the dais, surrounded by well-wishers who peppered him with questions. I took my seat next to a congenial-looking woman at the head table. "You must be *thrilled*," she said.

I smiled and nodded. "Yes, I am."

"Do you have children?"

I kept my smile intact. "So far, just a dog." Though I had just turned thirty-seven, my dream of starting our family was still on hold. Joel Lees had cautioned that we needed to wait at least three months for Cliff to recover from the effects of starvation. After being malnourished, a man's body needs at least that long to produce healthy sperm with a normal count. I tried to hide my impatience about having a baby from Cliff. Exhausted from speaking obligations, he didn't need another burden on him.

Earlier that night, at the cocktail party preceding the Sacramento banquet, a long line had formed of people wanting their pictures taken with Cliff and Guy. The line inched forward as Guy and Cliff were introduced, shook hands, then smiled for the camera as it flashed in their faces over and over. Watching them, my vision became speckled with flashbulbs.

After the photo session, more people gathered around Cliff. "Thank you," they said. "We admire your courage." "We're proud of you."

Always, Cliff's face relayed genuine appreciation. "I was just doing my job. I was glad to do it."

"There's the lovely wife," a man commented as he walked past.

I appreciated the few who acknowledged me, especially the one in a hundred who recognized any sacrifices I might have made. More often, people told me how relieved, thrilled, and excited I should be. "Yes, I am," I'd say over and over.

Another thirty minutes passed. The crowd around Cliff grew. I wondered how Cliff's hands were holding up under all the hand-shaking. The numbness, especially in his right hand, persisted, nearly four months after the original damage had been done. Doctors hoped the severed nerves would grow back, restoring the feeling, but so far they had shown no signs of regeneration. Though he rarely mentioned it, I knew Cliff worried he might never fly again.

A woman approached Cliff. "Aren't you *lucky?*" she asked kindly, squeezing his arm.

"Just once," I had asked Cliff one night after hearing again and again how lucky we were, "wouldn't you like to reply, 'Well, I'm not *that* lucky... where were *you* in January, February, and March?'"

But Cliff smiled back sincerely at the woman. "Yes, I am *very* lucky." Grateful to be alive, he meant every word.

It was against Cliff's nature and his military training to whine or complain. "I was only a prisoner for two months," Cliff often reminded me. "The Vietnam POWs did it for years and years."

When asked about his treatment, all he said was, "We were not treated very well."

Dr. Hardwig, the Navy psychiatrist, had tried to convince Cliff not to downplay his courage. "It's inspiring for people to hear," the doctor had argued. "It provides some meaning to the suffering you went through."

"I can't tell anyone how I resisted without feeling like I'm standing on a soapbox or boasting about my conduct."

"It's the truth," the doctor had said, "and the truth stands on its own. Part of the reason you are *here* is because of how brutally you were treated as a POW and how well you performed. If you had knuckled under, you wouldn't have been treated so severely."

"I'm proud that my eighteen years paid off," Cliff admitted. "But no one was there with us. No one knows what I did."

Cliff's bravery hadn't gone unnoticed by Guy. That morning, we had appeared on a Christian radio program with Guy and Mary while a reporter from the *Sacramento Union* listened in. After our one-hour interview concluded, Guy told the newspaper reporter, "Here's something to put in the paper we didn't talk about." He told them how their Iraqi captors had tried to force Cliff to repeat "President Bush is donkey."

"Colonel Acree told them, 'I cannot say that. He is my president.' His resistance gave me great strength." I turned to look at Cliff. His eyes were glistening.

Since few people could speak up for Cliff, I did so whenever possible. The day before, he and Guy had been recognized officially by the state of California. Governor Pete Wilson presented them each a plaque on behalf of the citizens of California. At the capitol in Sacramento, Cliff and Guy had been presented to the California Legislature and recognized "for the courageous manner with which [they] served and sacrificed in the safeguarding of our democratic principles worldwide. . . ."

In the assembly hall, covered with rich wood paneling, Cliff and Guy were presented with gold-framed copies of the Resolution Proclamation, which a member of the California Legislature read out loud. The many paragraphs of the identical resolutions for Cliff and Guy each started with "Whereas" and specified the challenges they had faced: being attacked by a missile; enduring interrogations, brutal treatment, and long periods of isolation; being forced to denounce the war. . . . That last one caught my attention.

I knew Cliff would never bring it to our hosts' attention that he hadn't denounced the war. Later that morning I took one of our hosts aside and pointed out that Cliff had not denounced the war. "And he suffered greatly for it," I added. He offered to strike that line from the resolution and send Cliff a revised copy. We received it two weeks later.

To limit the pain of recalling his ordeal, Cliff gave an abridged version of his captivity in his speeches. He began his story with preparing his squadron for war, skipped to the day he was shot down, then fast-forwarded to his arrival on the *Mercy.*

But during question-and-answer periods after speeches, and especially during meals, people asked him probing questions. His first bite of food had usually made it halfway to his mouth when the rapid-fire questions began.

Businessmen who had never fought for anything more important than a parking space seemed especially voyeuristic. "What were your interrogations like?" . . . "How did they torture you?" . . . "What was your worst moment?" Most people asked questions innocently, not realizing how difficult it was to eat while remembering being beaten. Cliff developed short, standard answers to their pointed questions. "Very brutal. Very violent."

It is human nature to want horrifying details. We all slow down to gawk at the remains of a car crash. A flawlessly dressed socialite at a $2,500-a-plate luncheon in Burbank fingered her chunky diamond necklace with elegantly manicured nails as she glanced at Cliff walking away from the table. Leaning toward me, she smiled coyly, as if to share a piece of gossip. "What *were* his injuries?" she asked.

A certain look came over some people's faces when Cliff left the table. I could almost predict their first words: "How is he—*really?*" ... "Does he have nightmares?" ... "Flashbacks?" ... "Is he *normal* yet?"

"He's doing *very* well, thank you," I'd answer. I wanted people to know the truth about Cliff's ordeal and his courageous response, but I felt uncomfortable answering tabloid-type questions from people I'd just met.

I was happy for Cliff to give his time to people who deserved it—whether they sent notes of encouragement to troops stationed in the Gulf, wore yellow ribbons of support, sent letters to the Iraqi ambassador, or otherwise showed support during Operation Desert Storm—but some didn't.

Some people treated him as if his evening and weekend public appearances were an extended obligation of his military service, not realizing he sacrificed personal time.

"Have you been making many appearances?" a man at our table asked at a veterans' benefit.

"Yes, I have," Cliff answered, "but I'm glad to do them."

"Well, you *owe* them," the man said.

I cut in. "Yes, as long as his health is good. . . . That should be his number-one priority."

"Oh, you've got years to get your health back!" he scoffed.

While most people thanked Cliff sincerely for his sacrifices, some treated him like a well-paid sports celebrity. "Kevin, John, Mike, and Susan," ordered a man at an air show as he slapped four programs on the table for autographs. At some fund-raisers and rallies, Cliff was treated like hired help, standing for long hours with few breaks and little to eat. He'd often come home from presentations and head straight to the refrigerator.

"Didn't they feed you?" I'd ask.

"They had food, but I never got to it."

One day I watched a TV interview with Wally Amos of the Famous Amos Cookie Company, the successful entrepreneur who also does volunteer and charity work. "It feels good to be giving back," he said. "Anyone could have had my success; now I can use my fame constructively."

"Is that how we can find some good in Cliff's ordeal?" I wondered. To use his notoriety to set a good example, be a role model, the hero our young people need? Like Wally Amos, Cliff could make sense of his experience by giving back.

But, not to diminish his contributions, Wally Amos had gained a great deal before giving back. Cliff had already given more than can reasonably be expected of even a Marine, and still more was being demanded of him. He had little privacy and almost no free time.

But however great the demands of the public or the Marine Corps, the demands Cliff placed upon himself were even greater. The ironclad sense of duty that had inspired Cliff to risk his life in captivity drove him still. I couldn't convince him otherwise, helpless to stem this tide nor that of the other forces threatening to sweep us apart again.

After the Sacramento banquet dinner, keynote speaker Oliver North, the retired Marine lieutenant colonel, a hero to some, took his place at the podium. "I am honored to be in this room with two *real* heroes." He turned to Cliff and Guy.

I agreed. Applied to everyone from sports figures to Hollywood celebrities, the term "hero" has almost lost its meaning. It has become associated more with image than with achievements, with what people have rather than who they are. In an era short on positive role models, too often our true heroes are overshadowed. I believe our society needs to raise its standards and reserve the title "hero" for courageous men and women who voluntarily take great personal risks to make life better for others. The sacrifices and contributions of these heroes will stand the test of time.

After his speech, Oliver North gathered his notes and moved quickly off the dais and out the door, where a driver waited to whisk him back to the airport.

One of the organizers stepped up to the microphone. He turned to Cliff. "Would you like to say a few words?"

Cliff nodded. Speaking from the heart without notes, he talked about the importance of freedom, a fragile gift. The crowd interrupted his sincere speech several times with applause.

As another round of applause swelled, I reflected that the greatest heroes are often the least recognized. Part of their heroism is their distaste for the limelight and their willingness to downplay what they have achieved.

One day Cliff had been scheduled to meet with his air wing commander. "This is a great opportunity to relate some of your captivity experiences," I had gently urged Cliff, especially knowing that this general was among the Marines he had tried to protect by withholding classified information.

At their meeting the next morning, the general surprised Cliff by bringing up Cliff's performance in captivity himself—but not in the way I had hoped. "Cliff," he said, "you have nothing to be ashamed of."

Because of Cliff's reluctance to talk about it, no one had learned the true story of his ordeal. His humility had done little to dispel the misconceptions the public had been fed by the media about Desert Storm POWs. An April 1, 1991, article in *People* magazine concluded, "Though they were fed only meager rations of watery gruel and stale bread and were prohibited from talking to each other, the POWs were not physically abused." In his 1991 book *Schwarzkopf: The Man, the Mission, the Triumph,* veteran war correspondent Richard Pyle concluded, "At first the pilots appeared to have been badly abused; this fear later would prove largely unfounded." Robert F. Dorr, in his 1991 book *Desert Storm Airwar,* came to the same conclusion:

"Though Small [a Marine pilot] had been beaten, the POWs generally were not treated as badly as the American public feared. Beatings of others took place, but none were ever tortured or drugged." My husband, systematically beaten to coerce him to reveal information, just happened to be one of the exceptions.

Simplified, Hollywood-style portrayals of the Gulf War perpetuated more falsehoods. The docudrama *Heroes of Desert Storm* included Guy Hunter as one of the heroes. In one scene, Guy defies his Iraqi guards by talking back and swinging his fists at them as they aim their AK-47s at him. In a later scene, Cliff and Guy are reunited after the Baghdad Biltmore bombing. Cliff—fit, healthy-looking, and clean-shaven—greets weakened, faltering Guy with a hearty slap on the back that causes him to groan and stumble. Cliff—speaking with a Southern accent—expresses surprise when gray-haired Guy moans and collapses into his arms.

"The only thing factual about that scene was the color of Guy's hair," Cliff said. Guy was embarrassed that the production company took such liberties with the information he had given them.

Only one person besides Cliff knew the true story of what he had endured in captivity. That singular knowledge felt like a heavy weight on me. I began to document his ordeal on the computer, adding to my notes each time he relayed another episode to me.

Cliff concluded his speech at the Sacramento banquet dinner: "I am forever grateful for the opportunity to serve my country and my fellow citizens, and grateful to God for giving me a second life in the land of the free. Thank you."

As the crowd gave him a standing ovation, I realized that he had already received one of his country's highest awards—public appreciation. He would have given his life to honor his deep commitment to his country and his fellow Marines—not for recognition or money, but to serve his country in a just cause. If only he could fly again.

Late that night in the hotel restaurant, Cliff indulged in one of his captivity food fantasies—a hot fudge sundae with Spanish peanuts. It was nearly midnight when we left the deserted restaurant and headed back to our hotel room. Walking side by side down the silent hallway, my hand accidentally brushed his. He stopped. His face held a look of contained excitement.

"I could *feel* that!"

"Honey, that's wonderful!" I hugged him. "I'm so glad for you."

Being medically grounded for flight left a void in Cliff's life. With any luck his medical problems would resolve and he'd be in the air soon. His hands were regaining their feeling. Even relegating Baghdad to the past had become less of an uphill battle. But I knew he hadn't left behind the memories of his ordeal. He had sealed them deeper behind the tough, uncomplaining Marine facade.

The next morning we packed quickly after breakfast, anxious to return home after three days in Sacramento. We waited with Guy and Mary in the hotel lobby for our overdue driver, one of the convention sponsors. Due to a miscommunication, he arrived late to take us to the airport.

Cliff climbed into the front of the black Mercedes sedan with the driver; Guy, Mary, and I squeezed into the back. Our seat belts were tucked underneath the seat, and though not using mine made me uneasy, I didn't want to delay our already-late departure by searching for it. As the heavy automobile pulled away, I noticed Cliff's unbuckled seat belt. Someone asked me a question, and I forgot to mention it.

A few minutes later, near the municipal airport, we exited off the interstate onto a street choked with cars. The snarled stop-and-go traffic frustrated our impatient driver, who followed closely behind the car in front, knowing he was late delivering us to the airport.

A horn honked. Suddenly, our driver slammed on the brakes. "What is that loud screeching sound?" I wondered. *BAM!* The sound of metal crunching metal announced the answer. A car rammed us from behind, propelling forward the car and everyone in it.

A second later I heard Cliff moaning. Bent toward the dashboard, he braced his head in his hands.

"Where's Guy?" he mumbled. "Is he bleeding?"

"Oh, no!" I thought. Though mild by comparison, the sensations of the crash had duplicated Cliff's shootdown. Adrenaline stung my arms and legs.

I hardly noticed my throbbing neck as I jumped out of the car and yanked open the front passenger-side door. Cliff held his head in his hands, unable to move without great pain. "Where's Guy? Where's Guy?" he kept repeating.

A starburst pattern on the cracked windshield showed where Cliff's head had hit. I knelt beside the car, not knowing how to help him, smelling oil and gasoline as cars detoured around ours.

"I heard a big explosion and felt the bang," Cliff muttered. "Something snapped. Suddenly my neck was in pain. All I could think of was Guy."

I squeezed his arm. "Honey, I'm so sorry you're hurt again."

"No, it's not as bad as the first time. No one was beating on me. . . . Are Guy and Mary okay?"

Luckily, the rest of us were uninjured. I asked our driver to call an ambulance, then turned back to Cliff. "Everything will be okay," I reassured him— words meant as much for me as for him.

An ambulance and medics arrived. "How much can one person take?" I wondered as two uniformed men hauled the long body board out.

Cliff didn't want to let go of his head. Somehow the medics got the cervical collar on him. When he finally tipped his head back onto the board, his feet and legs were shaking.

"I wonder if he has spinal problems," Guy speculated.

I knew better. The medics' protective equipment couldn't insulate Cliff from the horrors within. Reacting to the instant replay of his shootdown, he had gone back to Baghdad.

Oceanside, California
May 29, 1991

Cliff propped two bed pillows against the headboard behind him, then handed me the wrinkled sheets of his OV-10 cockpit emergency procedures. "Just ten minutes," he promised. Having quizzed him so many times over the past few nights, I was beginning to memorize the procedures myself.

The reinjuring of Cliff's neck in the car accident in Sacramento had been a major setback to his goal of flying by summertime. Fortunately, he had suffered no broken bones, and after receiving X rays, injections of a muscle relaxant, painkillers, and a new cervical collar, he had been released from the hospital.

Now, four weeks later, his neck and back pain had eased. He was off the giardia medication. His thick, hardened skin abrasions had diminished. His hands were steadily regaining feeling and all but seven pounds of the weight he had shed was back on. Working long hours and standing to give speeches didn't physically drain him as before; he had gained some reserve power.

As his health had improved, he set a goal of June 18 to be airborne again—five months after his shootdown. He was anxious to get some flight time under his belt before he gave up the squadron for a staff job—"flying a desk." He couldn't stay on as CO of VMO-2 forever; the normal tour for a squadron CO is eighteen months, and Cliff had taken command twelve months before.

As I listened to him recite the emergency procedures, I admitted to myself that although Cliff dreaded his change of command, I looked forward to the less hectic and more predictable schedule it would bring. But flying was part of who he was, and I would support him in finishing his goals as CO of VMO-2.

As Cliff approached his dream of flying again, I achieved some dreams of my own. The POW/MIA Liberty Alliance I had founded aimed for accountability and humane treatment of Coalition POWs/MIAs. Though Cliff and the other known POWs were home, our job would not be complete until all Desert Storm MIAs had been accounted for. We achieved a happy benchmark the day a letter arrived from General Schwarzkopf confirming that all Coalition MIAs had been accounted for. We closed our doors, knowing we had done all we could, and donated our few remaining funds to the Navy/Marine Corps Relief Society.

I went back to my duties as the CO's wife, writing the squadron wives' monthly newsletter, leading meetings, answering phone calls, and organizing fund-raising activities. The night of my first wives club meeting, I looked at the Marine wives seated around me. How far we'd come in the twelve months since we met. I had gone from the new kid on the block, trying hard to do the right thing, to an easy comfort and confidence.

In early June, Dr. Gerry Goyins, Joel Lees's replacement, gave Cliff an extensive flight physical to determine his physical fitness to pilot a plane. That same week, Dr. Hardwig, the Navy psychiatrist, evaluated Cliff's mental fitness to fly.

On June 11, Cliff—along with Guy, several Hollywood celebrities, and prominent Los Angeles businessmen—was named a Father of the Year by the National Father's Day Council to benefit the Juvenile Diabetes Foundation. The families of the honorees had secretly videotaped messages to the fathers earlier in the week. Stephany and I appeared on Cliff's tape with Cami and Murphy. "I'm so proud of you for winning the Father of the Year Award," Stephany told him. "You should have won the Nobel Peace Prize!"

On the morning of June 17, Cliff called from work, his voice unusually cheery. "I'm the proud new owner of an up chit! I can fly now!"

The flight surgeon who evaluated his medical condition later told me, "If I ever have a son, when he's sixteen, I won't have nearly as much fun giving him the car keys as I did giving Colonel Acree an up status."

Later that morning, Cliff briefed for his first flight at the controls of an OV-10 since being shot down. I drove to the airfield to see him launch. Several friends joined me, including Ken Barackman, who had served as treasurer of the POW/MIA Liberty Alliance. Cliff approached us looking excited and confident. Before he walked out to his plane, Ken handed him a blue POW bracelet; he had vowed to wear it until the day Cliff made his first flight. Cliff climbed into the cockpit. When he got into the air, I prayed his mind wouldn't flash back to his OV-10 going down in flames.

That night, Cliff fairly danced into the house when he returned home from work after that first flight. He grinned widely. "Did I tell you I flew today?" he teased. Anyone could see how thrilled he was at being back in the cockpit; flying was one of the great pleasures of his life.

"I felt uplifted being in the air again. Compared to the chaos ending my last flight, I felt serene and in control. But after I set the plane in cruise altitude, without thinking about it, I glanced over my left shoulder, expecting to see the engine torn off the aircraft."

Then his face took on a look of wistfulness. "When I flew today, I had the strangest feeling," he said. "I was in the right place but the wrong country—I should have been looking down at sand. I trained for months and after only two days in the war I was snatched away from where I belonged."

The grip Cliff's Iraqi captors held on our lives had loosened, but their handprints remained on both of us. For some reason, even I startled more easily now. After the unlucky events of the past, I had acquired superstitious rituals. Lifting weights at the gym, I never ended on thirteen repetitions. If a framed picture of a loved one overturned, I righted it immediately. I buckled my seat belt to drive across a parking lot.

The odds were against us, I'd been warned. Other wives, having survived the Gulf crisis and feeling a false sense of security, let their guard down. I fretted even more than normal. When Cliff came home late I worried. Even with him beside me, I jumped when the doorbell rang, a sound I now associated with dread.

That same week a helicopter mishap took the lives of two pilots in Cliff's air group, and Don and Kay Beaver made another official call—their sixth in 1991. Thinking of the widow and fatherless children one pilot left behind, I wrote in my journal:

> It almost happened to me. It *did* happen to them. Death is final. I had a second chance.

At the memorial service for the two pilots I had never met, I realized that having no clear picture in my mind of the deceased made it harder for me to relate to their loss as real people. What made the American people rally so strongly around the POWs was that the captives were shown on TV. They weren't just nameless, faceless people in crisis to these millions, but real people with real pain.

Our Independence Day celebration that year held new meaning. The next day we watched a videotape of Bob Simon's TV special *Back to Baghdad*. Partway through the tape, a large, white building came into view. Cliff's lips turned up in a strange smile. "I think that's the Biltmore!" He blew out a big puff of air. "A miserable place to live. See that wall? After the bombing, we were taken out there."

Fascinated, he replayed the Biltmore scene ten times. "I was right—three stories with a basement, so that would be four. A building I could very well have died in. It's strange to see that, I'll tell you."

He placed his fingers under his chin and closed his eyes, visualizing his days there. After a minute, he opened his eyes. "Looking at it now gives me a sense of liberty from that place. I made it home."

Other Marine pilots weren't so lucky. Tragedy struck again. "Do you remember...?" Cliff asked one night, and named two helicopter pilots.

"Yes, of course." One of their wives—Susan, a bright, friendly, talkative woman—had hosted the first wives club meeting I had ever attended. When Cliff was in captivity, she had brought me a full-course dinner on her lunch hour. Her husband was deployed to Saudi Arabia, too, and he stayed there nine months in all, missing the birth of their first child that spring.

"What about them?"

"They were killed with two other Marines in a Huey crash."

"What?" My heart sank. Susan, so good, so caring, had made it through the trauma of the war. Now, in peacetime, her husband left for work one morning and never came home. The aircraft had a mechanical failure; there was nothing the pilots could have done to prevent it.

As much as he loved flying, Cliff's transfer to a staff job would come as a relief to me. This mishap added to the list of people we had lost that year. Before the crash, Cliff had counted eleven Marine pilots he had known killed in crashes over the past twelve months. With each pilot friend we mourned, the fear that haunted me grew.

By fall, Cliff's speaking requests had dwindled to one or two a week. One Sunday, flying home from a speaking engagement, I realized his "fame" had begun to fade. "Ladies and gentlemen, we have two special guests on board," the captain declared over the loudspeaker.

Out of habit, I lowered my eyes, waiting for our names to be announced and for everyone to stare. The captain continued: "I'm proud to announce that we have *two* honeymoon couples on board." I smiled to myself and jotted a note in my journal:

> Times have changed. On a flight in April, Cliff was treated like a special guest and served champagne. Today no one recognized him and they pronounced his name wrong.

We had faded into welcome obscurity. Cashiers at the checkout counter no longer spotted Cliff's name on our checks with such frequency. Cliff could come and go as he pleased without being approached by strangers. Cliff was flying again and loving it. I was pregnant with our first child. A normal life was finally within our reach.

Or so I wished.

As the public demands on him lessened, Cliff immersed himself more deeply in his work, which stretched from 6:30 each morning till 8:00 at night. He kept himself overly busy and seemed never to relax. He slept restlessly at night and remained tired.

One September night, halfway through dinner, it suddenly struck me that Cliff and I hardly spoke to each other during meals anymore. Neither of us was as cheerful and outgoing as we once were. I searched Cliff's face.

It was hard to imagine him being lighthearted and happy. His memories had created an intolerable burden. Trying to forget them consumed his energy. Even at home with me he acted preoccupied, serious, and distant. I was losing him again.

In captivity, Cliff's iron-willed discipline and ability to deaden emotions had shielded him from the vulnerable emotions of fear, anger, and sadness. But now those long-practiced skills worked against him. Sadly, while they shielded him from pain, they also numbed the more-welcome emotions of joy, happiness, and contentment.

Only when he bowed his head in church to pray did he allow his true emotions to surface and the barrier to fall, as surely as the tears from his eyes. I had been the only person he allowed beyond that invisible barrier. Now the no-trespassing warning included me.

In October 1991, after considerable arm twisting, I convinced Cliff to accept a free vacation to the Caribbean. "It's the vacation of a lifetime," I pleaded. Pan American Airlines had offered all Desert Storm POWs free airfare to the Caribbean, the Secret Harbour Resort offered lodging, and the Virgin Islands Charter Yacht League in Saint Thomas offered five days of yachting. "The squadron will be fine without you," I urged. Reluctantly, he agreed to go.

For five days we cruised among lush tropical islands, the only passengers on the sixty-three-foot yacht *Zinja,* sailing on sapphire and aquamarine waters that sparkled in the sunshine. Away from populated areas, phones, or obligations, we had only each other and our solicitous crew of two.

Each afternoon, under a cloudless blue sky, we anchored in a different secluded bay for swimming and snorkeling in the warm, silky water. After breathtaking island sunsets, we enjoyed candlelit gourmet dinners under a romantic canopy of winking stars. If anything could transport us away from the past, this paradise could.

Though Cliff's body rested in paradise, his mind was not at peace. He had brought *Kiss the Boys Goodbye: How the United States Betrayed Its Own POWs in Vietnam,* the heartbreaking account of Vietnam POWs abandoned and families torn apart. He couldn't put the book down.

Late in the afternoon of the third day, the captain motored our boat into a small, hidden cove where clear aquamarine waters lapped on a white-sand beach. He turned off the key, and the steady chug of the engine stilled. The mysterious, hypnotic voice of the singer Enya drifted from the cabin as the boat bobbed at its anchor near the Sir Francis Drake Channel. I breathed deeply the warm, salty air that brushed our faces and the giant white sails luffing above our heads.

"This bay is *gorgeous,*" I gushed as the boat gently rocked beneath us. "Want to go snorkeling before . . . Oh look! . . . Cliff, did you see that huge turtle?"

No answer. I glanced over. Gripping the book in his lap, his hands had fallen still.

"Cliff?"

He stared at the rippling waters without seeing them. I'd lost him again.

"Cliff."

"What?" He shook his head as if coming out of a trance.

Seven months after the war, his memories still held him captive. The physical gulf that once separated us had been replaced by an emotional one, wide as the continents between us months before.

I did not see how I could ever cross that abyss and retrieve the closeness we once shared. As it turned out, the bridge would come in the form of a tiny child.

Oceanside, California
January 1992

Cinnamon scented the warm breeze as I walked onto the patio carrying a platter piled high with warm, cinnamon rolls dripping with cream cheese frosting. Setting the platter next to a basket of plump, ripe strawberries, I finally admitted I had enough food to feed our sixty guests.

A chain jingled, followed by the sound of a rapidly sniffing nose. I looked down to see Cami, her tail vigorously wagging and her mouth opened expectantly. I dropped a slice of turkey into her mouth, then turned to peruse our backyard preparations for our "one-year anniversary of Cliff's shootdown" party.

A large easel displayed photographs from events over the past year. Beyond the patio, tables and chairs dotted the lawn, their colorful coverings fluttering in the mild breeze. At the far end of the yard, a long table held the more interesting, amusing, or touching cards, letters, and drawings we had received from schoolchildren and the public.

Next to these, a box held the ten pounds of POW bracelets Cliff had received, many with touching notes enclosed. I had typed sixteen pages of selected comments, including:

From a nineteen-year-old firefighter in Preston, Washington: "I don't know if this is a 'corny' idea sending you this bracelet, or if it will be one of a few thousand you get. . . . I only hope that some day I will be able to support my country the way you have . . . [and] be the kind of hero that you are and will be for the rest of your life. . . . I will never forget you and your strength."

From a captain in the USMC Reserves: "Desert Storm is another proud chapter in Marine Corps history. I'm proud to say I was a part of that. . . . The bonding one experiences with his fellow Marines in combat is a unique high I will never forget. Of the thirty-five months I spent in Vietnam I never once said I was happy to be there, but being there I was happy it was with the Marines."

From Lorraine Durick of Monroe, Washington: "The bracelet dug into my flesh a bit and felt a little uncomfortable. I didn't mind because I knew your discomfort and pain as a POW was so much more. The uncomfortable feeling . . . was a constant reminder to pray for you and think of you as I did my entire waking hours."

From Rebecca Kimmel of Tumwater, Washington: "How can you tell someone that a small piece of metal made a difference? That small piece of metal made me watch, wait, wonder and again, pray that you would be returned home safely and quickly. . . . Maybe in some small way it will comfort you to know that we would have never let you down."

From George and Wanda Britton, New Port Richey, Florida: "When they showed you on CNN I was horrified. I went out and ordered POW bracelets the next day. Two weeks later I found out Lt Col Acree is the Commanding Officer for VMO-2—I was so surprised. My son is one of the Plane Captains for your unit over in Saudi."

From Susanne Schneider, Seattle, Washington: "Your POW bracelet is the first thing I put on and the last thing I take off together with my glasses. . . . We originally come from East Germany and were in jail there only for 1 day, but it was enough to find out what it means to be 'free.'"

From Joni and Michael Boness, Seattle, Washington: "Where do I begin—I guess I'll start with 19 years ago when Mike Boness, my husband (boyfriend then), got a job at Airways Rent A Car . . . While working there he met a nice guy named Cliff. You never forget a genuine nice person even if they only touch your life for a few years. . . . Our heart sank . . ."

I walked to a table in a corner of the yard where Cliff had arranged his POW memorabilia: a rough, hairy, rose-and-brown-colored blanket cut into a serape, his yellow POW shirt, and a pair of dirty canvas tennis shoes with rolled green threads for thin laces. The toes were inscribed with 2000040, his International Red Cross identification number.

Standing by the table, Cliff seemed lost in thought. I would learn that every January, his feelings would run close to the surface. When his release date, March 6, arrived, I would breathe a sigh of relief. Every year Cliff celebrated his Freedom Day with his Marine Corps colleagues by bringing them Middle Eastern tea and several dozen of my huge cinnamon rolls.

Reaching into the right hip pocket of the yellow shirt, Cliff pulled out three coarse, snarled threads of pink, green, and black. "This was a real treasure to me." From the left hip pocket he retrieved three hardened pieces of brown bread, each about the size of his thumb. "This is what kept me going at night. Knowing I'd have this to eat in the morning."

As he set the bread on the table next to the threads I glanced over my shoulder at the laden food table and said a silent prayer of thanks that he'd returned home alive. Hours later the food table was cleared and several of our guests formed a work party. We stamped and stuffed 1,300 letters from Cliff to people who had called, written, or sent POW bracelets to us.

Cliff's letters to them—adding to the more than 1,000 we had already sent—announced our exciting news: "Cindy and I are expecting a baby in March of 1992. We have yet to select a first name, but I chose its middle name immediately: 'Freedom.' I was given a second life when I returned from captivity, and without my freedom, we would not have had the opportunity to create this new life."

On February 2, the wives of VMO-2 hosted a going-away tea for me, and on February 7, 1992, Cliff relinquished command of VMO-2 after twenty months as CO. At his farewell party, VMO-2 Marines had presented him with the squadron colors—the unit flag that had flown over the tent encampment of VMO-2 in Saudi Arabia. The faded red flag was handsomely encased under glass within a huge wooden frame. Cliff was especially touched when the officers of VMO-2 presented him with a three-foot-long plaque of polished oak. On it was mounted an AK-47, much like those the Iraqis had tormented him with during captivity. The inscription etched on a brass plate read "Presented to LtCol Cliff Acree for inspirational leadership and courage during Operation Desert Storm. 'Semper Fidelis.'"

During the change of command ceremony, messages were read from Marine superiors that commended Cliff for the significant progress and improvements VMO-2 had made during his tenure. They had already awarded him the Bronze Star for his leadership and initiative during Desert Shield. The accompanying citation credited him with having "prepared for and conducted the longest self-deployment of a VMO squadron by moving eight OV-10 Broncos and associated personnel over 9,600 miles from Camp Pendleton, California, to Southwest Asia. Arriving in Saudi Arabia for Operation Desert Shield, his unit was immediately ready to conduct combat operations. . . ."

I enjoyed seeing him receive such recognition for his hard work and dedication before the war. I remained optimistic that his Marine superiors would someday investigate his conduct in captivity so others could benefit from his hard-earned lessons.

A week after his change of command ceremony, Cliff's nose was operated on at Naval Hospital San Diego, known as Balboa. His courage had been tested in hundreds of ways during captivity—now it was tested again as he dealt with the fallout of his ordeal. Lying in the recovery room after the four-and-a-half-hour procedure, Cliff shifted restlessly in his sleep, his mouth open and his bandaged nose stuffed with gauze plugs. The effects of the morphine gave his partially opened eyes a strange appearance. I watched the heart monitor beside his bed as it beeped reassuringly.

Kindhearted Doc Lees—now assigned at Balboa as the division head of general internal medicine—sat on the other side of Cliff, holding his limp right hand. I appreciated anew Joel's calm, comforting manner. Cliff had been so tense anticipating the surgical rebreaking of his nose that the anesthesiologist had given him an extralarge dose of medication to put him under. Even so, Cliff mumbled throughout the procedure. The surgery exposed many old emotional scars—as well as physical ones.

Looking at his bruised, swollen face, I wondered if that was how he'd looked after an interrogation. No matter that the pain he now endured would enable him to breathe through his nose again, watching him suffer was terrible.

"*How many* times did the Iraqis break your nose?" the surgeon, Dr. Riley, asked when he visited Cliff's hospital room that afternoon.

"I don't know," Cliff answered.

"It must have been fractured repeatedly," Dr. Riley said. "The infrastructure of your nose was nearly destroyed. The nasal bones on both sides were badly thickened and brittle over the fracture sites. Your bones had been traumatized to the point that new bone had nearly replaced the old fractured bone.

"Usually when we rebreak a nose to realign it, it breaks into two clean pieces, like two sides of a tepee," Dr. Riley explained. "Cliff's nose shattered into so many pieces it looked like it had been hit by a hammer.

The resident doctor who had been assisting Dr. Riley recognized the extensive damage. "I'm out of my league," he had said, and stepped back to let Dr. Riley, a surgeon with twenty years experience in reconstructive surgery, handle Cliff's case.

As if assembling a jigsaw puzzle, Dr. Riley reconstructed Cliff's nose. "I've done five hundred noses. And this had to be one of the most difficult. The top of your nose was almost gone," Dr. Riley continued. "Plus you had bone spurs occluding the airway. I removed all but the cartilage portion of your septum—the middle dividing bone—to reconstruct the top part of your nose. You may be able to push through skin and feel the parts and pieces I used to reconstruct."

Because Cliff remained weak, disoriented, and unable to keep food down on the day after his surgery, I stayed overnight in the hospital, sleeping on the brown vinyl recliner next to his bed. Eight months into my pregnancy, it was nearly impossible to find a comfortable position for my increased girth. But Cliff would have endured far more for me—or any of his Marines. When anyone in his squadron had surgery, gave birth, or became quite ill, no matter how long Cliff's day, he made the time to call or to visit that person at home or in the hospital.

The next morning, Dr. Riley visited again. The surgery had taken nearly twice as long as they had planned. "Before surgery, we didn't realize your skull had been fractured, too. Our surgery team had to align your rebuilt septum and airways over the scar tissue of your skull fracture."

Cliff was discharged the next day. The aftermath of his surgery proved worse than the surgery itself. Constant pain in his face and head brought back ugly memories of captivity. Medication lessened his pain, but the narcotics made him groggy and impatient with his debility.

Two weeks later, we returned to Dr. Riley for removal of Cliff's cast and bandages. For nearly an hour, I watched Cliff grimace as Dr. Riley removed stitches, adjusted, measured, readjusted, and taped Cliff's nose in position to his swollen face.

I studied Cliff's new nose. Was it only my imagination? The way Cliff's nose lined up with his eyes and mouth still didn't look right. "Something looks off," I told Dr. Riley.

"You're noticing his mid-face asymmetry," Dr. Riley explained. Cliff's beatings had also broken facial bones, and forced the top and bottom halves of his face out of alignment.

"Normally we align the nose with the top and bottom halves of the face." Dr. Riley gestured to Cliff's forehead. "With Cliff's, that was impossible, so I tried to align his forehead to the tip of his nose. Since I couldn't move the whole middle third of his face over to left, I tried to induce some crookedness into the tip so it angles over. It will look a little crooked to his forehead, but will look more normal for the lower third of his face—the mouth on down. If the nose alignment drifts, we'll cast it again."

To prevent Cliff's septum from deviating, Dr. Riley shoved four inches of hard gauze up Cliff's nose using metal prongs, a reminder of Cliff's beatings with a metal instrument. He clenched the muscles in his jaw so tightly that his cheek bulged. His foot tapped uncontrollably. It took all of his strength to hold still and not cry out. My heart went out to both Cliff and the doctor who had to cause him such physical and emotional pain.

When the doctor left us alone, Cliff broke down. "I felt myself back in the interrogation room, sitting in a chair." He shuddered convulsively. "Living my life a few seconds at a time—not knowing when I was going to get hammered again."

A week later, the nose packing—cemented inside Cliff's nose with dried blood and tissue—had to be wrenched out. Three days later, his bandages were removed. Then Dr. Riley delivered the bad news: "There's a chance this might not take and we'll have to go in there again." Seeing our crestfallen looks, he added, "But we won't have to tear it apart like the first time."

For several weeks after the surgery, Cliff's nose was "mobile." He had to shape it with his hands several times a day, pressing on the sides to keep it from healing crooked. He avoided Cami for fear she would bump his nose and undo the painful reconstruction before scar tissue had formed to support it.

Two weeks after Cliff's surgery, I gave birth to a boy at Camp Pendleton Naval Hospital with the help of my two coaches: Cliff and Rosana Martinez. My prolonged labor gave Mom enough time to fly down from Seattle to witness the birth. When the doctor laid him on my chest, our newborn baby opened the weary eyes in his tiny, reddened face and seemed to look into my soul. I felt intensely protective, as I had one year earlier when his father, too, had been delivered to my waiting arms. Both deliveries were miracles of new life.

We brought Stephen Freedom Acree home on March 6, the one-year anniversary of Cliff's release from captivity.

That spring Cliff learned he had been selected for Top Level School and was to attend the Air War College at Maxwell Air Force Base in Montgomery, Alabama. In March we received a letter from our Kuwaiti friend, Muhammed Mubarak. "Our dream could come true in going to school together in Alabama," Mo wrote. "Am crossing my fingers." Cliff and Mo shared an enduring brotherhood of mutual trust and loyalty, which Mo expressed in one of his letters by saying, "I do admire your personality. Am very lucky to have a brother and a true friend like you."

In April 1992, Cliff underwent a second nose surgery, or septo-rhinoplasty procedure. Afterward, Dr. Riley told Cliff, "I discovered bends in the bone so far back, you may not have survived. The back part of your nose had been shattered off and driven way posterior, farther back than most surgeons normally look."

Cliff's second nose surgery was a repeat of the pain he'd suffered in the first one. As his nose healed we were hopeful that this additional reconstructive work would support his nose structure and keep the airways open. But within weeks after the second surgery, his nasal passages collapsed. When he attempted to breathe through his blocked nose, he made a wheezing-whistling sound. His smell and taste abilities still functioned at only 20 to 30 percent of normal.

Dr. Riley recommended a third surgery to revise the septum and valves. Hesitant to put himself through those horrors again, Cliff said only, "I'll think about it." Besides, in May, movers were packing our household goods for our transfer to Montgomery, where Cliff would attend the Air War College. To our delight, our Kuwaiti friend Mo had also been selected to attend a Maxwell Air Force Base school, the Air Force Command and Staff College.

Two days after the movers left, Cliff underwent a third surgery at Balboa Naval Hospital. Only time would tell if this surgery would be successful at restoring normal breathing. But it would do nothing more for his sense of smell. After healing for sixteen months, it was as good as it would ever get.

Each surgery gave Cliff a new look—from a youthfully upturned nose to one with a too-large, rounded end—but always his nose was lopsided on his face and never straight. "I've had more noses than Michael Jackson," he joked. But his nose—welded together with scar tissue—and his breathing problems constantly reminded him of horrors he would have rather forgotten. Within months his nose caved in again, shutting off the right-side airway.

Still, he resumed his exercise regimen of lifting weights, running, and playing racquetball. That summer he confided in me that after a racquetball game he had felt a strange rapid beating of his heart, similar to what he had felt the night he was moved to the Biltmore prison. He didn't tell me when the erratic heartbeat happened several more times. Reluctant to confront another physical infirmity, Cliff dismissed the worrisome sensations. But, like his memories of captivity, they would have the power to spring up uninvited.

Pensacola, Florida, NAMI Special Studies
September 15, 1992

The door of the large testing room swung open and I was hastened into the room where Cliff had undergone a stress EKG. I found him lying on an examining table adjacent to a treadmill, surrounded by a group of people wearing white coats.

Cliff had reported to NAMI (since renamed the Naval Operational Medicine Institute, or NOMI) in Pensacola, Florida, for his annual physical. The thorough medical workup—including blood work, X rays, testing of pulmonary and heart function, and meetings with ear, nose, and throat specialists—strives to detect illness and prevent or reduce future medical problems.

The ENT doctor's report had discouraged us: Cliff's only hope of breathing well through his nose would be a fourth surgery that would rebreak his nose, then use bone from his hip or ribs to rebuild it. Several neuropsychological tests indicated slower functioning than expected, possibly due to limited brain damage.

Now, on the afternoon of his second day of testing, Cliff lay supine on the table, his bare chest still speckled with EKG electrodes, or "stickies."

"One minute into the recovery phase, the colonel's heart went into an abnormal cardiac rhythm," a doctor with a concerned expression informed me. "A rate of approximately two hundred beats per minute."

In his office later that afternoon, NAMI internist and flight surgeon Dr. Eric Bower explained the reason for Cliff's rapid heartbeat. "His heart entered into what is called a 'wide complex tachycardia,'" Dr. Bower, a gregarious, cheerful man in his mid-thirties explained. We discussed the possible causes of the arrythmia, but without further testing, Dr. Bower couldn't be sure of the exact diagnosis. The arrhythmia had also been precipitated in captivity by Cliff's physical abuse and sleep deprivation.

One of the possible diagnoses was ventricular tachycardia, which has potentially life-threatening consequences and is permanently disqualifying for piloting naval aircraft. The other possibility was a less dangerous condition, supraventricular tachycardia (SVT) that could be treated by lifelong antiarrhythmic drug therapy that nonetheless would also permanently disqualify Cliff for flight status.

Dr. Bower gently presented Cliff's options: begin a lifelong regimen of antiarrhythmic medication that would disqualify him for flight status, undergo a cardiac catheterization procedure to diagnose and correct the problem, or live with the possibility of sudden cardiac death. In sum, a series of unattractive options. Dr. Bower recommended that Cliff immediately undergo the cardiac catheter procedure. "I can't make a diagnosis based on the EKG information alone."

Weary of having his body battered or probed, Cliff was reluctant to undergo another invasive procedure. Dr. Bower had to press hard to get him to go along with his referral recommendation. "It's the only way to nail the diagnosis," Dr. Bower later confided in me. "And without a diagnosis, the colonel doesn't have a prayer of flying again."

"When will it end?" I wondered. Cliff's heart abnormality immediately disqualified him for flight status. The news of his infirmity had a disturbing, unsettling effect on Cliff. He doubted whether his body would ever heal and be normal again. As in captivity, he felt unable to control his own life.

A week later, we flew from Alabama to San Diego, where Cliff underwent cardiac catheterization at Balboa Naval Hospital. During the four-hour procedure, cardiologists inserted four leads into the veins of his thighs that snaked upward into his heart. Stimulating his heart, they re-created the arrythmia and determined the source of the problem. They then applied radio-frequency energy to the catheter tip to "burn" the abnormal pathway so his heart's electrical signals had no choice but to use the normal one.

After the interventional procedure, doctors pronounced Cliff "nearly cured"—any future arrhythmias should last only a few seconds. Corrected or not, Cliff's history of arrhythmia added another log on the pile of medical conditions that could interfere with his piloting a plane. Captain Baggett, the head of NAMI Special Studies, outlined them for Cliff in a letter: "(Moderately severe) History of closed-head injury with loss of consciousness; Tachycardia, wide complex; History of catheter ablation of heart lesion; and Post-traumatic stress syndrome, in remission. . . . All of which are considered permanent."

Cliff returned to his studies at the Air War College. In November 1992, we learned that he would be presented with the Meritorious Service Medal, an award given to many squadron COs upon completion of their tours. In my journal I speculated about the upcoming awards ceremony:

> The Commandant of the Marine Corps is coming to town to visit the school Cliff is attending and he will present the award. I've got my fingers crossed they're going to surprise him with some sort of recognition for his captivity experience. He has never received any recognition for his exemplary conduct during captivity—except the standard POW medal and Purple Heart. It would be wonderful if they had something planned. . . .

The Army, Navy, and Air Force had heralded the heroism of their POWs with coveted medals. Medals such as the Air Force Cross and the Silver Star, the nation's second- and third-highest medals awarded for bravery in combat—medals reserved for awarding high merit and bravery, medals to be passed on to grandchildren along with stories of how they were earned.

When I mentioned such honors to Cliff, he always replied, "I'm happy for them." Yet I was puzzled. To my knowledge, Cliff's own Marine Corps had yet to ask him about his captivity or examine his conduct as a POW. I had always been told by Cliff that the Corps "takes care of its own," yet the bravery of several Marine POWs in Desert Storm seemed to have gone unrecognized. Cliff had submitted the required paperwork to recognize Guy with a Bronze Star for his conduct in captivity. Guy's award was downgraded to a Navy Commendation Medal. Despite my feelings about his lack of recognition, Cliff remained quiet and intensely loyal.

The day of the awards ceremony arrived, and Cliff was honored when Marine Corps Commandant General Carl Mundy presented him with the Meritorious Service Medal for outstanding performance as a commanding officer—not related to his captivity.

Three weeks later Cliff underwent a series of extensive mental and physical examinations at NAMI in Pensacola to document his condition to the Special Board of Flight Surgeons. In December, the twenty-member board would convene to make a recommendation on Cliff's flying status.

The doctors' reports, along with his medical records from the USNS *Mercy,* Bethesda Naval Hospital, and Camp Pendleton, were sent to the Special Board of Flight Surgeons in Pensacola. In early December, Cliff traveled to Pensacola, bringing with him his two-inch-thick medical record and the "Request for waiver for flying status" prepared by his senior Marine officer at the Air War College.

Entering the meeting room, Cliff faced a lineup of doctors—a neurologist, a psychiatrist, an internist, and several other specialists in various branches of medicine, the majority of whom were flight surgeons with experience in aerospace. Prior to the board's convening, each doctor had reviewed

Cliff's records pertaining to his area of medical expertise and had prepared an extensive recommendation to the board.

As the "discussant" (Cliff's advocate), Dr. Bower presented Cliff's case, including the results of his recent examinations, his medical history, and his family, social, and military history. Members of the board asked clarifying questions, and once they were satisfied, it was Cliff's turn to make a statement. For ten minutes he gave a proud and unapologetic summarization of his accomplishments, trials, and potential as a Marine pilot.

Cliff was excused from the room. Dr. Bower presented additional information regarding the diagnosis, treatment, and implications of Cliff's condition. The Board deliberated his case. Finally, a roll call vote (excluding Dr. Bower) was taken. Whatever the outcome, Marine Corps Commandant Carl Mundy would make the final "go-no-go" call on Cliff's flying status.

Cliff was invited back into the room to hear the board's recommendation. A few moments later, he wore a relieved smile on his face. Considering his depth of experience as a Marine pilot, the Special Board of Flight Surgeons had recommended a return to flight status in a restricted capacity—pilot in command of dual-piloted aircraft only. Following a period of observation of at least one year, the board would entertain an upgrade of Cliff's waiver to include pilot-in-command status. Cliff's up chit was immediately written, and the recommendation was forwarded to General Mundy for final approval.

In May 1993, Cliff graduated from the Air War College at Maxwell Air Force Base and was assigned as a faculty member of the Marine Command and Staff College in Quantico, Virginia.

In May 1994, he reluctantly consented to undergo a fourth nose surgery, this one performed at Bethesda Naval Hospital by a premier nose reconstruction specialist, the best facial reconstruction surgeon in the U.S. Navy. This surgeon removed cartilage from Cliff's ear to create spreader grafts to keep the collapsed nasal passages open. I drove Cliff home from the hospital with high hopes about the results of this surgery.

That afternoon I sat next to Cliff on the living room couch. He slept upright, his breath coming in short jerks. More than three years had passed since Cliff's return from Iraq, three years filled with more highs and lows than many people experience in a lifetime. Cliff had made countless public speaking appearances, and I had made a few myself. I would always remember fondly those events that transported us to another world of celebrities, elegant meals, and wealthy, lavishly dressed people. But our most meaningful events involved causes and people we cared about. For me, those included speaking at a large veterans gathering in Los Angeles for National POW/MIA Recognition Day and being chosen Woman of the Year by a drug rehabilitation center for women. I was proud to be an example of someone who had found strength in adversity.

Other wives often ask, "How did you do it? I could never have done that."

"Yes, you could," I assure them. "When you live through something like this, you discover you can do just about anything."

Eleanor Roosevelt advised women in 1960, "You gain strength, courage, and confidence by every experience in which you really stop to look fear in the face. You are able to say to yourself, 'I lived through this horror. I can take the next thing that comes along.'" I had the benefit of supportive friends and family. I also learned that action is the best antidote to feeling helpless and a victim. You have a choice in how to respond, and you *can* make a difference in a seemingly helpless situation.

Over the years, we had met many former POWs and their families. I became painfully aware of the horrors these men and their families had endured without the government and public support Cliff and I received during the Gulf War. They have our deepest respect.

At some point in life everyone goes through something difficult. Individuals have endured ordeals far worse than ours—those permanently crippled in accidents, victims of random violence, sufferers in concentration camps—and displayed amazing courage. Their lengthy ordeals put ours into perspective.

Cliff had made countless speeches, but he especially enjoyed speaking to schoolchildren and youth groups about the importance of basic values and patriotism. After each speech, the kids mobbed him with questions. Number-one kid question: "What was it like, being a POW?" Number two: "What did you eat?" Cliff would especially remember the honor of meeting someone he deeply respected for his longtime service to military personnel—Bob Hope, who praised Cliff's impromptu speech on core values.

At several events, I had been happy to introduce Cliff to many people who had supported the POW/MIA Liberty Alliance. At a Marine Corps Scholarship Ball, Cliff and I met Shanna Reed, the actress in *Major Dad* who had offered her celebrity endorsement of the POW/MIA Liberty Alliance. "So *you're* the mystery wife!" she exclaimed, realizing that I was the anonymous POW wife who had founded the organization.

At a luncheon for the fiftieth anniversary of the USO, the band played "Hail to the Chief" and a serious-faced man in a dark suit placed the large, round presidential seal on the podium in front of the head table. I felt I was watching a *Saturday Night Live* skit as someone announced the arrival of President and Mrs. Bush. Mrs. Bush's eyes caught mine, then shifted to Cliff, sitting beside me. She nodded, smiling.

Our travels had introduced us to people around the country with hearts of gold who employ their wealth and fame to help others. Most touching were the ordinary people in the community we met whose incredible amount of caring and gratitude reminded us that we had never been alone.

Something warm and wet nudged my arm, shaking me from my thoughts. It was Cami's damp nose. She prodded Cliff's hand, then whined, her black tail wagging vigorously. Cliff groaned as he started to revive, breathing heavily through his mouth.

Light footsteps came down the stairs, picking up speed as they hit level ground. "Daddy!" Two-year-old Stephen Freedom Acree raced toward us. I braced my arm in front of the couch as slender, green-eyed Stephen lunged for Cliff's chest. "Careful, honey."

Cliff had devoted himself wholeheartedly to his son, becoming a loving, supportive, and nurturing father. In the soft glow of the night-light, he often placed his hands on Stephen's sleeping body and listened to his breathing rhythm.

Such is the tremendous healing power of a child. Wrapped in the safety of Stephen's love, Cliff had gradually dismantled the barrier he had erected to shield him from his painful memories. His POW experiences and their aftermath became less important as he put his energies elsewhere—into being a father.

With wide-eyed concern, Stephen looked up at Cliff's bruised, bandaged face. "Daddy thick, Daddy hopital," he said solemnly, patting Cliff's knee. He turned back to me. "Daddy bedder now?"

Cliff blinked his eyes, struggling to become lucid.

"Daddy loves you, Stephen," he said drowsily, groping for his son's tiny hand. As Stephen grew from a baby to a toddler, Cliff daily showed his son an example of manhood that encompassed tenderness as well as strength. Stephen reaped the benefits of the bond created and worshipped Cliff as a real-life, day-to-day hero.

Though Cliff's good deeds did not show to the world, he has the personal satisfaction of knowing, in his heart, that he did the right thing in resisting his captors. As Sir Francis Bacon observed, "Adversity doth best discover virtue."

I admired Cliff's courage and moral integrity, and believed his story needed to be told. Hoping to inspire other people with the courageous example he had set, I decided to write his story with details never revealed to anyone else. The difficulty of interesting a publisher in a book about courage and integrity—not a sensational scandal—would present many hurdles.

As I began to recount my experiences, a wealth of material aided my recall of events—my personal journal, several audiotapes of phone calls and interviews, notes of phone conversations, and reams of detailed notes. Cliff didn't have such records of his ordeal to draw upon. He didn't need them. Even without his injuries to remind him, the events of Cliff's captivity would be engraved in his memory forever.

Years later, he recalls details as if they happened yesterday. He watches CNN reports on Iraq with the eyes of a hawk for a face he recognizes. More than once, watching footage of Saddam Hussein surrounded by his top generals, Cliff has jumped up and pointed to the television, shouting, "I *know* that guy!" He would love to be asked to identify his captors one day. Believe me, he could. In 1992, Vice President Al Gore led a United Nations commission to indict Iraqi military leaders for war crimes, but the effort was not seriously pursued.

In July 1995, while stationed at Quantico, Virginia, Cliff was promoted to full colonel. After the Gulf War, each branch of the U.S. military experienced substantial drawdowns. In the Marine Corps, some cuts were made vertically, eliminating units rather than cutting across the board. All three OV-10 squadrons were eliminated and their missions were assigned to other units. In 1996, after attending six weeks of refresher training at Camp Pendleton, Cliff transitioned back to Cobra attack helicopters and happily took to the air again.

In July of that year, he became the commanding officer of Marine Aircraft Group 42, a unit consisting of five squadrons and two detachments of both fixed-wing and helicopter aircraft, primarily based at Naval Air Station Atlanta, in Marietta, Georgia.

By then, Cliff's nasal passageways had begun to collapse again, but after four reconstructions, he vowed that his days of surgery were over. He had also accepted the pain and stiffness from his neck injury that reappeared at irregular intervals. Though injuries remain, Cliff has returned to doing most of the things he loves, including flying, never forgetting how lucky he was to have a second chance at life. Cliff stays in touch with other Gulf War POWs through the 5th Allied POW Wing, the organization they formed that follows the 4th Allied POW Wing of the Vietnam era.

Guy Hunter, too, now retired and living in North Carolina, is sharply aware of how lucky he is to be alive. Guy often joked with Mary about his wallet, which remained lost somewhere in the Kuwaiti desert. "I sure could use that forty-seven dollars," he'd say, claiming that he knew exactly where he had buried it.

In December 1996, Guy received a package forwarded from Marine Corps Headquarters. In it he found a yellow envelope with a letter from a man named G. A. S. Santha, who identified himself as a worker in Kuwait.

Guy opened the envelope and was astonished to find his wallet and every mud-soaked item he'd kept in it—including the $47. "I felt a chill go through my body, like a voice from the past suddenly spoke to me," Guy said. "I realized how lucky I was to have survived."

Written in broken English, the letter spoke to the goodness of humanity.

Dear Sir:

   I am a Sri Lankan youth of 30 years. . . . I will glad to informed you that I was found the purse of Mr. Guy L. Hunter Jr. behind my house nearby the seaside. I checked and found it one I.D. card, three family photos, three bank cards and some dollar notes include. Herewith I am sending this valuable property your address by post. Therefore you may please noted and hand over to Mr. Guy.

Thinking of you, yours faithfully,

G. A. S. Santha

Guy sent a reply the next day, thanking Santha and inviting him to visit in the United States. Mary wanted to save the decaying currency as keepsakes. "I'm using it to buy some beer," Guy joked.

Looking back on this chapter of our lives as a growth experience has helped us integrate it into our lives and move forward. Facing adversity, Cliff discovered inner strength to sustain him that he couldn't have imagined before. I, too, became aware of the power of persistence. As a result, we are stronger and more focused on the important things in life. We never forget the importance of family and friends.

Our family was made all the more precious by the February 1996 arrival of our second son—named Mark Edward Acree, after Cliff's middle name (Mark) and my dad's middle name (Edward)—during a blizzard in Virginia.

In many ways, Cliff and I have been blessed. The ordeal we faced was short and had a happy ending. It brought lasting lessons and friendships. Today, the gulf between us is spanned by the bonds of our long friendship and our deep commitment to our marriage and family. We've learned that with love we can weather any storm—even a Desert Storm.

Epilogue

In the seven years since Cliff's return from Baghdad, we have traveled a long, eventful road. Much about our lives has changed since Cliff deployed to the Gulf. We'll never be the same people we were before his ordeal, but that's not entirely bad. Some of life's most powerful lessons come in a time of tragedy. I've learned that crisis brings out the best and worst in people. With more empathy for those in crisis, I dislike seeing the press invade the privacy of anyone in pain. I now know not to believe everything I see on television or in print news.

Our experience reaffirmed our values and left us with the realization of how important and precious life is; nothing is permanent. We have so much to be thankful for: I have a husband and two children I will never take for granted. Cliff will never take for granted his next meal, being warm at night, or the country that was determined not to abandon him.

Television, movies, and the tabloids these days are full of stories about horrible, depressing things. With war's evidence of man's inhumanity to man, it is reassuring to know that so many good people exist in this world. I have evidence of their love and warmth in the thousands of letters we received after Cliff was taken captive and the tens of thousands of letters sent to the Iraqi ambassador to the UN.

Did the letter-writing campaign help? We might never know what effect these letters had on the government of Iraq. We do know that this tremendous display of compassion notified Iraq that it had more to worry about than Coalition airpower. People around the world cared about our POWs/MIAs and wanted to hold the Iraqis accountable for their treatment.

If nothing else, contributing to the letter-writing campaign made people feel they were able to help. Our campaign gave us a measure of peace of mind and was a sign of the solidarity felt by the American people.

We will always be grateful to those who so patriotically supported the men and women of the United States military defending freedom on the other side of the world. After the Gulf War, our country was on a roll of loyalty and caring and pride in our military unseen since World War II. We hope this momentum continues.

Years after the euphoria faded, many people look back and ask, "Did the Gulf War make a difference?" The United States' success has received mixed reports. Compared to the nine years of the Vietnam conflict, victory was declared quickly in forty-three-day Desert Storm. And yes, the war did liberate Kuwait. In *The Generals' War,* retired Marine Corps General Bernard E. Trainor labeled the Gulf War an "incomplete victory" that left Saddam Hussein in power. Yet, he notes, to remove Hussein was beyond the mandate of the UN resolutions, the Coalition's agreed-upon military objective.

Seven years after the Gulf War, Saddam Hussein is still in power, and economic sanctions against Iraq remain in place. Concern continues about his labs' ability to develop weapons of mass destruction. Though Saddam has agreed to allow inspection of his suspected weapons sites, only time will tell if *this time* he keeps his promises.

The Gulf War did not solve all the problems in the Persian Gulf; no war could. But the bittersweet victory did prove that "a nation's people can unite after honorable debate and that countries can cooperate for their common good," as Mortimer Zuckerman pointed out in *U.S. News & World Report.* "Here," he noted, "is inspiration enough for the future."

In December 1997, Cliff met with Secretary of the Navy John Dalton regarding a possible assignment working for him at the Pentagon. "Do you think about your captivity much?" Secretary Dalton asked him during the interview. Cliff answered honestly: "I think about it every day."

One of the legacies of Cliff's captivity is that time does not heal all wounds. No acknowledgment ever came from Cliff's chain of command that his extensive debriefing after repatriation had been heard. The twelve hours of tapes remain locked in a classified vault in Fort Belvoir, Virginia.

Despite the sting I know he felt, Cliff remained devoted to the Marine Corps. And though he retained some physical injuries and other scars deep within, he regretted none of it. Given the chance, he would gladly make the same choices again to serve his country and his Corps.

As I type this, Cami is stretched out on the toy-scattered floor beside me, using as her pillow a copy of my five-inch-thick manuscript. When I began writing this book—nearly seven years ago—I did not foresee the magnitude of the project, nor the challenges of writing during six moves and the births of two children with a husband frequently gone.

Did our lives ever become normal? Insofar as any life in the military is normal—yes. Our frequent separations have continued, as has our nomadic lifestyle. Since Cliff's return from the Gulf, we have changed addresses six times, moving so often that many of our boxes are hauled back onto the moving van unopened. In June 1998, we moved again when Cliff completed his tour as the commanding officer of MAG-42 to begin an assignment at NATO headquarters in Brussels, Belgium.

Though our sons will frequently leave friends behind to start anew in homes in different parts of the world, they will learn lessons early in their lives about love of one's country and the gift of freedom. They will learn that heroes are not invincible but are ordinary people inspired by love in all its variety—love for one's family, one's country, one's military brethren, and love for one's ideals. We hope that after reading our story, you will recognize the unsung heroes in your life.

Index